First Person Singular

First Person Singular

STUART HIRSCHBERG

Rutgers: The State University of New Jersey, Newark

TERRY HIRSCHBERG

Allyn and Bacon
Boston ✦ London ✦ Toronto ✦ Sydney ✦ Tokyo ✦ Singapore

Executive Editor: Eben W. Ludlow
Editorial Assistant: Elisabeth Egan
Marketing Manager: Lisa Kimball
Editorial Production Service: MARBERN HOUSE
Manufacturing Buyer: Megan Cochran
Cover Administrator: Linda Knowles

Library of Congress Cataloging-in-Publication Data

Hirschberg, Stuart.
    First person singular / Stuart Hirschberg, Terry Hirschberg.
      p.   cm.
    Includes indexes.
    ISBN 0-205-19981-X (alk. paper)
    1. Readers—Autobiography.   2. Diaries—Authorship—Problems,
exercises, etc.   3. Autobiography—Problems, exercises, etc.
4. English language—Rhetoric.   5. College readers.   I. Hirschberg,
Terry.   II. Title.
PE1127.A9H57   1997
808'.0427—dc20   96-24862
                                          CIP

Acknowledgments

Acknowledgments are found on pages 453–456, which should be considered
extensions of the copyright page.

Printed in the United States of America
10 9 8 7 6 5 4 3 2 1   01 00 99 98 97 96

For Leo and Nicole

Contents

9 *Finding One's Place*   294

10 *Politics and Power*   328

Preface

◆

First Person Singular is intended for freshman composition, intermediate and advanced composition courses, creative writing courses, courses that consider the essay to be a form of literature, as well as autobiography-as-literature courses.

The book will introduce students to major traditions in autobiography and biography, illustrate how writers transform personal experiences for different audiences, and explore the relationship between the writer's voice and stylistic features that express the writer's attitude towards his or her personal experiences. The text will also provide guidance for students in developing writing skills and introduce them to various techniques writers use to interpret their experiences.

The book is thematically organized in order to bridge the gap between the expressive essays that students traditionally read and their own life experiences. Students are introduced to the reading and writing of autobiography as an interpretive process that aims at understanding or clarifying what was said, acted, or lived. Selections drawn from diaries, journals, letters, memoirs, autobiographical essays, and biographies illustrate how writers move through, and beyond, personal experience.

Chapters are organized by those themes that have traditionally elicited compelling autobiographical narratives and include accounts of personal growth, nature writing, prison literature, and narratives of religious and philosophical exploration. The text presents many different kinds of writing including diaries, journals, letters, biographies, memoirs, and expressive essays. *First Person Singular* is rich in a variety of perspectives by African American, Native American, Asian American, and Hispanic writers and offers cross-cultural and regional narratives as well as a core of selections by classic authors. Almost half of the 59 selections are by women.

Chapter Descriptions

The twelve chapters move from the most personal sphere of family life through influential people, male and female relationships, creatures great and small, adolescent turning points, education, and work, to the challenges posed by self-acceptance, finding one's place, the struggles of individuals against governmental power, and different perceptions of the spiritual dimension.

Chapter 1, "Family," introduces vivid recollections from childhood that offer insights into relationships between brothers, sisters and brothers, sons and fathers, daughters and fathers, and granddaughters and grandmothers.

Chapter 2, "Influential People," introduces memorable portraits of people who were important in the lives of the writers, and it presents a valuable opportunity to study the methods biographers use to analyze significant aspects of character.

Chapter 3, "Sexual Identity," explores the way we acquire sexual identities and the role that expectations, social pressures, and cultural values play in shaping the choices we make.

Chapter 4, "Creatures Great and Small," looks at the tradition of nature writing and features the observations and first-hand accounts of an entomologist, an ethologist, a wildlife film producer, and a well-known essayist.

Chapter 5, "Coming of Age," presents narratives in which writers come to understand decisive moments that irrevocably changed their lives. These recollections lead to an enlarged understanding of the self by conferring a measure of order and coherence on one's experiences.

Chapter 6, "Education and Self-Education," takes up the crucial issue of education in many different settings. Each essay offers insight into the role literacy and self-education play in self-discovery.

Chapter 7, "Our Working Lives," offers the reflections of an auto mechanic, financial trader, firefighter, and social activist that show how we define ourselves through the work we do.

Chapter 8, "Self-Acceptance," focuses on the importance of coming to terms with difficult life circumstances in which limitations may be personal, hereditary, or cultural.

Chapter 9, "Finding One's Place," shows writers who are compelled to redefine themselves in unfamiliar places. In each case, the look, sound, and feel of the environment elicit deeply felt responses that anchor values, ideals, and attitudes in tangible settings. The locations cover a wide range and include the newly acquired Louisiana territory, the ancient city of Ur, a mountainside in Wisconsin, Niagara Falls, and modern-day southern California.

Chapter 10, "Politics and Power," introduces a kind of autobiographical writing known as the literature of the witness. It consists of first-hand testimonies by writers whose accounts combine eyewitness reports, literary texts, and historical records.

Chapter 11, "Facing the Unknown," focuses on responses to the eternal questions of life and death. Letters, journals, diaries, and essays by people such as a Civil War soldier, a British explorer, a feminist poet, a student of Zen Buddhism, and a psychiatrist reveal an extraordinary multiplicity of reflections on questions of mortality.

Chapter 12, "Fictionalized Autobiography: A Boundary Genre," explores the boundary between the worlds of nonfiction and fiction. The freedom to restructure accounts, add to or take away from the known facts, expand or compress time, or even to create a narrator through whose eyes a life story is told, provides an additional means by which writers can get at the truth of their life experiences.

Editorial Apparatus

An Introduction discusses the history and significance of autobiography as a genre and introduces important aspects of journal writing. Chapter introductions discuss the theme of each chapter and its relation to the individual selections. Biographical sketches preceding each selection give background information on the writer's life and identify the personal and literary context in which the selection is written.

End-of-selection questions for discussion and writing are designed to encourage readers to discover relationships between their personal experiences and those described by the writers in the text, to explore points of agreement or areas of conflict sparked by the viewpoint of the authors, and to provide ideas for further inquiry and writing. These questions ask students to think critically about the content, meaning, and purpose of the selections as well as to evaluate the author's rhetorical strategy, the voice projected in relationship to the audience, evidence cited, and underlying assumptions. Many selections use journal writing suggestions to help students get started with writing their own diaries or journals.

Following each chapter a set of questions entitled "Connections" challenges readers to make associations and comparisons between selections within the chapter and throughout the book. These questions provide the opportunity to consider additional contrasting perspectives on a single theme or to explore a particular theme in depth.

A Rhetorical Index is included to allow the text to accommodate a variety of teaching approaches.

Instructor's Manual

An *Instructor's Manual* provides guidelines for using the text, suggested answers to questions in the text, and a filmography including filmstrips and video recordings of interviews with many of the writers in the anthology talking about their lives and art. An up-to-date bibliography of scholarship that addresses the personal essay as a genre and the uses of autobiographical writing and journal keeping for composition and literature classes will be provided. The *Instructor's Manual* will include sample syllabi for a ten-week course and a fifteen-week semester course, as well as teaching suggestions and class activities (including methods for peer critique and small group work) for individual selections.

Acknowledgments

No expression of thanks can adequately convey our gratitude to all those teachers of composition who offered thoughtful comments and gave this book the benefit of their scholarship and teaching experience. We would especially like to thank the instructors who reviewed the various stages of the manuscript, including Chris Anderson, Oregon State University, and Christopher C. Burnham, New Mexico State University.

For their dedication and skill, we owe much to the able staff at Allyn and Bacon, especially Elisabeth Egan, and, formerly with Allyn and Bacon, Marjorie Payne, production administrator.

We would like to thank Frederick T. Courtright and Amanda Sumner, permissions editors, for their skill in obtaining the rights to reprint selections in this text. To Eben W. Ludlow, we owe all the things that one owes to an extraordinarily gifted editor.

First Person Singular

◆

Introduction

Autobiography is the poor man's history.
—Raymond Carver, "Blackbird Pie," 1987

Personal narratives can take the form of journals or diaries written for oneself, letters written to others, and autobiographical essays written for an audience. Differences in the occasion, the audience addressed, and the writer's purpose can result in autobiographical writing of many different kinds, including meditations, memoirs, vignettes, eyewitness accounts, historical analyses, reveries, and confessions. In all these forms the writer's commitment to thoughtful reflection and analysis of personal experiences can yield worthwhile emotional and intellectual insights. Personal experience has always been seen as a particularly persuasive kind of evidence, especially when supported by statistics, the testimony of experts, and case histories. Writers may wish to relate life experiences to understand themselves better, to share these experiences with others, or to use them to make a point.

Journals and Diaries

There are many reasons why people keep journals. Journals offer a means for self-discovery and self-realization. Keeping a journal offers an opportunity to find out what you really think and feel about people, relationships, and events. Journal entries can be jotted down at the spur of the moment in response to immediate experiences, or they can take the form of more reflective observations and impressions written after the fact.

Journal writing can serve as a valuable means for creating a repository of thoughts and ideas on which to draw at a later time. A journal offers a place where you may think about the meaning of events in privacy. Keeping a journal also enables you to gain perspective on life experiences while simultaneously creating a record of observations and feelings over an extended period of time.

Having a record of this kind will enable you to observe recurring patterns in events in which you are involved, perceive their cumulative effect on you, and understand how your feelings and attitudes have changed in response to these events. Think how valuable it would be to have a written record of this kind to look back upon weeks, months, or even years later.

Journals are not only places for storing observations. They can become nonjudgmental friends in whom you may confide negative, as well as positive, feelings. This therapeutic function of journal-keeping has led some writers to give their journals names, as if they were speaking to a friend in whom they might totally confide. For example, Zlata Filipovic, a thirteen-year-old girl living with her parents in Sarajevo, began keeping a diary a few months before war broke out. Her entry for Monday, March 30, 1992, reads: "Hey Diary! You know what I think? Since Anne Frank called her diary Kitty, maybe I could give you a name too.... I'm thinking, thinking.... I've decided! I'm going to call you Mimmy." In a later entry, Zlata confides to Mimmy the bewilderment of an innocent child horrified by war: "Saturday, April 19, 1992. Dear Mimmy, They're shooting. Shells are falling. This really is WAR. Mommy and Daddy are worried, they sit up until late at night, talking. They're wondering what to do, but it's hard to know. Whether to leave and split up, or stay here together.... War has suddenly entered our town, our homes, our thoughts, our lives. It's terrible. It's also terrible that Mommy has packed my suitcase. Love, Zlata" (*Zlata's Diary* [New York: Penguin Books, 1994] 35). As the family spent day after day cowering in the cellar, without electricity or food, Zlata found that writing to Mimmy was the only way she could record her confusion, fears, and hopes.

Journal writing can be liberating in a purely technical sense because you do not have to worry about grammar, spelling, or punctuation. Without inhibition from fear of criticism, many people discover they are indeed writers. Moreover, you do not have to be consistent. Your journal does not require you to always be the same kind of person: you can try on different selves in a way that others might find disconcerting in real life. As a result, you have the freedom to explore different sides of your personality.

There is no prescribed form governing how journal entries should appear. You may wish to date them, or not, as you choose. It is important not to second-guess your initial observations by discarding or editing out what you have written, because you never know what might be useful to you later on. One technique you might want to try is writing quickly, so that your critical inner self does not have a chance to inhibit you. This process of free writing, or "brainstorming," can provide many impressions that you can sift through later. You might also try starting out with a question and letting your answer become the journal entry.

Both letters and autobiographical essays differ in important ways from typical journal entries (where you are free to start and stop discussions, change subjects, use colloquial language, and jot down spur-of-the-moment observations). In composing letters and essays, the knowledge that what you write will be read by others might make you exclude observations or thoughts some might find too personal or too revealing.

You may also have to curb the tendency to falsify or dramatize experiences to make them seem more interesting. To an audience, the underlying appeal of autobiographical writing ultimately rests on its belief that what is read reveals some measure of the truth.

Autobiographical Writing

From the writer's perspective, the need to clarify and interpret one's past may spring from many motives and may serve a multitude of purposes. First, a writer wants to understand the meaning of past events. Boston Celtics star basketball player Larry Bird observed that "sometimes when you look back at certain events, the reasons things happen the way they did seems pretty obvious. Yet, when something is actually happening and you are right in the middle of it you can't seem to get a handle on what's going on" (*Drive* [New York: Doubleday], page 32). Sigmund Freud expressed the same sentiment, albeit more theoretically, in 1927: "In general people experience the past naively without being able to form an estimate of its contents. They have first to put themselves at a distance from it—the present must become the past—before it can reveal points of vantage" ("The Future of an Illusion," in *Standard Edition* XXI [London: Hogarth Press, 1927], page 114). This shift in perspective requires the writer to go back into the past in order to reconstruct the meaning and significance of experiences *whose importance may not have been appreciated at the time they occured.* From these accounts, a reader gets the strange sense that the author is reliving events by conferring meanings on experiences he or she may not have had when the event first took place. These forays into a previously uncharted past may result in insights into those crucial turning points that created the writer's present self.

Traditions of Autobiographical Writing

The idea that one's own life is an appropriate object of self-examination can be said to have started with *The Confessions of St. Augustine* (circa A.D. 397–401), which demonstrated a new method for exploring the mysteries of the interior life. In St. Augustine's words we can hear the qualities of honesty, candor, and self-scrutiny that have remained distinguishing features of autobiographical writing:

Why do you mean so much to me? Help me to find words to explain. Why do I mean so much to you, that you should command me to love you? And if I fail to love you, you are angry and threaten me with great sorrow, as if not to love you were not sorrow enough in itself. Have pity on me and help me, O Lord my God. (*The Confessions of St. Augustine* [New York: Penguin Books, 1980] page 37.)

In St. Augustine's case, the assumption that recounting one's life was a necessary vehicle for self-understanding expressed itself as the need to to lay his soul bare before God.

Since writing autobiography is basically an interpretive act, the motives for refashioning oneself through imagination can serve many purposes. Each has yielded a rich tradition. Autobiographies in which the reader can see the role that acquisition of language plays in the creation of an identity are particularly fascinating. For example, in the accounts of Christy Brown, who was thought to be retarded, and Helen Keller, who was both deaf and blind, we can observe how being able to communicate led to acquiring a sense of identity. For them, the creation of a self and the ability to articulate a meaningful, coherent, and objective account of the world were simultaneous events.

Autobiographies also offer a means by which writers can define themselves as individuals, distinct from the self-images fostered by societal or cultural stereotyping. Narratives by Itabari Njeri, Sucheng Chan, Mary Crow Dog, and Gary Soto chart decisive moments when each writer came to terms with being African American, Asian American, Native American, or Hispanic within a culture that marginalizes minorities.

For other writers, the process of writing an autobiography offers a means to confront hidden or repressed memories that hold the key that will allow the writer to reconstruct an intelligible case history of his or her life. This cathartic or therapeutic function of autobiography cannot be overestimated. Mikal Gilmore, the brother of convicted mass murderer Gary Gilmore, confided that writing "My Brother, Gary Gilmore," was the only way to demystify the past and to understand why his relationships ended so disastrously.

Autobiographies of this kind allow writers to recover and confront repressed memories from childhood. For example, we can only imagine how painful it must have been for Richard Rhodes, in "A Hole in the World," to relive the circumstances of his childhood. Abused by his stepmother with his father's acquiescence, Rhodes knew there was something terribly wrong at the time. He was only able to confront the confusion and uncertainty of this experience through a conscious effort to reveal shameful secrets. For those with the courage to face the past, writing an autobiography can bring a sense of healing.

A particularly important kind of autobiographical writing, known as the literature of the witness, also aims at robbing the past of its power to control the present. These narratives are mixtures of eyewitness reports and historical accounts. They aim at breaking a silence that would be taken as complicity with the state in circumstances when only the state has the power to determine how reality will be perceived. For example, the account of Rigoberta Menchú, "Things Have Happened to Me as in a Movie," bears witness to incidents of arrest, interrogation, and torture that transform her personal experience into a public record. She literally provides a voice for those who would otherwise not be remembered. This tradition has yielded major works like Cervantes's *Don Quixote* and Oscar Wilde's *De Profundis*, both of which were written when the authors were in prison.

Other writers confront the abuses of a present regime in hopes of keeping alive the vision of what their country once was and might be again. Such is the case in Slavenka Drakulić's "The Balkan Express." In the unequal contest between the awesome governmental power and the isolated individual, autobiography offers one of the few means of keeping an accurate record the state cannot control.

Close and detailed observations of the natural world, based on personal research, have yielded an astonishingly rich body of work beginning with the journals of the eighteenth century Swedish botanist Linnæus and including Charles Darwin's *The Origin of Species* in the nineteenth century. Reflections on the complex interactions of living things, the study of animal behavior, concern for the environment and the extinction of species along with the concomitant value of wilderness are topics that occur frequently in the tradition of nature writing. Aldo Leopold's meditation "Thinking Like a Mountain" stands as one of the classics in the American tradition of this kind of writing, along with *Walden* by Thoreau (1845) and *The Yosemite* by John Muir (1912). Among studies of plants and animals, Jean Henri Fabre's engaging journal entries on the praying mantis are not just informative. They allow us to enter the private world of a distinguished researcher. Jane van Lawick-Goodall's pioneering research into chimpanzee behavior stands as a model of how personal experience can form the basis for objective scientific reporting.

Autobiographical writing's qualities of confidentiality, intimacy, and candor are well suited for revealing memories, thoughts, and desires that underly questions of sexual identity. The range of tone that writers achieve in these disclosures is especially striking. The candid recollections of Judith Ortiz Cofer, Kim Chernin, and Nawal el-Saadawi relentlessly expose prejudice towards women in various guises and in different cultures. We can share the sense of pride that Tepilit Ole Saitoti feels in meeting his tribe's rite of passage that ushers him into manhood. Conversely, Paul Monette's "Becoming a Man" depicts the difficulties of coping with societal and personal ambivalence towards sexual identity.

In the final analysis, nothing is more powerful in stripping away the mask of everyday preoccupations than the prospect of imminent death. Reflection on the end of life brings out a tendency in autobiographical writing, which is always there, to move from the intensely personal to the universal as basic doubts about the meaning and value of life are confronted. We can see the vulnerable self at the margins of existence facing the unknown in works by the Civil War soldier Sullivan Ballou, by the explorer Robert Falcon Scott, and by the African American feminist poet Audre Lorde. If these writers pose questions without answers, works by Peter Matthiessen, on a spiritual quest across the Himalayas, and psychiatrist Brian L. Weiss, M.D., whose patient under hypnotic regression experienced memories from past lives, suggest answers. These autobiographical writings can be distinguished from expressions of conventional theology because they are preeminently personal responses balanced on the edge of skepticism and faith.

Autobiographical fiction is at the furthest boundary of autobiographical writing; this form of writing draws on and spins out the implications of personal experience. Fiction writing of this kind emphasizes the first-person-singular "I" tradition of intimate revelation. The narrative voice we hear in these works sets up an immediate connection with the reader. It solicits understanding, empathy, and a persistent curiosity about the motives for behavior that otherwise might seem whimsical, eccentric, or tendentious. Just as they do when reading autobiographical writing, readers expect complete honesty and moments of self-recognition from fictionalized autobiographies. In practical terms, this means that the reader must perceive the narrator as reliable and credible. Narrators in these works are often thinly fictionalized projections of the writer's personality. Functioning as an alter ego or perhaps using the safety provided by this mask, or persona, the writer can be even more candid while seeming to be simply a character in a fictionalized work. Experiences related in this fashion may be harrowing, like those of Tadeusz Borowski; whimsical, like those of Natsume Soseki; painfully honest, as in Gary Soto's story; or ironic and self-mocking, as in Amy Tan's "Two Kinds."

1
Family

◆————————◆

*All happy families resemble one another, but each unhappy family
is unhappy in its own way.*

—Leo Tolstoy, *Anna Karenina*, 1873

The essays in this chapter serve as an introduction to the autobiographical process and illustrate how the writer's voice can be transferred to
the written page. We can understand that the desire to write about personal experiences is actually a way to make sense of one's life. Family is
a natural topic that provides a storehouse of memories, impressions,
and ideas that writers draw on when writing about their experiences.
Moreover, the process of drawing on these recollections from childhood often motivates writers to explore relationships they have had
with family members.

The family has been the most enduring basis of culture throughout
the world and has provided a stabilizing force in all societies. The complex network of dependencies, relationships, and obligations may extend outward from parents and children to include grandparents,
cousins, aunts and uncles, and more distantly related relatives. The
unique relationships developed among members of a family provide a
universal basis for common experiences, emotions, perceptions, and
expectations. It is in the context of the family that we first learn what it
means to experience love, hope, fear, anger, and contentment. At the
same time, each family is different, with its own unique characteristics
and bonds. The family continues to exist in the age-old role of nurtur-
ing, protecting, and instilling values and social mores. Family relationships also exert a profound influence on one's life long after childhood.

The selections in this chapter focus on the relationships between
parent and child, among siblings, and between grandparent and
grandchild. The complex portraits of family life offered in this chapter
allow us to share the experiences writers have had in various relationships and to understand more completely our own family experiences.

Sylvia Plath's letter to her brother expresses the kaleidoscope of emotions she experienced on her first trip to New York City. In "My Father's Life," Raymond Carver confronts the decisive role his father played in shaping his son's life and career. Tennessee Williams offers a vivid recollection of a family he found hard to live with, but intriguing to observe, in "The Man in the Overstuffed Chair." Patricia Hampl offers, in "Grandmother's Sunday Dinner," a nostalgic account of the rituals surrounding the preparation and serving of these celebratory meals. "Number One!" brings questions of race, superiority, and achievement to the fore as Jill Nelson attempts to come to terms with her father's commandment that she always be first. In "My Brother, Gary Gilmore," Mikal Gilmore explores the turbulent relationship he had with his brother, a convicted mass murderer.

Sylvia Plath

The American poet Sylvia Plath was born in Winthrop. Massachusetts, in 1932, the older of two children. Throughout her life she maintained a close relationship with her brother, Warren. After graduating from Smith College, she became one of several guest editors at the New York fashion magazine Mademoiselle. *In 1953, she traveled to New York City to work there. In the following letter, from* Letters Home, *Plath tells her brother, Warren, about her experiences and feelings.*

As a poet, Plath mythologized and transformed life experiences, many of them traumatic (including the unexpected death of her father, her suicide attempts, and her separation from. her husband, English poet Ted Hughes). Plath's most influential poems include "The Colossus" (1959), "Daddy," "Ariel" and "Lady Lazarus," all of which were written in 1962 but published posthumously in Ariel *(1965), after she committed suicide in 1963.*

[Undated—Late June, 1953]

Dear Warren,

. . . I have learned an amazing lot here; the world has split open before 1
my gaping eyes and spilt out its guts like a cracked watermelon. I think it will not be until I have meditated in peace upon the multitude of things I have learned and seen that I will begin to comprehend what has happened to me this last month. I am worn out now with the strenuous days at the office and the heat and the evenings out. I want to come home and sleep and sleep and play tennis and get tan again (I am an unhealthy shade of yellow now) and learn what I have been doing this last year.

I don't know about you, but I've realized that the last weeks of 2
school were one hectic running for buses and trains and exams and appointments, and the shift to NYC has been so rapid that I can't think logically about who I am or where I am going. I have been very ecstatic, horribly depressed, shocked, elated, enlightened, and enervated—all of which goes to make up living very hard and newly. I want to come home and vegetate in peace this coming weekend, with the people I love around me for a change.

Somehow I can't talk about all that has happened this week at 3
length, I am too weary, too dazed. I have, in the space of six days, toured the second largest ad agency in the world and seen television, kitchens, heard speeches there, gotten ptomaine poisoning from crabmeat the agency served us in their "own special test kitchen" and wanted to die very badly for a day, in the midst of faintings and hypo-

9

dermics and miserable agony. Spent an evening in Greenwich Village with the most brilliant, wonderful man in the world, the simultaneous interpreter, Gary Karmirloff, who is tragically a couple of inches shorter than I am, but who is the most magnificent lovable person I have ever met in my life. I think I will be looking for his alter ego all over the world for the rest of my life. Spent an evening listening to an 18-year-old friend of Bob Cochran's read his poetry to me after a steak dinner, also at the Village. Spent an evening fighting with a wealthy, unscrupulous Peruvian delegate to the UN at a Forest Hills tennis club dance—and spent Saturday in the Yankee Stadium with all the stinking people in the world watching the Yankees trounce the Tigers, having our pictures taken with commentator Mel Allen; getting lost in the subway and seeing deformed men with short arms that curled like pink, boneless snakes around a begging cup stagger through the car; thinking to myself all the time that Central Park Zoo was only different in that there were bars on the windows—oh God, it is unbelievable to think of all this at once—my mind will split open.... do you suppose you could meet your soot-stained, grubby, weary, wise, ex-managing editor at the station to carry her home with her bags? I love you a million times more than any of these slick admen, these hucksters, these wealthy beasts who get dronk [sic] in foreign accents all the time. I will let you know what train my coffin will come in on.

4   Seriously, I am more than overjoyed to have been here a month; it is just that I realize how young and inexperienced I am in the ways of the world. Smith seems like a simple, enchanting, bucolic existence compared to the dry, humid, breathless wasteland of the cliffdwellers, where the people are, as D. H. Lawrence wrote of his society, "dead brilliant galls on the tree of life." By contrast, the good few friends I have seem like clear ice water after a very strong, scalding martini.

5   Best love to you—you wonderful textured honest real unpainted people. Your exhausted ecstatic, elegaic New Yorker,

Sivvy

✦ Questions for Discussion and Writing

1. What impression of herself does Plath communicate in this letter?

2. Which of the experiences Plath relates seems to be especially important to her?

3. How would you characterize the tone of this letter? What does it tell you about her relationship to her brother, Warren?

4. How do the kind of observations Plath makes and the literal and figurative language she uses to express them suggest the qualities that distinguish her as a poet?

5. If you have ever kept a diary or journal in which you recorded your impressions of visiting a new place, use these as a basis for (a) a letter to a trusted friend or family member, (b) an autobiographical essay that anyone might read. How would these two accounts of the same event differ from each other and from your diary/journal?

6. Plath's free associations in her letter are very much like the technique of stream of consciousness that James Joyce popularized in his 1922 novel *Ulysses*. In your journal/diary, you might wish to try this technique of letting your imagination move freely. This flow of images provides a channel through which unconscious or subconscious thoughts can come through without the constraints of logic. Plath's letter is a result of a literal journey; make yours a journey that has not yet happened.

Raymond Carver

My Father's Life

◆ ——————

Raymond Carver (1938–1988) grew up in a logging town in Oregon and was educated at Humboldt State College (B.A., 1963) and at the University of Iowa where he studied creative writing. His strong desire to become a writer sustained him through difficult times while he was supporting a family. He first received recognition in the 1970s with the publication of stories in The New Yorker, Esquire, *and* The Atlantic Monthly. *His first collection of short stories,* Will You Please Be Quiet, Please? *(1976), was nominated for the National Book Award. Subsequently, he published many collections distinguished for their conversational style and realism, including* What We Talk About When We Talk About Love *(1981),* Cathedral *(1983), and* Where I'm Calling From *(1988). "My Father's Life," which first appeared in* Esquire *(1984), displays Carver's uncanny knack for getting to the heart of human relationships.*

1   My dad's name was Clevie Raymond Carver. His family called him Raymond and friends called him C. R. I was named Raymond Clevie Carver Jr. I hated the "Junior" part. When I was little my dad called me Frog, which was okay. But later, like everybody else in the family, he began calling me Junior. He went on calling me this until I was thirteen or fourteen and announced that I wouldn't answer to that name any longer. So he began calling me Doc. From then until his death, on June 17, 1967, he called me Doc, or else Son.

2   When he died, my mother telephoned my wife with the news. I was away from my family at the time, between lives, trying to enroll in the School of Library Science at the University of Iowa. When my wife answered the phone, my mother blurted out, "Raymond's dead!" For a moment, my wife thought my mother was telling her that I was dead. Then my mother made it clear *which* Raymond she was talking about and my wife said, "Thank God. I thought you meant *my* Raymond."

3   My dad walked, hitched rides, and rode in empty boxcars when he went from Arkansas to Washington State in 1934, looking for work. I don't know whether he was pursuing a dream when he went out to Washington. I doubt it. I don't think he dreamed much. I believe he was simply looking for steady work at decent pay. Steady work was meaningful work. He picked apples for a time and then landed a construction laborer's job on the Grand Coulee Dam. After he'd put aside a little money, he bought a car and drove back to Arkansas to help his

12

folks, my grandparents, pack up for the move west. He said later that they were about to starve down there, and this wasn't meant as a figure of speech. It was during that short while in Arkansas, in a town called Leola, that my mother met my dad on the sidewalk as he came out of a tavern.

"He was drunk," she said. "I don't know why I let him talk to me. His eyes were glittery. I wish I'd had a crystal ball." They'd met once, a year or so before, at a dance. He'd had girlfriends before her, my mother told me. "Your dad always had a girlfriend, even after we married. He was my first and last. I never had another man. But I didn't miss anything."

They were married by a justice of the peace on the day they left for Washington, this big, tall country girl and a farmhand-turned-construction worker. My mother spent her wedding night with my dad and his folks, all of them camped beside the road in Arkansas.

In Omak, Washington, my dad and mother lived in a little place not much bigger than a cabin. My grandparents lived next door. My dad was still working on the dam, and later, with the huge turbines producing electricity and the water backed up for a hundred miles into Canada, he stood in the crowd and heard Franklin D. Roosevelt when he spoke at the construction site. "He never mentioned those guys who died building that dam," my dad said. Some of his friends had died there, men from Arkansas, Oklahoma, and Missouri.

He then took a job in a sawmill in Clatskanie, Oregon, a little town alongside the Columbia River. I was born there, and my mother has a picture of my dad standing in front of the gate to the mill, proudly holding me up to face the camera. My bonnet is on crooked and about to come untied. His hat is pushed back on his forehead, and he's wearing a big grin. Was he going in to work or just finishing his shift? It doesn't matter. In either case, he had a job and a family. These were his salad days.

In 1941 we moved to Yakima, Washington, where my dad went to work as a saw filer, a skilled trade he'd learned in Clatskanie. When war broke out, he was given a deferment because his work was considered necessary to the war effort. Finished lumber was in demand by the armed services, and he kept his saws so sharp they could shave the hair off your arm.

After my dad had moved us to Yakima, he moved his folks into the same neighborhood. By the mid-1940s the rest of my dad's family—his brother, his sister, and her husband, as well as uncles, cousins, nephews, and most of their extended family and friends—had come out from Arkansas. All because my dad came out first. The men went to work at Boise Cascade, where my dad worked, and the women packed apples in the canneries. And in just a little while, it seemed—according to my mother—everybody was better off than my dad. "Your dad couldn't keep money," my mother said. "Money burned a hole in his pocket. He was always doing for others."

10   The first house I clearly remember living in, at 1515 South Fifteenth Street, in Yakima, had an outdoor toilet. On Halloween night, or just any night, for the hell of it, neighbor kids, kids in their early teens, would carry our toilet away and leave it next to the road. My dad would have to get somebody to help him bring it home. Or these kids would take the toilet and stand it in somebody else's backyard. Once they actually set it on fire, but ours wasn't the only house that had an outdoor toilet. When I was old enough to know what I was doing, I threw rocks at the other toilets when I'd see someone go inside. This was called bombing the toilets. After a while, though, everyone went to indoor plumbing until, suddenly, our toilet was the last outdoor one in the neighborhood. I remember the shame I felt when my third-grade teacher, Mr. Wise, drove me home from school one day. I asked him to stop at the house just before ours, claiming I lived there.

11   I can recall what happened one night when my dad came home late to find that my mother had locked all the doors on him from the inside. He was drunk, and we could feel the house shudder as he rattled the door. When he'd managed to force open a window, she hit him between the eyes with a colander and knocked him out. We could see him down there on the grass. For years afterward, I used to pick up this colander—it was as heavy as a rolling pin—and imagine what it would feel like to be hit in the head with something like that.

12   It was during this period that I remember my dad taking me into the bedroom, sitting me down on the bed, and telling me that I might have to go live with my Aunt LaVon for a while. I couldn't understand what I'd done that meant I'd have to go away from home to live. But this, too—whatever prompted it—must have blown over, more or less, anyway, because we stayed together, and I didn't have to go live with her or anyone else.

13   I remember my mother pouring his whiskey down the sink. Sometimes she'd pour it all out and sometimes, if she was afraid of getting caught, she'd only pour half of it out and then add water to the rest. I tasted some of his whiskey once myself. It was terrible stuff, and I don't see how anybody could drink it.

14   After a long time without one, we finally got a car, in 1949 or 1950, a 1938 Ford. But it threw a rod the first week we had it, and my dad had to have the motor rebuilt.

15   "We drove the oldest car in town," my mother said. "We could have had a Cadillac for all he spent on car repairs." One time she found someone else's tube of lipstick on the floorboard, along with a lacy handkerchief. "See this?" she said to me. "Some floozy left this in the car."

16   Once I saw her take a pan of warm water into the bedroom where my dad was sleeping. She took his hand from under the covers and

held it in the water. I stood in the doorway and watched. I wanted to know what was going on. This would make him talk in his sleep, she told me. There were things she needed to know, things she was sure he was keeping from her.

Every year or so, when I was little, we would take the North Coast Limited across the Cascade Range from Yakima to Seattle and stay in the Vance Hotel and eat, I remember, at a place called the Dinner Bell Cafe. Once we went to Ivar's Acres of Clams and drank glasses of warm clam broth.

In 1956, the year I was to graduate from high school, my dad quit his job at the mill in Yakima and took a job in Chester, a little sawmill town in northern California. The reasons given at the time for his taking the job had to do with a higher hourly wage and the vague promise that he might, in a few years' time, succeed to the job of head filer in this new mill. But I think, in the main, that my dad had grown restless and simply wanted to try his luck elsewhere. Things had gotten a little too predictable for him in Yakima. Also, the year before, there had been the deaths, within six months of each other, of both his parents.

But just a few days after graduation, when my mother and I were packed to move to Chester, my dad penciled a letter to say he'd been sick for a while. He didn't want us to worry, he said, but he'd cut himself on a saw. Maybe he'd got a tiny sliver of steel in his blood. Anyway, something had happened and he'd had to miss work, he said. In the same mail was an unsigned postcard from somebody down there telling my mother that my dad was about to die and that he was drinking "raw whiskey."

When we arrived in Chester, my dad was living in a trailer that belonged to the company. I didn't recognize him immediately. I guess for a moment I didn't want to recognize him. He was skinny and pale and looked bewildered. His pants wouldn't stay up. He didn't look like my dad. My mother began to cry. My dad put his arm around her and patted her shoulder vaguely, like he didn't know what this was all about, either. The three of us took up life together in the trailer, and we looked after him as best we could. But my dad was sick, and he couldn't get any better. I worked with him in the mill that summer and part of the fall. We'd get up in the mornings and eat eggs and toast while we listened to the radio, and then go out the door with our lunch pails. We'd pass through the gate together at eight in the morning, and I wouldn't see him again until quitting time. In November I went back to Yakima to be closer to my girlfriend, the girl I'd made up my mind I was going to marry.

He worked at the mill in Chester until the following February, when he collapsed on the job and was taken to the hospital. My mother asked if I would come down there and help. I caught a bus from Yakima to Chester, intending to drive them back to Yakima. But now, in

17

18

19

20

21

addition to being physically sick, my dad was in the midst of a nervous breakdown, though none of us knew to call it that at the time. During the entire trip back to Yakima, he didn't speak, not even when asked a direct question. ("How do you feel, Raymond?" "You okay, Dad?") He'd communicate if he communicated at all, by moving his head or by turning his palms up as if to say he didn't know or care. The only time he said anything on the trip, and for nearly a month afterward, was when I was speeding down a gravel road in Oregon and the car muffler came loose. "You were going too fast," he said.

22   Back in Yakima a doctor saw to it that my dad went to a psychiatrist. My mother and dad had to go on relief, as it was called, and the county paid for the psychiatrist. The psychiatrist asked my dad, "Who is the President?" He'd had a question put to him that he could answer. "Ike," my dad said, Nevertheless, they put him on the fifth floor of Valley Memorial Hospital and began giving him electroshock treatments. I was married by then and about to start my own family. My dad was still locked up when my wife went into this same hospital, just one floor down, to have our first baby. After she had delivered, I went upstairs to give my dad the news. They let me in through a steel door and showed me where I could find him. He was sitting on a couch with a blanket over his lap. *Hey,* I thought. *What in hell is happening to my dad?* I sat down next to him and told him he was a grandfather. He waited a minute and then said, "I feel like a grandfather." That's all he said. He didn't smile or move. He was in a big room with a lot of other people. Then I hugged him, and he began to cry.

23   Somehow he got out of there. But now came the years when he couldn't work and just sat around the house trying to figure what next and what he'd done wrong in his life that he'd wound up like this. My mother went from job to crummy job. Much later she referred to that time he was in the hospital, and those years just afterward, as "when Raymond was sick." The word *sick* was never the same for me again.

24   In 1964, through the help of a friend, he was lucky enough to be hired on at a mill in Klamath, California. He moved down there by himself to see if he could hack it. He lived not far from the mill, in a one-room cabin not much different from the place he and my mother had started out living in when they went west. He scrawled letters to my mother, and if I called she'd read them aloud to me over the phone. In the letters, he said it was touch and go. Every day that he went to work, he felt like it was the most important day of his life. But every day, he told her, made the next day that much easier. He said for her to tell me he said hello. If he couldn't sleep at night, he said, he thought about me and the good times we used to have. Finally, after a couple of months, he regained some of his confidence. He could do the work and didn't think he had to worry that he'd let anybody down ever again. When he was sure, he sent for my mother.

He'd been off from work for six years and had lost everything in   25
that time—home, car, furniture, and appliances, including the big
freezer that had been my mother's pride and joy. He'd lost his good
name too—Raymond Carver was someone who couldn't pay his
bills—and his self-respect was gone. He'd even lost his virility. My
mother told my wife, "All during that time Raymond was sick we slept
together in the same bed, but we didn't have relations. He wanted to a
few times, but nothing happened. I didn't miss it, but I think he wanted
to, you know."

During those years I was trying to raise my own family and earn a   26
living. But, one thing and another, we found ourselves having to move
a lot. I couldn't keep track of what was going down in my dad's life.
But I did have a chance one Christmas to tell him I wanted to be a
writer. I might as well have told him I wanted to become a plastic sur-
geon. "What are you going to write about?" he wanted to know. Then,
as if to help me out, he said, "Write about stuff you know about. Write
about some of those fishing trips we took." I said I would, but I knew I
wouldn't. "Send me what you write," he said, I said I'd do that, but
then I didn't. I wasn't writing anything about fishing, and I didn't
think he'd particularly care about, or even necessarily understand,
what I was writing in those days. Besides, he wasn't a reader. Not the
sort, anyway, I imagined I was writing for.

Then he died. I was a long way off, in Iowa City, with things still to   27
say to him. I didn't have the chance to tell him goodbye, or that I
thought he was doing great at his new job. That I was proud of him for
making a comeback.

My mother said he came in from work that night and ate a big sup-   28
per. Then he sat at the table by himself and finished what was left of a
bottle of whiskey, a bottle she found hidden in the bottom of the garbage under some coffee grounds a day or so later. Then he got up and
went to bed, where my mother joined him a little later. But in the night
she had to get up and make a bed for herself on the couch. "He was
snoring so loud I couldn't sleep," she said. The next morning when she
looked in on him, he was on his back with his mouth open, his cheeks
caved in. *Graylooking,* she said. She knew he was dead—she didn't
need a doctor to tell her that. But she called one anyway, and then she
called my wife.

Among the pictures my mother kept of my dad and herself during   29
those early days in Washington was a photograph of him standing in
front of a car, holding a beer and a stringer of fish. In the photograph he
is wearing his hat back on his forehead and has this awkward grin on
his face. I asked her for it and she gave it to me, along with some others.
I put it up on my wall, and each time we moved, I took the picture
along and put it up on another wall. I looked at it carefully from time to
time, trying to figure out some things about my dad, and maybe myself

in the process. But I couldn't. My dad just kept moving further and further away from me and back into time. Finally, in the course of another move, I lost the photograph. It was then that I tried to recall it, and at the same time make an attempt to say something about my dad, and how I thought that in some important ways we might be alike. I wrote the poem when I was living in an apartment house in an urban area south of San Francisco, at a time when I found myself, like my dad, having trouble with alcohol. The poem was a way of trying to connect up with him.

30 ### *Photograph of My Father*
in His Twenty-Second Year

October. Here in this dank, unfamiliar kitchen
I study my father's embarrassed young man's face.
Sheepish grin, he holds in one hand a string
of spiny yellow perch, in the other
a bottle of Carlsberg beer.

In jeans and flannel shirt, he leans
against the front fender of a 1934 Ford.
He would like to pose brave and hearty for his posterity,
wear his old hat cocked over his ear.
All his life my father wanted to be bold.

But the eyes give him away, and the hands
that limply offer the string of dead perch
and the bottle of beer. Father, I love you,
yet how can I say thank you, I who can't hold my liquor either
and don't even know the places to fish.

31   The poem is true in its particulars, except that my dad died in June and not October, as the first word of the poem says. I wanted a word with more than one syllable to it to make it linger a little. But more than that, I wanted a month appropriate to what I felt at the time I wrote the poem—a month of short days and failing light, smoke in the air, things perishing. June was summer nights and days, graduations, my wedding anniversary, the birthday of one of my children. June wasn't a month your father died in.

32   After the service at the funeral home, after we had moved outside, a woman I didn't know came over to me and said, "He's happier where he is now." I stared at this woman until she moved away. I still remember the little knob of a hat she was wearing. Then one of my dad's cousins— I didn't know the man's name—reached out and took my hand, "We all miss him," he said, and I knew he wasn't saying it just to be polite.

33   I began to weep for the first time since receiving the news. I hadn't been able to before. I hadn't had the time, for one thing. Now, suddenly,

I couldn't stop. I held my wife and wept while she said and did what she could do to comfort me there in the middle of that summer afternoon.

I listened to people say consoling things to my mother, and I was glad that my dad's family had turned up, had come to where he was. I thought I'd remember everything that was said and done that day and maybe find a way to tell it sometime. But I didn't. I forgot it all, or nearly. What I do remember is that I heard our name used a lot that afternoon, my dad's name and mine. But I knew they were talking about my dad. *Raymond,* these people kept saying in their beautiful voices out of my childhood. *Raymond.*

34

✦ *Questions for Discussion and Writing*

1. How would you characterize the relationship between Carver and his father? Was it distant? close? amiable? etc. What details suggest Carver is attempting to be as honest as possible in his account?

2. To what extent does Carver wish to understand his father's life in order to understand his own? What characteristics does Carver share with his father and in what ways do they differ?

3. What is the purpose of the poem in Carver's narrative? Would you consider writing a poem or story that expressed feelings towards a person if you found it difficult to express them face to face?

4. What relative of yours has had the most influence in shaping your life? Describe this relationship.

5. Describe a person from a photograph so that someone who has not seen the photograph would be able to recognize him or her from your detailed description.

6. For much of his life Raymond Carver struggled to come to terms with being a child of an alcoholic parent. If you keep a journal and can relate to Carver's situation, try free writing, using any of the following terms to trigger associations from your childhood: denial, abuse, unkept promises, fear, isolation, compulsive behavior, drunkenness, shame, or any other terms you may wish to use.

Tennessee Williams

The Man in the Overstuffed Chair

◆

Tennessee Williams (1911–1983), the preeminent American playwright, was born Thomas Lanier Williams in Columbus, Mississippi, to an Episcopalian minister's daughter and a traveling salesman. His family, including a brother and sister, moved to St. Louis in 1918, where he grew up and attended the University of Missouri and Washington University. He later received his B.A. degree from the University of Iowa. The 1945 production of The Glass Menagerie *gained Williams instant recognition as a significant playwright, a judgment reconfirmed with the Broadway success two years later of* A Streetcar Named Desire. *Other major plays include* Summer and Smoke *(1948),* Cat on a Hot Tin Roof *(1955), and* Sweet Bird of Youth *(1959). Williams's "The Man in the Overstuffed Chair" is a sympathetic account of the relationships in his family. It helps us to understand the themes and characters such as Amanda Winfield, Blanche Dubois, Stanley Kowalski, and Big Daddy Pollitt in his plays.*

1   He always enters the house as though he were entering it with the intention of tearing it down from inside. That is how he always enters it except when it's after midnight and liquor has put out the fire in his nerves. Then he enters the house in a strikingly different manner, almost guiltily, coughing a little, sighing louder than he coughs, and sometimes talking to himself as someone talks to someone after a long, fierce argument has exhausted the anger between them but not settled the problem. He takes off his shoes in the living room before he goes upstairs where he has to go past my mother's closed door, but she never fails to let him know she hears him by clearing her throat very loudly or "Ah, me, ah, me!" Sometimes I hear him say "Ah, me" in response as he goes on down the hall to where he sleeps, an alcove sunroom connected to the bedroom of my young brother, Dakin, who is at this time, the fall and winter of 1943, with the Air Force in Burma.

2   These months, the time of this story, enclose the end of the life of my mother's mother.

3   My father's behavior toward my maternal grandmother is scrupulously proper but his attitude toward my grandfather Dakin is so in-

sulting that I don't think the elderly gentleman could have endured it without the insulation of deafness and near-blindness.

Although my grandmother is dying, she is still quite sound of sight 4 and hearing, and when it is approaching the time for my father to return from his office to the house, my grandmother is always downstairs to warn her husband that Cornelius is about to storm in the front door. She hears the Studebaker charging up the drive and cries out to my grandfather, *"Walter, Cornelius is coming!"* She cries out this warning so loudly that Grandfather can't help but hear it. My grandfather staggers up from his chair by the radio and starts for the front stairs, but sometimes he doesn't make them in time and there is an awkward encounter in the downstairs hall. My grandfather says, "Good evening, Cornelius" and is lucky if he receives, in answer, a frigid "Hello, Mr. Dakin" instead of a red-eyed glare and a grunt.

It takes him, now that he's in his eighties with cataracts on both 5 eyes, quite a while to get up the stairs, shepherded by his wife, and sometimes my father will come thundering up the steps behind them as if he intended to knock the old couple down. What is he after? A drink, of course, from a whiskey bottle under his bed in the sunroom, or the bathroom tub.

"Walter, watch out!" 6

"Excuse me, Mrs. Dakin," my father grunts breathlessly as he 7 charges past them on the stairs.

They go to their bedroom, close the door. I don't hear just what 8 they say to each other, but I know that "Grand" is outdone with Grandfather for lingering too long downstairs to avoid this humiliating encounter. Of course Grandfather finds the encounter distasteful, too, but he dearly loves to crouch by the downstairs radio at this hour when the news broadcasters come on, now that he can't read newsprint.

They are living with us because my grandmother's strength is so 9 rapidly failing. She has been dying for ten years and her weight has dropped to eighty-six pounds. Any other person would be confined to bed, if not the terminal ward of a hospital, but my grandmother is resolved to remain on her feet, and actively helpful about the house. She is. She still does most of the laundry in the basement and insists on washing the dishes. My mother begs her to rest, but "Grand" is determined to show my father that she is not a dependent. And I have come home, this late autumn of 1943, because my mother wrote me, "Your grandmother has had to give up the house in Memphis because she is not strong enough to take care of it and your grandfather, too."

Between the lines of the letter, I read that my mother is expecting 10 the imminent death of her mother and I ought to stop in Saint Louis on my bus trip between the West and East coasts, so I have stopped there.

11   I arrive there late one night in November and as I go up the front
walk I see, through the curtains of the front room windows, my grandmother stalking across the living room like a skeleton in clothes. It
shocks me so that I have to set down my luggage on the front walk and
wait about five minutes before I can enter the house.

12   Only my grandmother has stayed up to receive me at this midnight
hour, the others thinking that I had probably driven on through to New
York, as I had so often before after promising to come home.

13   She makes light of her illness, and actually she manages to seem almost well for my benefit. She has kept a dinner plate on the stove for
me over a double boiler and a low flame, and the living room fire is
alive, and no reference is made to my failure in Hollywood, the humiliating termination of my six-months option as a screenwriter at MGM
studios.

14   "Grand" says she's come here to help Edwina, my mother, who is
suffering from nervous exhaustion and is very disturbed over Cornelius's behavior. Cornelius has been drinking heavily. Mother found five
empty bottles under his bed and several more under the bathtub, and
his position as sales manager of a branch of The International Shoe
Company is in jeopardy due to a scandalous poker fight in which half
of his left ear was bitten off, yes, actually bitten off, so that he had to go
to a hospital and have a plastic-surgery operation, taking cartilage from
a rib to be grafted onto the ear, and in spite of elaborate precautions to
keep it under wraps, the story has come out. Mr. J., the head executive
and my father's immediate superior, has at last lost all patience with
my father, who may have to retire in order to avoid being dismissed.
But otherwise everything is fine, she is telling me about these things
because Edwina may be inclined to exaggerate the seriousness of the
family situation when we talk in the morning. And now I ought to go
up to bed after a long, hard trip. Yes, I ought to, indeed. I will have to
sleep in brother Dakin's old room rather than in my usual retreat in the
attic, since the bed in the attic has been dismantled so that I won't insist
on sleeping up there and getting pneumonia.

15   I don't like the idea of taking Dakin's room since it adjoins my father's doorless appendage to it.

16   I enter the bedroom and undress in the dark.

17   Strange sounds come from my father's sunroom, great sighs and
groans and inebriate exclamations of sorrow such as, "Oh, God, oh,
God!" He is unaware of my sleepless presence in the room adjoining.
From time to time, at half-hour intervals, he lurches and stumbles out
of bed to fetch a bottle of whiskey from some place of naive concealment, remarking to himself, "How terrible!"

18   At last I take a sleeping pill so that my exhaustion can prevail over
my tension and my curiously mixed feelings of disgust and pity for my
father, Cornelius Coffin Williams, the Mississippi drummer who was

removed from the wild and free road and put behind a desk like a jungle animal put in a cage in a zoo.

At supper the following evening an awful domestic scene takes   19
place.

My father is one of those drinkers who never stagger or stumble but   20
turn savage with liquor, and this next evening after my homecoming he
comes home late and drunk for supper. He sits at one end of the table,
my mother at the other, and she fixes on him her look of silent suffering
like a bird dog drawing a bead on a covey of quail in the bushes.

All at once he explodes into maniacal fury.   21

His shouting goes something like this: "What the hell, why the hell   22
do you feel so sorry for yourself? I'm keeping your parents here,
they're not paying board!"

The shout penetrates my grandfather's deafness and he says,   23
"Rose, let's go to our room." But my grandmother Rose remains at the
table as Edwina and Grandfather retire upstairs. I stay as if rooted or
frozen to the dining-room chair, the food turning sick in my stomach.

Silence.   24

My father crouches over his plate, eating like a wild beast eats his   25
kill in the jungle.

Then my grandmother's voice, quiet and gentle: "Cornelius, do   26
you want us to pay board here?"

Silence again.   27

My father stops eating, though. He doesn't look up as he says in a   28
hoarse, shaky voice: "No, I don't, Mrs. Dakin."

His inflamed blue eyes are suddenly filled with tears. He lurches   29
up from the table and goes to the overstuffed chair in the living room.

This overstuffed chair, I don't remember just when we got it. I sus-   30
pect it was in the furnished apartment that we took when we first came
to Saint Louis. To take the apartment we had to buy the furniture that
was in it, and through this circumstance we acquired a number of
pieces of furniture that would be intriguing to set designers of films
about lower-middle-class life. Some of these pieces have been gradually weeded out through successive changes of address, but my father
was never willing to part with the overstuffed chair. It really doesn't
look like it could be removed. It seems too fat to get through a doorway.
Its color was originally blue, plain blue, but time has altered the blue to
something sadder than blue, as if it had absorbed in its fabric and stuffing all the sorrows and anxieties of our family life and these emotions
had become its stuffing and its pigmentation (if chairs can be said to
have a pigmentation). It doesn't really seem like a chair, though. It
seems more like a fat, silent person, not silent by choice but simply unable to speak because if it spoke it would not get through a sentence
without bursting into a self-pitying wail.

31   Over this chair still stands another veteran piece of furniture, a floor lamp that must have come with it. It rises from its round metal base on the floor to half a foot higher than a tall man sitting. Then it curves over his head one of the most ludicrous things a man has ever sat under, a sort of Chinesey-looking silk lamp shade with a fringe about it, so that it suggests a weeping willow. Which is presumably weeping for the occupant of the chair.

32   I have never known whether Mother was afraid to deprive my father of his overstuffed chair and weeping-willow floor lamp or if it simply amused her to see him with them. There was a time, in her younger years, when she looked like a fairy-tale princess and had a sense of style that exceeded by far her power to indulge it. But now she's tired, she's about sixty now, and she lets things go. And the house is now filled not only with its original furnishings but with the things inherited from my grandparents' house in Memphis. In fact, the living room is so full of furniture that you have to be quite sober to move through it without a collision ... and still there is the overstuffed chair.

33   A few days after the awful scene at the dinner table, my dearly loved grandmother, Rose Otte Dakin, bled to death in the house of my parents.

34   She had washed the dinner dishes, had played Chopin on the piano, which she'd brought with her from Memphis, and had started upstairs when she was overtaken by a fit of coughing and a lung hemorrhage that wouldn't stop.

35   She fought death for several hours, with almost no blood left in her body to fight with.

36   Being a coward, I wouldn't enter the room where this agony was occurring. I stood in the hall upstairs. My grandmother Rose was trying to deliver a message to my mother. She kept flinging out a wasted arm to point at a bureau.

37   It was not till several days after this death in the house that my mother found out the meaning of that gesture.

38   My grandmother was trying to tell my mother that all her savings were sewn up in a corset in a drawer of the bureau.

39   Late that night, when my grandmother had been removed to a mortuary, my father came home.

40   "Cornelius," said Mother, "I have lost my mother."

41   I saw him receive this announcement, and a look came over his face that was even more deeply stricken than that of my mother when she closed the eyelids of "Grand" after her last fight for breath.

42   He went to his overstuffed chair, under the weeping-willow floor lamp, like a man who has suddenly discovered the reality in a night-

mare, and he said, over and over again, "How awful, oh, God, oh, God, how awful!"

He was talking to himself.   43

At the time of my grandmother's death I had been for ten years   44
more an irregular and reluctant visitor to the house than a member of
the household. Sometimes my visits would last the better part of a year,
sometimes, more usually, they would last no more than a week. But for
three years after my years at college I was sentenced to confinement in
this house and to hard labor in "The World's Largest Shoe Company" in
which my father was also serving time, perhaps as unhappily as I was.
We were serving time in quite different capacities. My father was the
sales manager of that branch that manufactures, most notably, shoes
and booties for kiddies, called "Red Goose Shoes," and never before
and probably not to this day has "The World's Largest" had so gifted a
manager of salesmen. As for me, I was officially a clerk-typist but what
I actually did was everything that no one else wanted to do, and since
the boss wanted me to quit, he and the straw boss made sure that I had
these assignments. I was kept on my feet most of the time, charging
back and forth between the office and the connecting warehouse of this
world's largest wholesale shoe company, which gave me capable legs
and a fast stride. The lowliest of my assigned duties was the one I liked
most, dusting off the sample shoes in three brightly mirrored sample
rooms each morning; dusting off the mirrors as well as the shoes in
these rooms that were intended to dazzle the eyes of retailers from all
over the States. I liked this job best because it was so private. It was performed before the retailers came in: I had the rooms and the mirrors to
myself, dusting off the sample shoes with a chamois rag was something
that I could do quickly and automatically, and the job kept me off the
noisy floor of the office. I regretted that it took only about an hour, even
when I was being most dreamily meticulous about it. That hour having
been stretched to its fullest, I would have to take my desk in the office
and type out great sheaves of factory orders. It was nearly all numerals,
digits. I made many mistakes, but for an amusing reason I couldn't be
fired. The head of the department had gotten his job through the influence of my father, which was still high at that time. I could commit the
most appalling goofs and boners and still I couldn't be fired, however
much I might long to be fired from this sixty-five-dollar-a-month position. I left my desk more often than anyone else. My branch of "The
World's Largest" was on the top floor but I had discovered a flight of
stairs to the roof of the twelve-story building and every half hour or so I
would go up those stairs to have a cigarette, rather than retiring to the
smelly men's room. From this roof I could look across the Mississippi

River to the golden wheat fields of Illinois, and the air, especially in autumn, was bracingly above the smog of Saint Louis, so I used to linger up there for longer than a cigarette to reflect upon a poem or short story that I would finish that weekend.

45   I had several enemies in the office, especially the one called "The Straw Boss," a tall, mincing creature who had acquired the valuable trick of doing nasty things nicely. He was not at all bright, though. He didn't realize that I liked dusting the shoes and running the errands that took me out of "The World's Largest." And he always saw to it that the sample cases that I had to carry about ten blocks from "The World's Largest" to its largest buyer, which was J. C. Penney Company, were almost too heavy for a small man to carry. So did I build up my chest and slightly damage my arterial system, a damage that was soon to release me from my period of bondage. This didn't bother me, though. (I've thought a good deal about death but doubt that I've feared it very much, then or now.)

46   The thing I most want to tell you about is none of this, however; it is something much stranger. It is the ride downtown that my father and I would take every morning in his Studebaker. This was a long ride, it took about half an hour, and seemed much longer for neither my father nor I had anything to say to each other during the ride. I remember that I would compose one sentence to deliver to my father, to break just once the intolerable silence that existed between us, as intolerable to him, I suspect, as it was to me. I would start composing this one sentence during breakfast and I would usually deliver it halfway downtown. It was a shockingly uninteresting remark. It was delivered in a shockingly strained voice, a voice that sounded choked. It would be a comment on the traffic or the smog that enveloped the streets. The interesting thing about it was his tone of answer. He would answer the remark as if he understood how hard it was for me to make it. His answer would always be sad and gentle. "Yes, it's awful," he'd say. And he didn't say it as if it was a response to my remark. He would say it as if it referred to much larger matters than traffic or smog. And looking back on it, now, I feel that he understood my fear of him and forgave me for it, and wished there was some way to break the wall between us.

47   It would be false to say that he was ever outwardly kind to his fantastic older son, myself. But I suspect, now, that he knew that I was more of a Williams than a Dakin, and that I would be more and more like him as I grew older, and that he pitied me for it.

48   I often wonder many things about my father now, and understand things about him, such as his anger at life, so much like my own, now that I'm old as he was.

49   I wonder for instance, if he didn't hate and despise "The World's Largest Shoe Company" as much as I did. I wonder if he wouldn't have liked, as much as I did, to climb the stairs to the roof.

I understand that he knew that my mother had made me a sissy, 50
but that I had a chance, bred in his blood and bone, to some day rise
above it, as I had to and did.

His branch of "The World's Largest" was three floors down from 51
the branch I worked for, and sometimes an errand would take me
down to his branch.

He was always dictating letters in a voice you could hear from the 52
elevator before the door of it opened.

It was a booming voice, delivered on his feet as he paced about his 53
stenographer at the desk. Occupants of the elevator, hearing his voice,
would smile at each other as they heard it booming out so fiercely.

Usually he would be dictating a letter to one of his salesmen, and 54
not the kind of letter that would flatter or please them.

Somehow he dominated the office with his loud dictation. The let- 55
ters would not be indulgent.

"Maybe you're eating fried chicken now," he'd boom out, "but I 56
reckon you remember the days when we'd go around the corner for a
cigarette for breakfast. Don't forget it. I don't. Those days can come
back again..."

His boss, Mr. J., approved of C. C.'s letters, but had a soundproof 57
glass enclosure built about his corner in "The World's Largest."...

A psychiatrist once said to me, You will begin to forgive the world 58
when you've forgiven your father.

I'm afraid it is true that my father taught me to hate, but I know 59
that he didn't plan to, and, terrible as it is to know how to hate, and to
hate, I have forgiven him for it and for a great deal else.

Sometimes I wonder if I have forgiven my mother for teaching me 60
to expect more love from the world, more softness in it, than I could
ever offer?

The best of my work, as well as the impulse to work, was a gift 61
from the man in the overstuffed chair, and now I feel a very deep kin-
ship to him, I almost feel as if I am sitting in the overstuffed chair where
he sat, exiled from those I should love and those that ought to love me.
For love I make characters in plays. To the world I give suspicion and
resentment, mostly. I am not cold. I am never deliberately cruel. But after my morning's work, I have little to give but indifference to people. I
try to excuse myself with the pretense that my work justifies this lack of
caring much for almost everything else. Sometimes I crack through the
emotional block. I touch, I embrace, I hold tight to a necessary companion. But the breakthrough is not long lasting. Morning returns, and
only work matters again.

Now a bit more about my father whom I have come to know and 62
understand so much better.

My mother couldn't forgive him. A few years after the years that I 63
have annotated a little in this piece of writing, my mother became fi-

nancially able to cut him out of her life, and cut him out she did. He had been in a hospital for recovery from a drunken spree. When he returned to the house, she refused to see him. My brother had returned from the latest war, and he would go back and forth between them, arranging a legal separation. I suspect it was not at all a thing that my father wanted. But once more he exhibited a gallantry in his nature that I had not then expected. He gave my mother the house and half of his stock in the International Shoe Company, although she was already well set up by my gift to her of half of my earnings from *The Glass Menagerie.* He acquiesced without protest to the terms of the separation, and then he went back to his native town of Knoxville, Tennessee, to live with his spinster sister, our Aunt Ella. Aunt Ella wasn't able to live with him, either, so after a while he moved into a hotel at a resort called Whittle Springs, close to Knoxville, and somehow or other he became involved with a widow from Toledo, Ohio, who became his late autumn love which lasted till the end of his life.

64   I've never seen this lady but I am grateful to her because she stuck with Dad through those last years.

65   Now and then, during those years, my brother would be called down to Knoxville to see Dad through an illness brought on by his drinking, and I think it was the Toledo Widow who would summon my brother.

66   My brother, Dakin, is more of a Puritan than I am, and so I think the fact that he never spoke harshly of the Toledo Widow is a remarkable compliment to her. All I gathered from his guarded references to this attachment between Dad and the Toledo Widow was that she made him a faithful drinking companion. Now and then they would fly down to Biloxi and Gulfport, Mississippi, where Dad and Mother had spent their honeymoon, and it was just after one of these returns to where he had been happy with Mother, and she with him, that he had his final illness. I don't know what caused his death, if anything caused it but one last spree. The Toledo Widow was with him at the end, in a Knoxville hospital. The situation was delicate for Aunt Ella. She didn't approve of the widow and would only go to my father's deathbed when assured there would be no encounter between the widow and herself in the hospital room. She did pass by her once in the hospital corridor, but she made no disparaging comment on her when I flew down to Knoxville for the funeral of my father.

67   The funeral was an exceptionally beautiful service. My brother, Aunt Ella, and I sat in a small room set apart for the nearest of kin and listened and looked on while the service was performed.

68   Then we went out to "Old Gray," as they called the Knoxville Cemetery, and there we sat in a sort of tent with the front of it open, to witness the interment of the man of the overstuffed chair.

69   Behind us, on chairs in the open, was a very large congregation of more distant kinfolk and surviving friends of his youth, and somewhere among them was the Toledo Widow, I've heard.

After the interment, the kinfolk all came up to our little tent to offer   70
condolences that were unmistakably meant.

The widow drove off in his car which he had bequeathed to her,   71
her only bequest, and I've heard of her nothing more.

He left his modest remainder of stock in the International Shoe   72
Company in three parts to his sister, and to his daughter and to my
brother, a bequest which brought them each a monthly income of a
hundred dollars. He left me nothing because, as he had told Aunt Ella,
it didn't seem likely that I would ever have need of inherited money.

I wonder if he knew, and I suspect that he did, that he had left me   73
something far more important, which was his blood in my veins? And
of course I wonder, too, if there wasn't more love than hate in his blood,
however tortured it was.

Aunt Ella is gone now, too, but while I was in Knoxville for Dad's   74
funeral, she showed me a newspaper photograph of him outside a
movie house where a film of mine, *Baby Doll*, was being shown. Along
with the photograph of my father was his comment on the picture.

What he said was: "I think it's a very fine picture and I'm proud of   75
my son."

✦ Questions for Discussion and Writing

1. What character traits define Cornelius? What is Williams's attitude to-
    wards him?

2. What details suggest that Williams is aware of how different his family
    is from others?

3. What attributes does the "overstuffed chair" come to symbolize for
    Williams?

4. What is so significant about Williams's need to prepare a comment in
    advance before speaking with his father?

5. Write about one of your parents or grandparents in relationship to an
    object that you associate with him or her. Describe the circumstances in
    which you first encountered this object, and tell what significance it
    has for you in connection with this person.

6. Williams infers a good deal about his father's character from his over-
    stuffed chair, lamp, arrangement of furniture, etc. In your journal, you
    might try to write about your own room, house, or apartment as if you
    were trying to decipher the identity and character of the person who
    lives there. Try to take into account such elements as significant fea-
    tures and contents, clutter or lack of it, knickknacks, souvenirs, food in
    the refrigerator and pantry, records, CDs, videotapes, computers, soft-
    ware, and clothes in the closet.

Patricia Hampl

Grandmother's Sunday Dinner

◆

Patricia Hampl was born in 1946 and grew up in St. Paul, Minnesota. She graduated from the University of Minnesota, where she currently teaches, and studied at the Iowa Writer's Workshop. Hampl has often written about her connection to her Czech heritage, a theme that emerges in her autobiographical essay "Grandmother's Sunday Dinner." This account is drawn from her book A Romantic Education *(1981).*

1   Food was the potent center of my grandmother's life. Maybe the immense amount of time it took to prepare meals during most of her life accounted for her passion. Or it may have been her years of work in various kitchens on the hill and later, in the house of Justice Butler: after all, she was a professional. Much later, when she was dead and I went to Prague, I came to feel the motto I knew her by best—*Come eat*—was not, after all, a personal statement, but a racial one, the *cri de coeur* of Middle Europe.

2   Often, on Sundays, the entire family gathered for dinner at her house. Dinner was 1 P.M. My grandmother would have preferred the meal to be at the old time of noon, but her children had moved their own Sunday dinner hour to the more fashionable (it was felt) 4 o'clock, so she compromised. Sunday breakfast was something my mother liked to do in a big way, so we arrived at my grandmother's hardly out of the reverie of waffles and orange rolls, before we were propped like rag dolls in front of a pork roast and sauerkraut, dumplings, hot buttered carrots, rye bread and rollikey, pickles and olives, apple pie and ice cream. And coffee.

3   Coffee was a food in that house, not a drink. I always begged for some because the magical man on the Hills Brothers can with his turban and long robe scattered with stars and his gold slippers with pointed toes, looked deeply happy as he drank from his bowl. The bowl itself reminded me of soup, Campbell's chicken noodle soup, my favorite food. The distinct adultness of coffee and the robed man with his deep-drinking pleasure made it clear why the grownups lingered so long at the table. The uncles smoked cigars then, and the aunts said, "Oh, those cigars."

My grandmother, when she served dinner, was a virtuoso hanging   4
on the edge of her own ecstatic performance. She seemed dissatisfied,
almost querulous until she had corralled everybody into their chairs
around the table, which she tried to do the minute they got into the
house. No cocktails, no hors d'oeuvres (pronounced, by some of the
family, "horse's ovaries"), just business. She was a little power crazed:
she had us and, by God, we were going to eat. She went about it like a
goose breeder forcing pellets down the gullets of those dumb birds.

She flew between her chair and the kitchen, always finding more   5
this, extra that. She'd given you the *wrong* chicken breast the first time
around; now she'd found the *right* one: eat it too, eat it fast, because after the chicken comes the rhubarb pie. Rhubarb pie with a thick slice of
cheddar cheese that it was imperative every single person eat.

We had to eat fast because something was always out there in the   6
kitchen panting and charging the gate, champing at the bit, some
mound of rice or a Jell-O fruit salad or vegetable casserole or pie was
out there, waiting to be let loose into the dining room.

She had the usual trite routines: the wheedlings, the silent pout   7
("What! You don't like my brussels sprouts? I thought you liked *my*
brussels sprouts," versus your wife's/sister's/mother's. "I made that
pie just for you," etc., etc.). But it was the way she tossed around the
old cliches and the overused routines, mixing them up and dealing
them out shamelessly, without irony, that made her a pro. She tended to
peck at her own dinner. Her plate, piled with food, was a kind of stage
prop, a mere bending to convention. She liked to eat, she was even a
greedy little stuffer, but not on these occasions. She was a woman possessed by an idea, given over wholly to some phantasmagoria of food,
a mirage of stuffing, a world where the endless chicken and the infinite
lemon pie were united at last at the shore of the oceanic soup plate that
her children and her children's children alone could drain...if only
they would try.

She was there to bolster morale, to lead the troops, to give the   8
sharp command should we falter on the way. The futility of saying no
was supreme, and no one ever tried it. How could a son-in-law, already
weakened near the point of imbecility by the once, twice, thrice charge
to the barricades of pork and mashed potato, be expected to gather his
feeble wit long enough to ignore the final call of his old commander
when she sounded the alarm: "Pie, Fred?"

Just when it seemed as if the food-crazed world she had created   9
was going to burst, that she had whipped and frothed us like a sack of
boiled potatoes under her masher, just then she pulled it all together in
one easeful stroke like the pro she was.

She stood in the kitchen doorway, her little round Napoleonic self   10
sheathed in a cotton flowered pinafore apron, the table draped in its

white lace cloth but spotted now with gravy and beet juice, the troops mumbling indistinctly as they waited at their posts for they knew not what. We looked up at her stupidly, weakly. She said nonchalantly, "Anyone want another piece of pie?" No, no more pie, somebody said. The rest of the rabble grunted along with him. She stood there with the coffeepot and laughed and said, "Good! Because there *isn't* any more pie."

11   No more pie. We'd eaten it all, we'd put away everything in that kitchen. We were exhausted and she, gambler hostess that she was (but it was her house she was playing), knew she could offer what didn't exist, knew us, knew what she'd wrought. There was a sense of her having won, won something. There were no divisions among us now, no adults, no children. Power left the second and third generations and returned to the source, the grandmother who reduced us to mutters by her art.

12   That wasn't the end of it. At 5 P.M. there was "lunch"—sandwiches and beer; the sandwiches were made from the left-overs (mysteriously renewable resources, those roasts). And at about 8 P.M. we were at the table again for coffee cake and coffee, the little man in his turban and his coffee ecstasy and his pointed shoes set on the kitchen table as my grandmother scooped out the coffee and dumped it into a big enamel pot with a crushed eggshell. By then everyone was alive and laughing again, the torpor gone. My grandfather had been inviting the men, one by one, into the kitchen during the afternoon where he silently (the austere version of memory—but he must have talked, must have said *something*) handed them jiggers of whiskey, and watched them put the shot down in one swallow. Then he handed them a beer, which they took out in the living room. I gathered that the *little* drink in the tiny glass shaped like a beer mug was some sort of antidote for the *big* drink of beer. He sat on the chair in the kitchen with a bottle of beer on the floor next to him and played his concertina, allowing society to form itself around him—while he lived he was the center—but not seeking it, not going into the living room. And not talking. He held to his music and the kindly, medicinal administration of whiskey.

13   By evening, it seemed we could eat endlessly, as if we'd had some successful inoculation at dinner and could handle anything. I stayed in the kitchen after they all reformed in the dining room at the table for coffee cake. I could hear them, but the little man in his starry yellow robe was on the table in the kitchen and I put my head down on the oil cloth very near the curled and delighted tips of his pointed shoes, and I slept. Whatever laughter there was, there was. But something sweet and starry was in the kitchen and I lay down beside it, my stomach full, warm, so safe I'll live the rest of my life off the fat of that vast family security.

✦ Questions for Discussion and Writing

1. How do Hampl's descriptions of the actual food served and the manner in which it was served by her grandmother make the reader aware of the real objectives of the grandmother?

2. Evaluate and discuss Hampl's use of imaginative comparisons and analogies in depicting her grandmother. How effective did you find these?

3. How does Hampl, in her retrospective account, view her grandmother? What have these Sunday dinners come to mean to Hampl later in her life?

4. Describe a Sunday dinner or any other ritual event involved with food that is presided over by a member of your family. Describe your own behavior as a participant or an onlooker at these gatherings. If you keep a journal, you might wish to begin by freezing a moment in time during one of these events and focusing your full attention on the sights, sounds, tastes, smells, impressions, and feelings that can bring the reader into this moment.

5. Interview an older member of your family to discover how customs when they were growing up differ from current practices. Topics you might discuss include dating, courtship, marriage, child rearing, cures for illness, food preparation, and celebrations. Write an essay describing your findings.

Jill Nelson

Number One!

◆

Jill Nelson, born in 1952, is a native New Yorker and a graduate of the City College of New York and the Columbia University's School of Journalism. In 1983, she was a Charles N. Revson Fellow on the Future of the City of New York at Columbia University. A journalist for fifteen years, Nelson is a frequent contributor to Essence *magazine. Her work has also appeared in numerous other publications, including* U.S.A. Weekend, The Village Voice, *and* Ms. *The daughter of an affluent African American, Nelson attended private schools while growing up on New York's West Side. In 1986, she accepted a job at the* Washington Post's *new Sunday magazine. Her struggle with the paper's paternalistic corporate culture, as the only black woman reporter in a bastion of elite journalism, is described in* Volunteer Slavery: My Authentic Negro Experience *(1993). "Number One!" is an account drawn from the same book. In it Nelson describes her father's influence on her life and career.*

1   That night I dream about my father, but it is really more a memory than a dream.

2   "Number one! Not two! Number one!" my father intones from the head of the breakfast table. The four of us sit at attention, two on each side of the ten-foot teak expanse, our brown faces rigid. At the foot, my mother looks up at my father, the expression on her face a mixture of pride, anxiety, and, could it be, boredom? I am twelve. It is 1965.

3   "You kids have got to be, not number two," he roars, his dark face turning darker from the effort to communicate. He holds up his index and middle fingers. "But number—" here, he pauses dramatically, a preacher going for revelation, his four children a rapt congregation, my mother a smitten church sister. "Number one!"

4   These last words he shouts while lowering his index finger. My father has great, big black hands, long, perfectly shaped fingers with oval nails so vast they seem landscapes all their own. The half moons leading to the cuticle take up most of the nail and seem ever encroaching, threatening to swallow up first his fingertips, then his whole hand. I always wondered if he became a dentist just to mess with people by putting those enormous fingers in their mouths, each day surprising his patients and himself by the delicacy of the work he did.

5   Years later my father told me that when a woman came to him with an infant she asserted was his, he simply looked at the baby's hands. If

34

they lacked the size, enormous nails, and half-moon cuticles like an ocean eroding the shore of the fingers, he dismissed them.

Early on, what I remember of my father were Sunday morning   6
breakfasts and those hands, index finger coyly lowering, leaving the middle finger standing alone.

When he shouted "Number one!" that finger seemed to grow,   7
thicken and harden, thrust up and at us, a phallic symbol to spur us, my sister Lynn, fifteen, brothers Stanley and Ralph, thirteen and nine, on to greatness, to number oneness. My father's rich, heavy voice rolled down the length of the table, breaking and washing over our four trembling bodies.

When I wake up I am trembling again, but it's because the air con-   8
ditioner, a luxury in New York but a necessity in D.C., is set too high. I turn it down, check on Misu,[1] light a cigarette, and think about the dream.

It wasn't until my parents had separated and Sunday breakfasts   9
were no more that I faced the fact that my father's symbol for number one was the world's sign language for "fuck you." I know my father knew this, but I still haven't figured out what he meant by it. Were we to become number one and go out and fuck the world? If we didn't, would life fuck us? Was he intentionally sending his children a mixed message? If so, what was he trying to say?

I never went to church with my family. While other black middle-   10
class families journeyed to Baptist church on Sundays, both to thank the Lord for their prosperity and donate a few dollars to the less fortu- nate brethren they'd left behind, we had what was reverentially known as "Sunday breakfast." That was our church.

In the dining room of the eleven-room apartment we lived in, the   11
only black family in a building my father had threatened to file a dis- crimination suit to get into, my father delivered the gospel according to him. The recurring theme was the necessity that each of us be "number one," but my father preached about whatever was on his mind: current events, great black heroes, lousy black sell-outs, our responsibility as privileged children, his personal family history.

His requirements were the same as those at church: that we be on   12
time, not fidget, hear and heed the gospel, and give generously. But Daddy's church boasted no collection plate; dropping a few nickels into a bowl would have been too easy. Instead, my father asked that we absorb his lessons and become what he wanted us to be, number one. He never told us what that meant or how to get there. It was years be- fore I was able to forgive my father for not being more specific. It was even longer before I understood and accepted that he couldn't be.

---

[1]*Misu:* Nelson's daughter.

13   Like most preachers, my father was stronger on imagery, oratory, and instilling fear than he was on process. I came away from fifteen years of Sunday breakfasts knowing that to be number two was not enough, and having no idea what number one was or how to become it, only that it was better.

14   When I was a kid, I just listened, kept a sober face, and tried to understand what was going on. Thanks to my father, my older sister Lynn and I, usually at odds, found spiritual communion. The family dishwashers, our spirits met wordlessly as my father talked. We shared each other's anguish as we watched egg yolk harden on plates, sausage fat congeal, chicken livers separate silently from gravy.

15   We all had our favorite sermons. Mine was the "Rockefeller wouldn't let his dog shit in our dining room" sermon.

16   "You think we're doing well?" my father would begin, looking into each of our four faces. We knew better than to venture a response. For my father, even now, conversations are lectures. Please save your applause—and questions—until the end.

17   "And we are," he'd answer his own query. "We live on West End Avenue, I'm a professional, your mother doesn't *have* to work, you all go to private school, we go to Martha's Vineyard in the summer. But what we have, we have because 100,000 other black people haven't made it. Have nothing! Live like dogs!"

18   My father has a wonderfully expressive voice. When he said dogs, you could almost hear them whimpering. In my head, I saw an uncountable mass of black faces attached to the bodies of mutts, scrambling to elevate themselves to a better life. For some reason, they were always on 125th Street, under the Apollo Theatre marquee. Years later, when I got political and decided to be the number-one black nationalist, I was thrilled by the notion that my father might have been inspired by Claude McKay's[2] poem that begins, "If we must die, let it not be like dogs."

19   "There is a quota system in this country for black folks, and your mother and me were allowed to make it," my father went on. It was hard to imagine anyone allowing my six-foot-three, suave, smart, take-no-shit father to do anything. Maybe his use of the word was a rhetorical device.

20   "Look around you," he continued. With the long arm that supported his heavy hand he indicated the dining room. I looked around. At the eight-foot china cabinet gleaming from the weekly oiling administered by Margie, our housekeeper, filled to bursting with my maternal grandmother's china and silver. At the lush green carpeting, the

[2]*Claude McKay:* African American poet (1889–1948).

sideboard that on holidays sagged from the weight of cakes, pies, and cookies, at the paintings on the walls. We were living kind of good, I thought. That notion lasted only an instant.

My father's arm slashed left. It was as though he had stripped the room bare. I could almost hear the china crashing to the floor, all that teak splintering, silver clanging. 21

"Nelson Rockefeller wouldn't let his dog shit in here!" my father roared. "What we have, compared to what Rockefeller and the people who rule the world have, is nothing. Nothing! Not even good enough for his dog. You four have to remember that and do better than I have. Not just for yourselves, but for our people, black people. You have to be number one." 22

My father went on, but right about there was where my mind usually started drifting. I was entranced by the image of Rockefeller's dog—which I imagined to be a Corgi or Afghan or Scottish Terrier—bladder and rectum full to bursting, sniffing around the green carpet of our dining room, refusing to relieve himself. 23

The possible reasons for this fascinated me. Didn't he like green carpets? Was he used to defecating on rare Persian rugs and our 100 percent wool carpeting wasn't good enough? Was it because we were black? But weren't dogs colorblind? 24

I've spent a good part of my life trying to figure out what my father meant by number one. Born poor and dark in Washington, I think he was trying, in his own way, to protect us from the crushing assumptions of failure that he and his generation grew up with. I like to think he was simply saying, like the army, "Be all that you can be," but I'm still not sure. For years, I was haunted by the specter of number two gaining on me, of never having a house nice enough for Rockefeller dog shit, of my father's middle finger admonishing me. It's hard to move forward when you're looking over your shoulder. 25

When I was younger, I didn't ask my father what he meant. By the time I was confident enough to ask, my father had been through so many transformations—from dentist to hippie to lay guru—that he'd managed to forget, or convince himself he'd forgotten, those Sunday morning sermons. When I brought them up he'd look blank, his eyes would glaze over, and he'd say something like, "Jill, what are you talking about? With your dramatic imagination you should have been an actress." 26

But I'm not an actress. I'm a journalist, my father's daughter. I've spent a good portion of my life trying to be a good race woman and number one at the same time. Tomorrow, I go to work at the *Washington Post* magazine, a first. Falling asleep, I wonder if that's the same as being number one. 27

✦ Questions for Discussion and Writing

1. In what respects was Sunday breakfast transformed by Nelson's father into a secular church meeting? What message did he attempt to instill?

2. What portrait does Nelson create of her father? What part do personal strengths and character flaws play in her account of him?

3. To what extent is Nelson able to understand and act on the lessons her father taught? How has her view of him changed over the years?

4. Analyze Nelson's father's thesis concerning race and class relationships in the United States. To what extent do you agree or disagree with his assessment?

5. What family members have shaped your attitude towards failure and success, and how have their expectations influenced you?

6. If you keep a journal, try to create a list of ten to twenty things your parents or grandparents used to say to you. Then select one of these "messages," and describe how it played an enormous role in creating a subconscious expectation that has remained with you until today.

Mikal Gilmore

My Brother, Gary Gilmore

◆

Mikal Gilmore was born in 1951 in Salt Lake City, Utah, growing up there and in Portland, Oregon. He is currently a Senior Writer at Rolling Stone *magazine, where he has worked for the past twenty years. The following selection, "My Brother, Gary Gilmore," first appeared in GRANTA (Autumn 1991) and became the basis for his acclaimed autobiography* Shot Through the Heart *(1994).*

1   I am the brother of a man who murdered innocent men. His name was Gary Gilmore. After his conviction and sentencing, he campaigned to end his own life, and in January 1977 he was shot to death by a firing-squad in Draper, Utah. It was the first execution in America in over a decade.

2   Over the years, many people have judged me by my brother's actions as if in coming from a family that yielded a murderer I must be formed by the same causes, the same sins, must by my brother's actions be responsible for the violence that resulted, and bear the mark of a frightening and shameful heritage. It's as if there is guilt in the fact of the blood-line itself. Maybe there is.

3   Pictures in the family scrap-book show my father with his children. I have only one photograph of him and Gary together. Gary is wearing a sailor's cap. He has his arms wrapped tightly around my father's neck, his head bent towards him, a look of broken need on his face. It is heart-breaking to look at this picture—not just for the look on Gary's face, the look that was the stamp of his future, but also for my father's expression: pulling away from my brother's cheek, he is wearing a look of distaste.

4   When my brother Gaylen was born in the mid forties, my father turned all his love on his new, beautiful brown-eyed son. Gary takes on a harder aspect in the pictures around this time. He was beginning to keep a greater distance from the rest of the family. Six years later, my father turned his love from Gaylen to me. You don't see Gary in the family pictures after that.

5   Gary had nightmares. It was always the same dream: he was being beheaded.

6   In 1953, Gary was arrested for breaking windows. He was sent to a juvenile detention home for ten months, where he saw young men

raped and beaten. Two years later, at age fourteen, he was arrested for car theft and sentenced to eighteen months in jail. I was four years old.

7   When I was growing up I did not feel accepted by, or close to, my brothers. By the time I was four or five, they had begun to find life and adventure outside the home. Frank, Gary and Gaylen signified the teenage rebellion of the fifties for me. They wore their hair in greasy pompadours and played Elvis Presley and Fats Domino records. They dressed in scarred motorcycle jackets and brutal boots. They smoked cigarettes, drank booze and cough syrup, skipped—and quit—school, and spent their evenings hanging out with girls in tight sweaters, racing souped-up cars along country roads outside Portland, or taking part in gang rumbles. My brothers looked for a forbidden life—the life they had seen exemplified in the crime lore of gangsters and killers. They studied the legends of violence. They knew the stories of John Dillinger, Bonnie and Clyde, and Leopold and Loeb; mulled over the meanings of the lives and executions of Barbara Graham, Bruno Hauptmann, Sacco and Vanzetti, the Rosenbergs; thrilled to the pleading of criminal lawyers like Clarence Darrow and Jerry Giesler. They brought home books about condemned men and women, and read them avidly.

8   I remember loving my brothers fiercely, wanting to be a part of their late-night activities and to share in their laughter and friendship. I also remember being frightened of them. They looked deadly, beyond love, destined to hurt the world around them.

9   Gary came home from reform school for a brief Christmas visit. On Christmas night I was sitting in my room, playing with the day's haul of presents, when Gary wandered in. 'Hey Mike, how you doing?' he asked, taking a seat on my bed. 'Think I'll just join you while I have a little Christmas cheer.' He had a six-pack of beer with him and was speaking in a bleary drawl. 'Look partner, I want to have a talk with you.' I think it was the first companionable statement he ever made to me. I never expected the intimacy that followed and could not really fathom it at such a young age. Sitting on the end of my bed, sipping at his Christmas beer, Gary described a harsh, private world and told me horrible, transfixing stories: about the boys he knew in the detention halls, reform schools and county farms where he now spent most of his time; about the bad boys who had taught him the merciless codes of his new life; and about the soft boys who did not have what it took to survive that life. He said he had shared a cell with one of the soft boys, who cried at night, wanting to disappear into nothing, while Gary held him in his arms until the boy finally fell into sleep, sobbing.

10   Then Gary gave me some advice. 'You have to learn to be hard. You have to learn to take things and feel nothing about them: no pain, no anger, nothing. And you have to realize, if anybody wants to beat you up, even if they want to hold you down and kick you, you have to let

them. You can't fight back. You *shouldn't* fight back. Just lie down in front of them and let them beat you, let them kick you. Lie there and let them do it. It is the only way you will survive. If you don't give in to them, they will kill you.'

He set aside his beer and cupped my face in his hands. 'You have to remember this, Mike,' he said. 'Promise me. Promise me you'll be a man. Promise me you'll let them beat you.' We sat there on that winter night, staring at each other, my face in his hands, and as Gary asked me to promise to take my beatings, his bloodshot eyes began to cry. It was the first time I had seen him shed tears.

I promised: Yes, I'll let them kick me. But I was afraid—afraid of betraying Gary's plea.

Gary and Gaylen weren't at home much. I came to know them mainly through their reputations, through the endless parade of grim policemen who came to the door trying to find them, and through the faces and accusations of bail bondsman and lawyers who arrived looking sympathetic and left disgusted. I knew them through many hours spent in waiting-rooms at city and county jails, where my mother went to visit them, and through the numerous times I accompanied her after midnight to the local police station on Milwaukie's Main Street to bail out another drunken son.

I remember being called into the principal's office while still in grammar school, and being warned that the school would never tolerate my acting as my brothers did; I was told to watch myself, that my brothers had already used years of the school district's good faith and leniency, and that if I was going to be like them, there were other schools I could be sent to. I came to be seen as an extension of my brothers' reputations. Once, I was waiting for a bus in the centre of the small town when a cop pulled over. 'You're one of the Gilmore boys, aren't you? I hope you don't end up like those two. I've seen enough shitheads from your family.' I was walking down the local main highway when a car pulled over and a gang of older teenage boys piled out, surrounding me, 'Are you Gaylen Gilmore's brother?' one of them asked. They shoved me into the car, drove me a few blocks to a deserted lot and took turns punching me in the face. I remembered Gary's advice—'You can't fight back; you *shouldn't* fight back'—and I let them beat me until they were tired. Then they spat on me, got back in their car and left.

I cried all the way back home, and I hated the world. I hated the small town I lived in, its ugly, mean people. For the first time in my life I hated my brothers. I felt that my future would be governed by them, that I would be destined to follow their lives whether I wanted to or not, that I would never know any relief from shame and pain and disappointment. I felt a deep impulse to violence: I wanted to rip the faces off the boys who had beat me up. 'I want to kill them,' I told myself. 'I want to *kill* them'—and as I realized what it was I was saying, and why I was feeling that way, I only hated my world, and my brothers, more.

16   Frank Gilmore, Sr died on 30 June 1962. Gary was in Portland's Rocky Butte Jail, and the authorities denied his request to attend the funeral. He tore his cell apart; he smashed a light bulb and slashed his wrists. He was placed in 'the hole'—solitary confinement—on the day of father's funeral. Gary was twenty-one. I was eleven.

17   I was surprised at how hard my mother and brothers took father's death. I was surprised they loved him enough to cry at all. Or maybe they were crying for the love he had so long withheld, and the reconciliation that would be forever denied them. I was the only one who didn't cry. I don't know why, but I never cried over my father's death—not then, and not now.

18   With my father's death Gary's crimes became more desperate, more violent. He talked a friend into helping him commit armed robbery. Gary grabbed the victim's wallet while the friend held a club; he was arrested a short time later, tried and found guilty. The day of his sentencing, during an afternoon when my mother had to work, he called me from the Clackamas County Courthouse. 'How you doing partner? I just wanted to let you and mom know: I got sentenced to fifteen years.'

19   I was stunned. 'Gary, what can I do for you?' I asked. I think it came out wrong, as if I was saying: I'm busy; what do you *want?*

20   'I...I didn't really want anything,' Gary said, his voice broken. 'I just wanted to hear your voice. I just wanted to say goodbye. You know, I won't be seeing you for a few years. Take care of yourself.' We hadn't shared anything so intimate since that Christmas night, many years before.

21   I didn't have much talent for crime (neither did my brothers, to tell the truth), but I also didn't have much appetite for it. I had seen what my brothers' lives had brought them. For years, my mother had told me that I was the family's last hope for redemption. 'I want *one* son to turn out right, one son I don't have to end up visiting in jail, one son I don't have to watch in court as his life is sentenced away, piece by piece.' After my father's death, she drew me closer to her and her religion, and when I was twelve, I was baptized a Mormon. For many years, the Church's beliefs helped to provide me with a moral centre and a hope for deliverance that I had not known before.

22   I think culture and history helped to save me. I was born in 1951, and although I remember well the youthful explosion of the 1950s, I was too young to experience it the way my brothers did. The music of Elvis Presley and others had represented and expressed my brothers' rebellion: it was hard-edged, with no apparent ideology. The music was a part of my childhood, but by the early sixties the spirit of the music had been spent.

Then, on 9 February 1964 (my thirteenth birthday, and the day I   23
joined the Mormon priesthood), the Beatles made their first appearance on the Ed Sullivan Show. My life would never be the same. The
Beatles meant a change, they promised a world that my parents and
brothers could not offer. In fact, I liked the Beatles in part because they
seemed such a departure from the world of my brothers, and because
my brothers couldn't abide them.

The rock culture and youth politics of the sixties allowed their ad-   24
herents to act out a kind of ritualized criminality: we could use drugs,
defy authority, or contemplate violent or destructive acts of revolt, we
told ourselves, *because we had a reason to.* The music aimed to foment a
sense of cultural community, and for somebody who had felt as disen-
franchised by his family as I did, rock and roll offered not just a sense of
belonging but empowered me with new ideals. I began to find rock's
morality preferable to the Mormon ethos, which seemed rigid and severe. One Sunday in the summer of 1967, a member of the local bishop-
ric—a man I admired, and had once regarded as something of a father
figure—drove over to our house and asked me to step outside for a
talk. He told me that he and other church leaders had grown concerned
about my changed appearance—the new length of my hair and my
style of dressing—and felt it was an unwelcome influence on other
young Mormons. If I did not reject the new youth culture, I would no
longer be welcome in church.

On that day a line was drawn. I knew that rock and roll had pro-   25
vided me with a new creed and a sense of courage. I believed I was taking part in a rebellion that mattered—or at least counted for more than
my brothers' rebellions. In the music of the Rolling Stones or Doors or
Velvet Underground, I could participate in darkness without submitting to it, which is something Gary and Gaylen had been unable to do.
I remember their disdain when I tried to explain to them why Bob
Dylan was good, why he mattered. It felt great to belong to a different
world from them.

And I did: my father and Gaylen were dead; Gary was in prison   26
and Frank was broken. I thought of my family as a cursed outfit, plain
and simple, and I believed that the only way to escape its debts and
legacies was to leave it. In 1969 I graduated from high school—the only
member of my family to do so. The next day, I moved out of the house
in Milwaukie and, with some friends, moved into an apartment near
Portland State University, in downtown Portland.

In the summer of 1976, I was working at a record store in down-   27
town Portland, making enough money to pay my rent and bills. I was
also writing free-lance journalism and criticism, and had sold my first
reviews and articles to national publications, including *Rolling Stone.*

On the evening of 30 July, having passed up a chance to go drink-   28
ing with some friends, I headed home. *The Wild Bunch,* Peckinpah's

genuflection to violence and honour, was on television, and as I settled back on the couch to watch it, I picked up the late edition of *The Oregonian*. I almost passed over a page-two item headlined OREGON MAN HELD IN UTAH SLAYINGS, but then something clicked inside me, and I began to read it. 'Gary Mark Gilmore, 35, was charged with the murders of two young clerks during the hold-up of a service station and a motel.' I read on, dazed, about how Gary had been arrested for killing Max Jensen and Ben Bushnell on consecutive nights. Both men were Mormons, about the same age as I, and both left wives and children behind.

29   I dropped the paper to the floor. I sat on the couch the rest of the night, alternately staring at *The Wild Bunch* and re-reading the sketchy account. I felt shocks of rage, remorse and guilt—as if I were partly responsible for the deaths. I had been part of an uninterested world that had shut Gary away. I had wanted to believe that Gary's life and mine were not entwined, that what had shaped him had not shaped me.

30   It had been a long time since I had written or visited Gary. After his re-sentencing in 1972, I heard news of him from my mother. In January 1975, Gary was sent to the federal penitentiary in Marion, Illinois. After his transfer, we exchanged a few perfunctory letters. In early April 1976, I learned of the Oregon State Parole Board's decision to parole Gary from Marion to Provo, Utah, rather than transfer him back to Oregon. The transaction had been arranged between the parole board, Brenda Nicol (our cousin) and her father, our uncle Vernon Damico, who lived in Provo. I remember thinking that Gary's being paroled into the heart of one of Utah's most devout and severe Mormon communities was not a great idea.

31   Between his release and those fateful nights in July, Gary held a job at Uncle Vernon's shoe store, and he met and fell in love with Nicole Barrett, a beautiful young woman with two children. But Gary was unable to deny some old, less wholesome appetites. Almost immediately after his release, he started drinking heavily and taking Fiorinal, a muscle and headache medication that, in sustained doses, can cause severe mood swings and sexual dysfunction. Gary apparently experienced both reactions. He became more violent. Sometimes he got rough with Nicole over failed sex, or over what he saw as her flirtations. He picked fights with other men, hitting them from behind, threatening to cave in their faces with a tyre iron that he twirled as handily as a baton. He lost his job and abused his Utah relatives. He walked into stores and walked out again with whatever he wanted under his arm, glaring at the cashiers, challenging them to try to stop him. He brought guns home, and sitting on the back porch would fire them at trees, fences, the sky. 'Hit the sun,' he told Nicole. 'See if you can make it sink.' Then he hit Nicole with his fist one too many times, and she moved out.

32   Gary wanted her back. He told a friend that he thought he might kill her.

On a hot night in late July, Gary drove over to Nicole's mother's   33
house and persuaded Nicole's little sister, April, to ride with him in his
white pick-up truck. He wanted her to join him in looking for her sister.
They drove for hours, listening to the radio, talking aimlessly, until
Gary pulled up by a service station in the small town of Orem. He told
April to wait in the truck. He walked into the station, where twenty-
six-year-old attendant Max Jensen was working alone. There were no
other cars there. Gary pulled a .22 automatic from his jacket and told
Jensen to empty the cash from his pockets. He took Jensen's coin
changer and led the young attendant around the back of the station
and forced him to lie down on the bathroom floor. He told Jensen to
place his hands under his stomach and press his face to the ground.
Jensen complied and offered Gary a smile. Gary pointed the gun at the
base of Jensen's skull. 'This one is for me,' Gary said, and he pulled the
trigger. And then: 'This one is for Nicole,' and he pulled the trigger
again.

The next night, Gary walked into the office of a motel just a few   34
doors away from his uncle Vernon's house in Provo. He ordered the
man behind the counter, Ben Bushnell, to lie down on the floor, and
then he shot him in the back of the head. He walked out with the motel's cashbox under his arm and tried to stuff the pistol under a bush.
But it discharged, blowing a hole in his thumb.

Gary decided to get out of town. First he had to take care of his   35
thumb. He drove to the house of a friend named Craig and telephoned
his cousin. A witness had recognized Gary leaving the site of the second murder, and the police had been in touch with Brenda. She had the
police on one line, Gary on another. She tried to stall Gary until the police could set up a road-block. After they finished speaking, Gary got
into his truck and headed for the local airport. A few miles down the
road, he was surrounded by police cars and a SWAT team. He was arrested for Bushnell's murder and confessed to the murder of Max
Jensen.

Gary's trial began some months later. The verdict was never in   36
question. Gary didn't help himself when he refused to allow his attor-
neys to call Nicole as a defence witness. Gary and Nicole had been rec-
onciled; she felt bad for him and visited him in jail every day for hours.
Gary also didn't help his case by staring menacingly at the jury members or by offering belligerent testimony on his own behalf. He was
found guilty. My mother called me on the night of Gary's sentencing, 7
October, to tell me that he had received the death penalty. He told the
judge he would prefer being shot to being hanged.

On Saturday 15 January, I saw Gary for the last time. Camera crews   37
were camped in the town of Draper, preparing for the finale.

During our other meetings that week, Gary had opened with   38
friendly remarks or a joke or even a handstand. This day, though, he

was nervous and was eager to deny it. We were separated by a glass partition. 'Naw, the noise in this place gets to me sometimes, but I'm as cool as a cucumber,' he said, holding up a steady hand. The muscles in his wrists and arms were taut and thick as rope.

39   Gary showed me letters and pictures he'd received, mainly from children and teenage girls. He said he always tried to answer the ones from the kids first, and he read one from an eight-year-old boy: 'I hope they put you some place and make you live forever for what you did. You have no right to die. With all the malice in my heart. [*name*.]'

40   'Man, that one shook me up for a long time,' he said.

41   I asked him if he'd replied to it.

42   'Yeah, I wrote, "You're too young to have malice in your heart. I had it in mine at a young age and look what it did for me."'

43   Gary's eyes nervously scanned some letters and pictures, finally falling on one that made him smile. He held it up. A picture of Nicole. 'She's pretty, isn't she?' I agreed. 'I look at this picture every day. I took it myself; I made a drawing from it. Would you like to have it?'

44   I said I would. I asked him where he would have gone if he had made it to the airport the night of the second murder.

45   'Portland.'

46   I asked him why.

47   Gary studied the shelf in front of him. 'I don't want to talk about that night any more,' he said. 'There's no point in talking about it.'

48   'Would you have come to see me?'

49   He nodded. For a moment his eyes flashed the old anger. 'And what would *you* have done if I'd come to you?' he asked. 'If I had come and said I was in trouble and needed help, needed a place to stay? Would *you* have taken me in? Would you have hidden me?'

50   The question had been turned back on me. I couldn't speak. Gary sat for a long moment, holding me with his eyes, then said steadily: 'I think I was coming to kill you. I think that's what would have happened; there may have been no choice for you, no choice for me.' His eyes softened. 'Do you understand why?'

51   I nodded. Of course I understood why: I had escaped the family— or at least thought I had. Gary had not.

52   I felt terror. Gary's story could have been mine. Then terror became relief—Jensen and Bushnell's deaths, and Gary's own impending death, had meant my own safety. I finished the thought, and my relief was shot through with guilt and remorse. I felt closer to Gary than I'd ever felt before. I understood why he wanted to die.

53   The warden entered Gary's room. They discussed whether Gary should wear a hood for the execution.

54   I rapped on the glass partition and asked the warden if he would allow us a final handshake. At first he refused but consented after Gary explained it was our final visit, on the condition that I agree to a skin

search. After I had been searched by two guards, two other guards brought Gary around the partition. They said that I would have to roll up my sleeve past my elbow, and that we could not touch beyond a handshake. Gary grasped my hand, squeezed it tight and said, 'Well, I guess this is it.' He leaned over and kissed me on the cheek.

On Monday morning, 17 January, in a cannery warehouse out behind Utah State Prison, Gary met his firing-squad. I was with my mother and brother and girl-friend when it happened. Just moments before, we had seen the morning newspaper with the headline EXECUTION STAYED. We switched on the television for more news. We saw a press conference. Gary's death was being announced. 55

There was no way to be prepared for that last see-saw of emotion. You force yourself to live through the hell of knowing that somebody you love is going to die in an expected way, at a specific time and place, and that there is nothing you can do to change that. For the rest of your life, you will have to move around in a world that wanted this death to happen. You will have to walk past people every day who were heartened by the killing of somebody in your family—somebody who you knew had long before been murdered emotionally. 56

You turn on the television, and the journalist tells you how the warden put a black hood over Gary's head and pinned a small, circular cloth target above his chest, and how five men pumped a volley of bullets into him. He tells you how the blood flowed from Gary's devastated heart and down his chest, down his legs, staining his white pants scarlet and dripping to the warehouse floor. He tells you how Gary's arm rose slowly at the moment of the impact, how his fingers seemed to wave as his life left him. 57

Shortly after Gary's execution, *Rolling Stone* offered me a job as an assistant editor at their Los Angeles bureau. It was a nice offer. It gave me the chance to get away from Portland and all the bad memories it represented. 58

I moved to Los Angeles in April 1977. It was not an easy life at first. I drank a pint of whisky every night, and I took Dalmane, a sleeping medication that interfered with my ability to dream—or at least made it hard to remember my dreams. There were other lapses: I was living with one woman and seeing a couple of others. For a season or two my writing went to hell. I didn't know what to say or how to say it; I could no longer tell if I had anything *worth* writing about. I wasn't sure how you made words add up. Instead of writing, I preferred reading. I favoured hard-boiled crime fiction—particularly the novels of Ross Macdonald—in which the author tried to solve murders by explicating labyrinthine family histories. I spent many nights listening to punk rock. I liked the music's accommodation with a merciless world. One of the most famous punk songs of the period was by the Adverts. It was called 'Gary Gilmore's Eyes.' What would it be like, the song asked, to 59

see the world through Gary Gilmore's dead eyes? Would you see a
world of murder?

60   All around me I had Gary's notoriety to contend with. During my
first few months in LA—and throughout the years that followed—
most people asked me about my brother. They wanted to know what
Gary was like. They admired his bravado, his hardness. I met a woman
who wanted to sleep with me because I was his brother. I tried to avoid
these people.

61   I also met women who, when they learned who my brother was,
would not see me again, not take my calls again. I received letters from
people who said I should not be allowed to write for a young audience.
I received letters from people who thought I should have been shot
alongside my brother.

62   There was never a time without a reminder of the past. In 1979,
Norman Mailer's *The Executioner's Song* was published. At the time, I
was living with a woman I loved very much. As she read the book, I
could see her begin to wonder about who she was sleeping with, about
what had come into her life. One night, a couple of months after the
book had been published, we were watching *Saturday Night Live*. The
guest host was doing a routine of impersonations. He tied a bandana
around his eyes and gleefully announced his next subject: 'Gary
Gilmore!' My girl-friend got up from the sofa and moved into the bedroom, shutting the door. I poured a glass of whisky. She came out a few
minutes later. 'I'm sorry,' she said, 'I can't live with you any more. I
can't stand being close to all this stuff.' She was gone within a week.

63   I watched as a private and troubling event continued to be the subject of public sensation and media scrutiny; I watched my brother's
life—and in some way, my life—become too large to control. I tried not
to surrender to my feelings because my feelings wouldn't erase the
pain or shame or bad memories or unresolved love and hate. I was
waiting to be told what to feel.

64   Only a few months before, I had gone through one of the worst
times of my life—my brief move to Portland and back. What had gone
wrong, I realized, was because of my past, something that had been set
in motion long before I was born. It was what Gary and I shared, more
than any blood tie: we were both heirs to a legacy of negation that was
beyond our control or our understanding. Gary had ended up turning
the nullification outward—on innocents, on Nicole, on his family, on
the world and its ideas of justice, finally on himself. I had turned the
ruin inward. Outward or inward—either way, it was a powerfully destructive legacy, and for the first time in my life, I came to see that it had
not really finished its enactment. To believe that Gary had absorbed all
the family's dissolution, or that the worst of that rot had died with him
that morning in Draper, Utah, was to miss the real nature of the legacy

that had placed him before those rifles: what that heritage or patri-
mony was about, and where it had come from.

We tend to view murders as solitary ruptures in the world around   65
us, outrages that need to be attributed and then punished. There is a
motivation, a crime, an arrest, a trial, a verdict and a punishment.
Sometimes—though rarely—that punishment is death. The next day,
there is another murder. The next day, there is another. There has been
no punishment that breaks the pattern, that stops this custom of one
murder following another.

Murder has worked its way into our consciousness and our culture   66
in the same way that murder exists in our literature and film: we consume each killing until there is another, more immediate or gripping
one to take its place. When *this* murder story is finished, there will be
another to intrigue and terrify that part of the world that has survived
it. And then there will be another. Each will be a story, each will be
treated and reported and remembered as a unique incident. Each murder will be solved, but murder itself will never be solved. You cannot
solve murder without solving the human heart or the history that has
rendered that heart so dark and desolate.

This murder story is told from inside the house where murder was   67
born. It is the house where I grew up, and it is a house that I have never
been able to leave.

As the night passed, I formed an understanding of what I needed   68
to do. I would go back into my family—into its stories, its myths, its
memories, its inheritance—and find the real story and hidden propel-
lants behind it. I wanted to climb into the family story in the same way
I've always wanted to climb into a dream about the house where we all
grew up.

In the dream, it is always night. We are in my father's house—a   69
charred-brown, 1950s-era home. Shingled, two-storey and weather-
worn, it is located on the far outskirts of a dead-end American town,
pinioned between the night-lights and smoking chimneys of towering
industrial factories. A moonlit stretch of railroad track forms the border
to a forest I am forbidden to trespass. A train whistle howls in the distance. No train ever comes.

People move from the darkness outside the house to the darkness   70
inside. They are my family. They are all back from the dead. There is
my mother, Bessie Gilmore, who, after a life of bitter losses, died spitting blood, calling the names of her father and her husband—men who
had long before brutalized her hopes and her love—crying to them for
mercy, for a passage into the darkness that she had so long feared.
There is my brother Gaylen, who died young of knife-wounds, as his
new bride sat holding his hand, watching the life pass from his sunken
face. There is my brother Gary, who murdered innocent men in rage

against the way life had robbed him of time and love, and who died when a volley of bullets tore his heart from his chest. There is my brother Frank, who became quieter and more distant with each new death, and who was last seen in the dream walking down a road, his hands rammed deep into his pockets, a look of uncomprehending pain on his face. There is my father, Frank Sr, dead of the ravages of lung cancer. He is in the dream less often than the other family members, and I am the only one happy to see him.

71 One night, years into the same dream, Gary tells me why I can never join my family in its comings and goings, why I am left alone sitting in the living-room as they leave: it is because I have not yet entered death. I cannot follow them across the tracks, into the forest where their real lives take place, until I die. He pulls a gun from his coat pocket. He lays it on my lap. There is a door across the room, and he moves towards it. Through the door is the night. I see the glimmer of the train tracks. Beyond them, my family.

72 I do not hesitate. I pick the pistol up. I put its barrel in my mouth. I pull the trigger. I feel the back of my head erupt. It is a softer feeling than I expected. I feel my teeth fracture, disintegrate and pass in a gush of blood out of my mouth. I feel my life pass out of my mouth, and in that instant, I collapse into nothingness. There is darkness, but there is no beyond. There is *never* any beyond, only the sudden, certain rush of extinction. I know that it is death I am feeling—that is, I know this is how death must truly feel and I know that this is where beyond ceases to be a possibility.

73 I have had the dream more than once, in various forms. I always wake up with my heart hammering hard, hurting after being torn from the void that I know is the gateway to the refuge of my ruined family. Or is it the gateway to hell? Either way, I want to return to the dream, but in the haunted hours of the night there is no way back.

✦ Questions for Discussion and Writing

1. From Mikal's account of the murders, what might you conclude was Gary Gilmore's motivation in committing them?

2. Chart the phases in the relationship between Mikal and Gary in terms of their feelings toward each other before and after the murders.

3. What effect has Gary's crime and the consequent trial and public exposure had on Mikal's life?

4. How does Mikal's allusion to the mystery writer Ross MacDonald provide insight into his literary model for this account?

5. Describe an experience in which you were held accountable for something done by a family member.

6. Have you ever constructed a family tree? Describe the methods you used to interview family members and to corroborate details. Describe what you learned as a result of your research. What was the most interesting discovery?

7. If you keep a journal, create a short biographical sketch of someone who, when you were a child, seemed to be unpredictable and whose personality seemed to be composed of conflicting character traits. You might wish to try a sketch of a current acquaintance, friend, teacher, or employer.

Connections

1. Compare Sylvia Plath's relationship with her brother, Warren, to Mikal Gilmore's relationship with his brother Gary.

2. Compare the influence of the fathers on the lives of Raymond Carver and Tennessee Williams. To what extent did both Carver and Williams have difficulty relating to their fathers? To what extent did each author need to understand his father's effect on his own life (in terms of alcoholism, choosing to become writers, etc.)?

3. What similarities can you discover between Patricia Hampl's grandmother and Jill Nelson's father during mealtimes on Sundays? How did their "messages" differ?

4. In what respects do both Sylvia Plath and Annie Dillard ("So This Was Adolescence," Chapter 5) reveal a distinctive psychology of the adolescent?

5. Compare Raymond Carver's upbringing with that of Richard Rhodes's ("A Hole in the World," Chapter 5) in terms of each author's relationship with his father.

6. How do the issue of self-esteem and the messages received from adults play a crucial role in the accounts of Jill Nelson and Maya Angelou ("Liked for Myself," Chapter 8)?

7. What can you discover about the causes of violence in individuals and in groups from the accounts of Mikal Gilmore and Tadeusz Borowski ("This Way for the Gas, Ladies and Gentlemen," Chapter 12)?

2

Influential People

———————◆———————

The influence of others in shaping one's life is a topic that has provided ample opportunities for writers to recall those who have served as important role models for them. These recollections often take the form of autobiographical accounts or biographical sketches.

Writers frequently reflect on their own experiences in connection with the influence of friends, teachers, or others who have been important in their lives. The impulse underlying these accounts is the desire to know the answer to this question: how much of what I am today is the consequence of knowing this person?

This kind of writing offers a unique opportunity to study the methods writers use to characterize others. In each of these accounts, the authors identify qualities, actions, gestures, physical characteristics, and habits that they associate with a particular person. They isolate important qualities and dramatize significant actions that demonstrate unique character traits along with detailed physical and psychological descriptions that support these characterizations. Frequently, writers relate how they came to know a person and recall incidents that allow the reader to understand why this person is so important in their lives. Writers sometimes relate several episodes that provide revealing insight into patterns of behavior. Whatever form these memories take, they usually support the writer's assessment of the person's character in ways that readers find compelling and convincing.

In the chapter that follows, James Boswell provides unequaled insight into the character of his famous friend, Dr. Samuel Johnson. A childhood encounter with an African American friend reveals to Melton McLaurin the extent of his unconscious racism. Agnes De Mille assesses the inspiring influence that the famous Russian ballerina Pavlova had on her life. The impact of a remarkable preacher lies at the heart of Luis Alberto Urrea's eye-opening account. Fritz Peters recollects a humorous and offbeat experience with his boyhood teacher, a mystic philosopher, whose influence greatly shaped his life.

James Boswell

The Character of
Samuel Johnson

◆

James Boswell (1740–1795) was born in Edinburgh, Scotland, educated at Edinburgh University, and, while studying civil law at Glasgow, began his lifelong pursuit of literary and political fame by publishing numerous pamphlets and verses. At the age of twenty, he went to London, befriended the Duke of York, took the first of many mistresses, and, on May 16, 1763, at Tom Davie's Bookshop in Russell Street, met the famous Dr. Samuel Johnson for the first of the 276 occasions they would see each other. Boswell raised "social climbing" to an art form, introducing himself to such literary notables as Voltaire and Rousseau (whose advocacy of Corsican liberty inspired Boswell's first full-fledged work, in 1768, An Account of Corsica). *During 1773, he toured Scotland and the Hebrides with Dr. Johnson, was elected to Johnson's famous literary club, and began his* Journal of a Tour of the Hebrides, *which appeared in 1785 after Johnson's death. The perplexing contradictions within his illustrious friend's personality are described in "The Character of Samuel Johnson," an excerpt that concludes Boswell's major work,* The Life of Samuel Johnson *(1891), one of the greatest biographies ever written.*

1 The character of SAMUEL JOHNSON has, I trust, been so developed in the course of this work, that they who have honored it with a perusal, may be considered as well acquainted with him. As, however, it may be expected that I should collect into one view the capital and distinguishing features of this extraordinary man, I shall endeavor to acquit myself of that part of my biographical undertaking,[1] however difficult it it may be to do that which many of my readers will do better for themselves.

2 His figure was large and well formed, and his countenance of the cast of an ancient statue; yet his appearance was rendered strange and somewhat uncouth by convulsive cramps, by the scars of that distemper which it was once imagined the royal touch could cure, and by a slovenly mode of dress. He had the use only of one eye; yet so much does mind govern and even supply the deficiency of organs, that his vi-

---

[1]As I do not see any reason to give a different character of my illustrious friend now, from what I formerly gave, the greatest part of the sketch of him in my "Journal of a Tour to the Hebrides" is here adopted.—B.

sual perceptions, as far as they extended, were uncommonly quick and accurate. So morbid was his temperament that he never knew the natural joy of a free and vigorous use of his limbs: when he walked, it was like the struggling gait of one in fetters; when he rode, he had no command or direction of his horse, but was carried as if in a balloon. That with his constitution and habits of life he should have lived seventy-five years, is a proof that an inherent *vivida vis*[2] is a powerful preservative of the human frame.

3   Man is, in general, made up of contradictory qualities; and these will ever show themselves in strange succession, where a consistency in appearance at least, if not reality, has not been attained by long habits of philosophical discipline. In proportion to the native vigor of the mind, the contradictory qualities will be the more prominent, and more difficult to be adjusted; and, therefore, we are not to wonder that Johnson exhibited an eminent example of this remark which I have made upon human nature. At different times he seemed a different man, in some respects; not, however, in any great or essential article, upon which he had fully employed his mind, and settled certain principles of duty, but only in his manners, and in the display of argument and fancy in his talk. He was prone to superstition, but not to credulity. Though his imagination might incline him to a belief of the marvelous and the mysterious, his vigorous reason examined the evidence with jealousy. He was a sincere and zealous Christian, of high Church-of-England and monarchial principles, which he would not tamely suffer to be questioned; and had, perhaps, at an early period, narrowed his mind somewhat too much, both as to religion and politics. His being impressed with the danger of extreme latitude in either, though he was of a very independent spirit, occasioned his appearing somewhat unfavorable to the prevalence of that noble freedom of sentiment which is the best possession of man. Nor can it be denied, that he had many prejudices; which, however, frequently suggested many of his pointed sayings, that rather show a playfulness of fancy than any settled malignity. He was steady and inflexible in maintaining the obligations of religion and morality; both from a regard for the order of society, and from a veneration for the GREAT SOURCE of all order; correct, nay, stern in his taste; hard to please, and easily offended, impetuous and irritable in his temper, but of a most humane and benevolent heart[3] which showed itself not only in a most liberal charity, as far as his cir-

[2]Lucretius, i. 72.

[3]In the *Olla Podrida*, a collection of essays published at Oxford, there is an admirable paper upon the character of Johnson, written by the Reverend Dr. Horne, the last excellent Bishop of Norwich. The following passage is eminently happy: "To reject wisdom, because the person of him who communicates it is uncouth, and his manners are inelegant; what is it but to throw away a pineapple, and assign for a person the roughness of its coat?"—B.

cumstances would allow, but in a thousand instances of active benevolence. He was afflicted with a bodily disease which made him often restless and fretful; and with a constitutional melancholy, the clouds which darkened the brightness of his fancy, and gave a gloomy cast to his whole course of thinking: we, therefore, ought not to wonder at his sallies of impatience and passion at any time; especially when provoked by obtrusive ignorance, or presuming petulance; and allowance must be made for his uttering hasty and satirical sallies even against his best friends. And, surely, when it is considered, that, "amidst sickness and sorrow," he exerted his faculties in so many works for the benefit of mankind, and particularly that he achieved the great and admirable DICTIONARY of our language, we must be astonished at his resolution. The solemn text, "of him to whom much is given, much will be required," seems to have been ever present to his mind, in a rigorous sense, and to have made him dissatisfied with his labors and acts of goodness, however comparatively great; so that the unavoidable consciousness of his superiority was, in that respect, a cause of disquiet. He suffered so much from this, and from the gloom which perpetually haunted him and made solitude frightful, that it may be said of him, "If in this life only he had hope, he was of all men most miserable." He loved praise, when it was brought to him; but was too proud to seek for it. He was somewhat susceptible of flattery. As he was general and unconfined in his studies, he cannot be considered as master of any one particular science; but he had accumulated a vast and various collection of learning and knowledge, which was so arranged in his mind, as to be ever in readiness to be brought forth. But his superiority over other learned men consisted chiefly in what may be called the art of thinking, the art of using his mind: a certain continual power of seizing the useful substance of all that he knew, and exhibiting it in a clear and forcible manner; so that knowledge, which we often see to be no better than lumber in men of dull understanding, was in him true, evident, and actual wisdom. His moral precepts are practical; for they are drawn from an intimate acquaintance with human nature. His maxims carry conviction; for they are founded on the basis of common sense, and a very attentive and minute survey of real life. His mind was so full of imagery, that he might have been perpetually a poet; yet it is remarkable, that, however rich his prose is in this respect, his poetical pieces, in general, have not much of that splendor, but are rather distinguished by strong sentiment, and acute observation, conveyed in harmonious and energetic verse, particularly in heroic couplets. Though usually grave, and even awful in his deportment, he possessed uncommon and peculiar powers of wit and humor; he frequently indulged himself in colloquial pleasantry; and the heartiest merriment was often enjoyed in his company; with this great advantage, that as it was entirely free from any poisonous tincture of vice or impiety, it was salutary to those who shared in it. He had accustomed himself to such accuracy in his common conversation,[4] that he at all times expressed his thoughts with great force, and an elegant choice of language, the effect of which was aided by his having a loud voice and a slow deliberate utterance. In him were united a most logical head with a most fertile imagination, which gave him an extraordinary advantage in arguing: for he could reason close or wide, as he saw best for the moment. Exulting in his intellectual strength and dexterity, he could, when he pleased, be the greatest sophist that ever contended in the lists of declamation; and, from a spirit of contradiction and a delight in showing his powers, he would often maintain the wrong side with equal warmth and ingenuity; so that when there was an audience, his real opinions could seldom be gathered from his talk; though when he was in company with a single friend, he would discuss a subject with genuine fairness; but he was too conscientious to make error permanent and pernicious by deliberately writing it; and, in all his numerous works he earnestly inculcated what appeared to him to be the truth; his piety being constant, and the ruling principle of all his conduct.

[4]Though a perfect resemblance of Johnson is not to be found in any age, parts of his character are admirably expressed by Clarendon in drawing that of Lord Falkland, whom the noble and masterly historian describes at his seat near Oxford: "Such an immenseness of wit, such a solidity of judgment, so infinite a fancy bound in by a most logical ratiocination. His acquaintance was cultivated by the most polite and accurate men, so that his house was a University in less volume, whither they came, not so much for repose as study, and to examine and refine those grosser propositions, which laziness and consent made current in conversation." Bayle's account of *Menage* may also be quoted as exceedingly applicable to the great subject of this work. "His illustrious friends erected a very glorious monument to him in the collection entitled "Menagiana." Those who judge of things aright, will confess that this collection is very proper to show the extent of genius and learning which was the character of Menage. And I may be bold to say, that *the excellent works he published will not distinguish him from other learned men so advantageously as this*. To publish books of great learning, to make Greek and Latin verses exceedingly well turned, is not a common talent, I own; neither is it extremely rare. It is incomparably more difficult to find men who can furnish discourse about an infinite number of things, and who can diversify them a hundred ways. How many authors are there who are admired for their works, on account of the vast learning that is displayed in them, who are not able to sustain a conversation. Those who know Menage only by his books, might think he resembled those learned men; but if you show the MENAGIANA, you distinguish him from them, and make him known by a talent which is given to very few learned men. There it appears that he was a man who spoke offhand a thousand good things. His memory extended to what was ancient and modern; to the court and to the city; to the dead and to the living languages; to things serious and things jocose; in a word, to a thousand sorts of subjects. That which appeared a trifle to some readers of the "Menagiana," who did not consider circumstances, caused admiration in other readers, who minded the difference between what a man speaks without preparation, and that which he prepares for the press. And, therefore, we cannot sufficiently commend the care which his illustrious friends took to erect a monument so capable of giving him immortal glory. They were not obliged to rectify what they had heard him say; for, in so doing, they had not been faithful historians of his conversation."—B.

Such was SAMUEL JOHNSON, a man whose talents, acquirements, and   4
virtues, were so extraordinary, that the more his character is considered, the more he will be regarded by the present age, and by posterity,
with admiration and reverence.

✦ Questions for Discussion and Writing

1. What aspects of Dr. Johnson's character does Boswell find striking and
   commendable?

2. What evidence does Boswell present to support his contention that Dr.
   Johnson lived his life according to the principle that "of him to whom
   much is given, much will be required"?

3. What character trait does Boswell emphasize by telling his readers
   that, although Dr. Johnson could argue equally well on both sides of an
   issue, he would never set down in writing an opinion to which he did
   not subscribe?

4. How does Boswell organize his character sketch, within each paragraph and from sentence to sentence, to convey the extreme contradictions operating in Dr. Johnson's personality?

5. Describe a person you know whose character seems made up of many
   contradictions. Organize your character sketch to emphasize each side
   of the person's nature.

Melton A. McLaurin

Bobo

◆

Melton McLaurin is a professor and chairman of the Department of History at the University of North Carolina at Wilmington. He is the author of four books on southern history and Separate Pasts: Growing Up White in the Segregated South *(1987), from which the following account is drawn. McLaurin's uncommon honesty about and insight into racial relationships in the rural south in the 1950s is based on his experiences growing up in Wade, North Carolina.*

1   His name was James Robert Fuller, Jr., but everyone called him Bobo. He was a year younger than I, and I had known him all my life. He lived in a small white frame house in the black neighborhood behind Granddaddy's store. There seemed to be nothing unusual or special about Bobo; he was just another black boy in the community, of no more or less consequence than any other black child. Nevertheless, it was Bobo, a child I often looked down upon because of his blackness and his poverty, who showed me the emotional power that racial prejudice and segregation held over whites as well as blacks.

2   I knew his entire family. James Robert, his father, was a huge man, nearly six and a half feet tall, who appeared even taller to a thirteen-year-old white boy. He had the physique of many fine black athletes—long, thickly muscled arms, long legs sweeping upward to a short waist above which rested a powerful, well-formed torso. James Robert drove a truck for the Tart Lumber Company, making short runs to scores of hamlets in eastern North Carolina and Virginia to deliver dressed lumber to local building-and-supply dealers. He was a soft-spoken man with a gentle voice and blue-gray eyes. I remember his climbing down from his cab, his great long legs stretching to meet the ground, and I recall the easy, loping strides that moved him away from the truck. I also remember him drunk, for like many of Wade's poor male residents, black and white, he turned to the bottle to escape his problems, however briefly. Especially on weekends, but occasionally on weekdays, James Robert would enter our store after downing more than a few drinks. At such times he was a sad figure even to a white youth: he was a giant to be pitied, his physical size somehow overwhelmed by the circumstances of his life, few of which he determined and most of which he could not avoid. When he drank he withdrew

into himself, and in doing so he revealed his alienation from the world whites controlled—a world in which this huge man with smooth, copper-brown skin was just another menial laborer.

Jeanette was Bobo's mother. She had four children. Bobo was the oldest. Her second child, Jennifer, some two years younger, was a slight, timid girl with large mournful eyes. Two years younger than Jennifer was Chris, a small energetic boy whose black eyes shone with curiosity and intelligence. The youngest child, a girl whose name I can't recall, was an infant. Although Jeanette was still young, probably less than thirty when Bobo was twelve, she, like most black women of the village, had few skills that the society valued. In Wade there were not many jobs for black women, even for those who had completed high school or received some additional training. For women like Jeanette, who possessed little formal education, there was but one opportunity for employment: she "worked days" as a domestic, as did scores of her black sisters. For years she served a single white household two days a week—washing, ironing, cleaning, doing the heavy household chores. Other days she "picked up" work in the homes of Wade's more affluent families, including ours. She was a big woman, tall and long-limbed like her husband, already heavy in the hips. She did not strike me as pretty, although she had a pleasant face with nice eyes, a coffee-brown complexion, and an easy smile.

Jeanette was quiet, gentle, unobtrusive; all in all she seemed a terribly vulnerable figure. Yet she held her family together. She looked after James Robert, mothered her children, maintained the household, and brought home a supplemental income. When the family fell behind in its payments for the groceries purchased on credit from Granddaddy's store, it was Jeanette who had to beg "Mr. Lonnie" for additional time. Her supplications followed a centuries-old script that was undoubtedly as humiliating as it was successful. It was a charade often played in the segregated South, a drama in which all the characters knew perfectly their lines and postures. This drama I frequently saw staged, several times with Jeanette in the female lead, sometimes with other women in the role. On the few occasions on which I observed a male playing the supplicant, the script was revised slightly to allow the player a bit more dignity.

The role required that Jeanette project an image of childlike naiveté and innocence in order to deserve the beneficence of her superior. When she sought an extension of credit or time in which to pay her debt, Jeanette would ease into the store, head bent slightly forward, eyes downcast, her face a sorrowful study of helplessness, and with short, gliding steps she would move toward my grandfather. Standing across a wooden counter from him, she would pause and begin to shift her weight gently from foot to foot, her body swaying almost imperceptibly as in hushed tones she pled her case.

6   "Mr. Lonnie, I needs some things, and I ain't got no money, nothing, Mr. Lonnie. I knows we owe you, and I'll pay you as soon as I can, Mr. Lonnie, honest I will, but I needs some things right now."

7   After her appeal was delivered, without noticeable change of facial expression Granddaddy would turn and pick up his ledger book from the counter and read from Jeanette's account. "Jeanette, you owe me seventy-five dollars on this account. That's a lot of money. I can't keep letting you have groceries without getting paid."

8   Jeanette would then acknowledge Granddaddy's admonition and continue to press her case.

9   "I know it seems a lot, Mr. Lonnie. But I'll pay—just as soon as I can get the money. James Robert'll get paid next week, and I'll try and get an extra day's work somewhere. We'll catch up, Mr. Lonnie. You knows we pays you when we can. But the children needs some things now, Mr. Lonnie."

10   Granddaddy would then lay the ledger on the counter and shake his head, as if puzzled by the entire transaction and baffled by Jeanette's inability to obtain more income. Jeanette would continue to sway as she awaited his response, her eyes still searching the floor. After a long silence Granddaddy, like a judge sentencing a convicted felon, would deliver his verdict.

11   "Well, all right. This time. But no more than five dollars. Not a nickel more. And I want something on your account next week, you hear?"

12   "Thank you, Mr. Lonnie, thank you." Jeanette would snap her head up, stop swaying, then step smartly backward while bending forward slightly at the waist in an impromptu curtsy. "We'll be sure and pay some next week, Mr. Lonnie, just you wait and see."

13   "Well, just be sure you do," he would reply, and turn to me and command, "Boy, get Jeanette here what she wants—up to five dollars, no more."

14   "Yes, sir." And I would come to the counter to take her order.

15   I accepted such episodes and others equally demeaning to blacks as normal events of daily life, certainly nothing to cause concern. I assumed that James Robert and Jeanette and their family, and many other black families that I knew, always behaved in the way my father and grandfather, and most other white adults, expected them to. I knew, for I had been told since birth, that whites were superior to blacks (and for that matter, that members of my family were superior to most whites). On the other hand, I had also been taught that one should never mistreat a black, insult a black, or purposely be rude to a black. One was never to behave badly toward blacks, partially because of moral imperatives.

16   "Colored people have souls too," my grandmother, whom my brothers and sisters and I called Ma Ma, reminded us more than once.

"Some of them will go to heaven with us." Ma Ma, of course, was bent upon getting as many people into heaven as possible. I suspect that she believed that white Christians would require a servant class in the hereafter, although she never elaborated upon her concept of the social status of blacks in the New Jerusalem.

Such moral considerations, however, rarely influenced the behavior of upper class whites toward blacks. The more compelling reason why one was expected never to abuse blacks—unless, of course, they acted in a manner that whites deemed worthy of chastisement—had little to do with the admission that blacks were fellow humans. Rather, it was because superior people never treated their inferiors in an unseemly manner. For example, one didn't say "nigger," not because the use of that word caused blacks pain but because to do so indicated "poor breeding." "We don't use that word in our family"—this was the standard response of women in our family to men who did use that word in front of children.   17

In the South of my youth "good breeding" was still extremely important. Adults who abused blacks "for no good reason" were held in contempt by my family, and as late as the 1950s the older generation talked disparagingly about whites who "treated their colored people mean," as if whites still owned blacks and were compelled by some social code to handle their laborers gently. *Nigger* was a word poor whites used, a term they hurled at blacks (whom the adults in my family always referred to as "colored people") the way my childhood friends from less affluent families hurled pieces of granite from the railway track beds at hapless black children their age or younger. Despite linguistic niceties, however, all whites knew that blacks were, really, servants. It was their destiny to work at menial tasks, supervised, of course, by benevolent whites. All this was according to God's plan and was perfectly obvious to all but dimwitted Yankees and Communists. As a young child I could sit in church with the other white children of the village and sing "Jesus loves the little children... Red and yellow, black and white" and never know why no black children were in our group. Until I began to work at the store the thought that they should have been in church with us never occurred to me. It also probably never occurred to the adult church members, including the minister.   18

Race, then, was something I rarely thought about and never pondered—that is, until a single incident, a commonplace occurrence involving Bobo, made me aware of the tremendous impact a segregated society had upon my life. Unlike schoolmates like my best friend, Howard Lee Baker (named for Clarence Lee Tart, who owned the house in which Howard was born and in whose mill his father worked), or Linda Daughtery, the vivacious, sharp-tongued girl down the street who disliked me as much as I disliked her throughout adolescence, Bobo was never an important part of my life. Bobo was merely   19 there, a child whom I saw frequently and played with on occasion, but who was of no real consequence to me. Because of his relative unimportance, because I had known him all my life, because he had been a part of my childhood environment in the same way as the trees and the school playgrounds and the dusty streets, because, like them, he had always been there, Bobo changed that comfortable, secure racist world for me. He did so unintentionally, yet irrevocably, in the fall of my thirteenth year.

20   I knew Bobo as well as I knew any black child in Wade. He sometimes came to our house with his mother; although Jeanette didn't work for us as often as several other black women of the village did, it was not unusual for her to be hired to assist with the wash, housecleaning, or other heavy chores. Sometimes she brought her children with her, especially on pleasant days when all the children, black and white, could play outside while she worked, freed from the distractions of child care. The children of the two families were approximately the same age and played together well, although even in play the special status of the white children was understood, if rarely acknowledged verbally.

21   Playing with Bobo and other black youths was a natural part of my life, and seldom very meaningful. Much of the time our play, especially team games and horseplay among boys and occasional displays of developing male prowess, involved physical contact with blacks, and I thought nothing of it. In my childhood physical proximity to blacks was natural and accepted in the society. If someone had told me that I could not touch Bobo because he was black, I would have been as shocked as if I had been told that Bobo was my equal. Neither concept was a part of the village mentality or of the belief system of the segregated South. Had such notions been proposed to me as a child, I would have rejected both, but as a child I never encountered them.

22   There was certainly nothing extraordinary about physical contact with Bobo. As a child I played football and basketball with him, wrestled with him, and competed against him in other games that were actually boyhood tests of physical strength. One such incident occurred when I was twelve or thirteen. Bobo, my brother Tim, and I were at the store. There were no customers, and we began to play a version of King of the Mountain. The object of the game was simple—to knock the king from his position atop one of the store's counters. The king, by bracing himself with his back to the wall and his feet pushed against a second counter, could absorb some stiff blows to the body without yielding an inch. Since I was the oldest, I was king first. I wedged myself between the counters and Bobo and Tim threw their bodies at me, pushing and shoving, struggling to unseat me. I could feel Bobo's body slam against mine, feel the competitive tension with each blow. He was a heavy child, not fat and, as I knew from encounters in past games of physical

contact, not very strong either. During the contest I was aware of his blackness, conscious that his was a black body pushing against my white skin, but that fact did not concern me and I was not repulsed or upset by it. The game was short, broken up by Granddaddy, who returned and in unmistakable terms informed us that he failed to appreciate three boys tussling on his counter-tops.

We each enjoyed the physical nature of the contest, the straining of 23 muscles and the measuring contact of young bodies, the sense of manliness that such exertions evoked. I had struggled to remain king to prove my strength, my power as a male, without any conscious understanding of a need to best Bobo because he was black, or to triumph because I was white. Such racial innocence, or perhaps naiveté, soon departed, and with its departure came the realization that segregation fundamentally affected everyone in Wade, whites and blacks, that no one was immune, and that it was a constant force, controlling our present and dictating our future.

The realization occurred in a comfortable, familiar setting on the 24 playground. It was one of those uncommon common incidents of ordinary life which, because of some inexplicable turn of events or perhaps because of their timing, unmask some aspect of our life that we have always accepted as a given, place it in another perspective, and cause it to assume an entirely different face. Often such perceptions are not a result of either education or training but are instead mere happenstances, accidents of understanding, and are as unwelcome as they are unintended.

A basketball court was as appropriate as any place to gain some 25 understanding of the larger implications of segregation and racism. In Wade basketball was the premier sport, played continually by boys, black and white, from September through May. The consolidated high schools, black and white, were too small and too poor to field football teams, but they could afford basketball programs. The goal of most male students was to make their school's varsity basketball team. On weekends the village boys played on the asphalt court of the white elementary school, a court that ate up the jeans and shirts and knees and hands of those who fell on it. Weekday afternoon games of one-on-one or two-on-two were contested to the bitter end on dirt courts, one of which could be found in the yard of nearly every house with a teenage boy.

Pickup games between integrated teams were nothing unusual; in 26 fact, they were the norm when blacks and whites played on the same court. Teams composed of boys of only one race rarely played one another, because teams were selected by team captains who took turns choosing one player at a time. Since both captains wanted winning teams and since from years of playground experience they knew the individual skills of each participant, they selected the best players first, regardless of race. Although race was not completely ignored on the courts, it rarely influenced the conduct of a game. In all the years I played in such integrated contests, I never saw a fight provoked for racial reasons, though disputes over fouls, out-of-bounds plays, and other technicalities occurred with monotonous regularity during practically every game. The lack of racial tensions on the court probably stemmed from the fact that the society accepted, and in many ways encouraged, the practice of integrated play. Young southern males had traditionally engaged in integrated informal sports events, especially such outdoor sports as hunting and fishing. Integrated pickup basketball games, as opposed to organized play, were merely an extension of this practice. It was only contact with females of the opposite race that was proscribed, and that only after puberty.

27   Although my court skills were average at best, I loved the game and played at every opportunity. I had a good eye for the basket but neither speed nor height, and I was usually chosen somewhere in the middle of the selection process. In pickup games in which Bobo and I were on opposing teams we were often matched against one another since we were roughly the same size and age. I relished the chance to play opposite Bobo because he was no quicker or taller than I and couldn't shoot as well. I knew that I could count on a good game against him, and that I would score some points—a welcome prospect for one not blessed with physical grace in an adolescent male culture that stressed athletic prowess.

28   More than most white boys, I played pickup games on the dirt court of the black elementary school. Games there were especially easy to join on Saturday afternoons. Within an hour or two after lunch several black kids would gather on the court and, if a basketball could be found, would begin shooting at an iron hoop nailed to a battered and often-repaired plywood backboard. This "warmup" would continue for about fifteen to twenty minutes, the players dropping their best shots through the cords of the imaginary net beneath the rim. During play the composition of teams changed constantly as members were called by younger siblings to complete some chore left undone at home or as players tired of the game. If things were slow at the store, as they often were by late afternoon, I could sneak out to join the play, sometimes with a white friend or two who had come by on the chance that I could get away. Since individual games were short and team membership constantly changing, we could usually get into a game within minutes of arriving at the court.

29   One fall Saturday afternoon six of us were matched in a hotly contested game, neither of the equally untalented threesomes able to gain much of an advantage. Howard Lee and I, the only whites in the game, were joined by an awkward young black named Curtis, whose reasonably accurate jump shot was negated by his general lack of coordina-

tion. Bobo played on the other team, opposite me as usual. To a casual observer the game would have seemed thoroughly integrated, void of racial tensions. In fact we were unconcerned about race as we played, our attention focused on completing a pass, sinking a shot, grabbing a rebound. Yet the racial dynamics of this particular game, like those of all the other integrated games in which I played, were exactly the same as those of the village: the whites dictated the rules.

We were using Howard Lee's ball, which presented a challenge because it leaked air and had to be reinflated every thirty minutes or so. Since there was an air compressor at the store, I was charged with keeping the ball inflated. Although we played on a black playground, the white kids controlled the situation because we controlled the ball. None of the black players had a ball, so without us there was no game. Under the circumstances it made little difference which team won. However, had the black players challenged what Howard and I perceived as our rights on the court, we probably would have taken the ball and left the game.

We played into the afternoon, our play interrupted by frequent trips to the air compressor. When enough air leaked from the ball to cause it to lose its bounce and begin to interfere with the game, I would take it to the air compressor to pump it up. Some of the other boys, their game halted and lacking even a flat ball to shoot at the basket in the meantime, would accompany me from the playground to the store. On what turned out to be our last trip, Bobo and Howard strolled over with me as I went to inflate the ball. As we walked the three of us created brilliant passes and incredible moves with the flabby sphere, all of which we dreamed we would someday employ in the perfect game. When we reached the air compressor I pulled from my pocket the needle required to inflate the ball and without thinking handed it to Bobo.

The procedure followed for inserting a needle into a basketball had long been sanctioned by the rituals of kids playing on dirt and asphalt courts. First, someone wet the needle by sticking it into his mouth or spitting on it. Thus lubricated, the instrument was popped neatly into the small rubber valve through which the ball was inflated. This time chance dictated that playground procedure would fail; we couldn't insert the needle into the valve. Bobo stuck the needle in his mouth, applied the usual lavish amount of saliva, and handed it to Howard Lee, who held the ball. Howard struggled to push the needle into the valve, with no luck. Irritated by what struck me as their incompetence and anxious to return to the game I decided to inflate the ball myself. I took the ball from Howard, pulled the needle from the valve, and placed it in my mouth, convinced that my spit would somehow get the needle into the ball and us back onto the court. A split second after placing the needle in my mouth, I was jolted by one of the most shattering emotional experiences of my young life. Instantaneously an awareness of the shared racial prejudices of generations of white society coursed through every nerve in my body. Bolts of prejudice, waves of prejudice that I could literally feel sent my head reeling and buckled my knees.

33   The realization that the needle I still held in my mouth had come directly from Bobo's mouth, that it carried on it Bobo's saliva, transformed my prejudices into a physically painful experience. I often had drunk from the same cup as black children, dined on food prepared by blacks. It never occurred to me that such actions would violate my racial purity. The needle in my mouth, however, had been purposely drenched with Negro spit, and that substance threatened to defile my entire being. It threatened me with germs which, everyone said, were common among blacks. These black germs would ravage my body with unspeakable diseases, diseases from the tropics, Congo illnesses that would rot my limbs, contort my body with pain. Visions pulled from foreign missions films occasionally shown at the Presbyterian church flashed through my mind. I saw the white jungle doctor, Schweitzer at Lambarene, dressed in a white linen suit, walking among row on row of rickety cots, each occupied by some wretched, rotting black. Those awful African diseases, I now imagined, would claim me as a victim.

34   The tainted substance on the needle also threatened, in a less specific but equally disturbing manner, my white consciousness, my concept of what being white meant. Bobo's spit threatened to plunge me into a world of voodoo chants and tribal drums. Suddenly the *Saturday Evening Post* cartoon world of black savages dancing about boiling cauldrons filled with white hunters and missionaries seemed strangely real. I felt deprived of the ability to reason, to control the situation. All threats to mind and body, however, faded to compare to the ultimate danger posed by the saliva on the needle. It placed in jeopardy my racial purity, my existence as a superior being, the true soul of all southern whites. The needle was the ultimate unclean object, carrier of the human degeneracy that black skin represented. It transmitted to me Bobo's black essence, an essence that degraded me and made me, like him, less than human.

35   I felt compelled to jerk the needle from my mouth, to spit it to the ground and rid myself of the unclean thing. I wanted desperately to wipe my mouth with the back of my hand, to remove with my pure white skin any trace of this defiling substance. The urge to gag, to lean over and vomit out any of the black saliva that might remain to spread its contamination throughout my body, was almost unbearable. Yet I could neither gag nor vomit, nor could I wipe my mouth with the back of my hand. Ironically, the same prejudices that filled me with loathing and disgust also demanded that I conceal my feelings. The emotional turmoil exploding inside me had to be contained, choked off. Not for a second could I allow Bobo to suspect that I was in the least upset, or to

comprehend the anguish his simple act of moistening the needle with his saliva had caused me. The rules of segregation which I had absorbed every waking moment of my life, and which were now an essential part of my consciousness, demanded that I retain my position as the superior, that I remain in control of the situation. More than the poison of Bobo's saliva I feared the slightest indication of loss of self-control, the merest hint that this black child I knew so well had the power to cut me to the emotional quick, to reach the innermost regions of my being and challenge the sureties of my white world. He could never be allowed to cause me to deviate in the least from the prescribed pattern of white behavior.

Thirteen years of conditioning in a segregationist society squelched my confusion. The unswerving assurance of racial dogma suppressed any instinct to flinch, any inclination to hesitate. Infuriated with myself because I had momentarily allowed a black—even worse, a black my age—to intimidate me, I grabbed the needle from my mouth and slammed it through the valve into the basketball. I jerked the air hose from its rack and inflated the ball to its normal hardness. Still angry, I flung the ball at Bobo, striking him in the stomach. Startled, he clutched the ball with both hands, holding it tightly against his midriff. He and Howard Lee glanced at me, Bobo's eyes filled with anger, Howard's with surprise, as each probed to find a reason for my outburst. No one spoke, and I met their gaze. Bobo turned, bounced the ball once, hard, caught it, and moved toward the basketball court. He paused and glanced at me again, this time his eyes expressing puzzlement rather than anger. Howard followed him. My white heritage defended, I stood and watched them walk toward the three black boys who nonchalantly awaited our return and the resumption of the game.

I had triumphed. I had preserved my status as the superior. I had prevented Bobo from guessing that his actions had destroyed my emotional composure. I had challenged him in front of another white and forced him to confront my claim to superiority. By refusing to question my actions and returning to the game, he had acquiesced in that claim, though he never acknowledged it. I had upheld the doctrine of white supremacy and observed the rules of segregated society. And I suspect that Bobo realized, as I did, that those same rules governed his response to me. He must have understood that he could not respond to my challenge because of who he was within the village social structure, and because we stood in the shadow of Granddaddy's store, in a white world.

Yet my vindication of white supremacy was incomplete. While I had asserted my superiority and my right to that status because of my skin color, I still felt defiled. The thought that some residual contamination, some fingering trace of the essence of Bobo's blackness remained with me became an obsession. I could feel his germs crawling through my body, spreading their black pestilence from head to toe. I had to cleanse myself—to purify my body of Bobo's contaminants and to rid my person of any remaining trace of his negritude. Only then could I fully reclaim my racial purity and restore my shaken sense of superiority. And I had to do so quickly, without the knowledge of others, before I could return to the game.

39　　　I walked to the other side of the store, out of sight of the five boys on the basketball court who had begun to shoot goals at random while waiting for my return. From the side of the budding protruded a faucet, used by thirsty ball players who had no money for Cokes. Bending over, I turned the tap and watched the clear, clean water burst from the spigot and spatter into the sand. I cupped my hands beneath the flow, watched them fill with the crystal liquid, then splashed it to my face, felt it begin to cleanse me of Bobo's black stain. Bending farther, I placed my mouth against the grooved lip of the faucet. I filled my mouth with water, swished the water from cheek to cheek, then forced it through my teeth and onto the ground. Tilting my head, mouth still against the faucet, I let the cleansing stream trickle through my mouth, removing any remaining Negro contaminant. I splashed more water over my face and head, then washed my hands and forearms. Finally, I swallowed a large gulp of water, felt it slide down my throat, and in my mind's eye saw it wash away the last traces of Bobo's blackness. My rite of purification was completed. With this baptism of plain tap water I was reborn, my white selfhood restored. I stood straight, shook the water from my face and hands, and walked back to rejoin the game.

40　　　I don't remember if the game resumed at midpoint, if new sides were chosen, or who won or lost. What I remember is an awareness that things had changed. I knew that Bobo was black, that he would always be black, and that his blackness set him apart from me in ways that I had never understood. I realized, too, that his blackness threatened me, that in a way I did not comprehend it challenged my most securely held concepts about who I was and what I might become. For the first time I understood that Bobo and I belonged to two fundamentally different worlds, and that society demanded that we each stay in the world designated for us. And for the first time I understood that segregation was not a happenstance, an everyday reality of no import. I realized now that segregation was serious, as serious as life and death, perhaps as serious as heaven or hell. I knew, too, that Bobo was unchanged, that I was still me, that none of the blacks with whom I played or worked were any different than they had been. I also knew that there was something very wrong, even sinister, about this power Bobo held over me, this ability to confound my world simply because he was black. None of it made much sense at the time. But the knowledge, the understanding that segregation was so powerful a force, that it could provoke such violent emotional responses within me, for the first time raised questions in my mind about the institution, serious questions that adults didn't want asked and, as I would later discover, that they never answered.

✦ Questions for Discussion and Writing

1. Why does McLaurin begin his account of Bobo with such an extensive description of James Robert and Jeanette Fuller, Bobo's parents?

2. How do any of the incidents McLaurin describes give you insight into the social forces between races at that time in the South?

3. What unquestioned assumptions about the relationship between the races help explain the narrator's violent reaction to the incident on the playground with his friend Bobo?

4. What insight did the narrator gain about himself and the society in which he lived as a result of this incident with Bobo?

5. Describe an incident that gave you insight into the psychological roots of racism in contemporary American society.

Agnes De Mille

Pavlova

◆

Agnes De Mille, a principal figure in American dance, was born in New York City in 1908. She created distinctive American ballets, such as Rodeo *(1942) and* Tally-Ho *(1944), and brought her talents as an innovative choreographer to* Oklahoma! *(1943 and 1980),* Carousel *(1945),* Brigadoon *(1947),* Paint Your Wagon *(1951),* Gentlemen Prefer Blondes *(1949), and other musicals. De Mille's entertaining autobiographies,* Dance to the Piper *(1952) and* Reprieve: A Memoir *(1981) describe many exciting moments in her life. "Pavlova," from* Dance to the Piper, *contains De Mille's recollection of what she felt when she saw Anna Pavlova, the famed Russian ballerina, for the first time.*

1   Anna Pavlova! My life stops as I write that name. Across the daily preoccupation of lessons, lunch boxes, tooth brushings and quarrelings with Margaret flashed this bright, unworldly experience and burned in a single afternoon a path over which I could never retrace my steps. I had witnessed the power of beauty, and in some chamber of my heart I lost forever my irresponsibility. I was as clearly marked as though she had looked me in the face and called my name. For generations my father's family had loved and served the theater. All my life I had seen actors and actresses and had heard theater jargon at the dinner table and business talk of box-office grosses. I had thrilled at Father's projects and watched fascinated his picturesque occupations. I took a proprietary pride in the profitable and hasty growth of "The Industry." But nothing in his world or my uncle's prepared me for theater as I saw it that Saturday afternoon.

2   Since that day I have gained some knowledge in my trade and I recognize that her technique was limited; that her arabesques were not as pure or classically correct as Markova's, that her jumps and batterie were paltry, her turns not to be compared in strength and number with the strenuous durability of Baronova or Toumanova. I know that her scenery was designed by second-rate artists, her music was on a level with restaurant orchestrations, her company definitely inferior to all the standards we insist on today, and her choreography mostly hack. And yet I say that she was in her person the quintessence of theatrical excitement.

3   As her little bird body revealed itself on the scene, either immobile in trembling mystery or tense in the incredible arc which was her lift,

72

her instep stretched ahead in an arch never before seen, the tiny bones of her hands in ceaseless vibration, her face radiant, diamonds glittering under her dark hair, her little waist encased in silk, the great tutu balancing, quickening and flashing over her beating, flashing, quivering legs, every man and woman sat forward, every pulse quickened. She never appeared to rest static, some part of her trembled, vibrated, beat like a heart. Before our dazzled eyes, she flashed with the sudden sweetness of a hummingbird in action too quick for understanding by our gross utilitarian standards, in action sensed rather than seen. The movie cameras of her day could not record her allegro. Her feet and hands photographed as a blur.

Bright little bird bones, delicate bird sinews! She was all fire and steel wire. There was not an ounce of spare flesh on her skeleton, and the life force used and used her body until she died of the fever of moving, gasping for breath, much too young.

She was small, about five feet. She wore a size one and a half slipper, but her feet and hands were large in proportion to her height. Her hand could cover her whole face. Her trunk was small and stripped of all anatomy but the ciphers of adolescence, her arms and legs relatively long, the neck extraordinarily long and mobile. All her gestures were liquid and possessed of an inner rhythm that flowed to inevitable completion with the finality of architecture or music. Her arms seemed to lift not from the elbow or the arm socket, but from the base of the spine. Her legs seemed to function from the waist. When she bent her head her whole spine moved and the motion was completed the length of the arm through the elongation of her slender hand and the quivering reaching fingers. I believe there has never been a foot like hers, slender, delicate and of such an astonishing aggressiveness when arched as to suggest the ultimate in human vitality. Without in any way being sensual, being, in fact, almost sexless, she suggested all exhilaration, gaiety and delight. She jumped, and we broke bonds with reality. We flew. We hung over the earth, spread in the air as we do in dreams, our hands turning in the air as in water—the strong forthright taut plunging leg balanced on the poised arc of the foot, the other leg stretched to the horizon like the wing of a bird. We lay balancing, quivering, turning, and all things were possible, even to us, the ordinary people.

I have seen two dancers as great or greater since, Alicia Markova and Margot Fonteyn, and many other women who have kicked higher, balanced longer or turned faster. These are poor substitutes for passion. In spite of her flimsy dances, the bald and blatant virtuosity, there was an intoxicated rapture, a focus of energy, Dionysian in its physical intensity, that I have never seen equaled by a performer in any theater of the world. Also she was the *first* of the truly great in our experience.

I sat with the blood beating in my throat. As I walked into the bright glare of the afternoon, my head ached and I could scarcely swallow. I didn't wish to cry. I certainly couldn't speak. I sat in a daze in the car oblivious to the grownups' ceaseless prattle. At home I climbed the stairs slowly to my bedroom and, shutting myself in, placed both hands on the brass rail at the foot of my bed, then rising laboriously to the tips of my white buttoned shoes I stumped the width of the bed and back again. My toes throbbed with pain, my knees shook, my legs quivered with weakness. I repeated the exercise. The blessed, relieving tears stuck at last on my lashes. Only by hurting my feet could I ease the pain in my throat.

8   Standing on Ninth Avenue under the El, I saw the headlines on the front page of the *New York Times.* It did not seem possible. She was in essence the denial of death. My own life was rooted to her in a deep spiritual sense and had been during the whole of my growing up. It mattered not that I had only spoken to her once and that my work lay in a different direction. She was the vision and the impulse and the goal.

✦ *Questions for Discussion and Writing*

1. How did seeing Pavlova's performance change Agnes De Mille's life?

2. What impression of Pavlova does the reader gain from De Mille's description?

3. What details does De Mille include to draw the reader's attention to Pavlova's diminutive size and ability to express emotion through gestures?

4. Describe a person who might be as exciting a role model for you as Pavlova was for De Mille.

5. If you could appear on the cover of any magazine, which one would you choose—*Sports Illustrated, Time's* "Man of the Year," *Rolling Stone, Bon Appetit, Wired, Business Week, Ms.,* etc.—and for what achievement or quality would you be celebrated?

6. Describe any rock, country, jazz, or classical performer, paying special attention to gestures, physical appearance, voice, the mood he or she creates, instrumentation, and how the audience responds.

Luis Alberto Urrea

My Story

———————◆———————

Luis Alberto Urrea was born in Tijuana to an American mother and a Mexican father. He was raised in San Diego and graduated from the University of California in 1977. After working as a film extra, he worked as a volunteer from 1978 to 1982 with Spectrum Ministries, a Protestant organization with headquarters in San Diego that provided food, clothing, and medicine to the poor on the Mexican side of the border. In 1982, he went to Massachusetts, where he taught expository writing at Harvard. He currently lives in Boulder, Colorado. His latest work is a novel entitled In Search of Snow *(1994).* Across the Wire: Life and Hard Times on the Mexican Border *(1993), from which "My Story" is taken, offers a compassionate and unprecedented account of what life is like for those refugees living on the Mexican side of the border.*

I was born in Tijuana, to a Mexican father and an American mother. 1
I was registered with the U.S. government as an American Citizen, Born Abroad. Raised in San Diego, I crossed the border all through my boyhood with abandon, utterly bilingual and bicultural. In 1977, my father died on the border, violently. (The story is told in detail in a chapter entitled "Father's Day.")

In the Borderlands, anything can happen. And if you're in Tijuana 2
long enough, anything *will* happen. Whole neighborhoods appear and disappear seemingly overnight. For example, when I was a boy, you got into Tijuana by driving through the Tijuana River itself. It was a muddy floodplain bustling with animals and belching old cars. A slum that spread across the riverbed was known as "Cartolandia." In borderspeak, this meant "Land of Cardboard."

Suddenly, it was time for Tijuana to spruce up its image to attract 3
more American dollars, and Cartolandia was swept away by a flash flood of tractors. The big machines swept down the length of the river, crushing shacks and toppling fences. It was like magic. One week, there were choked multitudes of sheds; the next, a clear, flat space awaiting the blank concrete of a flood channel. Town—no town.

The inhabitants of Cartolandia fled to the outskirts, where they 4
were better suited to Tijuana's new image as Shopping Mecca. They had effectively vanished. Many of them homesteaded the Tijuana municipal garbage dump. The city's varied orphanages consumed many of their children.

5   Tijuana's characteristic buzz can be traced directly to a mixture of dread and expectation: there's always something coming.

6   I never intended to be a missionary. I didn't go to church, and I had no reason to believe I'd be involved with a bunch of Baptists. But in 1978, I had occasion to meet a remarkable preacher known as Pastor Von (Erhardt George von Trutzschler III, no less): as well as being a minister, he was a veteran of the Korean War, a graphic artist, a puppeteer, a German baron, an adventurer, and a practical joker. Von got me involved in the hardships and discipline he calls "Christian Boot Camp."

7   After working as a youth pastor in San Diego for many years, he had discovered Mexico in the late sixties. His work there began with the typical church do-good activities that everyone has experienced at least once: a bag of blankets for the orphans, a few Christmas toys, alms for the poor. As Protestantism spread in Mexico, however, interest in Von's preaching grew. Small churches and Protestant orphanages and Protestant *barrios*, lacking ministers of their own, began asking Von to teach. Preaching and pastoring led to more work; work led to more needs; more needs pulled in more workers. On it went until Von had put in thirty or so years slogging through the Borderlands mud, and his little team of die-hard renegades and border rats had grown to a nonprofit corporation (Spectrum Ministries, Inc.), where you'll find him today.

8   Von's religious ethic is similar in scope to Teresa of Calcutta's. Von favors actual works over heavy evangelism. Spectrum is based on a belief Christians call "living the gospel." This doctrine is increasingly rare in America, since it involves little lip service, hard work, and no glory.

9   Von often reminds his workers that they are "ambassadors of Christ" and should comport themselves accordingly. Visitors are indelicately stripped of their misconceptions and prejudices when they discover that the crust on Von and his crew is a mile thick: the sight of teenybopper Bible School girls enduring Von's lurid pretrip briefing is priceless. Insouciantly, he offers up his litany: lice, worms, pus, blood; diarrhea, rattletrap outhouses, no toilet paper; dangerous water and food; diseased animals that will leave you with scabies; rats, maggots, flies; *odor*. Then he confuses them by demanding love and respect for the poor. He caps his talk with: "Remember—you are not going to the zoo. These are people. Don't run around snapping pictures of them like they're animals. Don't rush into their shacks saying, 'Ooh, gross!' They live there. Those are their homes."

10   Because border guards often "confiscate" chocolate milk, the cartons must be smuggled into Mexico under bags of clothes. Because the floors of the vans get so hot, the milk will curdle, so the crew must first freeze it. The endless variations of challenge in the Borderlands keep Von constantly alert—problems come three at a time and must be solved on the run.

Like the time a shipment of tennis shoes was donated to Spectrum. 11
They were new, white, handsome shoes. The only problem was that no
two shoes in the entire shipment matched. Von knew there was no way
the Mexican kids could use *one* shoe, and they—like teens everywhere—were fashion-conscious and wouldn't be caught dead in un-
matching sneakers.

Von's solution was practical and witty. He donned unmatched 12
shoes and made his crew members wear unmatched shoes. Then he announced that it was the latest California surfer rage; kids in California
weren't considered hip unless they wore unmatched shoes. The shipment was distributed, and shoeless boys were shod in the *faux* fashion
craze begun by Chez Von.

Von has suffered for his beliefs. In the ever more conservative at- 13
mosphere of American Christianity (read: Protestantism), the efforts of
Spectrum have come under fire on several occasions. He was once denounced because he refused to use the King James Bible in his sermon—clearly the sign of a heretic.

Von's terse reply to criticism: "It's hard to 'save' people when 14
they're dead."

Von has a Monday night ministerial run into Tijuana, and in his 15
heyday, he was hitting three or four orphanages a night. I was curious,
unaware of the severity of the poverty in Tijuana. I knew it was there,
but it didn't really mean anything to me. One night, in late October
1978, my curiosity got the better of me. I didn't believe Von could show
me anything about my hometown that I didn't know. I was wrong. I
quickly began to learn just how little I really knew.

He managed to get me involved on the first night. Actually, it was 16
Von and a little girl named América. América lived in one of the orphanages barely five miles from my grandmother's house in the hills
above Tijuana.

She had light hair and blue eyes like mine—she could have been 17
my cousin. When she realized I spoke Spanish, she clutched my fingers
and chattered for an hour without a break. She hung on harder when
Von announced it was time to go. She begged me not to leave. América
resorted to a tactic many orphanage children master to keep visitors
from leaving—she wrapped her legs around my calf and sat on my
foot. As I peeled her off, I promised to return on Von's next trip.

He was waiting for me in the alley behind the orphanage. 18

"What did you say to that girl?" he asked. 19

"I told her I'd come back next week." 20

He glared at me. "Don't *ever* tell one of my kids you're coming 21
back," he snapped. "Don't you know she'll wait all week for you? Then
she'll wait for months. Don't say it if you don't mean it."

"I mean it!" I said. 22

23   I went back the next time to see her. Then again. And, of course, there were other places to go before we got to América's orphanage, and there were other people to talk to after we left. Each location had people waiting with messages and questions to translate. It didn't take long for Von to approach me with a proposition. It seemed he had managed the impressive feat of spending a lifetime in Mexico without picking up any Spanish at all. Within two months, I was Von's personal translator.

24   It is important to note that translation is often more delicate an art than people assume. For example, Mexicans are regularly amused to read *TV Guide* listings for Spanish-language TV stations. If one were to leave the tilde (~) off the word años, or "years," the word becomes the plural for "anus." Many cheap laughs are had when "The Lost Years" becomes "The Lost Butt Holes."

25   It was clear that Von needed reliable translating. Once, when he had arranged a summer camping trip for *barrio* children, he'd written a list of items the children needed to take. A well-meaning woman on the team translated the list for Von, and they Xeroxed fifty or sixty copies.

26   The word for "comb" in Spanish is *peine,* but leave out a letter, and the word takes on a whole new meaning. Von's note, distributed to every child and all their families, read:

27   You must bring CLEAN CLOTHES
          TOOTH PASTE
          SOAP
          TOOTHBRUSH
          SLEEPING BAG
          and BOYS—You Must Remember
          to BRING YOUR PENIS!

28   Von estimates that in a ten-year period his crew drove several *million* miles in Mexico without serious incident. Over five hundred people came and went as crew members. They transported more than sixty thousand visitors across the border.

29   In my time with him, I saw floods and three hundred-mile-wide prairie fires, car wrecks and gang fights, monkeys and blood and shit. I saw human intestines and burned flesh. I saw human fat through deep red cuts. I saw people copulating. I saw animals tortured. I saw birthday parties in the saddest sagging shacks. I looked down throats and up wombs with flashlights. I saw lice, rats, dying dogs, rivers black with pollywogs, and a mound of maggots three feet wide and two feet high. One little boy in the back country cooked himself with an overturned pot of boiling *frijoles;* when I asked him if it hurt, he sneered like Pancho Villa and said, "Nah." A maddened Pentecostal tried to heal our broken-down van by laying hands on the engine block. One girl who lived in a brickyard accidentally soaked her dress in diesel fuel

and lit herself on fire. When I went in the shed, she was standing there, naked, her entire front burned dark brown and red. The only part of her not burned was her vulva; it was a startling cleft, a triangular island of white in a sea of burns.

I saw miracles, too. A boy named Chispi, deep in a coma induced   30
by spinal meningitis, suffered a complete shutdown of one lobe of his brain. The doctors in the intensive care unit, looking down at his naked little body hard-wired to banks of machinery and pumps, just shook their heads. He was doomed to be a vegetable, at best. His mother, fished out of the cantinas in Tijuana's red-light district, spent several nights sitting in the hospital cafeteria sipping vending-machine coffee and telling me she hoped there were miracles left for people like her.

Chispi woke up. The machines were blipping and pinging, and he   31
sat up and asked for Von. His brain had regenerated itself. They un-hitched him, pulled out the catheters, and pulled the steel shunt out of his skull. He went home. There was no way anybody could explain it. Sometimes there were happy endings, and you spent as much time wondering about them as grieving over the tragedies.

God help me—it was fun. It was exciting and nasty. I strode, fearless,   32
through the Tijuana garbage dumps and the Barrio of Shallow Graves. I was doing good deeds, and the goodness thrilled me. But the squalor, too, thrilled me. Each stinking gray *barrio* gave me a wicked charge. I was arrested one night by Tijuana cops; I was so terrified that my knees wobbled like Jell-O. After they let me go, I was happy for a week. Mexican soldiers pointed machine guns at my testicles. I thought I was going to die. Later, I was so relieved, I laughed about it for days. Over the years, I was cut, punctured, sliced: I love my scars. I had girlfriends in every village, in every orphanage, at each garbage dump. For a time, I was a hero. And at night, when we returned, caked in dried mud, smelly, exhausted, and the good Baptists of Von's church looked askance at us, we felt dangerous. The housewives, grandmothers, fundamentalists, rock singers, bikers, former drug dealers, schoolgirls, leftists, republi-cans, jarheads, and I were all transformed into *The Wild Bunch*.

It added a certain flair to my dating life as well. It was not uncom-   33
mon for a Mexican crisis to track me down in the most unlikely places. I am reminded of the night I was sitting down to a fancy supper at a woman's apartment when the phone rang. A busload of kids from one of our orphanages had flipped over, killing the American daughter of the youth minister in charge of the trip. All the *gringos* had been ar-rested. The next hour was spent calling Tijuana cops, Mexican lawyers, cousins in Tijuana, and Von. I had to leave early to get across the border.

Incredibly, in the wake of this tragedy, the orphanage kids were   34
taken to the beach by yet another *gringo* church group, and one of the boys was hit by a car and killed.

My date was fascinated by all this, no doubt.   35

36   Slowly, it became obvious that nobody outside the experience understood it. Only among ourselves was hunting for lice in each other's hair considered a nice thing. Nobody but us found humor in the appalling things we saw. No one else wanted to discuss the particulars of our bowel movements. By firsthand experience, we had become diagnosticians in the area of gastrointestinal affliction. Color and content spoke volumes to us: pale, mucus-heavy ropes of diarrhea suggested amoebas. Etc.

37   One of Von's pep talks revolved around the unconscionable wealth in the United States. "Well," he'd say to some unsuspecting *gringo,* "you're probably not rich. You probably don't even have a television. Oh, you *do?* You have three televisions? One in each room? Wow. But surely you don't have furniture? You do? Living room furniture and beds in the bedrooms? Imagine that!

38   "But you don't have a floor, do you? Do you have carpets? Four walls? A roof! What do you use for light—candles? *Lamps!* No way. Lamps.

39   "How about your kitchen—do you have a stove?"

40   He'd pick his way through the kitchen: the food, the plates and pots and pans, the refrigerator, the ice. Ice cream. Soda. Booze. The closets, the clothes in the closets. Then to the bathroom and the miracle of indoor plumbing. Whoever lived in that house suddenly felt obscenely rich.

41   I was never able to reach Von's level of commitment. The time he caught scabies, he allowed it to flourish in order to grasp the suffering of those from whom it originated. He slept on the floor because the majority of the world's population could not afford a bed.

✦ Questions for Discussion and Writing

1. What portrait does Urrea create of the environment in which he, Von, and the other missionaries had to function? What kinds of problems did they face, and how did they solve them?

2. What qualities made Von such an influential leader and guide for the group?

3. Of the many dreadful and inspiring experiences described by Urrea, which made the greatest impression on you, and why?

4. What features of Urrea's account suggest that he is exceptionally honest and that he does not delude himself about his own motives?

5. Have you ever had occasion to sacrifice your own comfort, energy, or time in volunteer work or in a similar endeavor? Describe your experience, especially in terms of the meaning it had at the time, and tell how it changed you.

6. Write a character sketch of a person whom you admire (and perhaps even envy), drawing on incidents, events, and memories as a basis for your characterization.

7. In the process of examining his relationship to Von, Urrea becomes aware of how much he sees the minister as a hero. Write a letter to your hero or heroine, making clear what characteristics you admire and would like to emulate.

Fritz Peters

Gurdjieff Remembered

———————◆———————

Fritz Peters (born in 1916) began his association with the philosopher and mystic George Gurdjieff when he attended a school founded by Gurdjieff in Fontainebleau, France, where he spent four and a half years between 1924 and 1929. His highly unconventional education and unusual adventures there are recounted in his book Boyhood with Gurdjieff *(1964). A subsequent book,* Gurdjieff Remembered *(1965), in which the following account first appeared, captures the flavor of his relationship with Gurdjieff, an experience he found to be unpredictable, sometimes hilarious, enigmatic, but always rewarding.*

1   After seeing Mr. Gurdjieff in Chicago in 1932, there was an interval of about two years during which I did not see him again. I had moved to New York in the fall of 1933, and one Saturday afternoon when I came home from work my landlord told me that a very strange man, with a heavy, foreign accent had come to see me and wanted me to get in touch with him. The landlord, however, had not been able to understand him, did not know his name, and only knew that whoever he was, he was living at the Henry Hudson Hotel in New York. I thought of Gurdjieff at once, although it was difficult for me to believe that he had gone to the trouble of finding my address and then coming to search for me in person. I went to the hotel immediately and, as I had expected, found him there.

2   When I got to his apartment in the hotel, he told me that he had tried to find me earlier in the day, but that now it was too late and that he had no further need of—or use for—me. There was no affection in his greeting and he merely looked bored and very tired. In spite of this, and because I was glad to see him and worried about his great weariness, I did not leave but reminded him that he had once told me that "it was never too late to make reparations in life", and that while I was sorry not to have been home earlier, there was surely something I could do now that I had arrived.

3   He looked at me with a tired smile and said that perhaps there was something I could do. He led me into the kitchen, indicated an enormous pile of dirty dishes and said they needed to be washed; he then pointed to another equally enormous pile of vegetables and said they needed to be prepared for a dinner he was going to give that evening. After showing these to me, he asked me if I had the time to help him.

When I had assured him that I did, he told me to wash the dishes first and then prepare the vegetables. Before leaving the kitchen, to rest, he said that he hoped he would be able to count on me to finish both jobs—otherwise he would not be able to rest properly. I told him not to worry and went to work on the dishes. He watched me for a few minutes and then said that several people had promised to help him that day but that there were no members of the New York group who were able to keep their promises. I told him that he had better rest while he had the opportunity and not waste his time talking to me, and he laughed and left the kitchen.

I was finished with my work when he returned and he was very pleased. He then began to cook the evening meal and told me to set the table for fifteen people, adding that some very important people—important for his work—were coming to dinner and that when the food was in the oven he would need me to help him by giving him an English lesson as it was essential that he talk to these people in a certain way—in a language that they would understand correctly.

When we had finished our work, he sat down at the table, told me to sit next to him and then began asking me questions about the English language. It turned out that he wanted to learn, before the guests arrived, all the words for the various parts and functions of the body "that were not in the dictionary". We spent perhaps two hours repeating every four-letter word that I knew, plus every obscene phrase I could think of. By about seven o'clock he felt that he was reasonably proficient with our "slang" vocabulary which he, apparently, needed for his dinner. Inevitably, I began to wonder what sort of people would be coming to dinner. At the conclusion of this "lesson" he told me that it was for that lesson that he had been trying to find me, because I was the first person who, some years before in Chicago, had given him the real flavour and meaning of the words "phony" and "leery"; it seems that these words, in the interim, had become very useful in his conversations with his American students. "These very good words," he said, "raw... like your America."

When the guests did arrive, they turned out to be a group of well-dressed, well-mannered New Yorkers, and, since Gurdjieff had gone to "prepare" himself for dinner, I greeted them and, according to his precise instructions, served them drinks.

He did not appear until most of them had been there for about half an hour, and when he greeted them, he was very apologetic for the delay and extremely effusive about how beautiful the ladies looked and how much they were all honoring him by consenting to be the guests of a poor, humble man like himself. I was actually embarrassed by what seemed to me a very crude form of flattery and by his presentation of himself as an unworthy and very obsequious host. But, to my surprise, it seemed to work. By the time they were seated at the dinner table, all the guests were in a very mellow mood (they had had only one drink so it was not due to liquor) and they began, in a somewhat jocular and superior way, to ask him questions about his work and his reasons for coming to America. The general tone of the questions was bored—many of the people present were reporters or journalists—and they behaved as if they were carrying out an assignment to interview some crank. I could already see them making mental notes and could imagine the sort of "funny" interview or feature story they might write. After some questioning by this group, I noticed that Gurdjieff's voice changed in tone, and as I watched him he gave me a sudden, sly wink.

8　　　　He then proceeded to tell them that since they were all very superior people that they of course knew—since a simple person like himself knew it, then obviously they did—that humanity in general was in a very sad state and could only be considered as having degenerated into real waste matter, or to use a term that was familiar to all of them, pure "shit". That this transformation of humankind into something worthless was especially apparent in America—which was why he had come there to observe it. He went on to say that the main cause of this sad state of affairs was that people—especially Americans—were never motivated by intelligence or good feelings, but only by the needs—usually dirty—of their genital organs, using, of course (as he talked) only the four-letter words which he had practised with me earlier. He indicated one very well-dressed, handsome woman, complimented her on her coiffure, her dress, her perfume, etc., and then said that while she, of course, might not want everyone to know her motives or her desires, he and she could be honest with each other—that her reasons for turning herself out so elaborately were because she had a strong sexual urge (as he put it "wish to fuck") for some particular person and was so tormented by it that she was using every means and every wile she could think of in order to get that person into a bed with her. He said that her urge was particularly, especially strong because she had a very fertile imagination and could already picture herself performing various sexual acts with this man—"such as, how you say in English? 'Sixty-nine'?"—so that, aided by her imagination, she was now at the point where she would do *anything* to achieve her aim. While the company was somewhat startled with this dissertation (not to say "titillated"), before anyone had time to react, he began a description of his own sexual abilities and of his highly imaginative mind, and described himself as capable of sustained sexual acts of incredible variety—such as even the lady in question would not be able to imagine.

9　　　　He then launched into a detailed description of the sexual habits of various races and nations, during the course of which he pointed out that while the French had a world-wide reputation for amorous prowess, it would be well for the people present to make a note of the fact that those highly civilized French used such words as "Mama" and "Mimi" to describe some of their unnatural and perverted sexual practices. He added, however, that in all justice to the French they were, in reality, very moral people and sexually misunderstood and misrepresented.

The guests had all been drinking heavily during dinner—good old   10
Armagnac as always—and after about two hours of unadulterated four-letter word conversation, their behaviour became completely un-inhibited. Whether they had all come to believe and accept that they had been invited to an orgy, or for whatever reasons, an orgy—or the beginning of one—was the result. Gurdjieff egged them on by giving them elaborate descriptions of the male and female organs, and of some imaginative uses for them, and finally most of the guests were physically entangled in groups in various rooms of the apartment, and in various states of undress. The handsome lady had manœuvred her-self into a small bar with Gurdjieff and was busily making "passes" of a rather inventive nature, at him.

As for me, I was cornered in the kitchen by an overblown, attrac-   11
tive lady who told me that she was outraged that Gurdjieff should use such words in my presence—I did not look more than about seventeen. I explained, quite honestly, that I had taught them all to him—or at least most of them, and she found this suddenly hilarious and promptly made a pass at me. I backed away and told her that, unfortu-nately, I had to do the dishes. Rebuffed, she glared at me, called me var-ious dirty names and said that the only reason I had turned her down was because I was "that dirty old man's little faggot", and only wanted him to "screw" me. I was somewhat startled at this, but remembered Gurdjieff's reputation for sexual depravity and made no response.

While the other guests were still hard at it, Gurdjieff suddenly dis-   12
entangled himself from the lady and told them all, in loud, stentorian tones, that they had already confirmed his observations of the deca-dence of the Americans and that they need no longer demonstrate for him. He pointed at various individuals, mocked their behaviour and then told them that if they were, thanks to him, now partly conscious of what sort of people they really were, it was an important lesson for them. He said that he deserved to be paid for this lesson and that he would gladly accept cheques and cash from them as they left the apart-ment. I was not particularly surprised, knowing him and having watched the performance of the evening, to find that he had collected *several thousand dollars*. I was even less surprised when one man told me—as it were, "man to man"—that Gurdjieff, posing as a philosopher, had the best ideas about sex, and the safest "cover" for his orgies, of anyone he had ever known.

When everyone had left, I finished washing the dishes, and to my   13
surprise Gurdjieff came into the kitchen to dry them and put them away. He asked me how I had enjoyed the evening and I said, youth-fully and righteously, that I was disgusted. I also told him about my en-

counter with the lady in the kitchen and her description of my relationship with him. He shrugged his shoulders and said that in such cases the facts were what constituted the truth and that I should never consider or worry about opinions. Then he laughed and gave me a piercing look. "Is fine feeling you have—this disgust," he said. "But now is necessary ask yourself one question. With who you disgusted?"

14   When I was ready to leave the apartment, he stopped me and referred again to my experience with the lady. "Such lady have in self many homosexual tendencies, one reason she pick on you—young-looking boy, seem almost like girl to her. Not worry about this thing she say to you. Gossip about sex only give reputation for sexiness in your country, so not important, maybe even feather in hat, as you say. Some day you will learn much more about sex, but this you can learn by self, not from me."

✦ Questions for Discussion and Writing

1. How would you characterize the relationship between the narrator and Mr. Gurdjieff?

2. What preparations does Mr. Gurdjieff make for his dinner party?

3. How is the way in which Gurdjieff conducts the proceedings designed to (a) manipulate the guests in ways that produce a tangible benefit for him, and (b) educate the narrator about human nature?

4. What does the narrator learn about himself and other people from Gurdjieff's "experiment"?

5. Describe a belief you once held that you no longer hold because of the influence of another person. Create a character sketch of this person, and describe the role he or she played (and related experiences) in leading you to change your mind.

6. At the end of the evening, Gurdjieff punctures Fritz Peters's self-righteous indignation by asking him "is fine feeling you have—this disgust . . . but now is necessary ask yourself one question. With who you disgusted"? In your journal/diary, you may wish to pose and answer a question that might be phrased, What is there about this person that disgusts/repels/angers me so much that it is likely that I see qualities in them that I fear I possess?

Connections

1. Compare the kind of influence exerted on James Boswell by Dr. Samuel Johnson with Von's influence on Luis Alberto Urrea or Bobo's influence on Melton McLaurin. What insights were gained and what illusions dispelled?

2. Evaluate the techniques of James Boswell and Agnes De Mille as biographers in terms of the way they select significant details that reveal a pattern of important character traits descriptive of their subjects.

3. How do Von and Gurdjieff teach important lessons to Luis Alberto Urrea and Fritz Peters, respectively? What are these lessons?

4. What techniques for describing influential people do James Boswell and Mark Salzman ("Lessons," Chapter 6) use in their respective portrayals of Dr. Samuel Johnson and Pan?

5. What insights do Melton McLaurin and Mary Crow Dog ("Civilize Them with a Stick," Chapter 6) offer into the mechanisms and consequences of racism?

6. What biographical techniques do Agnes De Mille and Jill Nelson ("Number One!" Chapter 1) employ in depicting those who were instrumental in their choice of careers?

7. What common elements link Luis Alberto Urrea's and Jo Goodwin Parker's accounts ("What Is Poverty?" Chapter 10) of the effects of poverty?

8. What common features that define a "guru" emerge from the accounts of Fritz Peters and Mark Salzman ("Lessons," Chapter 6)?

3

Sexual Identity

◆

Women have served all these centuries as looking-glasses possessing the magic and delicious power of reflecting the figure of man at twice its natural size.

— Virginia Woolf, *A Room of One's Own*, 1929

One particularly revealing kind of autobiographical writing consists of forays into the perplexing realm of sexual identity. The desire to understand the changing psychological and social expectations produced by redrawing the boundaries of gender roles, marriage, and parenting have produced works that are surprising, and often humorous and sardonic. These very personal accounts offer insights expressed in language that is sometimes eloquent, often witty, and always idiosyncratic.

The authors in this chapter explore how we acquire sexual identities, and they reveal the role social and cultural expectations play in shaping the choices we make. The observations of these writers display a broad range of styles and voices. We can observe how differences in style result from unique word choices, figurative language, diction, rhythm, and syntax. The voices we hear, whether sympathetic, indifferent, amused, or outraged, vividly show the role tone plays in guiding readers' perceptions.

How we feel about ourselves and our life experiences reveals the powerful role gender stereotypes play in shaping our personal development. The social meanings attached to specific behavior for men and women begin with the fairy tales told to children. They are reinforced by conceptions of masculinity and femininity promulgated by the media. Some writers in this chapter speak out against the constricting effects of the rigid expectations that enforce inflexible images of masculine and feminine behavior. Other writers draw attention to the strikingly different ways societal expectations about gender roles vary from culture to culture.

Being treated as a Latina stereotype underlies Judith Ortiz Cofer's rueful appraisal in "The Myth of the Latin Woman: I Just Met a Girl Named Maria." Kim Chernin draws on personal observations to support her indictment of society's obsession with an ultra-thin female body image in "The Flesh and the Devil." In the first autobiographical account ever written by a Masai, Tepilit Ole Saitoti describes, in "The Initiation of a Masai Warrior," the circumcision ceremony that served as his rite of passage into adulthood. An Egyptian physician, Nawal el-Saadawi, draws on her own experiences and investigates the practice of female circumcision in Mideastern cultures in "Circumcision of Girls." Paul Monette's struggle to come to terms with his homosexuality while a student at Yale is the basis of his autobiographical account "Becoming a Man."

Judith Ortiz Cofer

The Myth of the Latin Woman: I Just Met a Girl Named Maria

◆

Judith Ortiz Cofer, a poet and novelist, was born in 1952 in Hormigueros, Puerto Rico. After her father, a career Navy officer, retired, the family settled in Georgia, where Cofer attended Augusta College. During college Cofer married, and, with her husband and daughter, she moved to Florida, where she finished a master's degree in English at Florida Atlantic University. A fellowship allowed her to pursue graduate work at Oxford University, after which she returned to Florida and began teaching English and writing poetry. Her first volume of poetry, Peregrina *(1985), won the Riverstone International Poetry Competition. It was followed by two poetry collections,* Reaching for the Mainland *(1987), and* Terms of Survival *(1988). Cofer's first novel,* The Line of the Sun *(1989), was listed as one of the year's "25 books to remember" by the New York City Public Library System. In the following essay, drawn from her collection,* The Latin Deli: Prose and Poetry *(1993), Cofer explores the destructive effects of the Latina stereotype.*

1   On a bus trip to London from Oxford University where I was earning some graduate credits one summer, a young man, obviously fresh from a pub, spotted me and as if struck by inspiration went down on his knees in the aisle. With both hands over his heart he broke into an Irish tenor's rendition of "Maria" from *West Side Story*. My politely amused fellow passengers gave his lovely voice the round of gentle applause it deserved. Though I was not quite as amused, I managed my version of an English smile: no show of teeth, no extreme contortions of the facial muscles—I was at this time of my life practicing reserve and cool. Oh, that British control, how I coveted it. But "Maria" had followed me to London, reminding me of a prime fact of my life: you can leave the island, master the English language, and travel as far as you can, but if you are a Latina, especially one like me who so obviously belongs to Rita Moreno's gene pool, the island travels with you.

2   This is sometimes a very good thing—it may win you that extra minute of someone's attention. But with some people, the same things can make *you* an island—not a tropical paradise but an Alcatraz, a

90

place nobody wants to visit. As a Puerto Rican girl living in the United States and wanting like most children to "belong," I resented the stereotype that my Hispanic appearance called forth from many people I met.

Growing up in a large urban center in New Jersey during the 1960s, I suffered from what I think of as "cultural schizophrenia." Our life was designed by my parents as a microcosm of their *casas* on the island. We spoke in Spanish, ate Puerto Rican food bought at the *bodega*, and practiced strict Catholicism at a church that allotted us a one-hour slot each week for mass, performed in Spanish by a Chinese priest trained as a missionary for Latin America.

As a girl I was kept under strict surveillance by my parents, since my virtue and modesty were, by their cultural equation, the same as their honor. As a teenager I was lectured constantly on how to behave as a proper *senorita*. But it was a conflicting message I received, since the Puerto Rican mothers also encouraged their daughters to look and act like women and to dress in clothes our Anglo friends and their mothers found too "mature" and flashy. The difference was, and is, cultural; yet I often felt humiliated when I appeared at an American friend's party wearing a dress more suitable to a semi-formal than to a playroom birthday celebration. At Puerto Rican festivities, neither the music nor the colors we wore could be too loud.

I remember Career Day in our high school, when teachers told us to come dressed as if for a job interview. It quickly became obvious that to the Puerto Rican girls "dressing up" meant wearing their mother's ornate jewelry and clothing, more appropriate (by mainstream standards) for the company Christmas party than as daily office attire. That morning I had agonized in front of my closet, trying to figure out what a "career girl" would wear. I knew how to dress for school (at the Catholic school I attended, we all wore uniforms), I knew how to dress for Sunday mass, and I knew what dresses to wear for parties at my relatives' homes. Though I do not recall the precise details of my Career Day outfit, it must have been a composite of these choices. But I remember a comment my friend (an Italian American) made in later years that coalesced my impressions of that day. She said that at the business school she was attending, the Puerto Rican girls always stood out for wearing "everything at once." She meant, of course, too much jewelry, too many accessories. On that day at school we were simply made the negative models by the nuns, who were themselves not credible fashion experts to any of us. But it was painfully obvious to me that to the others, in their tailored skirts and silk blouses, we must have seemed "hopeless" and "vulgar." Though I now know that most adolescents feel out of step much of the time, I also know that for the Puerto Rican girls of my generation that sense was intensified. The way our teachers and classmates looked at us that day in school was just a

taste of the cultural clash that awaited us in the real world, where pro-
spective employers and men on the street would often misinterpret our
tight skirts and jingling bracelets as a "come-on."

6   Mixed cultural signals have perpetuated certain stereotypes—for
example, that of the Hispanic woman as the "hot tamale" or sexual fire-
brand. It is a one-dimensional view that the media have found easy to
promote. In their special vocabulary, advertisers have designated "sizzling" and "smoldering" as the adjectives of choice for describing not
only the foods but also the women of Latin America. From conversations in my house I recall hearing about the harassment that Puerto
Rican women endured in factories where the "boss-men" talked to
them as if sexual innuendo was all they understood, and worse, often
gave them the choice of submitting to their advances or being fired.

7   It is custom, however, not chromosomes, that leads us to choose
scarlet over pale pink. As young girls, it was our mothers who influenced our decisions about clothes and colors—mothers who had
grown up on a tropical island where the natural environment was a riot
of primary colors, where showing your skin was one way to keep cool
as well as to look sexy. Most important of all, on the island, women perhaps felt freer to dress and move more provocatively since, in most
cases, they were protected by the traditions, mores, and laws of a
Spanish/Catholic system of morality and machismo whose main rule
was: *You may look at my sister, but if you touch her I will kill you.* The extended family and church structure could provide a young woman
with a circle of safety in her small pueblo on the island; if a man
"wronged" a girl, everyone would close in to save her family honor.

8   My mother has told me about dressing in her best party clothes on
Saturday nights and going to the town's plaza to promenade with her
girlfriends in front of the boys they liked. The males were thus given
an opportunity to admire the women and to express their admiration
in the form of *piropos*: erotically charged street poems they composed
on the spot. (I have myself been subjected to a few *piropos* while visiting the island, and they can be outrageous, although custom dictates
that they must never cross into obscenity.) This ritual, as I understand
it, also entails a show of studied indifference on the woman's part; if
she is "decent," she must not acknowledge the man's impassioned
words. So I do understand how things can be lost in translation. When
a Puerto Rican girl dressed in her idea of what is attractive meets a
man from the mainstream culture who has been trained to react to certain types of clothing as a sexual signal, a clash is likely to take place. I
remember the boy who took me to my first formal dance leaning over
to plant a sloppy, over-eager kiss painfully on my mouth; when I
didn't respond with sufficient passion, he remarked resentfully: "I
thought you Latin girls were supposed to mature early," as if I were expected to *ripen* like a fruit or vegetable, not just grow into womanhood
like other girls.

It is surprising to my professional friends that even today some 9
people, including those who should know better, still put others "in
their place." It happened to me most recently during a stay at a classy
metropolitan hotel favored by young professional couples for wed-
dings. Late one evening after the theater, as I walked toward my room
with a colleague (a woman with whom I was coordinating an arts program), a middle-aged man in a tuxedo, with a young girl in satin and
lace on his arm, stepped directly into our path. With his champagne
glass extended toward me, he exclaimed "Evita!"[1]

Our way blocked, my companion and I listened as the man half-re- 10
cited, half-bellowed "Don't Cry for Me, Argentina." When he finished,
the young girl said: "How about a round of applause for my daddy?"
We complied, hoping this would bring the silly spectacle to a close. I
was becoming aware that our little group was attracting the attention
of the other guests. "Daddy" must have perceived this too, and he once
more barred the way as we tried to walk past him. He began to shout-
sing a ditty to the tune of "La Bamba"—except the lyrics were about a
girl named Maria whose exploits rhymed with her name and gonor-
rhea. The girl kept saying "Oh, Daddy" and looking at me with pleading eyes. She wanted me to laugh along with the others. My
companion and I stood silently waiting for the man to end his offensive
song. When he finished, I looked not at him but at his daughter. I advised her calmly never to ask her father what he had done in the army.
Then I walked between them and to my room. My friend complimented me on my cool handling of the situation, but I confessed that I
had really wanted to push the jerk into the swimming pool. This same
man—probably a corporate executive, well-educated, even worldly by
most standards—would not have been likely to regale an Anglo
woman with a dirty song in public. He might have checked his impulse
by assuming that she could be somebody's wife or mother, or at least
somebody who might take offense. But, to him, I was just an Evita or a
Maria: merely a character in his cartoon-populated universe.

Another facet of the myth of the Latin woman in the United States 11
is the menial, the domestic—Maria the housemaid or countergirl. It's
true that work as domestics, as waitresses, and in factories is all that's
available to women with little English and few skills. But the myth of
the Hispanic menial—the funny maid, mispronouncing words and
cooking up a spicy storm in a shiny California kitchen—has been perpetuated by the media in the same way that "Mammy" from *Gone with
the Wind* became America's idea of the black woman for generations.
Since I do not wear my diplomas around my neck for all to see, I have
on occasion been sent to that "kitchen" where some think I obviously
belong.

---

[1]A musical about Eva Duarte de Peron, the former first lady of Argentina.

12   One incident has stayed with me, though I recognize it as a minor offense. My first public poetry reading took place in Miami, at a restaurant where a luncheon was being held before the event. I was nervous and excited as I walked in with notebook in hand. An older woman motioned me to her table, and thinking (foolish me) that she wanted me to autograph a copy of my newly published slender volume of verse, I went over. She ordered a cup of coffee from me, assuming that I was the waitress. (Easy enough to mistake my poems for menus, I suppose.) I know it wasn't an intentional act of cruelty. Yet of all the good things that happened later, I remember that scene most clearly, because it reminded me of what I had to overcome before anyone would take me seriously. In retrospect I understand that my anger gave my reading fire. In fact, I have almost always taken any doubt in my abilities as a challenge, the result most often being the satisfaction of winning a convert, of seeing the cold, appraising eyes warm to my words, the body language change, the smile that indicates I have opened some avenue for communication. So that day as I read, I looked directly at that woman. Her lowered eyes told me she was embarrassed at her faux pas, and when I willed her to look up at me, she graciously allowed me to punish her with my full attention. We shook hands at the end of the reading and I never saw her again. She has probably forgotten the entire incident, but maybe not.

13   Yet I am one of the lucky ones. There are thousands of Latinas without the privilege of an education or the entrees into society that I have. For them life is a constant struggle against the misconceptions perpetuated by the myth of the Latina. My goal is to try to replace the old stereotypes with a much more interesting set of realities. Every time I give a reading, I hope the stories I tell, the dreams and fears I examine in my work, can achieve some universal truth that will get my audience past the particulars of my skin color, my accent, or my clothes.

14   I once wrote a poem in which I called all Latinas "God's brown daughters." This poem is really a prayer of sorts, offered upward, but also, through the human-to-human channel of art, outward. It is a prayer for communication and for respect. In it, Latin women pray "in Spanish to an Anglo God/ with a Jewish heritage," and they are "fervently hoping/ that if not omnipotent,/ at least He be bilingual."

✦ Questions for Discussion and Writing

1. What characteristics define, from Cofer's perspective, the "Maria" stereotype in terms of style, clothes, and behavior? How has this stereotype been a source of harassment for Cofer?

2. How has the desire to destroy this stereotype and its underlying attitudes motivated Cofer to write the kinds of works that she has?

3. How does Cofer use her personal experiences as a springboard to understand sexual stereotyping of Latinas?

4. Restate in your own words Cofer's explanation of the cultural basis for the Latina stereotype as a cross-cultural misperception. How persuasive did you find her explanation?

5. Have you ever been the object of stereotyped perceptions? What signals, cues, behavior, or customs did others misperceive about you? What means, if any, did you take to correct this stereotype?

6. At different points in her narrative Cofer enters the minds of others to see things from their perspective. If you keep a journal, choose a person that you know whose point of view is different from yours. Put yourself in his or her shoes, and try to see the world through his or her eyes. Write your account in the form of a first-person narrative (using *I*).

7. The title of Cofer's narrative uses a phrase from the song lyrics of "Maria" (from Leonard Bernstein's *West Side Story*, 1957). In your journal, try using a song lyric that you often hear in your mind as a basis for free associating for at least ten minutes. What images, ideas, memories, and reflections does this lyric evoke?

Kim Chernin

The Flesh and the Devil

◆

Kim Chernin, born in 1940, is a freelance writer, editor, and self-described "feminist-humanist." Her account, "The Flesh and the Devil," is a chapter from The Obsession: Reflection on the Tyranny of Slenderness *(1981). In this essay, Chernin draws on her personal experiences as well as surveys, research studies, and life stories of friends to support her incisive analysis of the extent to which cultural stereotypes dominate women's lives.*

> *We know that every woman wants to be thin. Our images of womanhood are almost synonymous with thinness.*
>
> —Susie Orbach

> *. . . I must now be able to look at my ideal, this ideal of being thin, of being without a body, and to realize: "it is a fiction."*
>
> —Ellen West

> *When the body is hiding the complex, it then becomes our most immediate access to the problem.*
>
> —Marian Woodman

1   The locker room of the tennis club. Several exercise benches, two old-fashioned hair dryers, a mechanical bicycle, a treadmill, a reducing machine, a mirror, and a scale.

2   A tall woman enters, removes her towel; she throws it across a bench, faces herself squarely in the mirror, climbs on the scale, looks down.

3   A silence.

4   "I knew it," she mutters, turning to me. "I knew it."

5   And I think, before I answer, just how much I admire her, for this courage beyond my own, this daring to weigh herself daily in this way. And I sympathize. I know what she must be feeling. Not quite candidly, I say: "Up or down?" I am hoping to suggest that there might be people and cultures where gaining weight might not be considered a disaster. Places where women, stepping on scales, might be horrified to notice that they had reduced themselves. A mythical, almost unimaginable land.

96

"Two pounds," she says, ignoring my hint. "Two pounds." And 6 then she turns, grabs the towel and swings out at her image in the mirror, smashing it violently, the towel spattering water over the glass. "Fat pig," she shouts at her image in the glass. "You fat, fat pig...."

Later, I go to talk with this woman. Her name is Rachel and she be- 7 comes, as my work progresses, one of the choral voices that shape its vision.

Two girls come into the exercise room. They are perhaps ten or 8 eleven years old, at that elongated stage when the skeletal structure seems to be winning its war against flesh. And these two are particularly skinny. They sit beneath the hair dryers for a moment, kicking their legs on the faded green upholstery; they run a few steps on the eternal treadmill, they wrap the rubber belt of the reducing machine around themselves and jiggle for a moment before it falls off. And then they go to the scale.

The taller one steps up, glances at herself in the mirror, looks down 9 at the scale. She sighs, shaking her head. I see at once that this girl is imitating someone. The sigh, the headshake are theatrical, beyond her years. And so, too, is the little drama enacting itself in front of me. The other girl leans forward, eager to see for herself the troubling message imprinted upon the scale. But the older girl throws her hand over the secret. It is not to be revealed. And now the younger one, accepting this, steps up to confront the ultimate judgment. "Oh God," she says, this growing girl. "Oh God," with only a shade of imitation in her voice: "Would you believe it? I've gained five pounds."

These girls, too, become a part of my work. They enter, they per- 10 form their little scene again and again; it extends beyond them and in it I am finally able to behold something that would have remained hidden—for it does not express itself directly, although we feel its pressure almost every day of our lives. Something, unnamed as yet, struggling against our emergence into femininity. This is my first glimpse of it, out there. And the vision ripens.

I return to the sauna. Two women I have seen regularly at the club 11 are sitting on the bench above me. One of them is very beautiful, the sort of woman Renoir would have admired. The other, who is probably in her late sixties, looks, in the twilight of this sweltering room, very much an adolescent. I have noticed her before, with her tan face, her white hair, her fashionable clothes, her slender hips and jaunty walk. But the effect has not been soothing. A woman of advancing age who looks like a boy.

I've heard about that illness, anorexia nervosa," the plump one is 12 saying, "and I keep looking around for someone who has it. I want to go sit next to her. I think to myself, maybe I'll catch it...."

"Well," the other woman says to her, "I've felt the same way my- 13 self. One of my cousins used to throw food under the table when no one was looking. Finally, she got so thin they had to take her to the hospital.... I always admired her."

14   What am I to understand from these stories? The woman in the locker room who swings out at her image in the mirror, the little girls who are afraid of the coming of adolescence to their bodies, the woman who admires the slenderness of the anorexic girl. Is it possible to miss the dislike these women feel for their bodies?

15   And yet, an instant's reflection tells us that this dislike for the body is not a biological fact of our condition as women—we do not come upon it by nature, we are not born to it, it does not arise for us because of anything predetermined in our sex. We know that once we loved the body, delighting in it the way children will, reaching out to touch our toes and count over our fingers, repeating the game endlessly as we come to knowledge of this body in which we will live out our lives. No part of the body exempt from our curiosity, nothing yet forbidden, we know an equal fascination with the feces we eliminate from ourselves, as with the ear we discover one day and the knees that have become bruised and scraped with falling and that warm, moist place between the legs from which feelings of indescribable bliss arise.

16   From that state to the condition of the woman in the locker room is a journey from innocence to despair, from the infant's naive pleasure in the body, to the woman's anguished confrontation with herself. In this journey we can read our struggle with natural existence—the loss of the body as a source of pleasure. But the most striking thing about this alienation from the body is the fact that we take it for granted. Few of us ask to be redeemed from this struggle against the flesh by overcoming our antagonism toward the body. We do not rush about looking for someone who can tell us how to enjoy the fact that our appetite is large, or how we might delight in the curves and fullness of our own natural shape. We hope instead to be able to reduce the body, to limit the urges and desires it feels, to remove the body from nature. Indeed, the suffering we experience through our obsession with the body arises precisely from the hopeless and impossible nature of this goal.

17   Cheryl Prewitt, the 1980 winner of the Miss America contest, is a twenty-two-year-old woman, "slender, bright-eyed, and attractive."[1] If there were a single woman alive in America today who might feel comfortable about the size and shape of her body, surely we would expect her to be Ms. Prewitt? And yet, in order to make her body suitable for the swimsuit event of the beauty contest she has just won, Cheryl Prewitt "put herself through a grueling regimen, jogging long distances down back-country roads, pedaling for hours on her stationary bicycle." The bicycle is still kept in the living room of her parents' house so that she can take part in conversation while she works out.

[1]Sally Hegelson, *TWA Ambassador*, July 1980.

This body she has created, after an arduous struggle against nature, in conformity with her culture's ideal standard for a woman, cannot now be left to its own desires. It must be perpetually shaped, monitored, and watched. If you were to visit her at home in Ackerman, Mississippi, you might well find her riding her stationary bicycle in her parents' living room, "working off the calories from a large slice of homemade coconut cake she has just had for a snack."

And so we imagine a woman who will never be Miss America, a [18] next-door neighbor, a woman down the street, waking in the morning and setting out for her regular routine of exercise. The eagerness with which she jumps up at six o'clock and races for her jogging shoes and embarks upon the cold and arduous toiling up the hill road that runs past her house. And yes, she feels certain that her zeal to take off another pound, tighten another inch of softening flesh, places her in the school of those ancient wise men who formulated that vision of harmony between mind and body. "A healthy mind in a healthy body," she repeats to herself and imagines that it is love of the body which inspires her this early morning. But now she lets her mind wander and encounter her obsession. First it had been those hips, and she could feel them jogging along there with their own rhythm as she jogged. It was they that had needed reducing. Then, when the hips came down it was the thighs, hidden when she was clothed but revealing themselves every time she went to the sauna, and threatening great suffering now that summer drew near. Later, it was the flesh under the arms—this proved singularly resistant to tautness even after the rest of the body had become gaunt. And finally it was the ankles. But then, was there no end to it? What had begun as a vision of harmony between mind and body, a sense of well-being, physical fitness, and glowing health, had become now demonic, driving her always to further exploits, running farther, denying herself more food, losing more weight, always goaded on by the idea that the body's perfection lay just beyond her present achievement. And then, when she began to observe this driven quality in herself, she also began to notice what she had been thinking about her body. For she would write down in her notebook, without being aware of the violence in what she wrote: "I don't care how long it takes. One day I'm going to get my body to obey me. I'm going to make it lean and tight and hard. I'll succeed in this, even if it kills me."

But what a vicious attitude this is, she realizes one day, toward a [19] body she professes to love. Was it love or hatred of the flesh that inspired her now to awaken even before it was light, and to go out on the coldest morning, running with bare arms and bare legs, busily fantasizing what she would make of her body? Love or hatred?

"You know perfectly well we hate our bodies," says Rachel, who [20] calls herself the pig. She grabs the flesh of her stomach between her hands. "Who could love this?"

21   There is an appealing honesty in this despair, an articulation of what is virtually a universal attitude among women in our culture today. Few women who diet realize that they are confessing to a dislike for the body when they weigh and measure their flesh, subject it to rigorous fasts or strenuous regimens of exercise. And yet, over and over again, as I spoke to women about their bodies, this antagonism became apparent. One woman disliked her thighs, another her stomach, a third the loose flesh under her arms. Many would grab their skin and squeeze it as we talked, with that grimace of distaste language cannot translate into itself. One woman said to me: "Little by little I began to be aware that the pounds I was trying to 'melt away' were my own flesh. Would you believe it? It never occurred to me before. These 'ugly pounds' which filled me with so much hatred were my body."

22   The sound of this dawning consciousness can be heard now and again among the voices I have recorded in my notebook, heralding what may be a growing awareness of how bitterly the women of this culture are alienated from their bodies. Thus, another woman said to me: "It's true, I never used to like my body." We had been looking at pictures of women from the nineteenth century; they were large women, with full hips and thighs. "What do you think of them?" I said. "They're like me," she answered, and then began to laugh. "Soft, sensual, and inviting."

23   The description is accurate; the women in the pictures, and the woman looking at them, share a quality of voluptuousness that is no longer admired by our culture:

24   When I look at myself in the mirror I see that there's nothing wrong with me—now! Sometimes I even think I'm beautiful. I don't know why this began to change. It might have been when I started going to the YWCA. It was the first time I saw so many women naked. I realized it was the fuller bodies that were more beautiful. The thin women, who looked so good in clothes, seemed old and worn out. Their bodies were gaunt. But the bodies of the larger women had a certain natural mystery, very different from the false illusion of clothes. And I thought, I'm like them; I'm a big woman like they are and perhaps my body is beautiful. I had always been trying to make my body have the right shape so that I could fit into clothes. But then I started to look at myself in the mirror. Before that I had always looked at parts of myself. The hips were too flabby, the thighs were too fat. Now I began to see myself as a whole. I stopped hearing my mother's voice, asking me if I was going to go on a diet. I just looked at what was really there instead of what should have been there. What was wrong with it? I asked myself. And little by little I stopped disliking my body.[2]

---

[2]Private communication.

This is the starting point. It is from this new way of looking at an old problem that liberation will come. The very simple idea that an obsession with weight reflects a dislike and uneasiness for the body can have a profound effect upon a woman's life. 25

I always thought I was too fat. I never liked my body. I kept trying to lose weight. I just tortured myself. But if I see pictures of myself from a year or two ago I discover now that I looked just fine. 26

I remember recently going out to buy Häagen Dazs ice cream. I had decided I was going to give myself something I really wanted to eat. I had to walk all the way down to the World Trade Center. But on my way there I began to feel terribly fat. I felt that I was being punished by being fat. I had lost the beautiful self I had made by becoming thinner. I could hear these voices saying to me: "You're fat, you're ugly, who do you think you are, don't you know you'll never be happy?" I had always heard these voices in my mind but now when they would come into consciousness I would tell them to shut up. I saw two men on the street. I was eating the Häagen Dazs ice cream. I thought I heard one of them say "heavy." I thought they were saying: "She's so fat." But I knew that I had to live through these feelings if I was ever to eat what I liked. I just couldn't go on tormenting myself any more about the size of my body. 27

One day, shortly after this, I walked into my house. I noticed the scales, standing under the sink in the bathroom. Suddenly, I hated them. I was filled with grief for having tortured myself for so many years. They looked like shackles. I didn't want to have anything more to do with them. I called my boyfriend and offered him the scales. Then, I went into the kitchen. I looked at my shelves. I saw diet books there. I was filled with rage and hatred of them. I hurled them all into a box and got rid of them. Then I looked into the ice box. There was a bottle of Weight Watchers dressing. I hurled it into the garbage and watched it shatter and drip down the plastic bag. Little by little, I started to feel better about myself. At first I didn't eat less, I just worried less about my eating. I allowed myself to eat whatever I wanted. I began to give away the clothes I couldn't fit into. It turned out that they weren't right for me anyway. I had bought them with the idea of what my body should look like. Now I buy clothes because I like the way they look on me. If something doesn't fit it doesn't fit. I'm not trying to make myself into something I'm not. I weigh more than I once considered my ideal. But I don't seem fat to myself. Now, I can honestly say that I like my body.[3] 28

Some weeks ago, at a dinner party, a woman who had recently gained weight began to talk about her body. 29

[3]Private communication.

30   "I was once very thin," she said, "but I didn't feel comfortable in my body. I fit into all the right clothes. But somehow I just couldn't find myself any longer."

31   I looked over at her expectantly; she was a voluptuous woman, who had recently given birth to her first child.

32   "But now," she said as she got to her feet, "now, if I walk or jog or dance, I feel my flesh jiggling along with me." She began to shake her shoulders and move her hips, her eyes wide as she hopped about in front of the coffee table. "You see what I mean?" she shouted over to me. "I love it."

33   This image of a woman dancing came with me when I sat down to write. I remembered her expression. There was in it something secretive, I thought, something knowing and pleased—the look of a woman who has made peace with her body. Then I recalled the faces of women who had recently lost weight. The haggard look, the lines of strain around the mouth, the neck too lean, the tendons visible, the head too large for the emaciated body. I began to reason:

34   There must be, I said, for every woman a correct weight, which cannot be discovered with reference to a weight chart or to any statistical norm. For the size of the body is a matter of highly subjective individual preferences and natural endowments. If we should evolve an aesthetic for women that was appropriate to women it would reflect this diversity, would conceive, indeed celebrate and even love, slenderness in a woman intended by nature to be slim, and love the rounded cheeks of another, the plump arms, broad shoulders, narrow hips, full thighs, rounded ass, straight back, narrow shoulders or slender arms, of a woman made that way according to her nature, walking with head high in pride of her body, however it happened to be shaped. And then Miss America, and the woman jogging in the morning, and the woman swinging out at her image in the mirror might say, with Susan Griffin in *Woman and Nature:*

35   And we are various, and amazing in our variety, and our differences multiply, so that edge after edge of the endlessness of possibility is exposed ... none of us beautiful when separate but all exquisite as we stand, each moment heeded in this cycle, no detail unlovely....[4]

✦ Questions for Discussion and Writing

1. How do the kinds and range of examples Chernin presents serve as evidence for her thesis?

2. According to Chernin, what kind of influences do cultural values play in determining how women see themselves? What is her attitude towards these values?

[4]Susan Griffin, *Woman and Nature: The Roaring Inside Her,* New York, 1978.

3. What alternative value system does Chernin present to replace the prevailing cultural norms?

4. Analyze some of the cultural messages of which you are aware that depict socially desirable values having to do with how you look. To what extent do these messages differ from your own values regarding appearance?

5. Have you ever gone without food and/or liquids for any extended length of time for reasons other than those Chernin describes (e.g., fasting for religious or spiritual reasons)? What did you discover about yourself that you did not know before?

Tepilit Ole Saitoti

The Initiation of a Maasai Warrior

◆

Named for the language they speak—Maa, a distinct, but unwritten African tongue—the Maasai of Kenya and Tanzania, a tall, handsome, and proud people, still live much as they always have, herding cattle, sheep, and goats in and around the Great Rift Valley. This personal narrative is unique—the first autobiographical account written by a Maasai, which vividly documents the importance of the circumcision ceremony that serves as a rite of passage into warrior rank. Tepilit Ole Saitoti studied animal ecology in the United States and has returned to Kenya, where he is active in conservation projects. His experiences formed the basis for a National Geographic Society film, Man of Serengeti *(1971). This account first appeared in Saitoti's autobiography,* The Worlds of a Maasai Warrior *(1986).*

1   "Tepilit, circumcision means a sharp knife cutting into the skin of the most sensitive part of your body. You must not budge; don't move a muscle or even blink. You can face only one direction until the operation is completed. The slightest movement on your part will mean you are a coward, incompetent and unworthy to be a Maasai man. Ours has always been a proud family, and we would like to keep it that way. We will not tolerate unnecessary embarrassment, so you had better be ready. If you are not, tell us now so that we will not proceed. Imagine yourself alone remaining uncircumcised like the water youth [white people]. I hear they are not circumcised. Such a thing is not known in Maasailand; therefore, circumcision will have to take place even if it means holding you down until it is completed."

2   My father continued to speak and every one of us kept quiet. "The pain you will feel is symbolic. There is a deeper meaning in all this. Circumcision means a break between childhood and adulthood. For the first time in your life, you are regarded as a grownup, a complete man or woman. You will be expected to give and not just to receive. To protect the family always, not just to be protected yourself. And your wise judgment will for the first time be taken into consideration. No family affairs will be discussed without your being consulted. If you are ready for all these responsibilities, tell us now. Coming into manhood is not simply a matter of growth and maturity. It is a heavy load on your shoulders and

104

especially a burden on the mind. Too much of this—I am done. I have said all I wanted to say. Fellows, if you have anything to add, go ahead and tell your brother, because I am through. I have spoken."

After a prolonged silence, one of my half-brothers said awkwardly, "Face it, man...it's painful. I won't lie about it, but it is not the end. We all went through it, after all. Only blood will flow, not milk." There was laughter and my father left. 3

My brother Lellia said, "Men, there are many things we must acquire and preparations we must make before the ceremony, and we will need the cooperation and help of all of you. Ostrich feathers for the crown and wax for the arrows must be collected." 4

"Are you *orkirekenyi?*" One of my brothers asked. I quickly replied no, and there was laughter. *Orkirekenyi* is a person who has transgressed sexually. For you must not have sexual intercourse with any circumcised woman before you yourself are circumcised. You must wait until you are circumcised. If you have not waited, you will be fined. Your father, mother, and the circumciser will take a cow from you as punishment. 5

Just before we departed, one of my closest friends said, "If you kick the knife, you will be in trouble." There was laughter. "By the way, if you have decided to kick the circumciser, do it well. Silence him once and for all." "Do it the way you kick a football in school." "That will fix him," another added, and we all laughed our heads off again as we departed. 6

The following month was a month of preparation. I and others collected wax, ostrich feathers, honey to be made into honey beer for the elders to drink on the day of circumcision, and all the other required articles. 7

Three days before the ceremony my head was shaved and I discarded all my belongings, such as my necklaces, garments, spear, and sword. I even had to shave my pubic hair. Circumcision in many ways is similar to Christian baptism. You must put all the sins you have committed during childhood behind and embark as a new person with a different outlook on a new life. 8

The circumciser came the following day and handed the ritual knives to me. He left drinking a calabash of beer. I stared at the knives uneasily. It was hard to accept that he was going to use them on my organ. I was to sharpen them and protect them from people of ill will who might try to blunt them, thus rendering them inefficient during the ritual and thereby bringing shame on our family. The knives threw a chill down my spine; I was not sure I was sharpening them properly, so I took them to my closest brother for him to check out, and he assured me that the knives were all right. I hid them well and waited. 9

Tension started building between me and my relatives, most of whom worried that I wouldn't make it through the ceremony valiantly. Some even snarled at me, which was their way of encouraging me. 10

Others threw insults and abusive words my way. My sister Loiyan in particular was more troubled by the whole affair than anyone in the whole family. She had to assume my mother's role during the circumcision. Were I to fail my initiation, she would have to face the consequences. She would be spat upon and even beaten for representing the mother of an unworthy son. The same fate would befall my father, but he seemed unconcerned. He had this weird belief that because I was not particularly handsome, I must be brave. He kept saying, "God is not so bad as to have made him ugly and a coward at the same time."

11   Failure to be brave during circumcision would have other unfortunate consequences: the herd of cattle belonging to the family still in the compound would be beaten until they stampeded; the slaughtered oxen and honey beer prepared during the month before the ritual would go to waste; the initiate's food would be spat upon and he would have to eat it or else get a severe beating. Everyone would call him Olkasiodoi, the knife kicker.

12   Kicking the knife of the circumciser would not help you anyway. If you struggle and try to get away during the ritual, you will be held down until the operation is completed. Such failure of nerve would haunt you in the future. For example, no one will choose a person who kicked the knife for a position of leadership. However, there have been instances in which a person who failed to go through circumcision successfully became very brave afterwards because he was filled with anger over the incident; no one dares to scold him or remind him of it. His agemates, particularly the warriors, will act as if nothing had happened.

13   During the circumcision of a woman, on the other hand, she is allowed to cry as long as she does not hinder the operation. It is common to see a woman crying and kicking during circumcision. Warriors are usually summoned to help hold her down.

14   For woman, circumcision means an end to the company of Maasai warriors. After they recuperate, they soon get married, and often to men twice their age.

15   The closer it came to the hour of truth, the more I was hated, particularly by those closest to me. I was deeply troubled by the withdrawal of all the support I needed. My annoyance turned into anger and resolve. I decided not to budge or blink, even if I were to see my intestines flowing before me. My resolve was hardened when newly circumcised warriors came to sing for me. Their songs were utterly insulting, intended to annoy me further. They tucked their wax arrows under my crotch and rubbed them on my nose. They repeatedly called me names.

16   By the end of the singing, I was fuming. Crying would have meant I was a coward. After midnight they left me alone and I went into the house and tried to sleep but could not. I was exhausted and numb but remained awake all night.

At dawn I was summoned once again by the newly circumcised 17
warriors. They piled more and more insults on me. They sang their
weird songs with even more vigor and excitement than before. The
songs praised warriorhood and encouraged one to achieve it at all
costs. The songs continued until the sun shone on the cattle horns
clearly. I was summoned to the main cattle gate, in my hand a ritual
cowhide from a cow that had been properly slaughtered during my
naming ceremony. I went past Loiyan, who was milking a cow, and she
muttered something. She was shaking all over. There was so much tension that people could hardly breathe.

I laid the hide down and a boy was ordered to pour ice-cold water, 18
known as *engare entolu* (ax water), over my head. It dripped all over my
naked body and I shook furiously. In a matter of seconds I was summoned to sit down. A large crowd of boys and men formed a semicircle
in front of me; women are not allowed to watch male circumcision and
vice-versa. That was the last thing I saw clearly. As soon as I sat down,
the circumciser appeared, his knives at the ready. He spread my legs
and said, "One cut," a pronouncement necessary to prevent an initiate
from claiming that he had been taken by surprise. He splashed a white
liquid, a ceremonial paint called *enturoto*, across my face. Almost immediately I felt a spark of pain under my belly as the knife cut through
my penis' foreskin. I happened to choose to look in the direction of the
operation. I continued to observe the circumciser's fingers working
mechanically. The pain became numbness and my lower body felt
heavy, as if I were weighed down by a heavy burden. After fifteen minutes or so, a man who had been supporting from behind pointed at
something, as if to assist the circumciser. I came to learn later that the
circumciser's eyesight had been failing him and that my brothers had
been mad at him because the operation had taken longer than was usually necessary. All the same, I remained pinned down until the operation was over. I heard a call for milk to wash the knives, which signaled
the end, and soon the ceremony was over.

With words of praise, I was told to wake up, but I remained seated. 19
I waited for the customary presents in appreciation of my bravery. My
father gave me a cow and so did my brother Lillia. The man who had
supported my back and my brother-in-law gave me a heifer. In all I had
eight animals given to me. I was carried inside the house to my own
bed to recuperate as activities intensified to celebrate my bravery.

I laid on my own bed and bled profusely. The blood must be re- 20
tained within the bed, for according to Maasai tradition, it must not
spill to the ground. I was drenched in my own blood. I stopped bleeding after about half an hour but soon was in intolerable pain. I was supposed to squeeze my organ and force blood to flow out of the wound,
but no one had told me, so the blood coagulated and caused unbearable pain. The circumciser was brought to my aid and showed me what
to do, and soon the pain subsided.

21   The following morning, I was escorted by a small boy to a nearby valley to walk and relax, allowing my wound to drain. This was common for everyone who had been circumcised, as well as for women who had just given birth. Having lost a lot of blood, I was extremely weak. I walked very slowly, but in spite of my caution I fainted. I tried to hang on to bushes and shrubs, but I fell, irritating my wound. I came out of unconsciousness quickly, and the boy who was escorting me never realized what had happened. I was so scared that I told him to lead me back home. I could have died without there being anyone around who could have helped me. From that day on, I was selective of my company while I was feeble.

22   In two weeks I was able to walk and was taken to join other newly circumcised boys far away from our settlement. By tradition Maasai initiates are required to decorate their headdresses with all kinds of colorful birds they have killed. On our way to the settlement, we hunted birds and teased girls by shooting them with our wax blunt arrows. We danced and ate and were well treated wherever we went. We were protected from the cold and rain during the healing period. We were not allowed to touch food, as we were regarded as unclean, so whenever we ate we had to use specially prepared sticks instead. We remained in this pampered state until our wounds healed and our headdresses were removed. Our heads were shaved, we discarded our black cloaks and bird headdresses and embarked as newly shaven warriors, Irkeleani.

23   As long as I live I will never forget the day my head was shaved and I emerged a man, a Maasai warrior. I felt a sense of control over my destiny so great that no words can accurately describe it. I now stood with confidence, pride, and happiness of being, for all around me I was desired and loved by beautiful, sensuous Maasai maidens. I could now interact with women and even have sex with them, which I not been allowed before. I was now regarded as a responsible person.

24   In the old days, warriors were like gods, and women and men wanted only to be the parent of a warrior. Everything else would be taken care of as a result. When a poor family had a warrior, they ceased to be poor. The warrior would go on raids and bring cattle back. The warrior would defend the family against all odds. When a society respects the individual and displays confidence in him the way the Maasai do their warriors, the individual can grow to his fullest potential. Whenever there was a task requiring physical strength or bravery, the Maasai would call upon their warriors. They hardly ever fall short of what is demanded of them and so are characterized by pride, confidence, and an extreme sense of freedom. But there is an old saying in Maasai: "You are never a free man until your father dies." In other words, your father is paramount while he is alive and you are obligated to respect him. My father took advantage of this principle and held a tight grip on all his warriors, including myself. He always

wanted to know where we all were at any given time. We fought against his restrictions, but without success. I, being the youngest of my father's five warriors, tried even harder to get loose repeatedly, but each time I was punished severely.

Roaming the plains with other warriors in pursuit of girls and adventure was a warrior's pastime. We would wander from one settlement to another, singing, wrestling, hunting, and just playing. Often I was ready to risk my father's punishment for this wonderful freedom.

One clear day my father sent me to take sick children and one of his wives to the dispensary in the Korongoro Highlands. We rode in the L.S.B. Leakey lorry. We ascended the highlands and were soon attended to in the local hospital. Near the conservation offices I met several acquaintances, and one of them told me of an unusual circumcision that was about to take place in a day or two. All the local warriors and girls were preparing to attend it.

The highlands were a lush green from the seasonal rains and the sky was a purple-blue with no clouds in sight. The land was overflowing with milk, and the warriors felt and looked their best, as they always did when there was plenty to eat and drink. Everyone was at ease. The demands the community usually made on warriors during the dry season when water was scarce and wells had to be dug were now not necessary. Herds and flocks were entrusted to youths to look after. The warriors had all the time for themselves. But my father was so strict that even at times like these he still insisted on overworking us in one way or another. He believed that by keeping us busy, he would keep us out of trouble.

When I heard about the impending ceremony, I decided to remain behind in the Korongoro Highlands and attend it now that the children had been treated. I knew very well that I would have to make up a story for my father upon my return, but I would worry about that later. I had left my spear at home when I boarded the bus, thinking that I would be coming back that very day. I felt lighter but now regretted having left it behind; I was so used to carrying it wherever I went. In gales of laughter resulting from our continuous teasing of each other, we made our way toward a distant kraal. We walked at a leisurely pace and reveled in the breeze. As usual we talked about the women we desired, among other things.

The following day we were joined by a long line of colorfully dressed girls and warriors from the kraal and the neighborhood where we had spent the night, and we left the highland and headed to Ingorienito to the rolling hills on the lower slopes to attend the circumcision ceremony. From there one could see Oldopai Gorge, where my parents lived, and the Inaapi hills in the middle of the Serengeti Plain.

Three girls and a boy were to be initiated on the same day, an unusual occasion. Four oxen were to be slaughtered, and many people would therefore attend. As we descended, we saw the kraal where the ceremony would take place. All those people dressed in red seemed from a distance like flamingos standing in a lake. We could see lines of other guests heading to the settlements. Warriors made gallant cries of happiness known as *enkiseer*. Our line of warriors and girls responded to their cries even more gallantly.

31   In serpentine fashion, we entered the gates of the settlement. Holding spears in our left hands, we warriors walked proudly, taking small steps, swaying like palm trees, impressing our girls, who walked parallel to us in another line, and of course the spectators, who gazed at us approvingly.

32   We stopped in the center of the kraal and waited to be greeted. Women and children welcomed us. We put our hands on the children's heads, which is how children are commonly saluted. After the greetings were completed, we started dancing.

33   Our singing echoed off the kraal fence and nearby trees. Another line of warriors came up the hill and entered the compound, also singing and moving slowly toward us. Our singing grew in intensity. Both lines of warriors moved parallel to each other, and our feet pounded the ground with style. We stamped vigorously, as if to tell the next line and the spectators that we were the best.

34   The singing continued until the hot sun was overhead. We recessed and ate food already prepared for us by other warriors. Roasted meat was for those who were to eat meat, and milk for the others. By our tradition, meat and milk must not be consumed at the same time, for this would be a betrayal of the animal. It was regarded as cruel to consume a product of the animal that could be obtained while it was alive, such as milk, and meat, which was only available after the animal had been killed.

35   After eating we resumed singing, and I spotted a tall, beautiful *esiankiki* (young maiden) of Masiaya whose family was one of the largest and richest in our area. She stood very erect and seemed taller than the rest.

36   One of her breasts could be seen just above her dress, which was knotted at the shoulder. While I was supposed to dance generally to please all the spectators, I took it upon myself to please her especially. I stared at and flirted with her, and she and I danced in unison at times. We complemented each other very well.

37   During a break, I introduced myself to the *esiankiki* and told her I would like to see her after the dance. "Won't you need a warrior to escort you home later when the evening threatens?" I said. She replied, "Perhaps, but the evening is still far away."

38   I waited patiently. When the dance ended, I saw her departing with a group of other women her age. She gave me a sidelong glance, and I

took that to mean come later and not now. With so many others around, I would not have been able to confer with her as I would have liked anyway.

With another warrior, I wandered around the kraal killing time until the herds returned from pasture. Before the sun dropped out of sight, we departed. As the kraal of the *esiankiki* was in the lowlands, a place called Enkoloa, we descended leisurely, our spears resting on our shoulders. 39

We arrived at the woman's kraal and found that cows were now being milked. One could hear the women trying to appease the cows by singing to them. Singing calms cows down, making it easier to milk them. There were no warriors in the whole kraal except for the two of us. Girls went around into warriors' houses as usual and collected milk for us. I was so eager to go and meet my *esiankiki* that I could hardly wait for nightfall. The warriors' girls were trying hard to be sociable, but my mind was not with them. I found them to be childish, loud, bothersome, and boring. 40

As the only warriors present, we had to keep them company and sing for them, at least for a while, as required by custom. I told the other warrior to sing while I tried to figure out how to approach my *esiankiki*. Still a novice warrior, I was not experienced with women and was in fact still afraid of them. I could flirt from a distance, of course. But sitting down with a woman and trying to seduce her was another matter. I had already tried twice to approach women soon after my circumcision and had failed. I got as far as the door of one woman's house and felt my heart beating like a Congolese drum; breathing became difficult and I had to turn back. Another time I managed to get in the house and succeeded in sitting on the bed, but then I started trembling until the whole bed was shaking, and conversation became difficult. I left the house and the woman, amazed and speechless, and never went back to her again. 41

Tonight I promised myself I would be brave and would not make any silly, ridiculous moves. "I must be mature and not afraid," I kept reminding myself, as I remembered an incident involving one of my relatives when he was still very young and, like me, afraid of women. He went to a woman's house and sat on a stool for a whole hour; he was afraid to awaken her, as his heart was pounding and he was having difficulty breathing. 42

When he finally calmed down, he woke her up, and their conversation went something like this: 43

"Woman, wake up." 44

"Why should I?" 45

"To light the fire." 46

"For what?" 47

48   "So you can see me."

49   "I already know who you are. Why don't *you* light the fire, as you're nearer to it than me?"

50   "It's your house and it's only proper that you light it yourself."

51   "I don't feel like it."

52   "At least wake up so we can talk, as I have something to tell you."

53   "Say it."

54   "I need you."

55   "I do not need one-eyed types like yourself."

56   "One-eyed people are people too."

57   "That might be so, but they are not to my taste."

58   They continued talking for quite some time, and the more they spoke, the braver he became. He did not sleep with her that night, but later on he persisted until he won her over. I doubted whether I was as strong-willed as he, but the fact that he had met with success encouraged me. I told my warrior friend where to find me should he need me, and then I departed.

59   When I entered the house of my *esiankiki*, I called for the woman of the house, and as luck would have it, my lady responded. She was waiting for me. I felt better, and I proceeded to talk to her like a professional. After much talking back and forth, I joined her in bed.

60   The night was calm, tender, and loving, like most nights after initiation ceremonies as big as this one. There must have been a lot of courting and lovemaking.

61   Maasai women can be very hard to deal with sometimes. They can simply reject a man outright and refuse to change their minds. Some play hard to get, but in reality are testing the man to see whether he is worth their while. Once a friend of mine while still young was powerfully attracted to a woman nearly his mother's age. He put a bold move on her. At first the woman could not believe his intention, or rather was amazed by his courage. The name of the warrior was Ngengeiya, or Drizzle.

62   "Drizzle, what do you want?"

63   The warrior stared her right in the eye and said, "You."

64   "For what?"

65   "To make love to you."

66   "I am your mother's age."

67   "The choice was either her or you."

68   This remark took the woman by surprise. She had underestimated the saying "There is no such thing as a young warrior." When you are a warrior, you are expected to perform bravely in any situation. Your age and size are immaterial.

69   "You mean you could really love me like a grown-up man?"

70   "Try me, woman."

He moved in on her. Soon the woman started moaning with excite- 71
ment, calling out his name. "Honey Drizzle, Honey Drizzle, you *are* a
man." In a breathy, stammering voice, she said, "A real man."

Her attractiveness made Honey Drizzle ignore her relative old age. 72
The Maasai believe that if an older and a younger person have intercourse, it is the older person who stands to gain. For instance, it is believed that an older woman having an affair with a young man starts to
appear younger and healthier, while the young man grows older and
unhealthy.

The following day when the initiation rites had ended, I decided to 73
return home. I had offended my father by staying away from home
without his consent, so I prepared myself for whatever punishment he
might inflict on me. I walked home alone.

✦ Questions for Discussion and Writing

1. How is the candidate's life, reputation, and destiny dependent on the
   bravery he shows during the ceremony? What function does relentless
   taunting by warriors and those who are newly circumcised serve before the ceremony?

2. What is the significance of Tepilit throwing away his possessions and
   shaving his head three days before the ceremony? Explain the significance of the ceremonial white paint, with which the boy is splashed,
   and the milk used to wash the knives after the surgery.

3. Why is Tepilit careful not to allow the blood from his wound to spill
   onto the ground, as he lies on his bed after the surgery?

4. What responsibilities does Tepilit assume and what privileges is he allowed upon successful completion of the ceremony?

5. Have you ever undergone a religious ceremony or a rite of passage designed to unite you with your community and to ensure continuation
   of its traditions? Describe this initiation and the effect it had on you.

Nawal el-Saadawi

Circumcision of Girls

◆

Nawal el-Saadawi is an Egyptian physician and internationally ac-
claimed writer whose work publicizing the injustices and brutalities to
which Arab women are subject is well known throughout the world. Born
in the village of Kafrtahla on the banks of the Nile in 1931, she completed
her secondary and college education in Egypt and later studied at Colum-
bia University in New York. She has worked as a physician and psychia-
trist in both Cairo and rural areas of Egypt. She lost her position as
Egypt's director of education in the Ministry of Health because of the out-
spoken views expressed in her first nonfiction book, Women and Sex
(1972). In it, she openly challenged the restrictions placed on women in
Arab society. She was later imprisoned by Anwar Sadat, and her many
books, including seven novels, four collections of short stories, and five
works of nonfiction, are still banned in Egypt, Saudi Arabia, and Libya.
Since her release from prison in 1982, she has continued to write and is an
activist for women's rights in the Arab world. "Circumcision of Girls" is
drawn from The Hidden Face of Eve: Women in the Arab World,
translated and edited by el-Saadawi's husband, Dr. Sherif Hetata, in
1980. In this work, el-Saadawi investigates the cultural origins of the
widely practiced but rarely discussed procedure of female circumcision, an
operation she herself endured at the age of eight.

1   The practice of circumcising girls is still a common procedure in a
number of Arab countries such as Egypt, the Sudan, Yemen and some
of the Gulf states.

2   The importance given to virginity and an intact hymen in these societies is the reason why female circumcision still remains a very wide-
spread practice despite a growing tendency, especially in urban Egypt,
to do away with it as something outdated and harmful. Behind circumcision lies the belief that, by removing parts of girls' external genital organs, sexual desire is minimized. This permits a female who has
reached the "dangerous age" of puberty and adolescence to protect her
virginity, and therefore her honour, with greater ease. Chastity was imposed on male attendants in the female harem by castration which
turned them into inoffensive eunuchs. Similarly female circumcision is
meant to preserve the chastity of young girls by reducing their desire
for sexual intercourse.

114

Circumcision is most often performed on female children at the age of seven or eight (before the girl begins to get menstrual periods). On the scene appears the *daya* or local midwife. Two women members of the family grasp the child's thighs on either side and pull them apart to expose the external genital organs and to prevent her from struggling—like trussing a chicken before it is slain. A sharp razor in the hand of the *daya* cuts off the clitoris.

During my period of service as a rural physician, I was called upon many times to treat complications arising from this primitive operation, which very often jeopardized the life of young girls. The ignorant *daya* believed that effective circumcision necessitated a deep cut with the razor to ensure radical amputation of the clitoris, so that no part of the sexually sensitive organ would remain. Severe haemorrhage was therefore a common occurrence and sometimes led to loss of life. The *dayas* had not the slightest notion of asepsis, and inflammatory conditions as a result of the operation were common. Above all, the lifelong psychological shock of this cruel procedure left its imprint on the personality of the child and accompanied her into adolescence, youth and maturity. Sexual frigidity is one of the after-effects which is accentuated by other social and psychological factors that influence the personality and mental make-up of females in Arab societies. Girls are therefore exposed to a whole series of misfortunes as a result of outdated notions and values related to virginity, which still remains the fundamental criterion of a girl's honour. In recent years, however, educated families have begun to realize the harm that is done by the practice of female circumcision.

Nevertheless a majority of families still impose on young female children the barbaric and cruel operation of circumcision. The research that I carried out on a sample of 160 Egyptian girls and women showed that 97.5% of uneducated families still insisted on maintaining the custom, but this percentage dropped to 66.2% among educated families.[1]

When I discussed the matter with these girls and women it transpired that most of them had no idea of the harm done by circumcision, and some of them even thought that it was good for one's health and conducive to cleanliness and "purity." (The operation in the common language of the people is in fact called the cleansing or purifying operation.) Despite the fact that the percentage of educated women who have undergone circumcision is only 66.2%, as compared with 97.5% among uneducated women, even the former did not realize the effect that this amputation of the clitoris could have on their psychological and sexual health. The dialogue that occurred between these women and myself would run more or less as follows:

[1]This research study was carried out in the years 1973 and 1974 in the School of Medicine, Ein Shams University, under the title: *Women and Neurosis*.

7   "Have you undergone circumcision?"

8   "Yes."

9   "How old were you at the time?"

10   "I was a child, about seven or eight years old."

11   "Do you remember the details of the operation?"

12   "Of course. How could I possibly forget?"

13   "Were you afraid?"

14   "Very afraid. I hid on top of the cupboard [in other cases she would say under the bed, or in the neighbour's house], but they caught hold of me, and I felt my body tremble in their hands."

15   "Did you feel any pain?"

16   "Very much so. It was like a burning flame and I screamed. My mother held my head so that I could not move it, my aunt caught hold of my right arm and my grandmother took charge of my left. Two strange women whom I had not seen before tried to keep me from moving my thighs by pushing them as far apart as possible. The *daya* sat between these two women, holding a sharp razor in her hand which she used to cut off the clitoris. I was scared and suffered such great pain that I lost consciousness at the flame that seemed to sear me through and through."

17   "What happened after the operation?"

18   "I had severe bodily pains, and remained in bed for several days, unable to move. The pain in my external genital organs led to retention of urine. Every time I wanted to urinate the burning sensation was so unbearable that I could not bring myself to pass water. The wound continued to bleed for some time, and my mother used to change the dressing for me twice a day."

19   "What did you feel on discovering that a small organ in your body had been removed?"

20   "I did not know anything about the operation at the time, except that it was very simple, and that it was done to all girls for purposes of cleanliness, purity and the preservation of a good reputation. It was said that a girl who did not undergo this operation was liable to be talked about by people, her behaviour would become bad, and she would start running after men, with the result that no one would agree to marry her when the time for marriage came. My grandmother told me that the operation had only consisted in the removal of a very small piece of flesh from between my thighs, and that the continued existence of this small piece of flesh in its place would have made me unclean and impure, and would have caused the man whom I would marry to be repelled by me."

21   "Did you believe what was said to you?"

22   "Of course I did. I was happy the day I recovered from the effects of the operation, and felt as though I was rid of something which had to be removed, and so had become clean and pure."

Those were more or less the answers that I obtained from all those   23
interviewed, whether educated or uneducated. One of them was a
medical student from Ein Shams School of Medicine. She was preparing for her final examinations and I expected her answers to be different, but in fact they were almost identical to the others. We had quite a
long discussion which I reproduce here as I remember it.

"You are going to be a medical doctor after a few weeks, so how   24
can you believe that cutting off the clitoris from the body of a girl is a
healthy procedure, or at least not harmful?"

"This is what I was told by everybody. All the girls in my family   25
have been circumcised. I have studied anatomy and medicine, yet I
have never heard any of the professors who taught us explain that the
clitoris had any function to fulfill in the body of a woman, neither have
I read anything of the kind in the books which deal with the medical
subjects I am studying."

"That is true. To this day medical books do not consider the science   26
of sex as a subject which they should deal with. The organs of a woman
worthy of attention are considered to be only those directly related to
reproduction, namely the vagina, the uterus and the ovaries. The clitoris, however, is an organ neglected by medicine, just as it is ignored and
disdained by society."

"I remember a student asking the professor one day about the clito-   27
ris. The professor went red in the face and answered him curtly, saying
that no one was going to ask him about this part of the female body
during examinations, since it was of no importance."

My studies led me to try and find out the effect of circumcision on   28
the girls and women who had been made to undergo it, and to understand what results it had on the psychological and sexual life. The majority of the normal cases I interviewed answered that the operation
had no effect on them. To me it was clear that in the face of such questions they were much more ashamed and intimidated than the neurotic
cases were. But I did not allow myself to be satisfied with these answers, and would go on to question them closely about their sexual life
both before and after the circumcision was done. Once again I will try
to reproduce the dialogue that usually occurred.

"Did you experience any change of feeling or of sexual desire after   29
the operation?"

"I was a child and therefore did not feel anything."   30

"Did you not experience any sexual desire when you were a child?"   31

"No, never. Do children experience sexual desire?"   32

"Children feel pleasure when they touch their sexual organs, and   33
some form of sexual play occurs between them, for example, during
the game of bride and bridegroom usually practised under the bed.
Have you never played this game with your friends when still a
child?"

34   At these words the young girl or woman would blush, and her eyes would probably refuse to meet mine, in an attempt to hide her confusion. But after the conversation had gone on for some time, and an atmosphere of mutual confidence and understanding had been established, she would begin to recount her childhood memories. She would often refer to the pleasure she had felt when a man of the family permitted himself certain sexual caresses. Sometimes these caresses would be proffered by the domestic servant, the house porter, the private teacher or the neighbour's son. A college student told me that her brother had been wont to caress her sexual organs and that she used to experience acute enjoyment. However after undergoing circumcision she no longer had the same sensation of pleasure. A married woman admitted that during intercourse with her husband she had never experienced the slightest sexual enjoyment, and that her last memories of any form of pleasurable sensation went back twenty years, to the age of six, before she had undergone circumcision. A young girl told me that she had been accustomed to practise masturbation, but had given it up completely after removal of the clitoris at the age of ten.

35   The further our conversations went, and the more I delved into their lives, the more readily they opened themselves up to me and uncovered the secrets of childhood and adolescence, perhaps almost forgotten by them or only vaguely realized.

36   Being both a woman and a medical doctor I was able to obtain confessions from these women and girls which it would be almost impossible, except in very rare cases, for a man to obtain. For the Egyptian woman, accustomed as she is to a very rigid and severe upbringing built on a complete denial of any sexual life before marriage, adamantly refuses to admit that she has ever known, or experienced, anything related to sex before the first touches of her husband. She is therefore ashamed to speak about such things with any man, even the doctor who is treating her.

37   My discussions with some of the psychiatrists who had treated a number of the young girls and women in my sample, led me to conclude that there were many aspects of the life of these neurotic patients that remained unknown to them. This was due either to the fact that the psychiatrist himself had not made the necessary effort to penetrate deeply into the life of the woman he was treating, or to the tendency of the patient herself not to divulge those things which her upbringing made her consider matters not to be discussed freely, especially with a man.

38   In fact the long and varied interchanges I had over the years with the majority of practising psychiatrists in Egypt, my close association with a large number of my medical colleagues during the long periods I spent working in health centres and general or specialized hospitals and, finally, the four years I spent as a member of the National Board of the Syndicate of Medical Professions, have all led me to the firm con-

clusion that the medical profession in our society is still incapable of understanding the fundamental problems with which sick people are burdened, whether they be men or women, but especially if they are women. For the medical profession, like any other profession in society, is governed by the political, social and moral values which predominate, and like other professions is one of the institutions which is utilized more often than not to protect these values and perpetuate them.

Men represent the vast majority in the medical profession, as in most professions. But apart from this, the mentality of women doctors differs little, if at all, from that of the men, and I have known quite a number of them who were even more rigid and backward in outlook than their male colleagues.   39

A rigid and backward attitude towards most problems, and in particular towards women and sex, predominates in the medical profession, and particularly within the precincts of the medical colleges in the Universities.   40

Before undertaking my research study on "Women and Neurosis" at Ein Shams University, I had made a previous attempt to start it at the Kasr El Eini Medical College in the University of Cairo, but had been obliged to give up as a result of the numerous problems I was made to confront. The most important obstacle of all was the overpowering traditionalist mentality that characterized the professors responsible for my research work, and to whom the word "sex" could only be equated to the word "shame." "Respectable research" therefore could not possibly have sex as its subject, and should under no circumstances think of penetrating into areas even remotely related to it. One of my medical colleagues in the Research Committee advised me not to refer at all to the question of sex in the title of my research paper, when I found myself obliged to shift to Ein Shams University. He warned me that any such reference would most probably lead to fundamental objections which would jeopardize my chances of going ahead with it. I had initially chosen to define my subject as "Problems that confront the sexual life of modern Egyptian women," but after prolonged negotiations I was prevailed to delete the word "sexual" and replace it by "psychological." Only thus was it possible to circumvent the sensitivities of the professors at the Ein Shams Medical School and obtain their consent to go ahead with the research.   41

After I observed the very high percentages of women and girls who had been obliged to undergo circumcision, or who had been exposed to different forms of sexual violation or assault in their childhood, I started to look for research undertaken in these two areas, either in the medical colleges or in research institutes, but in vain. Hardly a single medical doctor or researcher had ventured to do any work on these subjects, in view of the sensitive nature of the issues involved. This can also be explained by the fact that most of the research   42 carried out in such institutions is of a formal and superficial nature, since its sole aim is to obtain a degree or promotion. The path of safety is therefore the one to choose, and safety means to avoid carefully all subjects of controversy. No one is therefore prepared to face difficulties with the responsible academic and scientific authorities, or to engage in any form of struggle against them, or their ideas. Nor is anyone prepared to face up to those who lay down the norms of virtue, morals and religious behaviour in society. All the established leaderships in the area related to such matters suffer from a pronounced allergy to the word "sex," and any of its implications, especially if it happens to be linked to the word "woman."

43   Nevertheless I was fortunate enough to discover a small number of medical doctors who had the courage to be different, and therefore to examine some of the problems related to the sexual life of women. I would like to cite, as one of the rare examples, the only research study carried out on the question of female circumcision in Egypt and its harmful effects. This was the joint effort of Dr. Mahmoud Koraim and Dr. Rushdi Ammar, both from Ein Shams Medical College, and which was published in 1965. It is composed of two parts, the first of which was printed under the title *Female Circumcision and Sexual Desire*,[2] and the second, under the title *Complications of Female Circumcision*.[3] The conclusions arrived at as a result of this research study, which covered 651 women circumcised during childhood, may be summarized as follows:

44   (1) Circumcision is an operation with harmful effects on the health of women, and is the cause of sexual shock to young girls. It reduces the capacity of a woman to reach the peak of her sexual pleasure (i.e., orgasm) and has a definite though lesser effect in reducing sexual desire.

45   (2) Education helps to limit the extent to which female circumcision is practised, since educated parents have an increasing tendency to refuse the operation for their daughters. On the other hand, uneducated families still go in for female circumcision in submission to prevailing traditions, or in the belief that removal of the clitoris reduces the sexual desire of the girl, and therefore helps to preserve her virginity and chastity after marriage.

46   (3) There is no truth whatsoever in the idea that female circumcision helps in reducing the incidence of cancerous disease of the external genital organs.

47   (4) Female circumcision in all its forms and degrees, and in particular the fourth degree known as Pharaonic or Sudanese excision, is

[2]*Female Circumcision and Sexual Desire*, Mahmoud Koraim and Rushdi Ammar (Ein Shams University Press, Cairo, 1965).

[3]*Complications of Female Circumcision*, the same authors (Cairo, 1965).

accompanied by immediate or delayed complications such as inflamma-
tions, haemorrhage, disturbances in the urinary passages, cysts or swellings that can obstruct the urinary flow or the vaginal opening.

(5) Masturbation in circumcised girls is less frequent than was ob-   48
served by Kinsey in girls who have not undergone this operation.

I was able to exchange views with Dr. Mahmoud Koraim during   49
several meetings in Cairo. I learnt from him that he had faced numerous difficulties while undertaking his research, and was the target of
bitter criticism from some of his colleagues and from religious leaders
who considered themselves the divinely appointed protectors of morality, and therefore required to shield society from such impious un-
dertakings, which constituted a threat to established values and moral
codes.

The findings of my research study coincided with some of the con-   50
clusions arrived at by my two colleagues on a number of points. There
is no longer any doubt that circumcision is the source of sexual and
psychological shock in the life of the girl, and leads to a varying degree
of sexual frigidity according to the woman and her circumstances. Education helps parents realize that this operation is not beneficial, and
should be avoided, but I have found that the traditional education
given in our schools and universities, whose aim is simply some certif-
icate, or degree, rather than instilling useful knowledge and culture, is
not very effective in combating the long-standing, and established traditions that govern Egyptian society, and in particular those related to
sex, virginity in girls, and chastity in women. These areas are strongly
linked to moral and religious values that have dominated and operated
in our society for hundreds of years.

Since circumcision of females aims primarily at ensuring virginity   51
before marriage, and chastity throughout, it is not to be expected that
its practice will disappear easily from Egyptian society or within a
short period of time. A growing number of educated families are, however, beginning to realize the harm that is done to females by this custom, and are therefore seeking to protect their daughters from being
among its victims. Parallel to these changes, the operation itself is no
longer performed in the old primitive way, and the more radical degrees approaching, or involving, excision are dying out more rapidly.
Nowadays, even in Upper Egypt and the Sudan, the operation is limited to the total, or more commonly the partial, amputation of the clitoris. Nevertheless, while undertaking my research, I was surprised to
discover, contrary to what I had previously thought, that even in educated urban families over 50% still consider circumcision as essential to
ensure female virginity and chastity.

Many people think that female circumcision only started with the   52
advent of Islam. But as a matter of fact it was well known and wide-
spread in some areas of the world before the Islamic era, including in

the Arab peninsula. Mahomet the Prophet tried to oppose this custom since he considered it harmful to the sexual health of the woman. In one of his sayings the advice reported as having been given by him to Om Attiah, a woman who did tattooings and circumcision, runs as follows: "If you circumcise, take only a small part and refrain from cutting most of the clitoris off . . . The woman will have a bright and happy face, and is more welcome to her husband, if her pleasure is complete."[4]

53   This means that the circumcision of girls was not originally an Islamic custom, and was not related to monotheistic religions, but was practised in societies with widely varying religious backgrounds, in countries of the East and the West, and among peoples who believed in Christianity, or in Islam, or were atheistic . . . Circumcision was known in Europe as late as the 19th century, as well as in countries like Egypt, the Sudan, Somaliland, Ethiopia, Kenya, Tanzania, Ghana, Guinea and Nigeria. It was also practised in many Asian countries such as Sri Lanka and Indonesia, and in parts of Latin America. It is recorded as going back far into the past under the Pharaonic Kingdoms of Ancient Egypt, and Herodotus mentioned the existence of female circumcision seven hundred years before Christ was born. This is why the operation as practised in the Sudan is called "Pharaonic excision."

54   For many years I tried in vain to find relevant sociological or anthropological studies that would throw some light on the reasons why such a brutal operation is practised on females. However I did discover other practices related to girls and female children which were even more savage. One of them was burying female children alive almost immediately after they were born, or even at a later stage. Other examples are the chastity belt, or closing the aperture of the external genital organs with steel pins and a special iron lock.[5] This last procedure is extremely primitive and very much akin to Sudanese circumcision where the clitoris, external lips and internal lips are completely excised, and the orifice of the genital organs closed with a flap of sheep's intestines leaving only a very small opening barely sufficient to let the tip of the finger in, so that the menstrual and urinary flows are not held back. This opening is slit at the time of marriage and widened to allow penetration of the male sexual organ. It is widened again when a child is born and then narrowed down once more. Complete closure of the aperture is also done on a woman who is divorced, so that she literally becomes a virgin once more and can have no sexual intercourse except in the eventuality of marriage, in which case the opening is restored.

---

[4]See *Dawlat El Nissa'a*, Abdel Rahman El Barkouky, first edition (Renaissance Bookshop, Cairo, 1945).

[5]Desmond Morris, *The Naked Ape* (Corgi, 1967). p. 76.

In the face of all these strange and complicated procedures aimed   55
at preventing sexual intercourse in women except if controlled by the
husband, it is natural that we should ask ourselves why women, in
particular, were subjected to such torture and cruel suppression. There
seems to be no doubt that society, as represented by its dominant
classes and male structure, realized at a very early stage that sexual desire in the female is very powerful, and that women, unless controlled
and subjugated by all sorts of measures, will not submit themselves to
the moral, social, legal and religious constraints with which they have
been surrounded, and in particular the constraints related to monog-
amy. The patriarchal system, which came into being when society had
reached a certain stage of development and which necessitated the im-
position of one husband on the woman whereas a man was left free to
have several wives, would never have been possible, or have been
maintained to this day, without the whole range of cruel and ingenious
devices that were used to keep her sexuality in check and limit her sexual relations to only one man, who had to be her husband. This is the
reason for the implacable enmity shown by society towards female sexuality, and the weapons used to resist and subjugate the turbulent force
inherent in it. The slightest leniency manifested in facing this "potential
danger" meant that woman would break out of the prison bars to
which marriage had confined her, and step over the steely limits of a
monogamous relationship to a forbidden intimacy with another man,
which would inevitably lead to confusion in succession and inheritance, since there was no guarantee that a strange man's child would
not step into the waiting line of descendants. Confusion between the
children of the legitimate husband and the outsider lover would mean
the unavoidable collapse of the patriarchal family built around the
name of the father alone.

History shows us clearly that the father was keen on knowing who   56
his real children were, solely for the purpose of handing down his
landed property to them. The patriarchal family, therefore, came into
existence mainly for economic reasons. It was necessary for society simultaneously to build up a system of moral and religious values, as
well as a legal system capable of protecting and maintaining these economic interests. In the final analysis we can safely say that female circumcision, the chastity belt and other savage practices applied to
women are basically the result of the economic interests that govern society. The continued existence of such practices in our society today sig-
nifies that these economic interests are still operative. The thousands of
dayas, nurses, paramedical staff and doctors, who make money out of
female circumcision, naturally resist any change in these values and
practices which are a source of gain to them. In the Sudan there is a ver-
itable army of dayas who earn a livelihood out of the series of operations performed on women, either to excise their external genital

organs, or to alternately narrow and widen the outer aperture according to whether the woman is marrying, divorcing, remarrying, having a child or recovering from labour.[6]

57   Economic factors and, concomitantly, political factors are the basis upon which such customs as female circumcision have grown up. It is important to understand the facts as they really are, the reasons that lie behind them. Many are the people who are not able to distinguish between political and religious factors, or who conceal economic and political motives behind religious arguments in an attempt to hide the real forces that lie at the basis of what happens in society and in history. It has very often been proclaimed that Islam is at the root of female circumcision, and is also responsible for the under-privileged and backward situation of women in Egypt and the Arab countries. Such a contention is not true. If we study Christianity it is easy to see that this religion is much more rigid and orthodox where women are concerned than Islam. Nevertheless, many countries were able to progress rapidly despite the preponderance of Christianity as a religion. This progress was social, economic, scientific and also affected the life and position of women in society.

58   That is why I firmly believe that the reasons for the lower status of women in our societies, and the lack of opportunities for progress afforded to them, are not due to Islam, but rather to certain economic and political forces, namely those of foreign imperialism operating mainly from the outside, and of the reactionary classes operating from the inside. These two forces cooperate closely and are making a concerted attempt to misinterpret religion and to utilize it as an instrument of fear, oppression and exploitation.

59   Religion, if authentic in the principles it stands for, aims at truth, equality, justice, love and a healthy wholesome life for all people, whether men or women. There can be no true religion that aims at disease, mutilation of the bodies of female children, and amputation of an essential part of their reproductive organs.

60   If religion comes from God, how can it order man to cut off an organ created by Him as long as that organ is not diseased or deformed? God does not create the organs of the body haphazardly without a plan. It is not possible that He should have created the clitoris in woman's body only in order that it be cut off at an early stage in life. This is a contradiction into which neither true religion nor the Creator could possibly fall. If God has created the clitoris as a sexually sensitive organ, whose sole function seems to be the procurement of sexual pleasure for women, it follows that He also considers such pleasure for women as normal and legitimate, and therefore as an integral part of

[6]Rose Oldfield, "Female genital mutilation, fertility control, women's roles, and patrilineage in modern Sudan," *American Ethnologist*, Vol. II, No. 4, November 1975.

mental health. The psychic and mental health of women cannot be complete if they do not experience sexual pleasure.

There are still a large number of fathers and mothers who are afraid of leaving the clitoris intact in the bodies of their daughters. Many a time they have said to me that circumcision is a safeguard against the mistakes and deviations into which a girl may be led. This way of thinking is wrong and even dangerous because what protects a boy or a girl from making mistakes is not the removal of a small piece of flesh from the body, but consciousness and understanding of the problems we face, and a worthwhile aim in life, an aim which gives it meaning and for whose attainment we exert our mind and energies. The higher the level of consciousness to which we attain, the closer our aims draw to human motives and values, and the greater our desire to improve life and its quality, rather than to indulge ourselves in the mere satisfaction of our senses and the experience of pleasure, even though these are an essential part of existence. The most liberated and free of girls, in the true sense of liberation, are the least preoccupied with sexual questions, since these no longer represent a problem. On the contrary, a free mind finds room for numerous interests and the many rich experiences of a cultured life. Girls that suffer sexual suppression, however, are greatly preoccupied with men and sex. And it is a common observation that an intelligent and cultured woman is much less engrossed in matters related to sex and to men than is the case with ordinary women, who have not got much with which to fill their lives. Yet at the same time such a woman takes much more initiative to ensure that she will enjoy sex and experience pleasure, and acts with a greater degree of boldness than others. Once sexual satisfaction is attained, she is able to turn herself fully to other important aspects of life.

In the life of liberated and intelligent women, sex does not occupy a disproportionate position, but rather tends to maintain itself within normal limits. In contrast, ignorance, suppression, fear and all sorts of limitations exaggerate the role of sex in the life of girls and women, and cause it to swell out of all proportion and to end up by occupying the whole, or almost the whole, of their lives.

✦ Questions for Discussion and Writing

1. How does the event el-Saadawi describes permanently change her relationship with her parents, husband, colleagues, and her professional role as a physician with her female patients?

2. Why do you think el-Saadawi chooses to describe the procedure in such precise detail and objective language, given her own personal experiences and feelings about it? How does el-Saadawi's use of diction, and choice of denotative rather than connotative language, encourage the reader to share the writer's perception of this subject?

3. How does el-Saadawi use case histories documenting the emotional and physical consequences of female circumcision?

4. To what factors does she attribute the hostility she encountered as a physician in Egypt as she continued with her investigation?

5. In el-Saadawi's view, what cultural attitudes explain the use of circumcision of social control intended to shape the attitude women have of themselves in Egyptian society?

6. Discuss the broad range of rhetorical means el-Saadawi uses to try to influence her readers to share her perspective of female circumcision. Consider her use of her own experiences, incidents and stories that bear on the subject, case histories as examples, an analysis of the prevailing cultural attitudes, and the linguistic means (style, tone, diction, imagery) she uses to express her views and shape the reader's response.

7. Is there any outdated custom or practice you would wish to make a case against in contemporary society? Provide evidence and reasons to support your views and respond to objections those holding the opposite view might raise.

Paul Monette

Becoming a Man

◆————————

Paul Monette is a distinguished writer of poetry, novels, and autobio-graphical volumes. He was born in 1945, attended Yale University, and first received critical attention in 1975 with the publication of his poetry collection The Carpenter at the Asylum. *His novels include* Taking Care of Mrs. Carroll *(1978),* The Gold Diggers *(1979),* The Long Shot *(1981),* Lightfall *(1982),* Afterlife *(1990), and* Halfway Home *(1991). Following the death from AIDS of his longtime lover, Roger Horwitz, Monette addressed the tragedy in a collection of poems* Love Alone: Eighteen Elegies for Rog *(1988) and wrote an acclaimed prose account,* Borrowed Time: An AIDS Memoir, *for which he received a National Book Critics Circle Award nomination for the best autobiography in 1988. At this time, Monette was diagnosed as being HIV-positive. Monette has also written* Becoming a Man: Half a Life Story *(1992), from which the following selection is taken, in which he recounts the difficulties he experienced coming to terms with his homosexuality and disclosing it to others. This memoir won the prestigious National Book Award for Nonfiction in 1992. Monette died in 1995.*

> *Audieris in quo, Flacce, balneo plausum,*
> *Maronis illic esse mentulam scito.*
>
> —*Martial (circa* A.D. *40–104)*

> *Lux et Veritas*
>
> *You ask at the Baths why all this sudden*
> *applause?*
> *It's their habit, Cabot.*
> *Another Yale type has stepped out of his drawers.*
>
> —*Translated by Dudley Fitts*

Assuming the judge's threat was real, I was lucky to get to Yale at all. That final summer before leaving home I worked at Nick's for the last time. I knew in my bones I was bound for a one-way trip, that as soon as I hung up my apron in the closet by the ice-cream maker, I would forfeit the inside track on life in a small town. That strange amalgam of Norman Rockwell folksiness and the quiet desperation of

127

Winesburg, Ohio. Vinnie O'Connor, having dropped out of Andover High at sixteen, was already picking up garbage door-to-door in his own truck, his bully days behind him. And I knew every bachelor and old maid on sight—the sensible shoes and the rubbers for rain, that wincing sense of apology for their very being. Going no place, the end of the line.

2   But if I was about to engineer my flight from same, I was more overwhelmed than I'd freely admit, especially to myself. I spent most of my working days with Alex, and after work as well, a ritual stack of records on the turntable, *Oklahoma* to *Candide.* Alex, whose high school C's were making it unlikely that he could take the college route of escape, was already talking cosmetology and hair. But not at the local level, please. His sights were on Madison Avenue and Beverly Hills, centers of style and chic, and not "this Ann Taylor woolen bullshit."

3   For all his queenly dish, or maybe because of it, Alex had a much more confident feel than I of a world out there to conquer. He had been noisily defying for so long his father's Greek ideal of manhood. "My son is a girl!" Nick would bellow as if accursed, Alex shaking his pompoms in retort. I can't say I actually envied him, but his raw, confrontive style had a certain antic charm about it. He was a drag queen without the dress and makeup, a caricature of a sissy, over the top in a town that had never seen genderfuck at all. Consequently the bullies gave him a sort of theatrical clearance,

4   In a way I couldn't begin to explain, Alex was defining himself more truly than I with all my school credentials. He said whatever came into his head, nothing to lose, go screw yourself if you didn't like it. Two months later I would have been mortified if any of my Yale friends had seen us laughing together, so desperate was I to pass. But in that summer of finishing life in the provinces I took a curious refuge in the camp of Alex Anestos, who might say absolutely anything and usually did.

5   "Good morning, sir," he'd greet a bleary customer. "You look like you need a little Ex-Lax, or is it a Kotex?" And they didn't quite hear it, because they couldn't believe it. There was something about these manic sendups, murmured just under his breath, that suggested a marvelous anarchy. Pinning a KICK ME sign on the seat of pompous WASP and shanty Irish alike.

6   Alex went with me to the mall one day, a half-hour's drive to Peabody. I was meant to buy clothes for school, but I'd been fretting that my summer savings weren't enough to steer me through the unchartered waters of starting college. We wandered around looking for sales, I wistfully passing up sweaters and jackets I couldn't afford. Without any premeditation I can recall, I found myself at the underwear counter at Kresge's, surreptitiously stuffing a package of Jockey shorts into my shopping bag. I think the idea was to rip off the little stuff so I could

buy a sexy sweater. Unless I was simply out to prove that Paul was no longer perfect.

With scant experience at thievery, I was blithely unaware of mall 7 security. In the next store I took my time picking a nice pair of flannel pajamas, then dropped them into my bag. (From that day on I never wore p.j.'s again.) Suddenly a hand grabbed my elbow, and I was dragged unceremoniously to the store's office, matrons gaping at me from every aisle. I broke into a cold sweat, half fainted. The plain-clothesman, who reminded me of my father, summoned a cop who formally arrested me. Both stores were pressing charges, and I was to appear the following morning at the Salem courthouse.

All the way home, Alex tried gently to laugh it off as an adventure, 8 but I was profoundly rattled. I told my mother with shamefaced tears. Though she was pained, she hugged me and promised we'd get through it. When Dad got home, he looked like he'd taken a punch in the gut, but as usual he was unbearably decent. The hardest thing was to drive to Salem at seven A.M., just he and I, the feeling I had of his sidelong looks, as if he didn't know what to make of me anymore.

The judge saw us in chambers. After hearing the cop's testimony 9 and a halting plea from Dad, he turned to me and said, "You realize, don't you, if Yale finds out about this, you're out." Now it was my turn to squirm and plead, how I understood the advantages I'd been given and would hereafter be a model citizen—a speech of Ciceronian clarity. He listened with pursed lips, a moment's silence as he toyed with my fate. Then gruffly dismissed the case, with a warning that I was *persona non grata* at the Northshore Mall forever.

We drove back to Andover wilted with relief. And yet I remember 10 being struck by the most perverse thought: *If Yale found out about this, I wouldn't have to go.* Unthinkable really, that I should seek a way to derail my glorious rise to privilege. I buried it rather than face it. But the incident shows how conflicted I was about sailing into the future, as well as an instinct for sabotage. Something in me didn't want more schooling, dreaded the claustrophobia of being one of the guys. Alex's life by contrast was utterly free to happen, changeable as the color of his hair.

But as I say, I buried all that along with my police record. Yale was 11 the next step, period. My mother and Nana dutifully sewed the nametags into my clothes, Nana's dignity much offended by the artificial leg and cane that had lately become her cross. She might have been going to Yale herself, so passionate was the vicarious thrill, for I was the first on the English side to ever get to college. The night before we left for New Haven, my Uncle Dan, with eight kids to feed, tucked ten bucks he couldn't afford into my shirt pocket. "Go buy a round of beers at Mory's," he said with a fond wink, sending the family hero off to claim his knighthood.

12   The next day, driving down, we stopped at a Hojo's just out of Hartford. ("Is that New York?" my brother asked in an awestruck voice as we swung by Hartford's three tall buildings. "No," we all laughed, though scarcely more worldly than he.) My father and I had a moment alone as he paid the bill, Bobby and Mother off to find the washroom. With an unsettling depth of feeling Dad put his arm around me and said, "Now remember, don't get involved with the wrong kind of girl. Okay?"

13   I nodded dumbly, seized by a rush of sorrow. Sad that my secrets kept us eternally out of phase, and hopeless of ever changing things.

14   The homesick blues were intolerable that first fall semester of '63, especially because I denied them. My life in 1068 Bingham Hall was a full-time job, chameleon and ventriloquist, so there wasn't a lot of time left over to feel how lonely I was. A two-bedroom suite, with bunk beds in each. The powers that be had paired me up with a studious lad from Andover, though we had barely been on nodding terms at school. This Russell (never Russ) had already decided on Chinese Studies, arriving at Yale with several thousand vocabulary cards and a placid air that was positively Confucian. He took the upper, I the lower.

15   Our two California roommates arrived in tandem: Sean and Jake, respectively a rock climber from Marin and a tennis jock from Santa Barbara. Outsize figures from the moment they walked through the door. They'd been buddies at the Trimble School—best of the West, old California gold, where every boy was required to keep a horse because it built character. Jake was third generation Trimble himself, grandson of the founding gentleman cowboy. He and Sean were smart as anybody from Andover, but not so polished, and proud of that. As to the mores and climate of Yale, everything struck them as being so *Eastern*, which only fortified their free-range superiority.

16   I was smitten by them both inside of twenty minutes. Not sexually, exactly—sexually was the least of it. Though they were strapping good athletes and frontier rugged, they never occupied a slot in the Olympian frieze of my fantasies. I needed them both to be more real than that, or else how would they ever transform my doggy life? For I quickly came to see them as my salvation, the pals I never had among the Apollo and Dionysus ranks of Andover. I'd never been on the inside before, shooting the breeze in a bull session. Never been anyone's confidant about women.

17   I took to the role with near-demented enthusiasm. To curry the favor of Sean and Jake I underwent a personality change—voluble where I'd been tongue-tied before, flattering them at every turn, adopting their sneering distaste for the East, I who'd never been west of the Hudson. I dressed like they did, took every meal I could with them. *Courtier* is far too pretty a term for my servile hero worship; *sycophant* is closer. Yet it wasn't at all unconscious: I saw my new friends as a last chance to leave behind the nothing I was in high school.

Thus I stopped answering Francis's letter from Georgetown, seal-   18
ing the tomb on our old playful style, because it felt tainted with fag-
gotry. Till the first snowfall I'd get up with Sean on Sunday mornings
and pile in a van with the Mountaineering Club, to spend hair-raising
afternoons climbing the sheer faces of northern Connecticut's bony
hills. Graceless and panting, biting the tongue of my acrophobia, I
clambered up the gorse till my knuckles bled, all for a macho nod from
Sean at the summit. Back at the dorm, I laughed myself hoarse at Jake's
razor wit, becoming his personal buffoon and comic foil. He wanted to
be a writer, and therefore so did I. Prose was his meat and potatoes, and
therefore I took poetry.

It amazes me now, that I made life choices for no other reason than   19
to get in Sean and Jake's good graces. Today I haven't a clue where they
live or what they've done since Yale. I realize college provides a classic
ground for reinvention of self, but self had nothing to do with this. The
very opposite: all I wanted to be was the two of them, burying every
trace of Paul Monette.

Bury especially the hungry voyeur with the secrets. Jake had what   20
amounted to a knee-jerk loathing of queers, every third remark a with-
ering bash of anybody who seemed the least bit eccentric. He'd pout
his lips and affect a nancy lisp and a wobbly wrist, dismissing whatever felt effete or even intellectual. Since there were so many closeted
teachers about, Yale was fertile territory for his HUAC-style snipery,
every bachelor guilty till proven innocent. And I was the first to go
along, frantic to hide my own fellow-traveling. Eagerly I learned how
to mock my brothers behind their backs—anything to make Jake laugh.

But more was required to prove one's manhood than just the put-   21
ting down of queers. In those pre-coed days, Yale men hardly talked of
anything except getting laid, unless it was getting drunk. The best of all
worlds therefore was scoring in both at once: a dream Saturday night
where you'd be shitfaced from the rotgut punch at a mixer and maul-
ing some poor townie girl. Jake and Sean were more than eager to get
in on the action, pestering me to set them up with dates since I was the
one with the East Coast connections. I could no more admit I'd never
dated than I could my heterosexual virginity. So I invented my own
modest tales of carnal prowess, cobbling details here and there from
other men's boasting.

For Dartmouth weekend I invited a girl I knew from Rosemary   22
Hall, who arrived with a blushing pair of her classmates. I hated attending the football game, having no idea what was going down on the
field, but the worst was the mixer that night. Guys throwing up in the
bushes outside and a general air of male entitlement, showing off their
women and making their moves in the shadows to the tawdry strains
of *Louie Louie.* I was engaged in the upstream battle of *not* scoring,
avoiding sex at all costs. Here my four-year schizophrenic pattern laid
itself out: the requisite girl on my arm, the looking good, the frenzied

round of sports and museums and parties, anything to avoid too much time *à deux,* the compulsory makeout.

23   I wasn't unaware even at the time what a grim sham I was putting the girls through. Oh, I made up for my carnal detachment with frantic charm and witticisms, and for a while at least found dates who seemed relieved not to be mauled. But I would almost never see a girl twice, for fear of the expectations. The girl from Rosemary Hall kept writing till Christmas, and I was too frozen to answer. Every minute of a date felt like a lie, but if you didn't date, you couldn't be one of the guys. My guys anyway, whose opinion I cared about more than my own.

24   For Harvard weekend I invited Missy Cabot to come down from Middlebury, spending my self-imposed month's allowance just on tickets for The Game. As Missy wasn't due in till six on Friday, I spent the afternoon out at the soccer field, timing the freshman match between Harvard and Yale. I hadn't suddenly developed a fondness for the sport that gave me chilblains all through four rotten autumns at Andover. It was because Sean and Jake were playing for Yale, and I their constant companion could get no closer than sitting on the bench with a stopwatch.

25   In the middle of the third quarter a campus policeman came up to huddle with the coach. From where I sat, the cop looked like he was crying. When he turned away, the coach walked over to me, who till now was as insignificant to him as a cockroach. "The President's been shot," he said, and at first I thought he meant the president of Yale. "He's still alive. I don't want the players told. We'll finish the game."

26   I don't think I could have been less political in those days. Because of my endless self-absorption and twenty-four-hour vigilance at the closet door, I never read the papers except for the theater page. The Cuban missile crisis had passed without causing a ripple in my pond. I'd only worn a Kennedy button in '60 because everyone in my family was voting for Nixon. I had no personal investment, in other words, and yet the coach's cavalier priorities offended me for the President's sake. Would he have stopped the game if the news had come in the *first* quarter?

27   By the time I bleated the horn at the end—a 3–3 tie—Kennedy was dead. Too late to stop Missy from coming. So the weekend proceeded, in New Haven as elsewhere, to the sound of muffled drums. We spent most of our time in front of the one snowy TV in the dorm, the world reduced to black and white. And yet what I remember most is the overriding sense of relief, as Missy cradled her head on my shoulder and cried softly into a handkerchief. Relief that I wouldn't have to make any carnal moves, wouldn't have to prove my hormonal mettle. A chaste goodnight kiss was more in keeping with national tragedy.

A grotesque perspective, to put it mildly. The self-obsession that
fears exposure will grab at almost anything to keep the closet door
shut. When I bundled Missy off on the bus on Sunday afternoon—just
after Ruby shot Oswald—the psychic pain had bonded us, travelers
thrown together by a crash. I wouldn't be inviting her again, of course,
though I basked for a few days after in Sean and Jake's praise of her
winsome beauty and Mayflower cheekbones. I had turned Missy into a
"beard" without knowing the term, like the artificial dates those closeted powers of Hollywood take in their limos to all the openings and
awards. Except in L.A., the starlets line up around the block for such an
honor.

✦ Questions for Discussion and Writing

1. In your opinion, did Paul shoplift to emulate the kind of daring behavior he admired in his friend Alex, or did he have some other motive? If
   so, what was this motive?

2. What explains Paul's attempt to ingratiate himself with his two roommates?

3. What happened that made Paul aware of how thoroughly he saw the
   world in terms of his own ambivalence towards his sexual identity?

4. In your view, what motivates Monette to tell his story? What do you
   think he hopes to achieve?

5. When you first started attending college, did you suppress certain
   parts of your nature in order to be accepted by a group? Was this
   stressful? Describe your experiences.

Connections

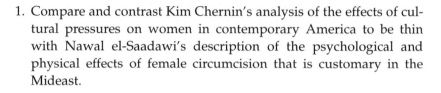

1. Compare and contrast Kim Chernin's analysis of the effects of cultural pressures on women in contemporary America to be thin with Nawal el-Saadawi's description of the psychological and physical effects of female circumcision that is customary in the Mideast.

2. To what extent is circumcision intended to physically and psychologically restrict girls in Mideastern cultures, as described by Nawal el-Saadawi, although it serves to confer authority on boys among the Masai, as related by Tepilit Ole Saitoti?

3. In what ways do both Judith Ortiz Cofer and Paul Monette challenge traditional societal and sexual stereotypes?

4. What different perspectives on sexual stereotyping emerge from the narratives by Judith Ortiz Cofer and Nora Ephron ("A Few Words About Breasts," Chapter 5)?

5. What similarities can you find in the perspectives of Kim Chernin and Mike Royko ("Farewell to Fitness," Chapter 8) on what society deems an acceptable body image?

6. What cross-cultural insights about societal control of women's bodies can you discover in the accounts of Nawal el-Saadawi and Margaret Sanger ("The Turbid Ebb and Flow of Misery," Chapter 7)?

7. What common assumptions about what it means to be a man underlie Paul Monette's and Tim O'Brien's ("If I Die in a Combat Zone," Chapter 10) accounts? What inner conflicts do societal expectations about manhood create for each writer?

4

*Creatures Great
and Small*

◆

*Animals are not brethren, they are not underlings; they are other
nations, caught with ourselves in the net of life and time.*

—Henry Beston, "Autumn, Ocean, and Birds,"
The Outermost House, 1928

Four legs good, two legs bad.

—George Orwell, *Animal Farm*, 1945

The works in this chapter reflect a rich tradition of observations of the
natural world that have been made by professionals and laypersons
alike. Whether recorded in journals, notebooks, or diaries, these observations form an indispensable storehouse of impressions that reveal
patterns of behavior that are often surprising.

The struggle to understand experiences we have with animals of
various kinds can produce thoughtful reflections that are both intellectually stimulating and dramatically compelling. Writing of this kind often moves beyond merely recording observations to considering the
varied relationships we have with "creatures great and small," to use
James Herriot's well-known phrase.

Jean Henri Fabre's journal entries in "The Praying Mantis" illustrate the kinds of detailed observations that characterize effective scientific writing. So, too, Jane van Lawick-Goodall's startling observations
of chimpanzee behavior alter previously held conceptions about pri-
mate capabilities. In "Playing Tag with Wild Dolphins," documentary
film producer Howard Hall describes an encounter with spotted dolphins that suggested some intriguing possibilities about the intelligence of these mammals. Although best known for his career at the
New Yorker magazine, essayist E. B. White, in "Death of a Pig," shares
his intimate knowledge of farm life.

Jean Henri Fabre

The Praying Mantis

◆

Jean Henri Fabre (1823–1915), considered the father of entomology, received a doctorate in natural sciences in 1864, in Paris. Fabre published the first of his many distinctive works on the biology and behavior of insects in 1855. In the following year, Fabre was awarded the Prix Montyon for experimental physiology by the Institute of France. Charles Darwin praised the value of Fabre's research, in 1859, in his On the Origin of Species. *Fabre disclosed the importance of instinct in the habits of many insects, including dung beetles, and discovered how wasps paralyze their prey in response to specific stimulating zones. Fabre's major scientific work, the ten-volume* Souvenirs Entomologiques *(1878–1907), was accomplished between his retirement from academic life and the time of his death at age ninety-two. In "The Praying Mantis," from* The Insect World *(1949), Fabre uses dramatic analogies to convey the cannibalistic mating habits of the praying mantis with his characteristic blend of meticulous observations and engaging style.*

1   Another creature of the south is at least as interesting as the Cicada, but much less famous, because it makes no noise. Had Heaven granted it a pair of cymbals, the one thing needed, its renown would eclipse the great musician's, for it is most unusual in both shape and habits. Folk hereabouts call it *lou Prègo-Diéu*, the animal that prays to God. Its official name is the Praying Mantis. . . .

2   The language of science and the peasant's artless vocabulary agree in this case and represent the queer creature as a pythoness[1] delivering her oracles or an ascetic rapt in pious ecstasy. The comparison dates a long way back. Even in the time of the Greeks the insect was called *Mántis*, the divine, the prophet. The tiller of the soil is not particular about analogies: where points of resemblance are not too clear, he will make up for their deficiencies. He saw on the sun-scorched herbage an insect of imposing appearance, drawn up majestically in a half-erect posture. He noticed its gossamer wings, broad and green, trailing like long veils of finest lawn; he saw its fore-legs, its arms so to speak, raised to the sky in a gesture of invocation. That was enough; popular imagination did the rest; and behold the bushes from ancient times stocked with Delphic priestesses, with nuns in orison.

[1]A reference to the priestess who served Apollo at Delphi and to the sacred serpent in the caves of Mount Parnassus from which the oracles were delivered.

Good people, with your childish simplicity, how great was your   3
mistake! Those sanctimonious airs are a mask for Satanic habits; those
arms folded in prayer are cut-throat weapons: they tell no beads, they
slay whatever passes within range. Forming an exception which one
would never have suspected in the herbivorous order of the Orthop-
tera, the Mantis feeds exclusively on living prey. She is the tigress of the
peaceable entomological tribes, the ogress in ambush who levies a trib-
ute of fresh meat. Picture her with sufficient strength; and her carnivorous appetites, combined with her traps of horrible perfection, would
make her the terror of the country-side. The *Prègo-Diéu* would become
a devilish vampire.

Apart from her lethal implement, the Mantis has nothing to inspire   4
dread. She is not without a certain beauty, in fact, with her slender figure, her elegant bust, her pale-green colouring and her long gauze
wings. No ferocious mandibles, opening like shears; on the contrary, a
dainty pointed muzzle that seems made for billing and cooing. Thanks
to a flexible neck, quite independent of the thorax, the head is able to
move freely, to turn to right or left, to bend, to lift itself. Alone among
insects, the Mantis directs her gaze; she inspects and examines; she almost has a physiognomy.

Great indeed is the contrast between the body as a whole, with its   5
very pacific aspect, and the murderous mechanism of the forelegs,
which are correctly described as raptorial.[2] The haunch is uncommonly
long and powerful. Its function is to throw forward the rat-trap, which
does not await its victim but goes in search of it. The snare is decked
out with some show of finery. The base of the haunch is adorned on the
inner surface with a pretty, black mark, having a white spot in the middle; and a few rows of bead-like dots complete the ornamentation.

The thigh, longer still, a sort of flattened spindle, carries on the   6
front half of its lower surface two rows of sharp spikes. In the inner row
there are a dozen, alternately black and green, the green being shorter
than the black. This alternation of unequal lengths increases the number of cogs and improves the effectiveness of the weapon. The outer
row is simpler and has only four teeth. Lastly, three spurs, the longest
of all, stand out behind the two rows. In short, the thigh is a saw with
two parallel blades, separated by a groove in which the leg lies when
folded back.

The leg, which moves very easily on its joint with the thigh, is like-   7
wise a double-edged saw. The teeth are smaller, more numerous and
closer together than those on the thigh. It ends in a strong hook whose
point vies with the finest needle for sharpness, a hook fluted underneath and having a double blade like a curved pruning-knife.

This hook, a most perfect instrument for piercing and tearing, has   8
left me many a painful memory. How often, when Mantis-hunting,

[2]Able to readily grasp victims.

clawed by the insect which I had just caught and not having both hands at liberty, have I been obliged to ask somebody else to release me from my tenacious captive! To try to free yourself by force, without first disengaging the claws implanted in your flesh, would expose you to scratches similar to those produced by the thorns of a rose-tree. None of our insects is so troublesome to handle. The Mantis claws you with her pruning-hooks, pricks you with her spikes, seizes you in her vice and makes self-defence almost impossible if, wishing to keep your prize alive, you refrain from giving the pinch of the thumb that would put an end to the struggle by crushing the creature.

9   When at rest, the trap is folded and pressed back against the chest and looks quite harmless. There you have the insect praying. But, should a victim pass, the attitude of prayer is dropped abruptly. Suddenly unfolded, the three long sections of the machine throw to a distance their terminal grapnel, which harpoons the prey and, in returning, draws it back between the two saws. The vice closes with a movement like that of the fore-arm and the upper arm; and all is over: Locusts, Grasshoppers and others even more powerful, once caught in the mechanism with its four rows of teeth, are irretrievably lost. Neither their desperate fluttering nor their kicking will make the terrible engine release its hold.

10   An uninterrupted study of the Mantis' habits is not practicable in the open fields; we must rear her at home. There is no difficulty about this: she does not mind being interned under glass, on condition that she be well fed. Offer her choice viands, served up fresh daily, and she will hardly feel her absence from the bushes.

11   As cages for my captives I have some ten large wire-gauze dishcovers, the same that are used to protect meat from the Flies. Each stands in a pan filled with sand. A dry tuft of thyme and a flat stone on which the laying may be done later constitute all the furniture. These huts are placed in a row on the large table in my insect laboratory, where the sun shines on them for the best part of the day. I install my captives in them, some singly, some in groups.

12   It is in the second fortnight of August that I begin to come upon the adult Mantis in the withered grass and on the brambles by the roadside. The females, already notably corpulent, are more frequent from day to day. Their slender companions, on the other hand, are rather scarce; and I sometimes have a good deal of difficulty in making up my couples, for there is an appalling consumption of these dwarfs in the cages. Let us keep these atrocities for later and speak first of the females.

13   They are great eaters, whose maintenance, when it has to last for some months, is none too easy. The provisions, which are nibbled at disdainfully and nearly all wasted, have to be renewed almost every day. I trust that the Mantis is more economical on her native bushes. When game is not plentiful, no doubt she devours every atom of her

catch; in my cages she is extravagant, often dropping and abandoning the rich morsel after a few mouthfuls, without deriving any further benefit from it. This appears to be her particular method of beguiling the tedium of captivity.

To cope with these extravagant ways I have to employ assistants.   14
Two or three small idlers, bribed by the promise of a slice of melon or bread-and-butter, go morning and evening to the grass-plots in the neighbourhood and fill their game-bags—cases made of reed-stumps—with live Locusts and Grasshoppers. I on my side, net in hand, make a daily circuit of my enclosure, in the hope of obtaining some choice morsel for my boarders.

These tit-bits are intended to show me to what lengths the Mantis'   15
strength and daring can go. They include the big Grey Locust . . ., who is larger than the insect that will consume him; the White-faced Decticus, armed with a vigorous pair of mandibles whereof our fingers would do well to fight shy; the quaint Tryxalis, who wears a pyramid-shaped mitre on her head; the Vine Ephippiger, who clashes cymbals and sports a sword at the bottom of her pot-belly. To this assortment of game that is not any too easy to tackle, let us add two monsters, two of the largest Spiders of the district: the Silky Epeira, whose flat, festooned abdomen is the size of a franc piece; and the Cross Spider, or Diadem Epeira, who is hideously hairy and obese.

I cannot doubt that the Mantis attacks such adversaries in the open,   16
when I see her, under my covers, boldly giving battle to whatever comes in sight. Lying in wait among the bushes, she must profit by the fat prizes offered by chance even as, in the wire cage, she profits by the treasures due to my generosity. Those big hunts, full of danger, are no new thing: they form part of her normal existence. Nevertheless they appear to be rare, for want of opportunity, perhaps to the Mantis' deep regret.

Locusts of all kinds, Butterflies, Dragon-flies, large Flies, Bees and   17
other moderate-sized captures are what we usually find in the lethal limbs. Still the fact remains that, in my cages, the daring huntress recoils before nothing. Sooner or later, Grey Locust and Decticus, Epeira and Tryxalis are harpooned, held tight between the saws and crunched with gusto. The facts are worth describing.

At the sight of the Grey Locust who has heedlessly approached   18
along the trelliswork of the cover, the Mantis gives a convulsive shiver and suddenly adopts a terrifying posture. An electric shock would not produce a more rapid effect. The transition is so abrupt, the attitude so threatening that the observer beholding it for the first time at once hesitates and draws back his fingers, apprehensive of some unknown danger. Old hand as I am, I cannot even now help being startled, should I happen to be thinking of something else.

You see before you, most unexpectedly, a sort of bogey-man or   19
Jack-in-the-box. The wing-covers open and are turned back on either

side, slantingly; the wings spread to their full extent and stand erect like parallel sails or like a huge heraldic crest towering over the back; the tip of the abdomen curls upwards like a crosier, rises and falls, relaxing with short jerks and a sort of sough, a "Whoof! Whoof!" like that of a Turkeycock spreading his tail. It reminds one of the puffing of a startled Adder.

20   Planted defiantly on its four hind-legs, the insect holds its long bust almost upright. The murderous legs, originally folded and pressed together upon the chest, open wide, forming a cross with the body and revealing the arm-pits decorated with rows of beads and a black spot with a white dot in the centre. These two faint imitations of the eyes in a Peacock's tail, together with the dainty ivory beads, are warlike ornaments kept hidden at ordinary times. They are taken from the jewel-case only at the moment when we have to make ourselves brave and terrible for battle.

21   Motionless in her strange posture, the Mantis watches the Locust, with her eyes fixed in his direction and her head turning as on a pivot whenever the other changes his place. The object of this attitudinizing is evident: the Mantis wants to strike terror into her dangerous quarry, to paralyze it with fright, for, unless demoralized by fear, it would prove too formidable.

22   Does she succeed in this? Under the shiny head of the Decticus, behind the long face of the Locust, who can tell what passes? No sign of excitement betrays itself to our eyes on those impassive masks. Nevertheless it is certain that the threatened one is aware of the danger. He sees standing before him a spectre, with uplifted claws, ready to fall upon him; he feels that he is face to face with death; and he fails to escape while there is yet time. He who excels in leaping and could so easily hop out of reach of those talons, he, the big-thighed jumper, remains stupidly where he is, or even draws nearer with a leisurely step.

23   They say that little birds, paralysed with terror before the open jaws of the Snake, spell-bound by the reptile's gaze, lose their power of flight and allow themselves to be snapped up. The Locust often behaves in much the same way. See him within reach of the enchantress. The two grapnels fall, the claws strike, the double saws close and clutch. In vain the poor wretch protests: he chews space with his mandibles and, kicking desperately, strikes nothing but the air. His fate is sealed. The Mantis furls her wings, her battle-standard; she resumes her normal posture; and the meal begins.

24   In attacking the Tryxalis and the Ephippiger, less dangerous game than the Grey Locust and the Decticus, the spectral attitude is less imposing and of shorter duration. Often the throw of the grapnels is sufficient. This is likewise so in the case of the Epeira, who is grasped round the body with not a thought of her poison-fangs. With the smaller Locusts, the usual fare in my cages as in the open fields, the mantis sel-

dom employs her intimidation-methods and contents herself with seizing the reckless one that passes within her reach.

When the prey to be captured is able to offer serious resistance, the Mantis has at her service a pose that terrorizes and fascinates her quarry and gives her claws a means of hitting with certainty. Her rat-traps close on a demoralized victim incapable of defence. She frightens her victim into immobility by suddenly striking a spectral attitude.

The wings play a great part in this fantastic pose. They are very wide, green on the outer edge, colourless and transparent every else-where. They are crossed lengthwise by numerous veins, which spread in the shape of a fan. Other veins, transversal and finer, intersect the first at right angles and with them form a multitude of meshes. In the spectral attitude, the wings are displaced and stand upright in two par-allel planes that almost touch each other, like the wings of a Butterfly at rest. Between them the curled tip of the abdomen moves with sudden starts. The sort of breath which I have compared with the puffing of an Adder in a posture of defence comes from this rubbing of the abdomen against the nerves of the wings. To imitate the strange sound, all that you need do is to pass your nail quickly over the upper surface of an unfurled wing.

Wings are essential to the male, a slender pigmy who has to wan-der from thicket to thicket at mating-time. He has a well-developed pair, more than sufficient for his flight, the greatest range of which hardly amounts to four or five of our paces. The little fellow is exceed-ingly sober in his appetites. On rare occasions, in my cages, I catch him eating a lean Locust, an insignificant, perfectly harmless creature. This means that he knows nothing of the spectral attitude which is of no use to an unambitious hunter of his kind.

On the other hand, the advantage of the wings to the female is not very obvious, for she is inordinately stout at the time when her eggs ripen. She climbs, she runs; but, weighed down by her corpulence, she never flies. Then what is the object of wings, of wings, too, which are seldom matched for breadth?

The question becomes more significant if we consider the Grey Mantis…, who is closely akin to the Praying Mantis. The male is winged and is even pretty quick at flying. The female, who drags a great belly full of eggs, reduces her wings to stumps and, like the cheesemakers of Auvergne and Savory, wears a short-tailed jacket. For one who is not meant to leave the dry grass and the stones, this abbre-viated costume is more suitable than superfluous gauze furbelows. The Grey Mantis is right to retain but a mere vestige of the cumbrous sails.

Is the other wrong to keep her wings, to exaggerate them, even though she never flies? Not at all. The Praying Mantis hunts big game. Sometimes a formidable prey appears in her hiding-place. A direct at-tack might be fatal. The thing to do is first to intimidate the new-comer, to conquer his resistance by terror. With this object she suddenly un-furls her wings into a ghost's winding-sheet. The huge sails incapable of flight are hunting-implements. This stratagem is not needed by the little Grey Mantis, who captures feeble prey, such as Gnats and new-born Locusts. The two huntresses, who have similar habits and, be-cause of their stoutness, are neither of them able to fly, are dressed to suit the difficulties of the ambuscade. The first, an impetuous amazon, puffs her wings into a threatening standard; the second, a modest fowler, reduces them to a pair of scanty coat-tails.

31   In a fit of hunger, after a fast of some days' duration, the Praying Mantis will gobble up a Grey Locust whole, except for the wings, which are too dry; and yet the victim of her voracity is as big as herself, or even bigger. Two hours are enough for consuming this monstrous head of game. An orgy of the sort is rare. I have witnessed it once or twice and have always wondered how the gluttonous creature found room for so much food and how it reversed in its favour the axiom that the cask must be greater than its contents. I can but admire the lofty privileges of a stomach through which matter merely passes, being at once digested, dissolved and done away with.

32   The usual bill of fare in my cages consists of Locusts of greatly var-ied species and sizes. It is interesting to watch the Mantis nibbling her Acridian, firmly held in the grip of her two murderous fore-legs. Not-withstanding the fine, pointed muzzle, which seems scarcely made for this gorging, the whole dish disappears, with the exception of the wings, of which only the slightly fleshy base is consumed. The legs, the tough skin, everything goes down. Sometimes the Mantis seizes one of the big hinder thighs by the knuckle-end, lifts it to her mouth, tastes it and crunches it with a little air of satisfaction. The Locust's fat and juicy thigh may well be a choice morsel for her, even as a leg of mutton is for us.

33   The prey is first attacked in the neck. While one of the two lethal legs holds the victim transfixed through the middle of the body, the other presses the head and makes the neck open upwards. The Mantis' muz-zle roots and nibbles at this weak point in the armour with some persis-tency. A large wound appears in the head. The Locust gradually ceases kicking and becomes a lifeless corpse; and, from this moment, freer in its movements, the carnivorous insect picks and chooses its morsel.

34   The Mantis naturally wants to devour the victuals in peace, with-out being troubled by the plunges of a victim who absolutely refuses to be devoured. A meal liable to interruptions lacks savour. Now the prin-cipal means of defence in this case are the hind-legs, those vigorous le-vers which can kick out so brutally and which moreover are armed with toothed saws that would rip open the Mantis' bulky paunch if by ill-luck they happen to graze it. What shalt we do to reduce them to helplessness, together with the others, which are not dangerous but troublesome all the same, with their desperate gesticulations?

Strictly speaking, it would be practicable to cut them off one by one. But that is a long process and attended with a certain risk. The Mantis has hit upon something better. She has an intimate knowledge of the anatomy of the spine. By first attacking her prize at the back of the half-opened neck and munching the cervical ganglia, she destroys the muscular energy at its main seat; and inertia supervenes, not suddenly and completely, for the clumsily-constructed Locust has not the Bee's exquisite and frail vitality, but still sufficiently, after the first mouthfuls. Soon the kicking and the gesticulating die down, all movements cease and the game, however big it be, is consumed in perfect quiet.

The little that we have seen of the Mantis' habits hardly tallies with what we might have expected from her popular name. To judge by the term *Prègo-Diéu*, we should look to see a placid insect, deep in pious contemplation; and we find ourselves in the presence of a cannibal, of a ferocious spectre munching the brain of a panic-stricken victim. Nor is even this the most tragic part. The Mantis has in store for us, in her relations with her own kith and kin, manners even more atrocious than those prevailing among the Spiders, who have an evil reputation in this respect.

To reduce the number of cages on my big table and give myself a little more space while still retaining a fair-sized menagerie, I install several females, sometimes as many as a dozen, under one cover. So far as accommodation is concerned, no fault can be found with the common lodging. There is room and to spare for the evolutions of my captives, who naturally do not want to move about much with their unwieldy bellies. Hanging to the trelliswork of the dome, motionless they digest their food or else await an unwary passer-by. Even so do they act when at liberty in the thickets.

Cohabitation has its dangers. I know that even Donkeys, those peace-loving animals, quarrel when hay is scarce in the manger. My boarders, who are less complaisant, might well, in a moment of dearth, become sour-tempered and fight among themselves. I guard against this by keeping the cages well supplied with Locusts, renewed twice a day. Should civil war break out, famine cannot be pleaded as the excuse.

At first, things go pretty well. The community lives in peace, each Mantis grabbing and eating whatever comes near her, without seeking strife with her neighbours. But this harmonious period does not last long. The bellies swell, the eggs are ripening in the ovaries, marriage and laying time are at hand. Then a sort of jealous fury bursts out, though there is an entire absence of males who might be held responsible for feminine rivalry. The working of the ovaries seems to pervert the flock, inspiring its members with a mania for devouring each other. There are threats, personal encounters, cannibal feasts. Once more the spectral pose appears, the hissing of the wings, the fearsome gesture of the grapnels outstretched and uplifted in the air. No hostile demonstration in front of a Grey Locust or White-faced Decticus could be more menacing.

40   For no reason that I can gather, two neighbors suddenly assume their attitude of war. They turn their heads to right and left, provoking each other, exchanging insulting glances. The "Puff! Puff!" of the wings rubbed by the abdomen sounds the charge. When the duel is to be limited to the first scratch received, without more serious consequences, the lethal fore-arms, which are usually kept folded, open like the leaves of a book and fall back sideways, encircling the long bust. It is a superb pose, but less terrible than that adopted in a fight to the death.

41   Then one of the grapnels, with a sudden spring, shoots out to its full length and strikes the rival; it is no less abruptly withdrawn and resumes the defensive. The adversary hits back. The fencing is rather like that of two Cats boxing each other's ears. At the first blood drawn from her flabby paunch, or even before receiving the last wound, one of the duellists confesses herself beaten and retires. The other furls her battle-standard and goes off elsewhither to meditate the capture of a Locust, keeping apparently calm, but ever ready to repeat the quarrel.

42   Very often, events take a more tragic turn. At such times, the full posture of the duels to the death is assumed. The murderous fore-arms are unfolded and raised in the air. Woe to the vanquished! The other seizes her in her vice and then and there proceeds to eat her, beginning at the neck, of course. The loathsome feast takes place as calmly as though it were a matter of crunching up a Grasshopper. The diner enjoys her sister as she would a lawful dish; and those around do not protest, being quite willing to do as much on the first occasion.

43   Oh, what savagery! Why, even Wolves are said not to eat one another. The Mantis has no such scruples; she banquets off her fellows when there is plenty of her favorite game, the Locust, around her. She practises the equivalent of cannibalism, that hideous peculiarity of man.

44   These aberrations, these child-bed cravings can reach an even more revolting stage. Let us watch the pairing and, to avoid the disorder of a crowd, let us isolate the couples under different covers. Each pair shall have its own home, where none will come to disturb the wedding. And let us not forget the provisions, with which we will keep them well supplied, so that there may be no excuse of hunger.

45   It is near the end of August. The male, that slender swain, thinks the moment propitious. He makes eyes at his strapping companion; he turns his head in her direction; he bends his neck and throws out his chest. His little pointed face wears an almost impassioned expression. Motionless, in this posture, for a long time he contemplates the object of his desire. She does not stir, is as though indifferent. The lover, however, has caught a sign of acquiescence, a sign of which I do not know the secret. He goes nearer; suddenly he spreads his wings, which quiver with a convulsive tremor. This is his declaration. He rushes,

small as he is, upon the back of his corpulent companion, clings on as best he can, steadies his hold. As a rule, the preliminaries last a long time. At last, coupling takes place and is also long drawn out, lasting for five or six hours.

Nothing worthy of attention happens between the two motionless partners. They end by separating, but only to unite again in a more intimate fashion. If the poor fellow is loved by his lady as the vivifier of her ovaries, he is also loved as a piece of highly-flavoured game. And, that same day, or at latest on the morrow, he is seized by his spouse, who first gnaws his neck, in accordance with precedent, and then eats him deliberately, by little mouthfuls, leaving only the wings. Here we have no longer a case of jealousy in the harem, but simply a depraved appetite.

I was curious to know what sort of reception a second male might expect from a recently fertilized female. The result of my enquiry was shocking. The Mantis, in many cases, is never sated with conjugal raptures and banquets. After a rest that varies in length, whether the eggs be laid or not, a second male is accepted and then devoured like the first. A third succeeds him, performs his function in life, is eaten and disappears. A fourth undergoes a like fate. In the course of two weeks I thus see one and the same Mantis use up seven males. She takes them all to her bosom and makes them all pay for the nuptial ecstasy with their lives.

Orgies such as this are frequent, in varying degrees, though there are exceptions. On very hot days, highly charged with electricity, they are almost the general rule. At such times the Mantes are in a very irritable mood. In the cages containing a large colony, the females devour one another more than ever; in the cages containing separate pairs, the males, after coupling, are more than ever treated as an ordinary prey,

I should like to be able to say, in mitigation of these conjugal atrocities, that the Mantis does not behave like this in a state of liberty; that the male, after doing his duty, has time to get out of the way, to make off, to escape from his terrible mistress, for in my cages he is given a respite, lasting sometimes until next day. What really occurs in the thickets I do not know, chance, a poor resource, having never instructed me concerning the love-affairs of the Mantis when at large. I can only go by what happens in the cages, when the captives, enjoying plenty of sunshine and food and spacious quarters, do not seem to suffer from homesickness in any way. What they do here they must also do under normal conditions.

Well, what happens there utterly refutes the idea that the males are given time to escape. I find, by themselves, a horrible couple engaged as follows. The male, absorbed in the performance of his vital functions, holds the female in a tight embrace. But the wretch has no head; he has no neck; he has hardly a body. The other, with her muzzle turned over her shoulder continues very placidly to gnaw what remains of his gentle swain. And, all the time, that masculine stump, holding on firmly, goes on with the business!

51   Love is stronger than death, men say. Taken literally, the aphorism has never received a more brilliant confirmation. A headless creature, an insect amputated down to the middle of the chest, a very corpse persists in endeavouring to give life. It will not let go until the abdomen, the seat of the procreative organs, is attacked.

52   Eating the lover after consummation of marriage, making a meal of the exhausted dwarf, henceforth good for nothing, can be understood, to some extent, in the insect world, which has no great scruples in matters of sentiment; but gobbling him up during the act goes beyond the wildest dreams of the most horrible imagination. I have seen it done with my own eyes and have not yet recovered from my astonishment.

✦ Questions for Discussion and Writing

1. Why, according to Fabre, has the name "praying" mantis led to misconceptions about its nature?

2. What natural features in the praying mantis's armory of weapons make it a terror in its own world?

3. What strategy does the mantis use to intimidate prey twice its size?

4. How does the female mantis treat her mate during and after reproduction?

5. Discuss the benefits of Fabre's dramatic methods of presenting the mantis according to the scale of its world, in which it appears huge and terrifying, as opposed to ours, in which it seems tiny and delicate.

6. How does the figurative comparison, or analogy, between the mantis and a fashionable lady (paragraph 4) make "her" behavior all the more shocking?

7. If you keep a journal, try to apply Fabre's method of description by analogy to highlight important and unusual features of an insect, bird, or small mammal you have observed.

Jane van Lawick-Goodall

First Observations

◆───────────◆

Jane van Lawick-Goodall, born in London, England, in 1934, first worked as an assistant to the late Louis Leakey, curator of the National Museum of Natural History in Nairobi, Kenya. Through his efforts, van Lawick-Goodall was able to obtain financial backing for what became the Gombe Stream Research Center, for studies of chimpanzees and other primates in Gombe, Tanzania. Her unique research into chimpanzee behavior relied on first-hand observations of individual primates over long periods to study relationships, communication, hunting, feeding, dominance, sexuality, and territoriality in chimpanzee society. Van Lawick-Goodall discovered that chimpanzees were not exclusively vegetarians and, surprisingly, were capable of modifying and using tools to procure food. In addition to many scientific papers, van Lawick-Goodall is the author of In the Shadow of Man *(1971) and* The Chimpanzees of Gombe *(1986). In "First Observations," from* In the Shadow of Man, *van Lawick-Goodall describes the first time she actually observed David Graybeard (one of the chimpanzees she had named) engaged in meat-eating and tool-using behavior.*

For about a month I spent most of each day either on the Peak or overlooking Mlinda Valley where the chimps, before or after stuffing themselves with figs, ate large quantities of small purple fruits that tasted, like so many of their foods, as bitter and astringent as sloes or crab apples. Piece by piece, I began to form my first somewhat crude picture of chimpanzee life. 1

The impression that I had gained when I watched the chimps at the msulula tree of temporary, constantly changing associations of individuals within the community was substantiated. Most often I saw small groups of four to eight moving about together. Sometimes I saw one or two chimpanzees leave such a group and wander off on their own or join up with a different association. On other occasions I watched two or three small groups joining to form a larger one. 2

Often, as one group crossed the grassy ridge separating the Kasekela Valley from the fig trees in the home valley, the male chimpanzee, or chimpanzees, of the party would break into a run, sometimes moving in an upright position, sometimes dragging a fallen branch, sometimes stamping or slapping the hard earth. These charging displays were always accompanied by loud pant-hoots and 3

147

afterward the chimpanzee frequently would swing up into a tree over-looking the valley he was about to enter and sit quietly, peering down and obviously listening for a response from below. If there were chimps feeding in the fig trees they nearly always hooted back, as though in answer. Then the new arrivals would hurry down the steep slope and, with more calling and screaming, the two groups would meet in the fig trees. When groups of females and youngsters with no males present joined other feeding chimpanzees, usually there was none of this excitement; the newcomers merely climbed up into the trees, greeted some of those already there, and began to stuff them-selves with figs.

4   While many details of their social behavior were hidden from me by the foliage, I did get occasional fascinating glimpses. I saw one fe-male, newly arrived in a group, hurry up to a big male and hold her hand toward him. Almost regally he reached out, clasped her hand in his, drew it toward him, and kissed it with his lips. I saw two adult males embrace each other in greeting. I saw youngsters having wild games through the treetops, chasing around after each other or jump-ing again and again, one after the other, from a branch to a springy bough below. I watched small infants dangling happily by themselves for minutes on end, patting at their toes with one hand, rotating gently from side to side. Once two tiny infants pulled on opposite ends of a twig in a gentle tug-of-war. Often, during the heat of midday or after a long spell of feeding, I saw two or more adults grooming each other, carefully looking through the hair of their companions.

5   At that time of year the chimps usually went to bed late, making their nests when it was too dark to see properly through binoculars, but sometimes they nested earlier and I could watch them from the peak. I found that every individual, except for infants who slept with their mothers, made his own nest each night. Generally this took about three minutes: the chimp chose a firm foundation such as an upright fork or crotch, or two horizontal branches. Then he reached out and bent over smaller branches onto this foundation, keeping each one in place with his feet. Finally he tucked in the small leafy twigs growing around the rim of his nest and lay down. Quite often a chimp sat up after a few minutes and picked a handful of leafy twigs, which he put under his head or some other part of his body before settling down again for the night. One young female I watched went on and on bending down branches until she had constructed a huge mound of greenery on which she finally curled up.

6   I climbed up into some of the nests after the chimpanzees had left them. Most of them were built in trees that for me were almost impos-sible to climb. I found that there was quite complicated interweaving of the branches in some of them. I found, too, that the nests were never fouled with dung; and later, when I was able to get closer to the

chimps, I saw how they were always careful to defecate and urinate over the edge of their nests, even in the middle of the night.

During that month I really came to know the country well, for I often went on expeditions from the Peak, sometimes to examine nests, more frequently to collect specimens of the chimpanzees' food plants, which Bernard Verdcourt had kindly offered to identify for me. Soon I could find my way around the sheer ravines and up and down the steep slopes of three valleys—the home valley, the Pocket, and Mlinda Valley—as well as a taxi driver finds his way about in the main streets and byways of London. It is a period I remember vividly, not only because I was beginning to accomplish something at last, but also because of the delight I felt in being completely by myself. For those who love to be alone with nature I need add nothing further; for those who do not, no words of mine could ever convey, even in part, the almost mystical awareness of beauty and eternity that accompanies certain treasured moments. And, though the beauty was always there, those moments came upon me unaware: when I was watching the pale flush preceding dawn; or looking up through the rustling leaves of some giant forest tree into the greens and browns and black shadows that occasionally ensnared a bright fleck of the blue sky; or when I stood, as darkness fell, with one hand on the still-warm trunk of a tree and looked at the sparkling of an early moon on the never still, sighing water of the lake.

One day, when I was sitting by the trickle of water in Buffalo Wood, pausing for a moment in the coolness before returning from a scramble in Mlinda Valley, I saw a female bushbuck moving slowly along the nearly dry streambed. Occasionally she paused to pick off some plant and crunch it. I kept absolutely still, and she was not aware of my presence until she was little more than ten yards away. Suddenly she tensed and stood staring at me, one small forefoot raised. Because I did not move, she did not know what I was—only that my outline was somehow strange. I saw her velvet nostrils dilate as she sniffed the air, but I was downwind and her nose gave her no answer. Slowly she came closer, and closer—one step at a time, her neck craned forward—always poised for instant flight. I can still scarcely believe that her nose actually touched my knee; yet if I close my eyes I can feel again, in imagination, the warmth of her breath and the silken impact of her skin. Unexpectedly I blinked and she was gone in a flash, bounding away with loud barks of alarm until the vegetation hid her completely from my view.

It was rather different when, as I was sitting on the Peak, I saw a leopard coming toward me, his tail held up straight. He was at a slightly lower level than I, and obviously had no idea I was there. Ever since arrival in Africa I had had an ingrained, illogical fear of leopards. Already, while working at the Gombe, I had several times nearly turned back when, crawling through some thick undergrowth, I had suddenly smelled the rank smell of cat. I had forced myself on, telling myself that my fear was foolish, that only wounded leopards charged humans with savage ferocity.

10   On this occasion, though, the leopard went out of sight as it started to climb up the hill—the hill on the peak of which I sat. I quickly hastened to climb a tree, but halfway there I realized that leopards can climb trees. So I uttered a sort of halfhearted squawk. The leopard, my logical mind told me, would be just as frightened of me if he knew I was there. Sure enough, there was a thudding of startled feet and then silence. I returned to the Peak, but the feeling of unseen eyes watching me was too much. I decided to watch for the chimps in Mlinda Valley. And, when I returned to the Peak several hours later, there, on the very rock which had been my seat, was a neat pile of leopard dung. He must have watched me go and then, very carefully, examined the place where such a frightening creature had been and tried to exterminate my alien scent with his own.

11   As the weeks went by the chimpanzees became less and less afraid. Quite often when I was on one of my food-collecting expeditions I came across chimpanzees unexpectedly, and after a time I found that some of them would tolerate my presence provided they were in fairly thick forest and I sat still and did not try to move closer than sixty to eighty yards. And so, during my second month of watching from the Peak, when I saw a group settle down to feed I sometimes moved closer and was thus able to make more detailed observations.

12   It was at this time that I began to recognize a number of different individuals. As soon as I was sure of knowing a chimpanzee if I saw it again, I named it. Some scientists feel that animals should be labeled by numbers—that to name them is anthropomorphic—but I have always been interested in the *differences* between individuals, and a name is not only more individual than a number but also far easier to remember. Most names were simply those which, for some reason or other, seemed to suit the individuals to whom I attached them. A few chimps were named because some facial expression or mannerism reminded me of human acquaintances.

13   The easiest individual to recognize was old Mr. McGregor. The crown of his head, his neck, and his shoulders were almost entirely devoid of hair, but a slight frill remained around his head rather like a monk's tonsure. He was an old male—perhaps between thirty and forty years of age (the longevity record for a captive chimp is forty-seven years). During the early months of my acquaintance with him, Mr. McGregor was somewhat belligerent. If I accidentally came across him at close quarters he would threaten me with an upward and backward jerk of his head and a shaking of branches before climbing down and vanishing from my sight. He reminded me, for some reason, of Beatrix Potter's old gardener in *The Tale of Peter Rabbit*.

Ancient Flo with her deformed, bulbous nose and ragged ears was   14
equally easy to recognize. Her youngest offspring at that time were
two-year-old Fifi, who still rode everywhere on her mother's back, and
her juvenile son, Figan, who was always to be seen wandering around
with his mother and little sister. He was then about six years old; it was
approximately a year before he would attain puberty. Flo often traveled
with another old mother, Olly. Olly's long face was also distinctive; the
fluff of hair on the back of her head—though no other feature—reminded me of my aunt, Olwen. Olly, like Flo, was accompanied by two
children, a daughter younger than Fifi, and an adolescent son about a
year older than Figan.

Then there was William, who, I am certain, must have been Olly's   15
blood brother. I never saw any special signs of friendship between
them, but their faces were amazingly alike. They both had long upper
lips that wobbled when they suddenly turned their heads. William had
the added distinction of several thin, deeply etched scar marks running
down his upper lip from his nose.

Two of the other chimpanzees I knew well by sight at that time   16
were David Graybeard and Goliath. Like David and Goliath in the Bible, these two individuals were closely associated in my mind because
they were very often together. Goliath, even in those days of his prime,
was not a giant, but he had a splendid physique and the springy movements of an athlete. He probably weighed about one hundred pounds.
David Graybeard was less afraid of me from the start than were any of
the other chimps. I was always pleased when I picked out his handsome face and well-marked silvery beard in a chimpanzee group, for
with David to calm the others, I had a better chance of approaching to
observe them more closely.

Before the end of my trial period in the field I made two really ex-   17
citing discoveries—discoveries that made the previous months of frus-
tration well worth while. And for both of them I had David Graybeard
to thank.

One day I arrived on the Peak and found a small group of chimps   18
just below me in the upper branches of a thick tree. As I watched I saw
that one of them was holding a pink-looking object from which he was
from time to time pulling pieces with his teeth. There was a female and
a youngster and they were both reaching out toward the male, their
hands actually touching his mouth. Presently the female picked up a
piece of the pink thing and put it to her mouth: it was at this moment
that I realized the chimps were eating meat.

After each bite of meat the male picked off some leaves with his   19
lips and chewed them with the flesh, Often, when he had chewed for
several minutes on this leafy wad, he spat out the remains into the
waiting hands of the female. Suddenly he dropped a small piece of
meat, and like a flash the youngster swung after it to the ground. Even
as he reached to pick it up the undergrowth exploded and an adult

bushpig charged toward him. Screaming, the juvenile leaped back into the tree. The pig remained in the open, snorting and moving backward and forward. Soon I made out the shapes of three small striped piglets. Obviously the chimps were eating a baby pig. The size was right and later, when I realized that the male was David Graybeard, I moved closer and saw that he was indeed eating piglet.

20   For three hours I watched the chimps feeding. David occasionally let the female bite pieces from the carcass and once he actually detached a small piece of flesh and placed it in her outstretched hand. When he finally climbed down there was still meat left on the carcass: he carried it away in one hand, followed by the others.

21   Of course I was not sure, then, that David Graybeard had caught the pig for himself, but even so, it was tremendously exciting to know that these chimpanzees actually ate meat. Previously scientists had believed that although these apes might occasionally supplement their diet with a few insects or small rodents and the like they were primarily vegetarians and fruit eaters. No one had suspected that they might hunt larger mammals.

22   It was within two weeks of this observation that I saw something that excited me even more. By then it was October and the short rains had begun. The blackened slopes were softened by feathery new grass shoots and in some places the ground was carpeted by a variety of flowers. The Chimpanzees' Spring, I called it. I had had a frustrating morning, trampling up and down three valleys with never a sign or sound of a chimpanzee. Hauling myself up the steep slope of Mlinda Valley I headed for the Peak, not only weary but soaking wet from crawling through dense undergrowth. Suddenly I stopped, for I saw a slight movement in the long grass about sixty yards away. Quickly focusing my binoculars I saw that it was a single chimpanzee, and just then he turned in my direction. I recognized David Graybeard.

23   Cautiously I moved around so that I could see what he was doing. He was squatting beside the red earth mound of a termite nest, and as I watched I saw him carefully push a long grass stem down into a hole in the mound. After a moment he withdrew it and picked something from the end with his mouth. I was too far away to make out what he was eating, but it was obvious that he was actually using a grass stem as a tool.

24   I knew that on two occasions casual observers in West Africa had seen chimpanzees using objects as tools: one had broken open palm-nut kernels by using a rock as a hammer, and a group of chimps had been observed pushing sticks into an underground bees' nest and licking off the honey. Somehow I had never dreamed of seeing anything so exciting myself.

25   For an hour David feasted at the termite mound and then he wandered slowly away. When I was sure he had gone I went over to examine the mound. I found a few crushed insects strewn about, and a

swarm of worker termites sealing the entrances of the nest passages into which David had obviously been poking his stems. I picked up one of his discarded tools and carefully pushed it into a hole myself. Immediately I felt the pull of several termites as they seized the grass, and when I pulled it out there were a number of worker termites and a few soldiers, with big red heads, clinging on with their mandibles. There they remained, sticking out at right angles to the stem with their legs waving in the air.

Before I left I trampled down some of the tall dry grass and constructed a rough hide—just a few palm fronds leaned up against the low branch of a tree and tied together at the top. I planned to wait there the next day. But it was another week before I was able to watch a chimpanzee "fishing" for termites again. Twice chimps arrived, but each time they saw me and moved off immediately. Once a swarm of fertile winged termites—the princes and princesses, as they are called—flew off on their nuptial flight, their huge white wings fluttering frantically as they carried the insects higher and higher. Later I realized that it is at this time of year, during the short rains, when the worker termites extend the passages of the nest to the surface, preparing for these emigrations. Several such swarms emerge between October and January. It is principally during these months that the chimpanzees feed on termites. 26

On the eighth day of my watch David Graybeard arrived again, together with Goliath, and the pair worked for two hours. I could see much better; I observed how they scratched open the sealed-over passage entrances with a thumb or forefinger. I watched how they bit the ends off their tools when they became bent, or used the other end, or discarded them in favor of new ones. Goliath once moved at least fifteen yards from the heap to select a firm-looking piece of vine, and both males often picked three or four stems while they were collecting tools, and put the spares beside them on the ground until they wanted them. 27

Most exciting of all, on several occasions they picked small leafy twigs and prepared them for use by stripping off the leaves. This was the first recorded example of a wild animal not merely *using* an object as a tool, but actually modifying an object and thus showing the crude beginnings of tool*making*. 28

Previously man had been regarded as the only tool-making animal. Indeed, one of the clauses commonly accepted in the definition of man was that he was a creature who "made tools to a regular and set pattern." The chimpanzees, obviously, had not made tools to any set pattern. Nevertheless, my early observations of their primitive toolmaking abilities convinced a number of scientists that it was necessary to redefine man in a more complex manner than before. Or else, as Louis Leakey put it, we should by definition have to accept the chimpanzee as Man. 29

I sent telegrams to Louis both of my new observations—the meat-eating and the toolmaking—and he was of course wildly enthusiastic. 30

In fact, I believe that the news was helpful to him in his efforts to find further financial support for my work. It was not long afterward when he wrote to tell me that the National Geographic Society in the United States had agreed to grant funds for another year's research.

✦ *Questions for Discussion and Writing*

1. What details of appearance and behavior led van Lawick-Goodall to assign descriptive names to individual chimpanzees? What was the advantage of this method, as opposed to the usual assignment of numbers?

2. Why did van Lawick-Goodall's observations of David Graybeard lead her to conclude that chimpanzees, contrary to previous thought, were not solely vegetarians?

3. In what way did van Lawick-Goodall's discoveries lead to a redefinition of the term *man*?

4. What previously unsuspected social interactions did van Lawick-Goodall observe? Why would her research have been more difficult to conduct if David Graybeard had not accepted her?

5. Van Lawick-Goodall's research changed previously held scientific views about chimpanzees. Have you ever observed surprising or unusual behavior in a pet that changed your previously held ideas about its capabilities and nature? Describe your observations and conclusions.

Howard Hall

Playing Tag
with Wild Dolphins

◆

Howard Hall is a wildlife film producer who specializes in marine sub-
jects. His films, including Seasons in the Sea *(1990) for the PBS series*
Nature, Shadows in a Desert Sea *(1992), and numerous specials for*
National Geographic Television, such as Jewels of the Caribbean Sea
(1994), have garnered four°Emmys for cinematography. Hall's books in-
clude Sharks: The Perfect Predator *(1993) and* A Charm of Dolphins
(1993). "Playing Tag with Wild Dolphins" first appeared in Skin Diver
Magazine *(July, 1986).*

It had been four years since I last knelt on the white sand of the Ba- 1
hamas Banks listening for the calls of wild spotted dolphins. In the silence, looking out across the empty, sandy plain, I couldn't help feeling
pessimistic. It seemed so very unlikely they would come racing from
miles away to have a visit with me. It was not typical behavior for wild
animals. But, then again, this was not a typical situation.

Hardy and Julia Whitty-Jones were more confident. They had been 2
returning to the banks every year for nearly a decade. Every year the
dolphins had been there and the relationship between humans and
wild dolphins had grown from mutual curiosity to something that may
approach mutual friendship. I had been along on several of the earlier
expeditions to photograph the school for a film the Jones' would produce. In those early years the dolphins had been curious, but tentative.
The encounters had been infrequent and brief. But Hardy and Julia explained that much has changed since my last dive with the "Spotters."
Many members of the school had grown up having regular summer
encounters with divers.

I heard the clicks and whistles. Moments later they surrounded me. 3
The dolphins immediately came in much closer than in years past and
moved with less trepidation. Nearest to me was a mother and her
young calf. The baby was a beautiful and perfect miniature of her
mother. She looked almost artificial. In years past the mothers never
brought their calves in so close. It was as if this one was proudly showing off her baby. Suddenly I understood why. The top half of the
mother's dorsal fin was missing. I couldn't believe it! It was Chopper, a
dolphin we had seen eight years earlier when she was only a juvenile.

155

Now she was an adult and had a calf of her own. She was one of many dolphins I would recognize from earlier times.

4   Julia swam over my shoulder carrying a bright red scarf. She dropped the scarf and swam back toward me. Then, just as the dolphins noticed it, Julia swam quickly back, grabbed the scarf, and made a big show of swimming away with it. The dolphins caught on fast. The next time Julia dropped the scarf the dolphins gave her no chance to retrieve it. A group of 20 or more rushed toward the scarf and the fastest one caught it on his pectoral fin. Somewhat less quickly than the animals, I realized we were playing "keep away." Julia, Hardy, several other divers, and I spent the next ten minutes trying to take the scarf from the dolphins. Of course, our swimming skills were non-existent compared to theirs, but they compensated by bringing the scarf to within inches of our fingertips.

5   The dolphin carrying the scarf would pass it from nose, to pectoral fin, to tail flukes with remarkable dexterity even while swimming at high speed. When a dolphin released the scarf, the other members of the group would compete for it at their top speed. Every time the scarf was dropped, we divers would go for it as fast as we could. This effort would have been futile except the dolphins seemed to have given us a handicap and would occasionally let one of us win. Once I even managed to take the scarf off the dolphin's pectoral fin! This was a remarkable demonstration of their physical control since the dolphins never permitted me to actually touch them.

6   I soon realized the dolphins had established rules to the game. Once a dolphin had the scarf it was his/hers until he/she chose to pass it on. No other dolphin would take it. Other dolphins would rub up against the scarf as it was carried by another, or even bite it, but it was against the rules to take it until released. Once released it was up for grabs, but it seemed understood that occasionally the divers should be given a turn.

7   We played "keep away" for nearly four hours. Although the dolphins seemed to be just warming up, we were exhausted. We swam back to the boat; trying to ignore the scarf that was being trailed on a dolphin's tail flukes right before our noses. The dolphins finally departed as the last diver dragged himself up on the swim step. As I watched the school swim away, silhouetted against the white sand below the boat, one dolphin broke away, turned and swam back toward the boat. It made a quick pass by the swim step to drop off the red scarf.

8   In the weeks that followed the dolphins allowed me to swim with them as they hunted for food, nursed their young, and played games among themselves. Often juveniles would repeat the "keep away" game using a frond of seaweed. At the time I felt rather pleased we had managed to teach the dolphins a new pastime. But in retrospect, I'm not so sure they would see it that way. Dolphins with brains as large

and as complex as our own have lived on this planet millions of years longer than we. It's quite possible the dolphins believe they taught us the game. And, I'm not sure they wouldn't be right.

✦ *Questions for Discussion and Writing*

1. What means does Hall use to let the audience share his anticipation?

2. How did the game known as "keep away" originate and evolve? What are the rules?

3. What experiences did Hall have that led him to conclude that dolphins possessed intelligence? To what extent do you agree with his evaluations of these experiences?

4. Have you ever had experiences with an animal in a game that led you to conclude it possessed intelligence beyond simple instinct? Describe these experiences and your conclusions.

E. B. White

Death of a Pig

◆───────────◆

Born Elwyn Brooks White in Mt. Vernon, New York, in 1899, the distinguished essayist graduated from Cornell University in 1922. He became an editor at The New Yorker *magazine in 1929. White's collections of essays include* One Man's Meat *(1942),* The Second Tree from the Corner *(1954), and* Essays *(1977). He is also the author of children's books, including the well-known* Stuart Little *and* Charlotte's Web. *In 1959, E. B. White and William Strunk, Jr. coauthored the influential guide* The Elements of Style. *As "Death of a Pig" reveals, E. B. White was familiar with every aspect of farm life, having lived on one in southern Maine for most of his life.*

Autumn 1947

1 I spent several days and nights in mid-September with an ailing pig and I feel driven to account for this stretch of time, more particularly since the pig died at last, and I lived, and things might easily have gone the other way round and none left to do the accounting. Even now, so close to the event, I cannot recall the hours sharply and am not ready to say whether death came on the third night or the fourth night. This uncertainty afflicts me with a sense of personal deterioration; if I were in decent health I would know how many nights I had sat up with a pig.

2 The scheme of buying a spring pig in blossomtime, feeding it through summer and fall, and butchering it when the solid cold weather arrives, is a familiar scheme to me and follows an antique pattern. It is a tragedy enacted on most farms with perfect fidelity to the original script. The murder, being premeditated, is in the first degree but is quick and skillful, and the smoked bacon and ham provide a ceremonial ending whose fitness is seldom questioned.

3 Once in a while something slips—one of the actors goes up in his lines and the whole performance stumbles and halts. My pig simply failed to show up for a meal. The alarm spread rapidly. The classic outline of the tragedy was lost. I found myself cast suddenly in the role of pig's friend and physician—a farcical character with an enema bag for a prop. I had a presentiment, the very first afternoon, that the play would never regain its balance and that my sympathies were now wholly with the pig. This was slapstick—the sort of dramatic treatment

158

that instantly appealed to my old dachshund, Fred, who joined the vigil, held the bag, and, when all was over, presided at the interment. When we slid the body into the grave, we both were shaken to the core. The loss we felt was not the loss of ham but the loss of pig. He had evidently become precious to me, not that he represented a distant nourishment in a hungry time, but that he had suffered in a suffering world. But I'm running ahead of my story and shall have to go back.

4   My pigpen is at the bottom of an old orchard below the house. The pigs I have raised have lived in a faded building that once was an icehouse. There is a pleasant yard to move about in, shaded by an apple tree that overhangs the low rail fence. A pig couldn't ask for anything better—or none has, at any rate. The sawdust in the icehouse makes a comfortable bottom in which to root, and a warm bed. This sawdust, however, came under suspicion when the pig took sick. One of my neighbors said he thought the pig would have done better on new ground—the same principle that applies in planting potatoes. He said there might be something unhealthy about that sawdust, that he never thought well of sawdust.

5   It was about four o'clock in the afternoon when I first noticed that there was something wrong with the pig. He failed to appear at the trough for his supper, and when a pig (or a child) refuses supper a chill wave of fear runs through any household, or ice-household. After examining my pig, who was stretched out in the sawdust inside the building, I went to the phone and cranked it four times. Mr. Dameron answered. "What's good for a sick pig?" I asked. (There is never any identification needed on a country phone; the person on the other end knows who is talking by the sound of the voice and by the character of the question.)

6   "I don't know, I never had a sick pig," said Mr. Dameron, "but I can find out quick enough. You hang up and I'll call Henry."

7   Mr. Dameron was back on the line again in five minutes. "Henry says roll him over on his back and give him two ounces of castor oil or sweet oil, and if that doesn't do the trick give him an injection of soapy water. He says he's almost sure the pig's plugged up, and even if he's wrong, it can't do any harm."

8   I thanked Mr. Dameron. I didn't go right down to the pig, though. I sank into a chair and sat still for a few minutes to think about my troubles, and then I got up and went to the barn, catching up on some odds and ends that needed tending to. Unconsciously I held off, for an hour, the deed by which I would officially recognize the collapse of the performance of raising a pig; I wanted no interruption in the regularity of feeding, the steadiness of growth, the even succession of days. I wanted no interruption, wanted no oil, no deviation. I just wanted to keep on raising a pig, full meal after full meal, spring into summer into fall. I didn't even know whether there were two ounces of castor oil on the place.

9   Shortly after five o'clock I remembered that we had been invited out to dinner that night and realized that if I were to dose a pig there was no time to lose. The dinner date seemed a familiar conflict: I move in a desultory society and often a week or two will roll by without my going to anybody's house to dinner or anyone's coming to mine, but when an occasion does arise, and I am summoned, something usually turns up (an hour or two in advance) to make all human intercourse seem vastly inappropriate. I have come to believe that there is in hostesses a special power of divination, and that they deliberately arrange dinners to coincide with pig failure or some other sort of failure. At any rate, it was after five o'clock and I knew I could put off no longer the evil hour.

10   When my son and I arrived at the pigyard, armed with a small bottle of castor oil and a length of clothesline, the pig had emerged from his house and was standing in the middle of his yard, listlessly. He gave us a slim greeting. I could see that he felt uncomfortable and uncertain. I had brought the clothesline thinking I'd have to tie him (the pig weighed more than a hundred pounds) but we never used it. My son reached down, grabbed both front legs, upset him quickly, and when he opened his mouth to scream I turned the oil into his throat—a pink, corrugated area I had never seen before. I had just time to read the label while the neck of the bottle was in his mouth. It said Puretest. The screams, slightly muffled by oil, were pitched in the hysterically high range of pig-sound, as though torture were being carried out, but they didn't last long: it was all over rather suddenly, and, his legs released, the pig righted himself.

11   In the upset position the corners of his mouth had been turned down, giving him a frowning expression. Back on his feet again, he regained the set smile that a pig wears even in sickness. He stood his ground, sucking slightly at the residue of oil; a few drops leaked out of his lips while his wicked eyes, shaded by their coy little lashes, turned on me in disgust and hatred. I scratched him gently with oily fingers and he remained quiet, as though trying to recall the satisfaction of being scratched when in health, and seeming to rehearse in his mind the indignity to which he had just been subjected. I noticed, as I stood there, four or five small dark spots on his back near the tail end, brown in color, each about the size of a housefly. I could not make out what they were. They did not look troublesome but at the same time they did not look like mere surface bruises or chafe marks. Rather they seemed blemishes of internal origin. His stiff white bristles almost completely hid them and I had to part the bristles with my fingers to get a good look.

12   Several hours later, a few minutes before midnight, having dined well and at someone else's expense, I returned to the pighouse with a flashlight. The patient was asleep. Kneeling, I felt his ears (as you

might put your hand on the forehead of a child) and they seemed cool, and then with the light made a careful examination of the yard and the house for sign that the oil had worked. I found none and went to bed.

We had been having an unseasonable spell of weather—hot, close   13 days, with the fog shutting in every night, scaling for a few hours in midday, then creeping back again at dark, drifting in first over the trees on the point, then suddenly blowing across the fields, blotting out the world and taking possession of houses, men, and animals. Everyone kept hoping for a break, but the break failed to come. Next day was another hot one. I visited the pig before breakfast and tried to tempt him with a little milk in his trough. He just stared at it, while I made a sucking sound through my teeth to remind him of past pleasures of the feast. With very small, timid pigs, weanlings, this ruse is often quite successful and will encourage them to eat, but with a large, sick pig the ruse is senseless and the sound I made must have made him feel, if anything, more miserable. He not only did not crave food, he felt a positive revulsion to it. I found a place under the apple tree where he had vomited in the night.

At this point, although a depression had settled over me, I didn't   14 suppose that I was going to lose my pig. From the lustiness of a healthy pig a man derives a feeling of personal lustiness; the stuff that goes into the trough and is received with such enthusiasm is an earnest of some later feast of his own, and when this suddenly comes to an end and the food lies stale and untouched, souring in the sun, the pig's imbalance becomes the man's, vicariously, and life seems insecure, displaced, transitory.

As my own spirits declined, along with the pig's, the spirits of my   15 vile old dachshund rose. The frequency of our trips down the footpath through the orchard to the pigyard delighted him, although he suffers greatly from arthritis, moves with difficulty, and would be bedridden if he could find anyone willing to serve him meals on a tray.

He never missed a chance to visit the pig with me, and he made   16 many professional calls on his own. You could see him down there at all hours, his white face parting the grass along the fence as he wobbled and stumbled about, his stethoscope dangling—a happy quack, writing his villainous prescriptions and grinning his corrosive grin. When the enema bag appeared, and the bucket of warm suds, his happiness was complete, and he managed to squeeze his enormous body between the two lowest rails of the yard and then assumed full charge of the irrigation. Once, when I lowered the bag to check the flow, he reached in and hurriedly drank a few mouthfuls of the suds to test their potency. I have noticed that Fred will feverishly consume any substance that is associated with trouble—the bitter flavor is to his liking. When the bag was above reach, he concentrated on the pig and was everywhere at once, a tower of strength and inconvenience. The pig, curiously enough, stood rather quietly through this colonic carnival, and the enema, though ineffective, was not as difficult as I had anticipated.

17   I discovered, though, that once having given a pig an enema there is no going back, no chance of resuming one of life's more stereotyped roles. The pig's lot and mine were inextricably bound now, as though the rubber tube were the silver cord. From then until the time of his death I held the pig steadily in the bowl of my mind; the task of trying to deliver him from his misery became a strong obsession. His suffering soon became the embodiment of all earthly wretchedness. Along toward the end of the afternoon, defeated in physicking, I phoned the veterinary twenty miles away and placed the case formally in his hands. He was full of questions, and when I casually mentioned the dark spots on the pig's back, his voice changed its tone.

18   "I don't want to scare you," he said, "but when there are spots, erysipelas has to be considered."

19   Together we considered erysipelas, with frequent interruptions from the telephone operator, who wasn't sure the connection had been established.

20   "If a pig has erysipelas can he give it to a person?" I asked.

21   "Yes, he can," replied the vet.

22   "Have they answered?" asked the operator.

23   "Yes, they have," I said. Then I addressed the vet again. "You better come over here and examine this pig right away."

24   "I can't come myself," said the vet, "but McFarland can come this evening if that's all right. Mac knows more about pigs than I do anyway. You needn't worry too much about the spots. To indicate erysipelas they would have to be deep hemorrhagic infarcts."

25   "Deep hemmorrhagic what?" I asked.

26   "Infarcts," said the vet.

27   "Have they answered?" asked the operator.

28   "Well," I said, "I don't know what you'd call these spots, except they're about the size of a housefly. If the pig has erysipelas I guess I have it, too, by this time, because we've been very close lately,"

29   "McFarland will be over," said the vet.

30   I hung up. My throat felt dry and I went to the cupboard and got a bottle of whiskey. Deep hemorrhagic infarcts—the phrase began fastening its hooks in my head. I had assumed that there could be nothing much wrong with a pig during the months it was being groomed for murder; my confidence in the essential health and endurance of pigs had been strong and deep, particularly in the health of pigs that belonged to me and that were part of my proud scheme. The awakening had been violent and I minded it all the more because I knew that what could be true of my pig could be true also of the rest of my tidy world.

I tried to put this distasteful idea from me, but it kept recurring. I took a short drink of the whiskey and then, although I wanted to go down to the yard and look for fresh signs, I was scared to. I was certain I had erysipelas.

It was long after dark and the supper dishes had been put away when a car drove in and McFarland got out. He had a girl with him. I could just make her out in the darkness—she seemed young and pretty. "This is Miss Owen," he said. "We've been having a picnic supper on the shore, that's why I'm late." 31

McFarland stood in the driveway and stripped off his jacket, then his shirt. His stocky arms and capable hands showed up in my flashlight's gleam as I helped him find his coverall and get zipped up. The rear seat of his car contained an astonishing amount of paraphernalia, which he soon overhauled, selecting a chain, a syringe, a bottle of oil, a rubber tube, and some other things I couldn't identify. Miss Owen said she'd go along with us and see the pig. I led the way down the warm slope of the orchard, my light picking out the path for them, and we all three climbed the fence, entered the pighouse, and squatted by the pig while McFarland took a rectal reading. My flashlight picked up the glitter of an engagement ring on the girl's hand. 32

"No elevation," said McFarland, twisting the thermometer in the light. "You needn't worry about erysipelas." He ran his hand slowly over the pig's stomach and at one point the pig cried out in pain. 33

"Poor piggledy-wiggledy!" said Miss Owen. 34

The treatment I had been giving the pig for two days was then repeated, somewhat more expertly, by the doctor, Miss Owen and I handing him things as he needed them—holding the chain that he had looped around the pig's upper jaw, holding the syringe, holding the bottle stopper, the end of the tube, all of us working in darkness and in comfort, working with the instinctive teamwork induced by emergency conditions, the pig unprotesting, the house shadowy, protecting, intimate. I went to bed tired but with a feeling of relief that I had turned over part of the responsibility of the case to a licensed doctor. I was beginning to think, though, that the pig was not going to live. 35

He died twenty-four hours later, or it might have been forty-eight—there is a blur in time here, and I may have lost or picked up a day in the telling and the pig one in the dying. At intervals during the last day I took cool fresh water down to him and at such times as he found the strength to get to his feet he would stand with head in the pail and snuffle his snout around. He drank a few sips but no more; yet it seemed to comfort him to dip his nose in water and bobble it about, sucking in and blowing out through his teeth. Much of the time, now, he lay indoors half buried in sawdust. Once, near the last, while I was 36 attending him I saw him try to make a bed for himself but he lacked the strength, and when he set his snout into the dust he was unable to plow even the little furrow he needed to lie down in.

37   He came out of the house to die. When I went down, before going to bed, he lay stretched in the yard a few feet from the door. I knelt, saw that he was dead, and left him there: his face had a mild look, expressive neither of deep peace nor of deep suffering, although I think he had suffered a good deal. I went back up to the house and to bed, and cried internally—deep hemorrhagic intears. I didn't wake till nearly eight the next morning, and when I looked out the open window the grave was already being dug, down beyond the dump under a wild apple. I could hear the spade strike against the small rocks that blocked the way. Never send to know for whom the grave is dug, I said to myself, it's dug for thee. Fred, I well knew, was supervising the work of digging, so I ate breakfast slowly.

38   It was a Saturday morning. The thicket in which I found the gravediggers at work was dark and warm, the sky overcast. Here, among alders and young hackmatacks, at the foot of the apple tree, Lennie had dug a beautiful hole, five feet long, three feet wide, three feet deep. He was standing in it, removing the last spadefuls of earth while Fred patrolled the brink in simple but impressive circles, disturbing the loose earth of the mound so that it trickled back in. There had been no rain in weeks and the soil, even three feet down, was dry and powdery. As I stood and stared, an enormous earthworm which had been partially exposed by the spade at the bottom dug itself deeper and made a slow withdrawal, seeking even remoter moistures at even lonelier depths. And just as Lennie stepped out and rested his spade against the tree and lit a cigarette, a small green apple separated itself from a branch overhead and fell into the hole. Everything about this last scene seemed overwritten—the dismal sky, the shabby woods, the imminence of rain, the worm (legendary bedfellow of the dead), the apple (conventional garnish of a pig).

39   But even so, there was a directness and dispatch about animal burial, I thought, that made it a more decent affair than human burial: there was no stopover in the undertaker's foul parlor, no wreath nor spray; and when we hitched a line to the pig's hind legs and dragged him swiftly from his yard, throwing our weight into the harness and leaving a wake of crushed grass and smoothed rubble over the dump, ours was a businesslike procession, with Fred, the dishonorable pallbearer, staggering along in the rear, his perverse bereavement showing in every seam in his face; and the postmortem performed handily and swiftly right at the edge of the grave, so that the inwards that had caused the pig's death preceded him into the ground and he lay at last resting squarely on the cause of his own undoing.

I threw in the first shovelful, and then we worked rapidly and 40
without talk, until the job was complete. I picked up the rope, made it
fast to Fred's collar (he is a notorious ghoul), and we all three filed back
up the path to the house, Fred bringing up the rear and holding back
every inch of the way, feigning unusual stiffness. I noticed that although he weighed far less than the pig, he was harder to drag, being
possessed of the vital spark.

The news of the death of my pig traveled fast and far, and I re- 41
ceived many expressions of sympathy from friends and neighbors, for
no one took the event lightly and the premature expiration of a pig is, I
soon discovered, a departure which the community marks solemnly on
its calendar, a sorrow in which it feels fully involved. I have written this
account in penitence and in grief, as a man who failed to raise his pig,
and to explain my deviation from the classic course of so many raised
pigs. The grave in the woods is unmarked, but Fred can direct the
mourner to it unerringly and with immense good will, and I know he
and I shall often revisit it, singly and together, in seasons of reflection
and despair, on flagless memorial days of our own choosing.

✦ Questions for Discussion and Writing

1. What motivates White to provide this account of the time he spent
   with his sick pig?

2. Of what significance is the dog, Fred, in this account?

3. How does the shift in tone from the beginning to the end of this essay
   underscore the larger implications White explores?

4. What function do literary allusions play in White's essay?

5. Have you ever experienced the death of a pet? Describe the circumstances, your feelings, and the larger implications apparent at the time
   or later.

6. Do you know someone whose pet expresses important, but submerged, aspects of its owner's personality? If so, describe both the person and the pet, and discuss the hidden traits that connect them (e.g., a
   person, with a meek, timid, and retiring nature who owns a pit bull).

Connections

1. How does anthropomorphism enter into the accounts by Jane van Lawick-Goodall and E. B. White?

2. How do the accounts by Jean Henri Fabre and Howard Hall reveal surprising behavior in insects and animals that points out differences between instinct and intelligence?

3. What role do precise observations play in establishing the credibility of the conclusions drawn by Jean Henri Fabre and Sir Leonard Woolley ("The Flood," Chapter 9)?

4. How do the accounts by Jane van Lawick-Goodall and Peter Matthiessen ("The Snow Leopard," Chapter 11) differ in the way in which they see animals within a scientific or metaphysical context?

5. How do the narratives of E. B. White and Aldo Leopold ("Thinking Like a Mountain," Chapter 9) reveal an unsuspected meaning and value for the pig and wolf, respectively?

5

Coming of Age

---◆---

The old believe everything. The middle-aged suspect everything.
The young know everything.
—Oscar Wilde, *The Picture of Dorian Gray*, 1890

The idea of coming of age has been a well-defined theme in autobiographical writing from *The Confessions of St. Augustine* (circa A.D. 397–
401) onward. In these accounts writers explore decisive moments of insight and illumination as they gaze back into the past from the perspective of the present. The process by which writers perceive or confer a
measure of order and coherence on past experiences is fascinating to
observe. The psychological honesty of these accounts is perhaps their
most striking feature.

Each essay in this chapter reveals a willingness to dispense with a
false image of oneself in the interest of gaining greater self-knowledge
and psychological insight. These moments of insight may be private
psychological turning points, or they may occur in the context of communal rites of passage. In this chapter, individuals move from a childhood innocence to an adult awareness, which often involves learning a
particular society's rules, values, and expectations. In the process of
growing up, people often assert their individuality by defining themselves in opposition to the values held by the societies in which they live.

Nora Ephron's experiences at the threshold of puberty, retold in "A
Few Words About Breasts," make for poignant and funny reading. In
"So This Was Adolescence," Annie Dillard explores the maelstrom of
emotions all teenagers experience. Richard Rhodes confronts the life-
long consequences of being abused as a child in "A Hole in the World."
An adventure turns life threatening in Douchan Gersi's account of his
encounter in Borneo in "Initiated into an Iban Tribe of Headhunters."
Barbara Grizzuti Harrison, in "Growing Up Apocalyptic," reveals the
psychological pressures that come from being raised among fervent
Jehovah's Witnesses.

167

Nora Ephron

A Few Words About Breasts

◆

Nora Ephron, born in 1941, attended Wellesley College and began her writing career as a reporter for The New York Post. *She became a columnist for* Esquire *magazine in 1972 and was named a senior editor in 1974. With Alice Arlen, she wrote the screenplay for* Silkwood *(1983), which was nominated for an Academy Award. Working on her own, Ephron wrote the screenplays for* When Harry Met Sally *(1989) and* Sleepless in Seattle *(1993), which she also directed. Her collected essays on popular culture include* Wallflower at the Orgy *(1970) and* Crazy Salad *(1975), the latter of which contains "A Few Words About Breasts."*

1   I have to begin with a few words about androgyny. In grammar school, in the fifth and sixth grades, we were all tyrannized by a rigid set of rules that supposedly determined whether we were boys or girls. The episode in *Huckleberry Finn* where Huck is disguised as a girl and gives himself away by the way he threads a needle and catches a ball—that kind of thing. We learned that the way you sat, crossed your legs, held a cigarette and looked at your nails, your wristwatch, the way you did these things instinctively was absolute proof of your sex. Now obviously most children did not take this literally, but I did. I thought that just one slip, just one incorrect cross of my legs or flick of an imaginary cigarette ash would turn me from whatever I was into the other thing; that would be all it took, really. Even though I was outwardly a girl and had many of the trappings generally associated with the field of girl-dom—a girl's name, for example, and dresses, my own telephone, an autograph book—I spent the early years of my adolescence absolutely certain that I might at any point gum it up. I did not feel at all like a girl. I was boyish. I was athletic, ambitious, outspoken, competitive, noisy, rambunctious. I had scabs on my knees and my socks slid into my loafers and I could throw a football. I wanted desperately not to be that way, not to be a mixture of both things but instead just one, a girl, a definite indisputable girl. As soft and as pink as a nursery. And nothing would do that for me, I felt, but breasts.

2   I was about six months younger than everyone in my class, and so for about six months after it began, for six months after my friends had begun to develop—that was the word we used, *develop*—I was not particularly worried. I would sit in the bathtub and look down at my breasts and know that any day now, any second now, they would start

168

growing like everyone else's. They didn't. "I want to buy a bra," I said to my mother one night. "What for?" she said. My mother was really hateful about bras, and by the time my third sister had gotten to that point where she was ready to want one, my mother had worked the whole business into a comedy routine, "Why not use a Band-Aid instead?" she would say. It was a source of great pride to my mother that she had never even had to wear a brassiere until she had her fourth child, and then only because her gynecologist made her. It was incomprehensible to me that anyone would ever be proud of something like that. It was the 1950s, for God's sake. Jane Russell. Cashmere sweaters. Couldn't my mother see that? *"I am too old to wear an undershirt."* Screaming. Weeping. Shouting. "Then don't wear an undershirt," said my mother. "But I want to buy a bra." "What for?"

I suppose that for most girls, breasts, brassieres, that entire thing,   3 has more trauma, more to do with the coming of adolescence, of becoming a woman, than anything else. Certainly more than getting your period, although that too was traumatic, symbolic. But you could *see* breasts; they were there; they were visible. Whereas a girl could claim to have her period for months before she actually got it and nobody would ever know the difference. Which is exactly what I did. All you had to do was make a great fuss over having enough nickels for the Kotex machine and walk around clutching your stomach and moaning for three to five days a month about The Curse and you could convince anybody. There is a school of thought somewhere in the women's lib/ women's mag/gynecology establishment that claims that menstrual cramps are purely psychological, and I lean toward it. Not that I didn't have them finally. Agonizing cramps, heating-pad cramps, go-down-to-the-school-nurse-and-lie-on-the-cot cramps. But unlike any pain I had ever suffered, I adored the pain of cramps, welcomed it, wallowed in it, bragged about it. "I can't go. I have cramps." "I can't do that. I have cramps." And most of all, gigglingly, blushingly: "I can't swim. I have cramps." Nobody ever used the hard-core word. Menstruation. God, what an awful word. Never that. "I have cramps."

The morning I first got my period, I went into my mother's bed-   4 room to tell her. And my mother, my utterly-hateful-about-bras mother, burst into tears. It was really a lovely moment, and I remember it so clearly not just because it was one of the two times I ever saw my mother cry on my account (the other was when I was caught being a six-year-old kleptomaniac), but also because the incident did not mean to me what it meant to her. Her little girl, her firstborn, had finally become a woman. That was what she was crying about. My reaction to the event, however, was that I might well be a woman in some scientific, textbook sense (and could at least stop faking every month and stop wasting all those nickels). But in another sense—in a visible sense—I was as androgynous and as liable to tip over into boyhood as ever.

5   I started with a 28AA bra. I don't think they made them any
smaller in those days, although I gather that now you can buy bras for
five year olds that don't have any cups whatsoever in them; trainer
bras they are called. My first brassiere came from Robinson's Department Store in Beverly Hills. I went there alone, shaking, positive they
would look me over and smile and tell me to come back next year. An
actual fitter took me into the dressing room and stood over me while I
took off my blouse and tried the first one on. The little puffs stood out
on my chest. "Lean over," said the fitter (to this day I am not sure what
fitters in bra departments do except to tell you to lean over). I leaned
over, with the fleeting hope that my breasts would miraculously fall
out of my body and into the puffs. Nothing.

6   "Don't worry about it," said my friend Libby some months later,
when things had not improved. "You'll get them after you're married."

7   "What are you talking about?" I said.

8   "When you get married," Libby explained, "your husband will
touch your breasts and rub them and kiss them and they'll grow."

9   That was the killer. Necking I could deal with. Intercourse I could
deal with. But it had never crossed my mind that a man was going to
touch my breasts, that breasts had something to do with all that, petting, my God they never mentioned petting in my little sex manual
about the fertilization of the ovum. I became dizzy. For I knew instantly—as naive as I had been only a moment before—that only part
of what she was saying was true: the touching, rubbing, kissing part,
not the growing part. And I knew that no one would ever want to
marry me. I had no breasts. I would never have breasts.

10   My best friend in school was Diana Raskob. She lived a block from
me in a house full of wonders. English muffins, for instance. The
Raskobs were the first people in Beverly Hills to have English muffins
for breakfast. They also had an apricot tree in the back, and a badminton
court, and a subscription to *Seventeen* magazine, and hundreds of games
like Sorry and Parcheesi and Treasure Hunt and Anagrams. Diana and I
spent three or four afternoons a week in their den reading and playing
and eating. Diana's mother's kitchen was full of the most colossal assortment of junk food I have ever been exposed to. My house was full of
apples and peaches and milk and homemade chocolate-chip cookies—
which were nice, and good for you, but-not-right-before-dinner-or-
you'll-spoil-your-appetite. Diana's house had nothing in it that was
good for you, and what's more, you could stuff it in right up until dinner and nobody cared. Bar-B-Q potato chips (they were the first in them,
too), giant bottles of ginger ale, fresh popcorn with melted butter, hot
fudge sauce on Baskin-Robbins jamoca ice cream, powdered-sugar
doughnuts from Van de Kamps. Diana and I had been best friends since

we were seven; we were about equally popular in school (which is to say, not particularly), we had about the same success with boys (extremely intermittent), and we looked much the same. Dark. Tall. Gangly.

It is September, just before school begins. I am eleven years old, 11 about to enter the seventh grade, and Diana and I have not seen each other all summer. I have been to camp and she has been somewhere like Banff with her parents. We are meeting, as we often do, on the street midway between our two houses and we will walk back to Diana's and eat junk and talk about what has happened to each of us that summer. I am walking down Walden Drive in my jeans and my father's shirt hanging out and my old red loafers with the socks falling into them and coming toward me is...I take a deep breath...a young woman. Diana. Her hair is curled and she has a waist and hips and a bust and she is wearing a straight skirt, an article of clothing I have been repeatedly told I will be unable to wear until I have the hips to hold it up. My jaw drops, and suddenly I am crying, crying hysterically, can't catch my breath sobbing. My best friend has betrayed me. She has gone ahead without me and done it. She has shaped up.

Here are some things I did to help: 12
Bought a Mark Eden Bust Developer. 13
Slept on my back for four years. 14
Splashed cold water on them every night because some French ac- 15 tress said in *Life* magazine that that was what she did for her perfect bustline.

Ultimately, I resigned myself to a bad toss and began to wear pad- 16 ded bras. I think about them now, think about all those years in high school I went around in them, my three padded bras, every single one of them with different sized breasts. Each time I changed bras I changed sizes: one week nice perky but not too obtrusive breasts, the next medium-sized slightly pointed ones, the next week knockers, true knockers; all the time, whatever size I was, carrying around this rubberized appendage on my chest that occasionally crashed into a wall and was poked inward and had to be poked outward—I think about all that and wonder how anyone kept a straight face through it. My parents, who normally had no restraints about needling me—why did they say nothing as they watched my chest go up and down? My friends, who would periodically inspect my breasts for signs of growth and reassure me—why didn't they at least counsel consistency?

And the bathing suits. I die when I think about the bathing suits. 17 That was the era when you could lay an uninhabited bathing suit on the beach and someone would make a pass at it. I would put one on, an absurd swimsuit with its enormous bust built into it, the bones from the suit stabbing me in the rib cage and leaving little red welts on my body, and there I would be, my chest plunging straight downward absolutely vertically from my collarbone to the top of my suit and then suddenly, wham, out came all that padding and material and wiring absolutely horizontally.

18   Buster Klepper was the first boy who ever touched them. He was my boyfriend my senior year of high school. There is a picture of him in my high-school yearbook that makes him look quite attractive in a Jewish, horn-rimmed glasses sort of way, but the picture does not show the pimples, which were air-brushed out, or the dumbness. Well, that isn't really fair. He wasn't dumb. He just wasn't terribly bright. His mother refused to accept it, refused to accept the relentlessly average report cards, refused to deal with her son's inevitable destiny in some junior college or other. "He was tested," she would say to me, apropos of nothing, "and it came out 145. That's near-genius." Had the word underachiever been coined, she probably would have lobbed that one at me, too. Anyway, Buster was really very sweet—which is, I know, damning with faint praise, but there it is. I was the editor of the front page of the high-school newspaper and he was editor of the back page; we had to work together, side by side, in the print shop, and that was how it started. On our first date, we went to see *April Love* starring Pat Boone. Then we started going together. Buster had a green coupe, a 1950 Ford with an engine he had handchromed until it shone, dazzled, reflected the image of anyone who looked into it, anyone usually being Buster polishing it or the gas-station attendants he constantly asked to check the oil in order for them to be overwhelmed by the sparkle on the valves. The car also had a boot stretched over the back seat for reasons I never understood; hanging from the rearview mirror, as was the custom, was a pair of angora dice. A previous girlfriend named Solange who was famous throughout Beverly Hills High School for having no pigment in her right eyebrow had knitted them for him. Buster and I would ride around town, the two of us seated to the left of the steering wheel. I would shift gears. It was nice.

19   There was necking. Terrific necking. First in the car, overlooking Los Angeles from what is now the Trousdale Estates. Then on the bed of his parents' cabana at Ocean House. Incredibly wonderful, frustrating necking, I loved it, really, but no further than necking, please don't, please, because there I was absolutely terrified of the general implications of going-a-step-further with a near-dummy and also terrified of his finding out there was next to nothing there (which he knew, of course; he wasn't that dumb).

20   I broke up with him at one point. I think we were apart for about two weeks. At the end of that time I drove down to see a friend at a boarding school in Palos Verdes Estates and a disc jockey played "April Love" on the radio four times during the trip. I took it as a sign. I drove straight back to Griffith Park to a golf tournament Buster was playing

in (he was the sixth-seeded teenage golf player in Southern California) and presented myself back to him on the green of the 18th hole. It was all very dramatic. That night we went to a drive-in and I let him get his hand under my protuberances and onto my breasts. He really didn't seem to mind at all.

"Do you want to marry my son?" the woman asked me.   21

"Yes," I said.   22

I was nineteen years old, a virgin, going with this woman's son, this big   23
strange woman who was married to a Lutheran minister in New Hampshire
and pretended she was Gentile and had this son, by her first husband, this total
fool of a son who ran the hero-sandwich concession at Harvard Business
School and whom for one moment one December in New Hampshire I said—
as much out of politeness as anything else—that I wanted to marry.

"Fine," she said. "Now, here's what you do. Always make sure you're on   24
top of him so you won't seem so small. My bust is very large, you see, so I al-
ways lie on my back to make it look smaller, but you'll have to be on top most
of the time."

I nodded. "Thank you," I said.   25

"I have a book for you to read," she went on. "Take it with you when you   26
leave. Keep it." She went to the bookshelf, found it, and gave it to me. It was a
book on frigidity.

"Thank you," I said.   27

That is a true story. Everything in this article is a true story, but I   28
feel I have to point out that that story in particular is true. It happened on December 30, 1960. I think about it often. When it first happened, I naturally assumed that the woman's son, my boyfriend, was responsible. I invented a scenario where he had had a little heart-to-heart with his mother and confessed that his only objection to me was that my breasts were small; his mother then took it upon herself to help out. Now I think I was wrong about the incident. The mother was acting on her own, I think: That was her way of being cruel and competitive under the guise of being helpful and maternal. You have small breasts, she was saying; therefore you will never make him as happy as I have. Or you have small breasts; therefore you will doubtless have sexual problems. Or you have small breasts; therefore you are less woman than I am. She was, as it happens, only the first of what seems to me to be a never-ending string of women who have made competitive remarks to me about breast size. "I would love to wear a dress like that," my friend Emily says to me, "but my bust is too big." Like that. Why do women say these things to me? Do I attract these remarks the way other women attract married men or alcoholics or homosexuals? This summer, for example. I am at a party in East Hampton and I am introduced to a woman from Washington. She is a minor celebrity, very pretty and Southern and blonde and outspoken and I am flattered because she has

read something I have written. We are talking animatedly, we have been talking no more than five minutes, when a man comes up to join us. "Look at the two of us," the woman says to the man, indicating me and her. "The two of us together couldn't fill an A cup." Why does she say that? It isn't even true, dammit, so why? Is she even more addled than I am on this subject? Does she honestly believe there is something wrong with her size breasts, which, it seems to me, now that I look hard at them, are just right? Do I unconsciously bring out competitiveness in women? In that form? What did I do to deserve it?

29   As for men.

30   There were men who minded and let me know they minded. There were men who did not mind. In any case, I always minded.

31   And even now, now that I have been countlessly reassured that my figure is a good one, now that I am grown up enough to understand that most of my feelings have very little to do with the reality of my shape, I am nonetheless obsessed by breasts. I cannot help it. I grew up in the terrible Fifties—with rigid stereotypical sex roles, the insistence that men be men and dress like men and women be women and dress like women, the intolerance of androgyny—and I cannot shake it, cannot shake my feelings of inadequacy. Well, that time is gone, right? All those exaggerated examples of breast worship are gone, right? Those women were freaks, right? I know all that. And yet, here I am, stuck with the psychological remains of it all, stuck with my own peculiar version of breast worship. You probably think I am crazy to go on like this: Here I have set out to write a confession that is meant to hit you with the shock of recognition and instead you are sitting there thinking I am thoroughly warped. Well, what can I tell you? If I had had them, I would have been a completely different person. I honestly believe that.

32   After I went into therapy, a process that made it possible for me to tell total strangers at cocktail parties that breasts were the hang-up of my life, I was often told that I was insane to have been bothered by my condition. I was also frequently told, by close friends, that I was extremely boring on the subject. And my girlfriends, the ones with nice big breasts, would go on endlessly about how their lives had been far more miserable than mine. Their bra straps were snapped in class. They couldn't sleep on their stomachs. They were stared at whenever the word *mountain* cropped up in geography. And *Evangeline*, good God what they went through every time someone had to stand up and recite the Prologue to Longfellow's *Evangeline*: *". . . stand like druids of eld . . . / With beards that rest on their bosoms."* It was much worse for them, they tell me. They had a terrible time of it, they assure me. I don't know how lucky I was, they say.

I have thought about their remarks, tried to put myself in their   33
place, considered their point of view. I think they are full of shit.

✦ Questions for Discussion and Writing

1. What does having breasts mean to Ephron? How did Ephron's experience lead her to understand the role culture plays in shaping gender expectations?

2. How would you characterize Ephron's relationship with Buster and with his mother?

3. What function does her description of her friendship with Diana Raskob play in Ephron's account?

4. Do your own experiences or those of your friends suggest that Ephron's observations are still valid?

5. You have brought home a date, not necessarily of the opposite sex, to meet your family. How do you think they will react? Identify important characteristics of the individuals involved so that your readers will understand each person's reaction.

6. It was important for Ephron to gain detachment about things that seemed bizarre, confusing, or inconsistent to her when she was growing up. If you keep a journal, try returning to an incident that occured when you were growing up, and describe everything that happened as if it were a scene in a play. Gain detachment by using the third person for yourself, for what you saw through your eyes as a child, as well as for what you observed in the behavior of others.

Annie Dillard

So This Was Adolescence

————————◆————————

Annie Dillard, born in 1945, won the Pulitzer Prize in 1974 for her book Pilgrim at Tinker Creek. *She served as contributing editor to* Harper's *magazine between 1973 and 1982. Since 1979, Dillard has taught creative writing at Wesleyan University. Her more recent books include* The Writing Life *(1989) and her autobiography,* An American Childhood *(1987), from which "So This Was Adolescence" is drawn.*

1   When I was fifteen, I felt it coming; now I was sixteen, and it hit.

2   My feet had imperceptibly been set on a new path, a fast path into a long tunnel like those many turnpike tunnels near Pittsburgh, turnpike tunnels whose entrances bear on brass plaques a roll call of those men who died blasting them. I wandered witlessly forward and found myself going down, and saw the light dimming; I adjusted to the slant and dimness, traveled further down, adjusted to greater dimness, and so on. There wasn't a whole lot I could do about it, or about anything. I was going to hell on a handcart, that was all, and I knew it and everyone around me knew it, and there it was.

3   I was growing and thinning, as if pulled. I was getting angry, as if pushed. I morally disapproved most things in North America, and blamed my innocent parents for them. My feelings deepened and lingered. The swift moods of early childhood—each formed by and suited to its occasion—vanished. Now feelings lasted so long they left stains. They arose from nowhere, like winds or waves, and battered at me or engulfed me.

4   When I was angry, I felt myself coiled and longing to kill someone or bomb something big. Trying to appease myself, during one winter I whipped my bed every afternoon with my uniform belt. I despised the spectacle I made in my own eyes—whipping the bed with a belt, like a creature demented!—and I often began halfheartedly, but I did it daily after school as a desperate discipline, trying to rid myself and the innocent world of my wildness. It was like trying to beat back the ocean.

5   Sometimes in class I couldn't stop laughing; things were too funny to be borne. It began then, my surprise that no one else saw what was so funny.

I read some few books with such reverence I didn't close them at   6
the finish, but only moved the pile of pages back to the start, without
breathing, and began again. I read one such book, an enormous novel,
six times that way—closing the binding between sessions, but not between readings.

On the piano in the basement I played the maniacal "Poet and Peas-   7
ant Overture" so loudly, for so many hours, night after night, I damaged
the piano's keys and strings. When I wasn't playing this crashing overture, I played boogie-woogie, or something else, anything else, in oc-
taves—otherwise, it wasn't loud enough. My fingers were so strong I
could do push-ups with them. I played one piece with my fists. I banged
on a steel-stringed guitar till I bled, and once on a particularly piercing
rock-and-roll downbeat I broke through one of Father's snare drums.

I loved my boyfriend so tenderly, I thought I must transmogrify   8
into vapor. It would take spectroscopic analysis to locate my molecules
in thin air. No possible way of holding him was close enough. Nothing
could cure this bad case of gentleness except, perhaps, violence: maybe
if he swung me by the legs and split my skull on a tree? Would that ease
this insane wish to kiss too much his eyelids' outer corners and his tem-
ples, as if I could love up his brain?

I envied people in books who swooned. For two years I felt myself   9
continuously swooning and continuously unable to swoon; the blood
drained from my face and eyes and flooded my heart; my hands emptied, my knees unstrung, I bit at the air for something worth breathing—but I failed to fall, and I couldn't find the way to black out. I had
to live on the lip of a waterfall, exhausted.

When I was bored I was first hungry, then nauseated, then furious   10
and weak. "Calm yourself," people had been saying to me all my life.
Since early childhood I had tried one thing and then another to calm
myself, on those few occasions when I truly wanted to. Eating helped;
singing helped. Now sometimes I truly wanted to calm myself. I
couldn't lower my shoulders; they seemed to wrap around my ears. I
couldn't lower my voice although I could see the people around me
flinch. I waved my arm in class till the very teachers wanted to kill me.

I was what they called a live wire. I was shooting out sparks that   11
were digging a pit around me, and I was sinking into that pit. Laughing
with Ellin at school recess, or driving around after school with Judy in
her jeep, exultant, or dancing with my boyfriend to Louis Armstrong
across a polished dining-room floor, I got so excited I looked around
wildly for aid; I didn't know where I should go or what I should do
with myself. People in books split wood.

When rage or boredom reappeared, each seemed never to have left.   12
Each so filled me with so many years' intolerable accumulation it

jammed the space behind my eyes, so I couldn't see. There was no room left even on my surface to live. My rib cage was so taut I couldn't breathe. Every cubic centimeter of atmosphere above my shoulders and head was heaped with last straws. Black hatred clogged my very blood. I couldn't peep, I couldn't wiggle or blink; my blood was too mad to flow.

13   For as long as I could remember, I had been transparent to myself, unselfconscious, learning, doing, most of every day. Now I was in my own way; I myself was a dark object I could not ignore. I couldn't remember how to forget myself. I didn't want to think about myself, to reckon myself in, to deal with myself every livelong minute on top of everything else—but swerve as I might, I couldn't avoid it. I was a boulder blocking my own path. I was a dog barking between my own ears, a barking dog who wouldn't hush.

14   So this was adolescence. Is this how the people around me had died on their feet—inevitably, helplessly? Perhaps their own selves eclipsed the sun for so many years the world shriveled around them, and when at last their inescapable orbits had passed through these dark egoistic years it was too late, they had adjusted.

15   Must I then lose the world forever, that I had so loved? Was it all, the whole bright and various planet, where I had been so ardent about finding myself alive, only a passion peculiar to children, that I would outgrow even against my will?

✦ *Questions for Discussion and Writing*

1. What picture of her adolescence does Dillard create? Evaluate the effectiveness of the metaphors she uses to express her experiences.

2. How does Dillard understand the nature of the crisis she experienced during her adolescence, and how does her attitude towards it change over the course of the essay?

3. What images are especially effective in communicating her perception of this crisis to her readers?

4. Compare Dillard's adolescent experiences with your own. Does her sense of an emerging self differ from or confirm your experiences?

5. What actions (and reactions) are reliable indicators that a person is in love? How does this behavior differ from what it normally is? How do these differences demonstrate that he or she is in love? In your opin-

ion, is there a difference between loving a person and being "in love" with someone?

6. If you keep a journal, use it to return to moments when you were growing up in which you might have had, as Dillard did, fantasies that would have been inappropriate to express to others. Put a few of these down without censoring yourself. Describe any insight you gained by completing this activity.

Richard Rhodes

A Hole in the World

---◆---

Richard Rhodes was born in 1937 in Kansas City, Kansas. After graduating with honors from Yale University in 1959, he worked for Hallmark Cards, Inc. and as a contributing editor for Harper's *magazine and* Playboy *magazine. Rhodes is the author of more than fifty articles and ten books, including* Looking for America: A Writer's Odyssey *(1979) and the acclaimed* The Making of the Atomic Bomb *(1987), which won the Pulitzer Prize, the National Book Award, and the National Book Critics Circle Award. When he was thirteen years old, his mother committed suicide. His father remarried and tried to raise him and his older brother. Rhodes's account from his 1990 autobiography,* A Hole in the World, *shares an intensely personal story of childhood abuse at the hands of his stepmother.*

1   Slapping, kicking us, bashing our heads with a broom handle or a mop or the stiletto heel of a shoe, slashing our backs and the backs of our legs with the buckle of a belt, our stepmother exerted one kind of control over us, battery that was immediately coercive but intermittent and limited in effect. We cowered, cringed, screamed, wrapped our poor heads protectively in our arms, danced the belt-buckle tango, but out of sight and reach we recovered our boundaries more or less intact. The bodily memory of the blows, the heat of the abrasions, the caution of pain, the indignation and the smoldering rage only demarcated those boundaries more sharply. More effective control required undermining our boundaries from within. As diseases do, our stepmother sought to harness our physiology to her own ends. Compelling us to eat food we didn't like—cayenne gravy, mint jelly, moldy bread—is hardly more coercion than most parents impose, not that custom justifies it. Our stepmother tinkered more radically with manipulating what we took into our bodies and what we expelled. The techniques she developed led eventually to a full-scale assault.

2   Colds and tonsillitis frequently kept us home from school and underfoot. To help prevent that inconvenience she might have improved our diet. Instead she began dosing us mornings with cod-liver oil. Stanley swallowed it down. It nauseated me. It tasted like bad fish. I clamped my jaw and balked. Even her jerking and slapping didn't always prevail. She had to stop pounding me to move the tablespoon of

oil to my mouth and by then I'd clamped my jaw again. Every morning was a fight. Goaded by stalemate, she devised an alternative. I loved school. It was my escape into the wide world. She fettered that love to my daily dose of oil. She forbade me to go to school until I'd swallowed it. I resisted until the last possible moment and then gagged it down.

We polished off the cod-liver oil. She remembered a bottle of mineral oil left over in the bathroom closet. She must have thought the two oils were equally invigorating. She substituted one for the other. The mineral oil might have been an improvement, but it had absorbed the acrid taint of its Bakelite lid, a taste even more nauseating than cod liver. Worse, since mineral oil is indigestible, drops of oil now dispersed on the surface of the toilet water after my bowel movements. I understood the connection between the oil I was gagging down and the oil shimmering above my stool, but I thought the phenomenon was pathological. It anguished me for weeks. Finally, on a morning when she seemed uncharacteristically sympathetic, I dared to reveal my problem. She inspected the evidence. "Oh, that's just the mineral oil," she dismissed my fears airily, but she cut my dose and eventually gave up dosing us.

I no longer wet the bed, but I needed the toilet at night. The only bathroom in the house opened directly inside her bedroom door. I used it whenever I had to, sometimes more than once a night, until she announced one day in a fury that I was getting up at night unnecessarily and disturbing her sleep. I should make sure I relieved myself before I went to bed, she told me, because from then on I was forbidden to use the bathroom at night. "I married your *father*, not you," she added mysteriously. I understood her to mean she wanted to be alone with him at night. She meant more. "Kidneys move a good deal, gets up often during night," the social worker whom the juvenile court appointed wrote of me a year and a half later in her investigation report. "Step mother accused him of being curious to know what was going on." There was only one bathroom, and only one way to access it. If she thought I was spying on her sex life she could have supplied me with a chamber pot.

Telling someone *not* to do something to induce him to do it is a powerful form of suggestion. Dutifully I went to the bathroom just before climbing to my upper bunk on the north wall of the sleeping porch, but as soon as Stanley turned out the light and we settled down to sleep I felt my bladder fill. I lay awake then for hours. I tried to redirect my thoughts, tell myself stories, recite numbers, count sheep. I clamped my sphincters until they cramped and burned. Lying on my back, hurting and urgent, I cried silently to the ceiling low overhead, tears running down my face without consolation, only reminding me of the other flow of body fluid that my commandant had blocked. When clamping my sphincters no longer worked I pinched my penis to red pain.

6   Sometimes I fell asleep that way and slept through. Once or twice, early in the chronology of this torture, I wet the bed. That villainy erupted in such monstrous humiliation that I learned not to repeat it. Thereafter I added struggling to stay awake to struggling to retain my urine.

7   One desperate night I decided to urinate out the window. There were two windows in the porch back wall. They opened ten feet above the yard. I waited until I was sure Stanley was solidly asleep, climbed down my ladder and slipped to the nearer window. Two spring-loaded pins had to be pulled and held out simultaneously to open it. That wasn't easy to coordinate, especially since I was bent over with cramping. The window fit its frame badly. It jammed and squeaked going up. I forced it up six inches and then a foot—high enough—stood on tiptoe, my little penis barely reaching over the sill, and let go. I'd hoped the hydraulic pressure would be sufficient to drive the stream of urine through the screen, missing the ledge and the frame, but the angle was bad. I dribbled. My urine ran down the ledge and out under the screen frame. That meant it would leave a telltale stain down the outside wall. I tried forcing the stream into a higher arc and managed to pulse it in splashes through the screen. It sprayed out into the night air below a blank silver moon.

8   I'd barely begun when I heard noise—the bedroom door, footsteps in the dining room, the kitchen door swinging. I clamped off the flow in a panic—it was hard to stop—popped my dripping penis back into my pajamas, warm urine running down my leg, and stood at the window waiting. I prayed to God it wasn't my stepmother.

9   Dad stepped through the doorway, half awake. "What's going on?" he said softly.

10   "It was stuffy in here," I improvised. "I opened the window to get some air."

11   "You don't want to disturb your Aunt Anne," he told me. "Better close that thing and get back to bed."

12   I wasn't sure if he knew what I was doing or not. Probably not. I closed the window. He padded off. I'd managed to alleviate my urgency enough to get to sleep. To my amazement—I suppose I believed her omniscient—my stepmother only grumbled the next morning about people up at night prowling around. Even so, I knew I couldn't use the window anymore. I'd have to find some other way.

13   I had plenty of time at night to think. I needed a way to store my urine, an equivalent to the Schonmeier chamber pot. The top of the closet Stanley and I shared formed a deep storage shelf, level with the head of my bed. Stanley and I stashed our junk there—books, comic

books, cigar boxes of crayons and pencils, homemade wooden swords. There were dozens of empty mason jars in the basement. I could bring up some jars, I worked out, urinate into them at night, hide them on the junk shelf and empty them the next day when no one was looking.

Accumulating jars was easy. I brought them up from the basement   14 one at a time. Stanley and I used them anyway to collect fireflies and bugs and they all looked alike. Arranging them in the dark to relieve my urgent bladder was harder. Dad's and our stepmother's bed was on the other side of the wall behind the closet. We couldn't hear through the wall unless she and Dad were fighting, but I didn't dare take chances. She hadn't only forbidden me to use the bathroom at night. Because she'd offered me no alternative receptacle, she'd effectively forbidden me to urinate at night, asserting by that fiat that she, not I, controlled my bladder. Devising an alternative, as I'd done, was challenging her authority over my body. My fear of being caught reflected the risk I felt I was taking. I also had every reason to believe that if she caught me with a mason jar of urine she'd forbid me that release as well and I'd be worse off than I was before.

So I didn't open a jar to relieve myself as soon as the house quieted   15 down. I continued my ritual of restraint, of clamping my sphincters and pinching my penis, until I could no longer bear the pain. Only then, an hour or more after bedtime, did I dare to ease a jar stealthily from its hiding place, slip it under the covers to muffle any sound and slowly unscrew its heavy zinc lid. After I'd waited a while longer to be sure no one had heard, I turned on my side, released my penis, bent it over the rough lip of the jar tilted down into the sag of my mattress and tentatively, squirting and clamping, emptied my bladder. I thought I could fill a jar and sometimes I nearly did. To avoid overflowing I pressed a finger down along the inside of the jar; when the warm urine wet it I knew I needed to stop. Hot with shame then I screwed the lid back on, struggling sometimes to start the threads straight. Then I had the concealment problem in reverse. I had to move the jar filled with urine back onto the junk shelf, and with the evidence now patent I was even more terrified of being heard. It didn't take me as long to return the jars to the shelf as it did to fetch them, but I worked tense with caution and froze every time my bunk springs squeaked.

Disposing of the jars turned out to be the hardest part. I was afraid   16 to move them when our stepmother was home and she seldom left the house after school or during the evening. Jars of urine began accumulating on the shelf behind the junk. They didn't smell—I screwed the lids tight enough to prevent that—but the liquid turned a darker yellow and grew gray cobwebs of mold. Once in a while I had a chance to dispose of them, one or two at a time. I let Stanley in on the secret. He didn't disapprove beyond warning me of the danger. "You better hadn't let her catch you," he told me. A dozen jars collected on the shelf.

17   I was away all one Saturday morning doing a job, running errands or cleaning out someone's garage. When I got home Stanley met me coming through the backyard and hissed me aside to a conference. "She almost found the jars," he whispered. I turned white. "It's okay," he said. "I got rid of them. She got mad about all the junk on the shelf and told me to clean it off. She was standing there watching me. I started cleaning stuff off but I kept moving it around to hide your jars. I got to where I didn't see how I could hide them any longer and just then the phone rang and she went off and starting jawing. I hurried up and ran the jars down the back steps and hid them out here under the old tarp. She went off after that and I came out and emptied them. Whew! they smelled bad. They smelled like dead fish." It was a close call and he wasn't happy with me for exposing him to it. After that he helped me keep them emptied.

18   To this day, forty years later, once a month or so, pain wakes me. Falling asleep with urine in my bladder or unmoved rectal stool, I still reflexively tighten my pelvic muscles until my sphincters cramp. My stepmother, my commandant, still intermittently controls my body even at this distant and safe remove. I sit on the toilet those nights in the silence of my house forcing my sphincters to relax, waiting out the pain in the darkness, remembering her.

✦ Questions for Discussion and Writing

1. In your view, what did Rhodes's stepmother hope to achieve through her psychological and physical abuse?

2. What can you tell about Rhodes from the different methods he used to stay one step ahead of his stepmother?

3. How were the issues of power, control, and rebellion experienced by Rhodes at the time each one occurred? How have these experiences affected his adult life?

4. Have you or anyone you know witnessed or experienced any of the problems encountered in a relationship with a stepparent like the one that Rhodes describes? Were the same dynamics of power and control operating in these incidents?

5. It may not have been possible to express the reactions you had as a child. If you keep a journal, use it to compose a letter (that is not intended to be sent) to an adult airing your grievances toward him or her.

Douchan Gersi

Initiated into an Iban Tribe of Headhunters

◆

Douchan Gersi is the producer of the National Geographic television se-
ries called Discovery. *He has traveled extensively throughout the Philip-*
pines, New Zealand, the Polynesian and Melanesian Islands, the Sahara
Desert, Africa, New Guinea, and Peru. "Initiated into an Iban Tribe of
Headhunters," from his book Explorer *(1987), tells of the harrowing ini-*
tiation process he underwent to become a member of the Iban Tribe in
Borneo.

The hopeful man sees success where others see shadows and storm.
—O. S. Marden

Against Tawa's excellent advice I asked the chief if I could become   1
a member of their clan. It took him a while before he could give me an
answer, for he had to question the spirits of their ancestors and wait for
their reply to appear through different omens: the flight of a blackbird,
the auguries of a chick they sacrificed. A few days after the question,
the answer came:

"Yes...but!"   2

The "but" was that I would have to undergo their initiation. With-   3
out knowing exactly what physical ordeal was in store, I accepted. I
knew I had been through worse and survived. It was to begin in one
week.

Late at night I was awakened by a girl slipping into my bed. She   4
was sweet and already had a great knowledge of man's morphology.
Like all the others who came and "visited" me this way every night,
she was highly skilled in the arts of love. Among the Iban, only unmar-
ried women offer sexual hospitality, and no one obliged these women
to offer me their favors. Sexual freedom ends at marriage. Unfaithful-
ness—except during yearly fertility celebrations when everything,
even incest at times, is permitted—is punished as an offense against
their matrimonial laws.

As a sign of respect to family and the elders, sexual hospitality is   5
not openly practiced. The girls always came when my roommates were
asleep and left before they awoke. They were free to return or give their
place to their girlfriends.

185

6   The contrast between the violence of some Iban rituals and the beauty of their art, their sociability, their kindness, and their personal warmth has always fascinated me. I also witnessed that contrast among a tribe of Papuans (who, besides being headhunters, practice cannibalism) and among some African tribes. In fact, tribes devoted to cannibalism and other human sacrifices are often among the most sociable of people, and their art, industry, and trading systems are more advanced than other tribes that don't have these practices.

7   For my initiation, they had me lie down naked in a four-foot-deep pit filled with giant carnivorous ants. Nothing held me there. At any point I could easily have escaped, but the meaning of this rite of passage was not to kill me. The ritual was intended to test my courage and my will, to symbolically kill me by the pain in order for me to be reborn as a man of courage. I am not sure what their reactions would have been if I had tried to get out of the pit before their signal, but it occurred to me that although the ants might eat a little of my flesh, the Iban offered more dramatic potentials.

8   Since I wore, as Iban do, a long piece of cloth around my waist and nothing more, I had the ants running all over my body. They were everywhere. The pain of the ants' bites was intense, so I tried to relax to decrease the speed of my circulation and therefore the effects of the poison. But I couldn't help trying to get them away from my face where they were exploring every inch of my skin. I kept my eyes closed, inhaling through my almost closed lips and exhaling through my nose to chase them away from there.

9   I don't know how long I stayed in the pit, waiting with anguish for the signal which would end my ordeal. As I tried to concentrate on my relaxing, the sound of the beaten gongs and murmurs of the assistants watching me from all around the pit started to disappear into a chaos of pain and loud heartbeat.

10   Then suddenly I heard Tawa and the chief calling my name. I removed once more the ants wandering on my eyelids before opening my eyes and seeing my friends smiling to indicate that it was over. I got out of the pit on my own, but I needed help to rid myself of the ants, which were determined to eat all my skin. After the men washed my body, the shaman applied an herbal mixture to ease the pain and reduce the swellings. I would have quit and left the village then had I known that the "pit" experience was just the hors d'oeuvre.

11   The second part of the physical test started early the next morning. The chief explained the "game" to me. It was Hide and Go Seek Iban-style. I had to run without any supplies, weapons, or food, and for three days and three nights escape a group of young warriors who would leave the village a few hours after my departure and try to find me. If I were caught, my head would be used in a ceremony. The Iban

would have done so without hate. It was simply the rule of their life. Birth and death. A death that always engenders new life.

When I asked, "What would happen if someone refused this part   12
of the initiation?" the chief replied that such an idea wasn't possible. Once one had begun, there was no turning back. I knew the rules governing imitations among the cultures of tradition but never thought they would be applied to me. Whether or not I survived the initiation, I would be symbolically killed in order to be reborn among them. I had to die from my present time and identity into another life. I was aware that, among some cultures, initiatory ordeals are so arduous that young initiates sometimes really die. These are the risks if one wishes to enter into another world.

I was given time to get ready and the game began. I ran like hell   13
without a plan or, it seemed to me, a prayer of surviving. Running along a path I had never taken, going I knew not where, I thought about every possible way I could escape from the young warriors. To hide somewhere. But where? Climb a tree and hide in it? Find a hole and squeeze in it? Bury myself under rocks and mud? But all of these seemed impossible. I had a presentiment they would find me anyway. So I ran straight ahead, my head going crazy by dint of searching for a way to safely survive the headhunters.

I would prefer staying longer with ants, I thought breathlessly. It   14
was safer to stay among them for a whole day since they were just simple pain and fear compared to what I am about to undergo. I don't want to die.

For the first time I realized the real possibility of death—no longer   15
in a romantic way, but rather at the hands of butchers.

Ten minutes after leaving the long house, I suddenly heard a call   16
coming from somewhere around me. Still running, I looked all around trying to locate who was calling, and why. At the second call I stopped, cast my gaze about, and saw a woman's head peering out from the bushes. I recognized her as one of my pretty lovers. I hesitated, not knowing if she were part of the hunting party or a goddess come to save me. She called again. I thought, God, what to do? How will I escape from the warriors? As I stood there truly coming into contact with my impossible situation, I began to panic. She called again. With her fingers she showed me what the others would do if they caught me. Her forefinger traced an invisible line from one side of her throat to the other. If someone was going to kill me, why not her? I joined her and found out she was in a lair. I realized I had entered the place where the tribe's women go to hide during their menstruation. This area is taboo for men. Each woman was her own refuge. Some have shelters made of branches, others deep covered holes hidden behind bushes with enough space to eat and sleep and wait until their time is past.

17   She invited me to make myself comfortable. That was quite difficult since it was just large enough for one person. But I had no choice.
And after all, it was a paradise compared to what I would have undergone had I not by luck crossed this special ground.

18   Nervously and physically exhausted by my run and fear and despair, I soon fell asleep. Around midnight I woke. She gave me rice and
meat. We exchanged a few words. Then it was her turn to sleep.

19   The time I spent in the lair with my savior went fast. I tried to sleep
all day long, an escape from the concerns of my having broken a taboo.
And I wondered what would happen to me if the headhunters were to
learn where I spent the time of my physical initiation.

20   Then, when it was safe, I snuck back to the village . . . in triumph. I
arrived before the warriors, who congratulated and embraced me
when they returned. I was a headhunter at last.

21   I spent the next two weeks quietly looking at the Iban through new
eyes. But strangely enough, instead of the initiation putting me closer
to them, it had the opposite effect. I watched them more and more from
an anthropological distance: my Iban brothers became an interesting
clan whose life I witnessed but did not really share. And then suddenly
I was bored and yearned for my own tribe. When Tawa had to go to an
outpost to exchange pepper grains for other goods, I took a place
aboard his canoe. Two days later I was in a small taxi-boat heading toward Sibu, the first leg in civilization on my voyage home.

22   I think of them often. I wonder about the man I tried to cure. I think
about Tawa and the girl who saved my life, and all the others sitting on
the veranda. How long will my adopted village survive before being
destroyed like all the others in the way of civilization? And what has
become of those who marked my flesh with the joy of their lives and offered me the best of their souls? If they are slowly vanishing from my
memories, I know that I am part of the stories they tell. I know that my
life among them will be perpetuated until the farthest tomorrow. Now
I am a story caught in a living legend of a timeless people.

✦ Questions for Discussion and Writing

1. What do the unusual sexual customs of hospitality bestowed on outsiders suggest about the different cultural values of the Iban? Do these
customs suggest that the initiation would be harsher or milder than
Gersi expected? Interpret this episode as it relates to the probable nature of Gersi's forthcoming initiation.

2. In a short paragraph, explain the nature of the hide-and-seek game that constituted the main test for a candidate. Explain why the use of the lighthearted term *game* is ironic in this context.

3. At what point did Gersi realize that his former ideas about death were based on fantasy and that in the present situation he might in fact be separated from his head? How did this realization change his previous attitudes?

4. How does the reappearance of one of the girls who had earlier paid a nocturnal "visit" to Gersi result in his finding a safe hiding place? What does the nature of the hiding place reveal about the tribe's taboos?

5. In terms of suspense, how effective is it for the reader to learn from Gersi that "I would have quit and left the village then had I known that the 'pit' experience was just the hors d'oeuvre"? How is the narrative shaped so as to put the reader through the same suspenseful moments that Gersi himself experienced?

6. If you can enter into the mind of the Iban, explain how the voluntary endurance of the pain of innumerable bites of carnivorous ants could serve as a ritual of symbolic death of the individual and subsequent rebirth as a member of the tribe.

7. Explain in what way the initiation resulted in Gersi feeling quite differently from what he had expected. That is, instead of feeling he was now part of the tribe, he actually felt more distant from them than he had felt before the initiation. To what factors do you attribute this unexpected sense of alienation? What did he discover about his own preconceptions during the initiation that stripped away certain romantic ideas he had had about the Iban and the ability of any outsider to truly become a member of the tribe?

8. If you have ever been initiated into a fraternity or sorority or another organization, compare the nature of Gersi's initiation with those you experienced. In particular, try to identify specific stages in these initiations that mark the "death" of the outsider and "rebirth" of the initiated member.

9. Have you ever had an experience of looking forward to being a member of a particular group, and, upon achieving this, discovered that you felt estranged from this group?

Barbara Grizzuti Harrison

Growing Up Apocalyptic

◆

Barbara Grizzuti Harrison was born in Brooklyn, New York, in 1934. Although she has written fiction, her non-fiction explorations of her life experiences have gained wide acceptance. Harrison's first book, Unlearning the Lie: Sexism in School *(1969), was based on her dissatisfactions with the education her children were receiving. Her next work,* Vision of Glory: A History and a Memory of Jehovah's Witnesses *(1978), confronted the traumatic effects of being enlisted into the Jehovah's Witnesses as an adolescent, a theme she returned to in "Growing Up Apocalyptic" in her next book,* Off Center *(1980).*

1   "The trouble with you," Anna said, in a voice in which compassion, disgust, and reproach fought for equal time, "is that you can't remember what it was like to be young. And even if you could remember—well, when you were my age, you were in that crazy Jehovah's Witness religion, and you probably didn't even play spin the bottle."

2   Anna, my prepubescent eleven-year-old, feels sorry for me because I did not have "a normal childhood." It has never occurred to her to question whether her childhood is "normal"... which is to say, she is happy. She cannot conceive of a life in which one is not free to move around, explore, argue, flirt with ideas and dismiss them, form passionate alliances and friendships according to no imperative but one's own nature and volition; she regards love as unconditional, she expects nurturance as her birthright. It fills her with terror and pity that anyone—especially her mother—could have grown up any differently—could have grown up in a religion where love was conditional upon rigid adherence to dogma and established practice... where approval had to be bought from authoritarian sources... where people did not fight openly and love fiercely and forgive generously and make decisions of their own and mistakes of their own and have adventures of their own.

3   "Poor Mommy," she says. To have spent one's childhood in love with/tyrannized by a vengeful Jehovah is not Anna's idea of a good time—nor is it her idea of goodness. As, in her considered opinion, my having been a proselytizing Jehovah's Witness for thirteen years was about as good a preparation for real life as spending a commensurate amount of time in a Skinner box on the North Pole, she makes allowances for me. And so, when Anna came home recently from a boy-girl

190

party to tell me that she had kissed a boy ("interesting," she pronounced the experiment), and I had heard my mouth ask that atavistic mother-question, "And what else did you do?" Anna was inclined to be charitable with me: "Oh, for goodness' sake, what do you think we did, screw? The trouble with you is . . ." And then she explained to me about spin the bottle.

I do worry about Anna. She is, as I once explained drunkenly to   4
someone who thought that she might be the better for a little vigorous repression, a teleological child. She is concerned with final causes, with ends and purposes and means; she would like to see evidence of design and order in the world; and all her adventures are means to that end. That, combined with her love for the music, color, poetry, ritual, and drama of religion, might, I think, if she were at all inclined to bow her back to authority—and if she didn't have my childhood as an example of the perils thereof—have made her ripe for conversion to an apocalyptic, messianic sect.

That fear may be evidence of my special paranoia, but it is not an   5
entirely frivolous conjecture. Ardent preadolescent girls whose temperament tends toward the ecstatic are peculiarly prone to conversion to fancy religions.

I know. My mother and I became Jehovah's Witnesses in 1944,   6
when I was nine years old. I grew up drenched in the dark blood-poetry of a fierce messianic sect. Shortly after my conversion, I got my first period. We used to sing this hymn: "Here is He who comes from Eden / all His raiment stained with blood." My raiments were stained with blood, too. But the blood of the Son of Man was purifying, redemptive, cleansing, sacrificial. Mine was filthy—proof of my having inherited the curse placed upon the seductress Eve. I used to "read" my used Kotexes compulsively, as if the secret of life—or a harbinger of death—were to be found in that dull, mysterious effluence.

My brother, at the time of our conversion, was four. After a few   7
years of listlessly following my mother and me around in our door-to-door and street-corner proselytizing, he allied himself with my father, who had been driven to noisy, militant atheism by the presence of two female religious fanatics in his hitherto patriarchal household. When your wife and daughter are in love with God, it's hard to compete—particularly since God is good enough not to require messy sex as proof or expression of love. As a child, I observed that it was not extraordinary for women who became Jehovah's Witnesses to remove themselves from their husband's bed as a first step to getting closer to God. For women whose experience had taught them that all human relationships were treacherous and capricious and frighteningly volatile, an escape from the confusions of the world into the certainties of a fundamentalist religion provided the illusion of safety and of rest. It is not too simple to say that the reason many unhappily married and sex-

ually embittered women fell in love with Jehovah was that they didn't have to go to bed with Him.

8   Apocalyptic religions are, by their nature, antierotic. Jehovah's Witnesses believe that the world—or, as they would have it, "this evil system under Satan the Devil"—will end in our lifetime. After the slaughter Jehovah has arranged for his enemies at Armageddon, say the Witnesses, this quintessentially masculine God—vengeful in battle, benevolent to survivors—will turn the earth into an Edenic paradise for true believers. I grew up under the umbrella of the slogan, "Millions Now Living Will Never Die," convinced that 1914 marked "the beginning of the times of the end." So firmly did Jehovah's Witnesses believe this to be true that there were those who, in 1944, refused to get their teeth filled, postponing all care of their bodies until God saw to their regeneration in His New World, which was just around the corner.

9   Some corner.

10   Despite the fact that their hopes were not immediately rewarded, Jehovah's Witnesses have persevered with increasing fervor and conviction, and their attitude toward the world remains the same: Because all their longing is for the future, they are bound to hate the present—the material, the sexual, the flesh. It's impossible, of course, truly to savor and enjoy the present, or to bend one's energies to shape and mold the world into the form of goodness, if you are only waiting for it to be smashed by God. There is a kind of ruthless glee in the way in which Jehovah's Witnesses point to earthquakes, race riots, heroin addiction, the failure of the United Nations, divorce, famine, and liberalized abortion laws as proof of the nearest Armageddon.

11   The world will end, according to the Witnesses, in a great shaking and rending and tearing of unbelieving flesh, with unsanctified babies swimming in blood—torrents of blood. They await God's Big Bang—the final orgasmic burst of violence, after which all things will come together in a cosmic orgasm of joy. In the meantime, they have disgust and contempt for the world; and freedom and spontaneity, even playfulness, in sex are explicitly frowned upon.

12   When I was ten, it would have been more than my life was worth to acknowledge, as Anna does so casually, that I knew what *screwing* was. (Ignorance, however, delivered me from that grave error.) Once, having read somewhere that Hitler had a mistress, I asked my mother what a mistress was. (I had an inkling that it was some kind of sinister superhousekeeper, like Judith Anderson in *Rebecca*.) I knew from my mother's silence, and from her cold, hard, and frightened face, that the question was somehow a grievous offense. I knew that I had done something terribly wrong, but as usual, I didn't know what. The fact was that I never knew how to buy God's—or my mother's—approval. There were sins I consciously and knowingly committed. That was

bad, but it was bearable. I could always pray to God to forgive me, say, for reading the Bible for its "dirty parts" (to prefer the Song of Solomon to all the begats of Genesis was proof absolute of the sinfulness of my nature). But the offenses that made me most cringingly guilty were those I had committed unconsciously; as an imperfect human being descended from the wretched Eve, I was bound—so I had been taught—to offend Jehovah seventy-seven times a day without my even knowing what I was doing wrong.

I knew that good Christians didn't commit "unnatural acts"; but I 13 didn't know what "unnatural acts" were. I knew that an increase in the number of rapes was one of the signs heralding the end of the world, but I didn't know what rape was. Consequently, I spent a lot of time praying that I was not committing unnatural acts or rape.

My ignorance of all things sexual was so profound that it fre- 14 quently led to comedies of error. Nothing I've ever read has inclined me to believe that Jehovah has a sense of humor, and I must say that I consider it a strike against Him that He wouldn't find this story funny: One night shortly after my conversion, a visiting elder of the congregation, as he was avuncularly tucking me in bed, asked me if I were guilty of performing evil practices with my hands under the covers at night. I was puzzled. He was persistent. Finally, I thought I understood. And I burst into wild tears of self-recrimination: What I did under the covers at night was bite my cuticles—a practice which, in fact, did afford me a kind of sensual pleasure. I didn't learn about masturbation—which the Witnesses call "idolatry" because "the masturbator's affection is diverted away from the Creator and is bestowed upon a coveted object . . . his genitals"—until much later. So, having confessed to a sin that I didn't even know existed, I was advised of the necessity of keeping one's body pure from sin; cold baths were recommended. I couldn't see the connection between cold baths and my cuticles, but no one ever questioned the imperatives of an elder. So I subjected my impure body, in midwinter, to so many icy baths that I began to look like a bleached prune. My mother thought I was demented. But I couldn't tell her that I'd been biting my cuticles, because to have incurred God's wrath—and to see the beady eye of the elder steadfastly upon me at every religious meeting I went to—was torment enough. There was no way to win.

One never questioned the imperatives of an elder. I learned as a very 15 small child that it was my primary duty in life to "make nice." When I was little, I was required to respond to inquiries about my health in this manner: "Fine and dandy, just like sugar candy, thank you." And to curtsy. If that sounds like something from a Shirley Temple movie, it's because it is. Having been brought up to be the Italian working-class Shirley Temple from Bensonhurst, it was not terribly difficult for me to learn to "make nice" for God and the elders. Behaving well was rela-

tively easy. The passionate desire to win approval guaranteed my con-
forming. But behaving well never made me feel good. I always felt as if
I were a bad person.

16   I ask myself why it was that my brother was not hounded by the
obsessive guilt and the desperate desire for approval that informed all
my actions. Partly, I suppose, luck, and an accident of temperament,
but also because of the peculiarly guilt-inspiring double message girls
received. Girls were taught that it was their nature to be spiritual, but
paradoxically that they were more prone to absolute depravity than
were boys.

17   In my religion, everything beautiful and noble and spiritual and
good was represented by a woman; and everything evil and depraved
and monstrous was represented by a woman. I learned that "God's organization," the "bride of Christ," or His 144,000 heavenly co-rulers were
represented by a "chaste virgin." I also learned that "Babylon the Great,"
or "false religion," was "the mother of the abominations or the 'disgusting things of the earth.'... She likes to get drunk on human blood....
Babylon the Great is... pictured as a woman, an international harlot."

18   Young girls were thought not to have the "urges" boys had. They
were not only caretakers of their own sleepy sexuality but protectors of
boys' vital male animal impulses as well. They were thus doubly responsible, and, if they fell, doubly damned. Girls were taught that, simply by existing, they were provoking male sexuality... which it was
their job then to subdue.

19   To be female, I learned, was to be Temptation; nothing short of
death—the transformation of your atoms into a lilac bush—could
change that. (I used to dream deliciously of dying, of being as inert—
and as unaccountable—as the dust I came from.) Inasmuch as males
naturally "wanted it" more, when a female "wanted it" she was doubly
depraved, unnatural as well as sinful. She was the receptacle for male
lust, "the weaker vessel." If the vessel, created by God for the use of
males, presumed to have desires of its own, it was perforce consigned
to the consuming fires of God's wrath. If then, a woman were to fall
from grace, her fall would be mighty indeed—and her willful nature
would lead her into that awful abyss where she would be deprived of
the redemptive love of God and the validating love of man. Whereas,
were a man to fall, he would be merely stumbling over his own feet of
clay.

20   (Can this be accident? My brother, when he was young, was always
falling over his own feet. I, on the other hand, to this day sweat with
terror at the prospect of going down escalators or long flights of stairs.
I cannot fly; I am afraid of the fall.)

21   I spent my childhood walking a religious tightrope, maintaining a
difficult dizzying balance. I was, for example, expected to perform well
at school, so that glory would accrue to Jehovah and "His organiza-

tion." But I was also made continually aware of the perils of falling prey to "the wisdom of this world which is foolishness to God." I had constantly to defend myself against the danger of trusting my own judgment. To question or to criticize God's "earthly representatives" was a sure sign of "demonic influence"; to express doubt openly was to risk being treated like a spiritual leper. I was always an honor student at school; but this was hardly an occasion for unqualified joy. I felt, rather, as if I were courting spiritual disaster: While I was congratulated for having "given a witness" by virtue of my academic excellence, I was, in the next breath, warned against the danger of supposing that my intelligence could function independently of God's. The effect of all this was to convince me that my intelligence was like some kind of tricky, predatory animal, which, if it were not kept firmly reined, would surely spring on and destroy me.

"Vanity, thy name is woman." I learned very early what happened   22
to women with "independent spirits" who opposed the will and imperatives of male elders. They were disfellowshipped (excommunicated) and thrown into "outer darkness." Held up as an example of such perfidious conduct was Maria Frances Russell, the wife of Charles Taze Russell, charismatic founder of the sect.

Russell charged his wife with "the same malady which has smitted   23
others—*ambition.*" Complaining of a "female conspiracy" against the Lord's organization, he wrote: "The result was a considerable stirring up of slander and misrepresentation, for of course it would not suit (her) purposes to tell the plain unvarnished truth, that Sister Russell was ambitious.... When she desired to come back, I totally refused, except upon a promise that she should make reasonable acknowledgment of the wrong course she had been pursuing." Ambition in a woman was, by implication, so reprehensible as to exact from Jehovah the punishment of death.

(What the Witnesses appeared less eager to publicize about the   24
Russells' spiritual-cum-marital problems is that in April 1906, Mrs. Russell, having filed suit for legal separation, told a jury that her husband had once remarked to a young orphan woman the Russells had reared: "I am like a jellyfish. I float around here and there. I touch this one and that one, and if she responds I take her to me, and if not I float on to others." Mrs. Russell was unable to prove her charge.)

I remember a line in *A Nun's Story:* "Dear God," the disaffected Bel-   25
gian nun anguished, "forgive me. I will never be able to love a Nazi." I, conversely, prayed tormentedly for many years, "Dear God, forgive me, I am not able to hate what you hate. I love the world." As a Witness I was taught that "friendship with the world" was "spiritual adultery." The world was crawling with Satan's agents. But Satan's agents— evolutionists, "false religionists," and all those who opposed, or were indifferent to, "Jehovah's message"—often seemed like perfectly nice,

decent, indeed lovable people to me. (They were certainly interesting.) As I went from door to door, ostensibly to help the Lord divide the "goats" from the "sheep," I found that I was more and more listening to *their* lives; and I became increasingly more tentative about telling them that I had *The* Truth. As I grew older, I found it more and more difficult to eschew their company. I entertained fantasies, at one time or another, about a handsome, ascetic Jesuit priest I had met in my preaching work and about Albert Schweitzer, J. D. Salinger, E. B. White, and Frank Sinatra; in fact, I was committing "spiritual adultery" all over the place. And then, when I was fifteen, I fell in love with an "unbeliever."

26   If I felt—before having met and loved Arnold Horowitz, English 31, New Utrecht High School—that life was a tightrope, I felt afterward that my life was perpetually being lived on a high wire, with no safety net to catch me. I was obliged, by every tenet of my faith, to despise him: to be "yoked with an unbeliever," an atheist and an intellectual ... the pain was exquisite.

27   He was the essential person, the person who taught me how to love, and how to doubt. Arnold became interested in me because I was smart; he loved me because he thought I was good. He nourished me. He nurtured me. He paid me the irresistible compliment of totally comprehending me. He hated my religion. He railed against the sect that would rather see babies die than permit them to have blood transfusions, which were regarded as unscriptural; he had boundless contempt for my overseers, who would not permit me to go to college— the "Devil's playground," which would fill my head with wicked, ungodly nonsense; he protested mightily, with the rage that springs from genuine compassion, against a religion that could tolerate segregation and apartheid, sneer at martyred revolutionaries, dismiss social reform and material charity as "irrelevant," a religion that—waiting for God to cure all human ills—would act by default to maintain the status quo, while regarding human pain and struggle without pity and without generosity. He loathed the world view that had been imposed on me, a black-and-white view that allowed no complexities, no moral dilemmas, that disdained metaphysical or philosophical or psychological inquiry; he loathed the bloated simplicities that held me in thrall. But he loved *me.* I had never before felt loved unconditionally.

28   This was a measure of his love: Jehovah's Witnesses are not permitted to salute the flag. Arnold came, unbidden, to sit with me at every school assembly, to hold my hand, while everyone else stood at rigid salute. We were very visible; and I was very comforted. And this was during the McCarthy era. Arnold had a great deal to lose, and he risked it all for me. Nobody had ever risked anything for me before. How could I believe that he was wicked?

29   We drank malteds on his porch and read T. S. Eliot and listened to Mozart. We walked for hours, talking of God and goodness and happi-

ness and death. We met surreptitiously. (My mother so feared and hated the man who was leading me into apostasy that she once threw a loaf of Arnold bread out the window; his very name was loathsome to her.) Arnold treated me with infinite tenderness; he was the least alarming man I had ever known. His fierce concentration on me, his solicitous care uncoupled with sexual aggression, was the gentlest—and most thrilling—love I had ever known. He made me feel what I had never felt before—valuable, and good.

It was very hard. All my dreams centered around Arnold, who was becoming more important, certainly more real to me, than God. All my dreams were blood-colored. I would fantasize about Arnold's being converted and surviving Armageddon and living forever with me in the New World. Or I would fantasize about my dying with Arnold, in fire and flames, at Armageddon. I would try to make bargains with God— my life for his. When I confessed my terrors to the men in charge of my spiritual welfare—when I said that I knew I could not rejoice in the destruction of the "wicked" at Armageddon—I was told that I was presuming to be "more compassionate than Jehovah," the deadliest sin against the holy spirit. I was reminded that, being a woman and therefore weak and sentimental, I would have to go against my sinful nature and listen to their superior wisdom, which consisted of my never seeing Arnold again. I was also reminded of the perils of being over-smart: If I hadn't been such a good student, none of this would have happened to me.

I felt as if I were leading a double life, as indeed I was. I viewed the world as beautifully various, as a blemished but mysteriously wonderful place, as savable by humans, who were neither good nor bad but imperfectly wise; but I *acted* as if the world were fit for nothing but destruction, as if all human efforts to purchase happiness and goodness were doomed to failure and deserving of contempt, as if all people could be categorized as "sheep" or "goats" and herded into their appropriate destinies by a judgmental Jehovah, the all-seeing Father who knew better than His children what was good for them.

As I had when I was a little girl, I "made nice" as best I could. I maintained the appearance of "goodness," that is, of religiosity, although it violated my truest feelings. When I left high school, I went into the full-time preaching work. I spent a minimum of five hours a day ringing doorbells and conducting home Bible studies. I went to three religious meetings a week. I prayed that my outward conformity would lead to inner peace. I met Arnold very occasionally, when my need to see him overcame my elders' imperatives and my own devastating fears. He was always accessible to me. Our meetings partook equally of misery and of joy. I tried, by my busyness, to lock all my doubts into an attic of my mind.

And for a while, and in a way, it "took." I derived sustenance from communal surges of revivalist fervor at religious conventions and from

30
31
32
33

the conviction that I was united, in a common cause, with a tiny minority of persecuted and comradely brothers and sisters whose approval became both my safety net and the Iron Curtain that shut me off from the world. I felt that I had chosen Jehovah, and that my salvation, while not assured, was at least a possibility; perhaps He would choose me. I vowed finally never to see Arnold again, hoping, by this sacrifice, to gain God's approval for him as well as for me.

34   I began to understand that for anyone so obviously weak and irresponsible as I, only a life of self-sacrifice and abnegation could work. I wanted to be consumed by Jehovah, to be locked so closely into the straitjacket of His embrace that I would be impervious to the devilish temptations my irritable, independent intelligence threw up in my path.

35   I wished to be eaten up alive; and my wish was granted. When I was nineteen, I was accepted into Bethel, the headquarters organization of Jehovah's Witnesses, where I worked and lived, one of twelve young women among two hundred and fifty men, for three years. "Making nice" had paid off. Every minute of my waking life was accounted for; there was no leisure in which to cultivate vice or reflection. I called myself happy. I worked as a housekeeper for my brothers, making thirty beds a day, sweeping and vacuuming and waxing and washing fifteen rooms a day (in addition to proselytizing in my "free time"); I daily washed the bathtub thirty men had bathed in. In fact, the one demurral I made during those years was to ask—I found it so onerous—if perhaps the brothers, many of whom worked in the Witnesses' factory, could not clean out their own bathtub (thirty layers of grease is a lot of grease). I was told by the male overseer who supervised housekeepers that Jehovah had assigned me this "privilege." And I told myself I was lucky.

36   I felt myself to be even luckier—indeed, blessed—when, after two years of this servant's work, one of Jehovah's middlemen, the president of the Watch Tower Bible and Tract Society, told me that he was assigning me to proofread Watch Tower publications. He accompanied this benediction with a warning: This new honor, I was told, was to be a test of my integrity—"Remember in all things to defer to the brothers; you will have to guard your spirit against pride and vanity. Satan will try now to tempt you as never before."

37   And defer I did. There were days when I felt literally as if my eternal destiny hung upon a comma: if the brother with whom I worked decided a comma should go out where I wanted to put one in, I prayed to Jehovah to forgive me for that presumptuous comma. I was perfectly willing to deny the existence of a split infinitive if that would placate my brother. I denied and denied—commas, split infinitives, my sexuality, my intelligence, my femaleness, my yearning to be part of the world—until suddenly with a great silent shifting and shuddering, and

with more pain than I had ever experienced or expect to experience again, I broke. I woke up one morning, packed my bags, and walked out of that place. I was twenty-two; and I had to learn how to begin to live. It required a great deal of courage; I do not think I will ever be capable of that much courage again.

The full story of life in that institution and the ramifications of my 38 decision to leave it is too long to tell here; and it will take me the rest of my life to understand fully the ways in which everything I have ever done since has been colored and informed by the guilt that was my daily bread for so many dry years, by the desperate need for approval that allowed me to be swallowed up whole by a devouring religion, by the carefully fostered desire to "make nice" and to be "a good girl," by the conviction that I was nothing and nobody unless I served a cause superior to that of my own necessities.

Arnold, of course, foresaw the difficulty; when I left religion, he 39 said, "Now you will be just like the rest of us." With no guiding passion, he meant; uncertain, he meant, and often muddled and confused, and always struggling. And he wept.

✦ Questions for Discussion and Writing

1. What circumstances led Harrison to become a Jehovah's Witness? What effect did being a Jehovah's Witness have on her?

2. How would you characterize Harrison's relationship with Arnold?

3. In Harrison's view, in what ways did the teachings of the Jehovah's Witnesses affect her self-image as a woman? From her perspective, how did the teachings employ negative female stereotypes?

4. Did you ever experience a moment of disillusionment with a relative, friend, or acquaintance that marked an important turning point in your relationship? Develop a short autobiographical narrative that includes dialogue to recreate this incident. Evaluate the experience, discussing how it influenced the overall pattern of your life.

5. What physical obstacles (such as separation or distance), psychological problems (such as your own jealousy or that of others), or social barriers (such as being of a different race, religion, or social class) have you had to overcome in order to maintain a romantic relationship?

6. There are times in Harrison's narrative in which she imagines herself in the future. If you keep a journal, try to go forward at least one year; imagine what you will be doing and where you will be living. Identify the challenges you have faced and the insights you have gained.

Connections

1. Compare Nora Ephron's account with Annie Dilliard's in terms of what each one reveals about the pressures of being an adolescent.

2. How do Richard Rhodes and Douchan Gersi use ingenuity to survive threatening circumstances?

3. Compare Douchan Gersi's account with Barbara Grizzuti Harrison's in terms of what each author reveals about the meaning and effects of being accepted into a select group.

4. Contrast how the experience Douchan Gersi describes is intended to produce a result quite opposite to that described by Nawal el-Saadawi ("Circumcision of Girls," Chapter 3).

5. How does Nawal el-Saadawi's analysis of Islamic attitudes towards concealment of the female body ("Circumcision of Girls," Chapter 3) reflect cultural values opposite to those described by Nora Ephron?

6. To what extent do the experiences of Nora Ephron and Annie Dillard confirm Kim Chernin's analysis of contemporary American social values ("The Flesh and the Devil," Chapter 3)?

7. What character traits enabled Richard Rhodes and Mary Crow Dog ("Civilize Them with a Stick," Chapter 6) to survive the abuse they were subjected to as children?

8. How do the accounts of Barbara Grizzuti Harrison and Peter Matthiessen ("The Snow Leopard," Chapter 11) point out dramatic differences between eastern and western religious beliefs and practices?

9. How do Douchan Gersi and Meriwether Lewis and William Clark ("The Journals," Chapter 9) cope with the challenge of being outsiders in a new territory?

6

Education and Self-Education

◆

Children have to be educated, but they also have to be left to educate themselves.

—Ernest Dimnet, *The Art of Thinking*, 1928

Accounts of education or self-education are often the records of voyages of self-discovery. In the past, education has served a variety of objectives, including socialization of the young, job preparation, citizenship training, the cultivation of moral values, and intellectual development. Questions as to what constitutes an educated person are answered differently by each of the writers in this chapter. Yet, all of them attest to the value of literacy and to the importance of the ability to communicate. Their detailed descriptions, careful analyses, and sharply rendered accounts of events cannot fail to impress us with the transforming effects of literacy in many different contexts. Autobiographies, in which the reader can see the role that the acquisition of language plays in the creation of an identity, are particularly fascinating. The articulating function of language gives writers who acquire it the possibility of remembering and communicating previous experiences that were frustrating, difficult, or painful. These reflections on past experiences, both inside and outside of formal school environments, may lead you to reflect on experiences you have had or hope to have in college.

Helen Keller describes the series of events that led her from the isolation of being deaf and blind into the world of language and communication in "The Day Language Came into My Life." Frederick Douglass's struggle to become literate required ingenuity and determination, a process we can see in "Learning to Read and Write." "Lessons" contains Mark Salzman's account of trading English lessons for martial arts instruction when he lived in China. In "Transformation," Lydia Minatoya retraces the sequence of events that led her to rebel against being cast in

201

the role of teacher's pet. Mary Crow Dog records her search for personal dignity in "Civilize Them with a Stick," an account in which she describes her rebellion against the way she was treated in a Bureau of Indian Affairs boarding school.

Helen Keller

The Day Language Came into My Life

———————◆———————

Helen Keller (1880–1968) was born without handicaps in Alabama, but she contracted a disease at the age of nineteen months that left her both blind and deaf. Through the extraordinary efforts of Annie Sullivan, Helen overcame her isolation and learned what words meant. She graduated with honors from Radcliffe College and devoted herself for most of her life to helping the blind and deaf through the American Foundation for the Blind. Helen Keller was awarded the Presidential Medal of Freedom by President Lyndon B. Johnson in 1964. Her autobiography, The Story of My Life *(1902), from which "The Day Language Came into My Life" is taken, served as the basis for the 1954 film* The Unconquered *as well as for the acclaimed 1959 play by William Gibson,* The Miracle Worker, *that was subsequently made into a movie.*

The most important day I remember in all my life is the one on which my teacher, Anne Mansfield Sullivan, came to me. I am filled with wonder when I consider the immeasurable contrast between the two lives which it connects. It was the third of March 1887, three months before I was seven years old.

On the afternoon of that eventful day, I stood on the porch, dumb, expectant. I guessed vaguely from my mother's signs and from the hurrying to and fro in the house that something unusual was about to happen, so I went to the door and waited on the steps. The afternoon sun penetrated the mass of honeysuckle that covered the porch and fell on my upturned face. My fingers lingered almost unconsciously on the familiar leaves and blossoms which had just come forth to greet the sweet southern spring. I did not know what the future held of marvel or surprise for me. Anger and bitterness had preyed upon me continually for weeks and a deep languor had succeeded this passionate struggle.

Have you ever been at sea in a dense fog, when it seemed as if a tangible white darkness shut you in, and the great ship, tense and anxious, groped her way toward the shore with plummet and sounding-line, and you waited with beating heart for something to happen? I was like that ship before my education began, only I was without compass or sounding-line and had no way of knowing how near the harbor was.

"Light! give me light!" was the wordless cry of my soul, and the light of love shone on me in that very hour.

4   I felt approaching footsteps. I stretched out my hand as I supposed to my mother. Someone took it, and I was caught up and held close in the arms of her who had come to reveal all things to me, and, more than all things else, to love me.

5   The morning after my teacher came she led me into her room and gave me a doll. The little blind children at the Perkins Institution had sent it and Laura Bridgman had dressed it; but I did not know this until afterward. When I had played with it a little while, Miss Sullivan slowly spelled into my hand the word "d-o-l-l." I was at once interested in this finger play and tried to imitate it. When I finally succeeded in making the letters correctly I was flushed with childish pleasure and pride. Running downstairs to my mother I held up my hand and made the letters for doll. I did not know that I was spelling a word or even that words existed; I was simply making my fingers go in monkeylike imitation. In the days that followed I learned to spell in this uncomprehending way a great many words, among them *pin, hat, cup* and a few verbs like *sit, stand* and *walk*. But my teacher had been with me several weeks before I understood that everything has a name.

6   One day, while I was playing with my new doll, Miss Sullivan put my big rag doll into my lap also, spelled "d-o-l-l" and tried to make me understand that "d-o-l-l" applied to both. Earlier in the day we had had a tussle over the words "m-u-g" and "w-a-t-e-r." Miss Sullivan had tried to impress it upon me that "m-u-g" is *mug* and that "w-a-t-e-r" is *water*, but I persisted in confounding the two. In despair she had dropped the subject for the time, only to renew it at the first opportunity. I became impatient at her repeated attempts and, seizing the new doll, I dashed it upon the floor. I was keenly delighted when I felt the fragments of the broken doll at my feet. Neither sorrow nor regret followed my passionate outburst. I had not loved the doll. In the still, dark world in which I lived there was no strong sentiment or tenderness. I felt my teacher sweep the fragments to one side of the hearth, and I had a sense of satisfaction that the cause of my discomfort was removed. She brought me my hat, and I knew I was going out into the warm sunshine. This thought, if a wordless sensation may be called a thought, made me hop and skip with pleasure.

7   We walked down the path to the well-house, attracted by the fragrance of the honeysuckle with which it was covered. Some one was drawing water and my teacher placed my hand under the spout. As the cool stream gushed over one hand she spelled into the other the word *water*, first slowly, then rapidly. I stood still, my whole attention fixed upon the motions of her fingers. Suddenly I felt a misty consciousness as of something forgotten—a thrill of returning thought; and somehow the mystery of language was revealed to me. I knew

then that "w-a-t-e-r" meant the wonderful cool something that was flowing over my hand. The living word awakened my soul, gave it light, hope, joy, set it free! There were barriers still, it is true, but barriers that could in time be swept away.

I left the well-house eager to learn. Everything had a name, and 8 each name gave birth to a new thought. As we returned to the house every object which I touched seemed to quiver with life. That was because I saw everything with the strange, new sight that had come to me. On entering the door I remembered the doll I had broken. I felt my way to the hearth and picked up the pieces. I tried vainly to put them together. Then my eyes filled with tears; for I realized what I had done, and for the first time I felt repentance and sorrow.

I learned a great many new words that day. I do not remember 9 what they all were; but I do know that *mother, father, sister, teacher* were among them—words that were to make the world blossom for me, "like Aaron's rod, with flowers." It would have been difficult to find a happier child than I was as I lay in my crib at the close of that eventful day and lived over the joys it had brought me, and for the first time longed for a new day to come.

✦ Questions for Discussion and Writing

1. Why is it important for the reader to know how angry Keller was before the events she described actually happened?

2. How does spelling by rote differ from the kind of understanding Keller experienced when she became conscious of the meaning of words?

3. How does language make it possible to understand experiences in a way that would be otherwise inaccessible?

4. What experiences have you had that revealed the importance of language to you in understanding and communicating your thoughts?

5. How does the change in Keller's attitude towards the broken doll reveal how much she has been transformed?

Frederick Douglass

Learning to Read and Write

◆

Frederick Douglass (1817–1895) was born into slavery in Maryland, where he worked as a field hand and servant. In 1838, after previous failed attempts to escape, for which he was beaten and tortured, he successfully made his way to New York using the identity papers of a freed black sailor. There he adopted the last name of Douglass and subsequently settled in New Bedford, Massachusetts. Douglass was the first black American to rise to prominence as a national figure. He gained renown as a speaker for the Massachusetts Anti-Slavery League and was an editor for the North Star, an abolitionist paper, from 1847–1860. He was a friend to John Brown, helped convince President Lincoln to issue the Emancipation Proclamation, and became ambassador to several foreign countries. The Narrative of the Life of Frederick Douglass, an American Slave *(1845) is one of the most illuminating of the many slave narratives written during the nineteenth century. The following account from this autobiography reveals his ingenuity and determination in teaching himself to read and write.*

1   I lived in Master Hugh's family about seven years. During this time, I succeeded in learning to read and write. In accomplishing this, I was compelled to resort to various stratagems. I had no regular teacher. My mistress, who had kindly commenced to instruct me, had, in compliance with the advice and direction of her husband, not only ceased to instruct, but had set her face against my being instructed by any one else. It is due, however, to my mistress to say of her, that she did not adopt this course of treatment immediately. She at first lacked the depravity indispensable to shutting me up in mental darkness. It was at least necessary for her to have some training in the exercise of irresponsible power, to make her equal to the task of treating me as though I were a brute.

2   My mistress was, as I have said, a kind and tender-hearted woman; and in the simplicity of her soul she commenced, when I first went to live with her, to treat me as she supposed one human being ought to treat another. In entering upon the duties of a slaveholder, she did not seem to perceive that I sustained to her the relation of a mere chattel, and that for her to treat me as a human being was not only wrong, but

dangerously so. Slavery proved as injurious to her as it did to me. When I went there, she was a pious, warm, and tender-hearted woman. There was no sorrow or suffering for which she had not a tear. She had bread for the hungry, clothes for the naked, and comfort for every mourner that came within her reach. Slavery soon proved its ability to divest her of these heavenly qualities. Under its influence, the tender heart became stone, and the lamb-like disposition gave way to one of tiger-like fierceness. The first step in her downward course was in her ceasing to instruct me. She now commenced to practise her husband's precepts. She finally became even more violent in her opposition than her husband himself. She was not satisfied with simply doing as well as he had commanded; she seemed anxious to do better. Nothing seemed to make her more angry than to see me with a newspaper. She seemed to think that here lay the danger. I have had her rush at me with a face made all up of fury, and snatch from me a newspaper, in a manner that fully revealed her apprehension. She was an apt woman; and a little experience soon demonstrated, to her satisfaction, that education and slavery were incompatible with each other.

From this time I was most narrowly watched. If I was in a separate room any considerable length of time, I was sure to be suspected of having a book, and was at once called to give an account of myself. All this, however, was too late. The first step had been taken. Mistress, in teaching me the alphabet, had given me the *inch*, and no precaution could prevent me from taking the *ell*. 3

The plan which I adopted, and the one by which I was most successful, was that of making friends of all the little white boys whom I met in the street. As many of these as I could, I converted into teachers. With their kindly aid, obtained at different times and in different places, I finally succeeded in learning to read. When I was sent of errands, I always took my book with me, and by going one part of my errand quickly, I found time to get a lesson before my return. I used also to carry bread with me, enough of which was always in the house, and to which I was always welcome; for I was much better off in this regard than many of the poor white children in our neighborhood. This bread I used to bestow upon the hungry little urchins, who, in return, would give me that more valuable bread of knowledge. I am strongly tempted to give the names of two or three of those little boys, as a testimonial of the gratitude and affection I bear them; but prudence forbids;—not that it would injure me, but it might embarrass them; for it is almost an unpardonable offence to teach slaves to read in this Christian country. It is enough to say of the dear little fellows, that they lived on Philpot Street, very near Durgin and Bailey's ship-yard. I used to talk this matter of slavery over with them. I would sometimes say to them, I wished I 4 could be as free as they would be when they got to be men. "You will be free as soon as you are twenty-one, *but I am a slave for life!* Have not I as good a right to be free as you have?" These words used to trouble them; they would express for me the liveliest sympathy, and console me with the hope that something would occur by which I might be free.

5   I was now about twelve years old, and the thought of being *a slave for life* began to bear heavily upon my heart. Just about this time, I got hold of a book entitled "The Columbian Orator." Every opportunity I got, I used to read this book. Among much of other interesting matter, I found in it a dialogue between a master and his slave. The slave was represented as having run away from his master three times. The dialogue represented the conversation which took place between them, when the slave was retaken the third time. In this dialogue, the whole argument in behalf of slavery was brought forward by the master, all of which was disposed of by the slave. The slave was made to say some very smart as well as impressive things in reply to his master—things which had the desired though unexpected effect; for the conversation resulted in the voluntary emancipation of the slave on the part of the master.

6   In the same book, I met with one of Sheridan's mighty speeches on and in behalf of Catholic emancipation. These were choice documents to me. I read them over and over again with unabated interest. They gave tongue to interesting thoughts of my own soul, which had frequently flashed through my mind, and died away for want of utterance. The moral which I gained from the dialogue was the power of truth over the conscience of even a slaveholder. What I got from Sheridan was a bold denunciation of slavery, and a powerful vindication of human rights. The reading of these documents enabled me to utter my thoughts, and to meet the arguments brought forward to sustain slavery; but while they relieved me of one difficulty, they brought on another even more painful than the one of which I was relieved. The more I read, the more I was led to abhor and detest my enslavers. I could regard them in no other light than a band of successful robbers, who had left their homes, and gone to Africa, and stolen us from our homes, and in a strange land reduced us to slavery. I loathed them as being the meanest as well as the most wicked of men. As I read and contemplated the subject, behold! that very discontentment which Master Hugh had predicted would follow my learning to read had already come, to torment and sting my soul to unutterable anguish. As I writhed under it, I would at times feel that learning to read had been a curse rather than a blessing. It had given me a view of my wretched condition, without the remedy. It opened my eyes to the horrible pit, but to no ladder upon which to get out. In moments of agony, I envied my fellow-slaves for their stupidity. I have often wished myself a beast. I preferred the condition of the meanest reptile to my own. Any thing,

no matter what, to get rid of thinking! It was this everlasting thinking of my condition that tormented me. There was no getting rid of it. It was pressed upon me by every object within sight or hearing, animate or inanimate. The silver trump of freedom had roused my soul to eternal wakefulness. Freedom now appeared, to disappear no more forever. It was heard in every sound, and seen in every thing. It was ever present to torment me with a sense of my wretched condition. I saw nothing without seeing it, I heard nothing without hearing it, and felt nothing without feeling it. It looked from every star, it smiled in every calm, breathed in every wind, and moved in every storm.

I often found myself regretting my own existence, and wishing myself dead; and but for the hope of being free, I have no doubt but that I should have killed myself, or done something for which I should have been killed. While in this state of mind, I was eager to hear any one speak of slavery. I was a ready listener. Every little while I could hear something about the abolitionists. It was some time before I found what the word meant. It was always used in such connections as to make it an interesting word to me. If a slave ran away and succeeded in getting clear, or if a slave killed his master, set fire to a barn, or did any thing very wrong in the mind of a slaveholder, it was spoken of as the fruit of *abolition*. Hearing the word in this connection very often, I set about learning what it meant. The dictionary afforded me little or no help. I found it was "the act of abolishing;" but then I did not know what was to be abolished. Here I was perplexed. I did not dare to ask any one about its meaning, for I was satisfied that it was something they wanted me to know very little about. After a patient waiting, I got one of our city papers, containing an account of the number of petitions from the north, praying for the abolition of slavery in the District of Columbia, and of the slave trade between the States. From this time I understood the words *abolition* and *abolitionist*, and always drew near when that word was spoken, expecting to hear something of importance to myself and fellow-slaves. The light broke in upon me by degrees. I went one day down on the wharf of Mr. Waters; and seeing two Irishmen unloading a scow of stone, I went, unasked, and helped them. When we had finished, one of them came to me and asked me if I were a slave. I told him I was. He asked, "Are ye a slave for life?" I told him that I was. The good Irishman seemed to be deeply affected by the statement. He said to the other that it was a pity so fine a little fellow as myself should be a slave for life. He said it was a shame to hold me. They both advised me to run away to the north; that I should find friends there, and that I should be free. I pretended not to be interested in what they said, and treated them as if I did not understand them; for I feared they might be treacherous. White men have been known to encourage slaves to escape, and then, to get the reward, catch them and return them to their masters. I was afraid that these seemingly good men might use me so;

7

but I nevertheless remembered their advice, and from that time I resolved to run away. I looked forward to a time at which it would be safe for me to escape. I was too young to think of doing so immediately; besides, I wished to learn how to write, as I might have occasion to write my own pass. I consoled myself with the hope that I should one day find a good chance. Meanwhile, I would learn to write.

8   The idea as to how I might learn to write was suggested to me by being in Durgin and Bailey's ship-yard, and frequently seeing the ship carpenters, after hewing, and getting a piece of timber ready for use, write on the timber the name of that part of the ship for which it was intended. When a piece of timber was intended for the larboard side, it would be marked thus—"L." When a piece was for the starboard side, it would be marked thus—"S." A piece for the larboard side forward, would be marked thus—"L. F." When a piece was for starboard side forward, it would be marked thus—"S. F." For larboard aft, it would be thus—"L. A." For starboard aft, it would be marked thus—"S. A." I soon learned the names of these letters, and for what they were intended when placed upon a piece of timber in the ship-yard. I immediately commenced copying them, and in a short time was able to make the four letters named. After that, when I met with any boy who I knew could write, I would tell him I could write as well as he. The next word would be, "I don't believe you. Let me see you try it." I would then make the letters which I had been so fortunate as to learn, and ask him to beat that. In this way I got a good many lessons in writing, which it is quite possible I should never have gotten in any other way. During this time, my copy-book was the board fence, brick wall, and pavement; my pen and ink was a lump of chalk. With these, I learned mainly how to write. I then commenced and continued copying the Italics in Webster's Spelling Book, until I could make them all without looking on the book. By this time, my little Master Thomas had gone to school, and learned how to write, and had written over a number of copy-books. These had been brought home, and shown to some of our near neighbors, and then laid aside. My mistress used to go to class meeting at the Wilk Street meetinghouse every Monday afternoon, and leave me to take care of the house. When left thus, I used to spend the time in writing in the spaces left in Master Thomas's copy-book, copying what he had written. I continued to do this until I could write a hand very similar to that of Master Thomas. Thus, after a long, tedious effort for years, I finally succeeded in learning how to write.

✦ Questions for Discussion and Writing

1. How did the institution of slavery transform Douglass's relationship with his mistress after she had initially made efforts to help him become literate?

2. What ingenious methods did Douglass use to obtain knowledge of reading and writing?

3. Douglass writes that "education and slavery were incompatible with each other." How does his account illustrate this assertion?

4. How does Douglass transform his narrative into a powerful statement about the value of literacy as an empowering force?

5. What would your life be like if you could not read or write? Describe a day in your life, with specific examples and details, that would dramatize this condition.

6. Douglass structures his narrative by identifying important markers, or milestones, in his struggle to learn to read and write. Using your journal, try to create a chronological list that identifies significant stages, or the milestones, in your education. Choose one of these stages; write for fifteen minutes; and expand the time period it refers to by describing all the feelings, images, and associations that made it such a significant step for you.

Mark Salzman

Lessons

◆

Mark Salzman graduated Phi Beta Kappa, summa cum laude from Yale in 1982 with a degree in Chinese language and literature. From 1982 to 1984, he lived in Chang-sha, Hunan, in the People's Republic of China, where he taught English at Hunan Medical College. There he studied under Pan Qingfu, one of China's greatest traditional boxers and martial arts masters. In October 1985, he was invited back to China to participate in the National Martial Arts Competition and Conference in Tianjin. Iron and Silk (1986) recounts his adventures and provides a fascinating behind-the-scenes glimpse into the workings of Chinese society. His experiences also formed the basis for a 1991 film of the same name starring the author. "Lessons," from this book, describes the extraordinary opportunity that studying martial arts with Pan Qingfu offered, along with the comic misunderstandings produced by their being from such different cultures.

1   I was to meet Pan at the training hall four nights a week, to receive private instruction after the athletes finished their evening workout. Waving and wishing me good night, they politely filed out and closed the wooden doors, leaving Pan and me alone in the room. First he explained that I must start from scratch. He meant it, too, for beginning that night, and for many nights thereafter, I learned how to stand at attention. He stood inches away from me and screamed, "Stand straight!" then bored into me with his terrifying gaze. He insisted that I maintain eye contact for as long as he stood in front of me, and that I meet his gaze with one of equal intensity. After as long as a minute of this silent torture, he would shout "At ease!" and I could relax a bit, but not smile or take my eyes away from his. We repeated this exercise countless times, and I was expected to practice it four to six hours a day. At the time, I wondered what those staring contests had to do with wushu, but I came to realize that everything he was to teach me later was really contained in those first few weeks when we stared at each other. His art drew strength from his eyes; this was his way of passing it on.

2   After several weeks I came to enjoy staring at him. I would break into a sweat and feel a kind of heat rushing up through the floor into my legs and up into my brain. He told me that when standing like that, I must at all times be prepared to duel, that at any moment he might attack, and I should be ready to defend myself. It exhilarated me to face

212

off with him, to feel his power and taste the fear and anticipation of the blow. Days and weeks passed, but the blow did not come.

One night he broke the lesson off early, telling me that tonight was special. I followed him out of the training hall, and we bicycled a short distance to his apartment. He lived with his wife and two sons on the fifth floor of a large, anonymous cement building. Like all the urban housing going up in China today, the building was indistinguishable from its neighbors, mercilessly practical and depressing in appearance. Pan's apartment had three rooms and a small kitchen. A private bathroom and painted, as opposed to raw, cement walls in all the rooms identified it as the home of an important family. The only decoration in the apartment consisted of some silk banners, awards and photographs from Pan's years as the national wushu champion and from the set of *Shaolin Temple*. Pan's wife, a doctor, greeted me with all sorts of homemade snacks and sat me down at a table set for two. Pan sat across from me and poured two glasses of baijiu. He called to his sons, both in their teens, and they appeared from the bedroom instantly. They stood in complete silence until Pan asked them to greet me, which they did, very politely, but so softly I could barely hear them. They were handsome boys, and the elder, at about fourteen, was taller than me and had a moustache. I tried asking them questions to put them at ease, but they answered only by nodding. They apparently had no idea how to behave toward something like me and did not want to make any mistakes in front of their father. Pan told them to say good night, and they, along with his wife, disappeared into the bedroom. Pan raised his glass and proposed that the evening begin.

He told me stories that made my hair stand on end, with such gusto that I thought the building would shake apart. When he came to the parts where he vanquished his enemies, he brought his terrible hand down on the table or against the wall with a crash, sending our snacks jumping out of their serving bowls. His imitations of cowards and bullies were so funny I could hardly breathe for laughing. He had me spellbound for three solid hours; then his wife came in to see if we needed any more food or baijiu. I took the opportunity to ask her if she had ever been afraid for her husband's safety when, for example, he went off alone to bust up a gang of hoodlums in Shenyang. She laughed and touched his right hand. "Sometimes I figured he'd be late for dinner." A look of tremendous satisfaction came over Pan's face, and he got up to use the bathroom. She sat down in his chair and looked at me. "Every day he receives tens of letters from all over China, all from people asking to become his student. Since he made the movie, it's been almost impossible for him to go out during the day." She refilled our cups, then looked at me again. "He has trained professionals for more than twenty-five years now, but in all that time he has accepted only one private student." After a long pause, she gestured at me with her chin. "You." Just then Pan came back into the room, returned to his seat and started a new story. This one was about a spear:

5   While still a young man training for the national wushu competition, Pan overheard a debate among some of his fellow athletes about the credibility of an old story. The story described a famous warrior as being able to execute a thousand spear-thrusts without stopping to rest. Some of the athletes felt this to be impossible: after fifty, one's shoulders ache, and by one hundred the skin on the left hand, which guides the spear as the right hand thrusts, twists and returns it, begins to blister. Pan had argued that surely this particular warrior would not have been intimidated by aching shoulders and blisters, and soon a challenge was raised. The next day Pan went out into a field with a spear, and as the other athletes watched, executed one thousand and seven thrusts without stopping to rest. Certain details of the story as Pan told it—that the bones of his left hand were exposed, and so forth—might be called into question, but the number of thrusts I am sure is accurate, and the scar tissue on his left palm indicates that it was not easy for him.

6   One evening later in the year, when I felt discouraged with my progress in a form of Northern Shaolin boxing called "Changquan," or "Long Fist," I asked Pan if he thought I should discontinue the training. He frowned, the only time he ever seemed genuinely angry with me, and said quietly, "When I say I will do something, I do it, exactly as I said I would. In my whole life, I have never started something without finishing it. I said that in the time we have, I would make your wushu better than you could imagine, and I will. Your only responsibility to me is to practice and to learn. My responsibility to you is much greater! Every time you think your task is great, think how much greater mine is. Just keep this in mind: if you fail"—here he paused to make sure I understood—"I will lose face."

7   Though my responsibility to him was merely to practice and to learn, he had one request that he vigorously encouraged me to fulfill—to teach him English. I felt relieved to have something to offer him, so I quickly prepared some beginning materials and rode over to his house for the first lesson. When I got there, he had a tape recorder set up on a small table, along with a pile of oversized paper and a few felt-tip pens from a coloring set. He showed no interest at all in my books, but sat me down next to the recorder and pointed at the pile of paper. On each sheet he had written out in Chinese dozens of phrases, such as "We'll need a spotlight over there," "These mats aren't springy enough," and "Don't worry—it's just a shoulder dislocation." He asked me to write down the English translation next to each phrase, which took a little over two and a half hours. When I was finished, I asked him if he could read my handwriting, and he smiled, saying that he was sure my handwriting was fine. After a series of delicate questions, I determined that

he was as yet unfamiliar with the alphabet, so I encouraged him to have a look at my beginning materials. "That's too slow for me," he said. He asked me to repeat each of the phrases I'd written down five times into the recorder, leaving enough time after each repetition for him to say it aloud after me. "The first time should be very slow—one word at a time, with a pause after each word so I can repeat it. The second time should be the same. The third time you should pause after every other word. The fourth time read it through slowly. The fifth time you can read it fast." I looked at the pile of phrase sheets, calculated how much time this would take, and asked if we could do half today and half tomorrow, as dinner was only three hours away. "Don't worry!" he said, beaming. "I've prepared some food for you here. Just tell me when you get hungry." He sat next to me, turned on the machine, then turned it off again. "How do you say, 'And now, Mark will teach me English'?" I told him how and he repeated it, at first slowly, then more quickly, twenty or twenty-one times. He turned the machine on. "And now, Mark will teach me English." I read the first phrase, five times as he had requested, and he pushed a little note across the table. "Better read it six times," it read, "and a little slower."

After several weeks during which we nearly exhausted the phrasal possibilities of our two languages, Pan announced that the time had come to do something new. "Now I want to learn routines." I didn't understand. "Routines?" "Yes. Everything, including language, is like wushu. First you learn the basic moves, or words, then you string them together into routines." He produced from his bedroom a huge sheet of paper made up of smaller pieces taped together. He wanted me to write a story on it. The story he had in mind was a famous Chinese folk tale, "How Yu Gong Moved the Mountain." The story tells of an old man who realized that, if he only had fields where a mountain stood instead, he would have enough arable land to support his family comfortably. So he went out to the mountain with a shovel and a bucket and started to take the mountain down. All his neighbors made fun of him, calling it an impossible task, but Yu Gong disagreed: it would just take a long time, and after several tens of generations had passed, the mountain would at last become a field and his family would live comfortably. Pan had me write this story in big letters, so that he could paste it up on his bedroom wall, listen to the tape I was to make and read along as he lay in bed.

Not only did I repeat this story into the tape recorder several dozen times—at first one word at a time, and so on—but Pan invited Bill, Bob and Marcy over for dinner one night and had them read it a few times for variety. After they had finished, Pan said that he would like to recite a few phrases for them to evaluate and correct. He chose some of his favorite sentences and repeated each seven or eight times without a pause. He belted them out with such fierce concentration we were all afraid to move lest it disturb him. At last he finished and looked at me, asking quietly if it was all right. I nodded and he seemed overcome with relief. He smiled, pointed at me and said to my friends, "I was very nervous just then. I didn't want him to lose face."

10   While Pan struggled to recite English routines from memory, he began teaching me how to use traditional weapons. He would teach me a single move, then have me practice it in front of him until I could do it ten times in a row without a mistake. He always stood about five feet away from me, with his arms folded, grinding his teeth, and the only time he took his eyes off me was to blink. One night in the late spring I was having a particularly hard time learning a move with the staff. I was sweating heavily and my right hand was bleeding, so the staff had become slippery and hard to control. Several of the athletes stayed on after their workout to watch and to enjoy the breeze that sometimes passed through the training hall. Pan stopped me and indicated that I wasn't working hard enough. "Imagine," he said, "that you are participating in the national competition, and those athletes are your competitors. Look as if you know what you are doing! Frighten them with your strength and confidence." I mustered all the confidence I could, under the circumstances, and flung myself into the move. I lost control of the staff, and it whirled straight into my forehead. As if in a dream, the floor raised up several feet to support my behind, and I sat staring up at Pan while blood ran down across my nose and a fleshy knob grew between my eyebrows. The athletes sprang forward to help me up. They seemed nervous, never having had a foreigner knock himself out in their training hall before, but Pan, after asking if I felt all right, seemed positively inspired. "Sweating and bleeding. Good."

11   Every once in a while, Pan felt it necessary to give his students something to think about, to spur them on to greater efforts. During one morning workout two women practiced a combat routine, one armed with a spear, the other with a *dadao,* or halberd. The dadao stands about six feet high and consists of a broadsword attached to a thick wooden pole, with an angry-looking spike at the far end. It is heavy and difficult to wield even for a strong man, so it surprised me to see this young woman, who could not weigh more than one hundred pounds, using it so effectively. At one point in their battle the woman with the dadao swept it toward the other woman's feet, as if to cut them off, but the other woman jumped up in time to avoid the blow. The first woman, without letting the blade of the dadao stop, brought it around in another sweep, as if to cut the other woman in half at the waist. The other woman, without an instant to spare, bent straight from the hips so that the dadao slashed over her back and head, barely an inch away. This combination was to be repeated three times in rapid

succession before moving on to the next exchange. The women practiced this move several times, none of which satisfied Pan. "Too slow, and the weapon is too far away from her. It should graze her back as it goes by." They tried again, but still Pan growled angrily. Suddenly he got up and took the dadao from the first woman. The entire training hall went silent and still. Without warming up at all, Pan ordered the woman with the spear to get ready, and to move fast when the time came. His body looked as though electricity had suddenly passed through it, and the huge blade flashed toward her. Once, twice the dadao flew beneath her feet, then swung around in a terrible arc and rode her back with flawless precision. The third time he added a little twist at the end, so that the blade grazed up her neck and sent a little decoration stuck in her pigtails flying across the room.

I had to sit down for a moment to ponder the difficulty of sending 12 an object roughly the shape of an oversized shovel, only heavier, across a girl's back and through her pigtails, without guide ropes or even a safety helmet. Not long before, I had spoken with a former troupe member who, when practicing with this instrument, had suddenly found himself on his knees. The blade, unsharpened, had twirled a bit too close to him and passed through his Achilles' tendon without a sound. Pan handed the dadao back to the woman and walked over to me. "What if you had made a mistake?" I asked. "I never make mistakes," he said, without looking at me.

✦ Questions for Discussion and Writing

1. Why is the standing-at-attention exercise so important in learning *wushu* (Kung Fu)? What abilities does this exercise develop?

2. What is the relevance of the Chinese folk tale "How Yu Gong Moved the Mountain" to Salzman's apprenticeship?

3. What evidence can you cite to show that Pan applies the same standard (based on fear of "losing face") to Mark as he does to himself? What part does the concept of "losing face" play in Chinese culture, and what values are expressed through this term?

4. What similarities can you discover between Pan's approach to learning English and his methods of teaching Chinese martial arts?

5. What factors do you believe might explain why Pan chooses Mark to be the only private student he has ever had? Why is this especially significant because Mark is an American and Pan has never taken one private student within China in twenty-five years?

6. To what extent was Pan's choice of Mark an expression of Pan's personality in terms of always taking on the hardest challenge possible? In view of this, what would have been involved for Pan if Mark were to perform his martial arts routine poorly and Pan were to "lose face"?

7. Why is Pan's performance with a heavy spear, without any warm-up, so impressive? How does the placement of this episode at the end of the chapter serve as an appropriate and dramatic conclusion?

8. Describe an experience that you have had, including martial arts instruction, that gave you an insight into Salzman's experiences.

9. If you could master anything you wished, what would it be, and who would you want to be your teacher? Would you want to learn from someone like Pan?

Lydia Minatoya

Transformation

◆

Lydia Minatoya was born in 1950 in Albany, New York, where she and her family experienced ethnic isolation during the late 1950s. She received a Ph.D. in psychology from the University of Maryland in 1981. From 1983 to 1985 she taught and traveled throughout Asia, including Hong Kong, Japan, China, and Nepal. She received the 1991 P.E.N./Jerard Fund Award and a grant from the Seattle Arts Commission for Talking to High Monks in the Snow, *published in 1992. This work is made up of memories of childhood, graduate school study in psychology, her career as a university professor, and her travels in Asia. She currently lives in Seattle, where she is a community college counselor and faculty member. "Transformation," the following chapter from her book, reveals an important moment in the author's journey toward self-discovery.*

Perhaps it begins with my naming. During her pregnancy, my mother was reading Dr. Spock. "Children need to belong," he cautioned. "An unusual name can make them the subject of ridicule." My father frowned when he heard this. He stole a worried glance at my sister. Burdened by her Japanese name, Misa played unsuspectingly on the kitchen floor. 1

The Japanese know full well the dangers of conspicuousness. "The nail that sticks out gets pounded down," cautions an old maxim. In America, Relocation was all the proof they needed. 2

And so it was, with great earnestness, my parents searched for a conventional name. They wanted me to have the full true promise of America. 3

"I will ask my colleague Froilan," said my father. "He is the smartest man I know." 4

"And he has poetic soul," said my mother, who cared about such things. 5

In due course, Father consulted Froilan. He gave Froilan his conditions for suitability. 6

"First, if possible, the full name should be alliterative," said my father. "Like Misa Minatoya." He closed his eyes and sang my sister's name. "Second, if not an alliteration, at least the name should have assonantal rhyme." 7

"Like Misa Minatoya?" said Froilan with a teasing grin. 8

219

9   "Exactly," my father intoned. He gave an emphatic nod. "Finally, most importantly, the name must be readily recognizable as conventional." He peered at Froilan with hope. "Do you have any suggestions or ideas?"

10   Froilan, whose own American child was named Ricardito, thought a while.

11   "We already have selected the name for a boy," offered my Father. "Eugene."

12   "Eugene?" wondered Froilan. "But it meets none of your conditions!"

13   "Eugene is a special case," said my father, "after Eugene, Oregon, and Eugene O'Neill. The beauty of the Pacific Northwest, the power of a great writer."

14   "I see," said Froilan, who did not but who realized that this naming business would be more complex than he had anticipated. "How about Maria?"

15   "Too common," said my father. "We want a *conventional* name, not a common one."

16   "Hmmm," said Froilan, wondering what the distinction was. He thought some more and then brightened. "Lydia!" he declared. He rhymed the name with media. "Lydia for *la bonita infanta!*"

17   And so I received my uncommon conventional name. It really did not provide the camouflage my parents had anticipated. I remained unalterably alien. For Dr. Spock had been addressing *American* families, and in those days, everyone knew all real American families were white.

18   Call it denial, but many Japanese Americans never quite understood that the promise of America was not truly meant for them. They lived in horse stalls at the Santa Anita racetrack and said the Pledge of Allegiance daily. They rode to Relocation Camps under armed guard, labeled with numbered tags, and sang "The Star-Spangled Banner." They lived in deserts or swamps, ludicrously imprisoned—where would they run if they ever escaped—and formed garden clubs, and yearbook staffs, and citizen town meetings. They even elected beauty queens.

19   My mother practiced her okoto and was featured in a recital. She taught classes in fashion design and her students mounted a show. Into exile she had carried an okoto and a sewing machine. They were her past and her future. She believed in Art and Technology.

20   My mother's camp was the third most populous city in the entire state of Wyoming. Across the barren lands, behind barbed wire, bloomed these little oases of democracy. The older generation bore the humiliation with pride. *"Kodomo no tame ni,"* they said. For the sake of

the children. They thought that if their dignity was great, then their
children would be spared. Call it valor. Call it bathos. Perhaps it was
closer to slapstick: a sweet and bitter lunacy.

Call it adaptive behavior. Coming from a land swept by savage ty-   21
phoons, ravaged by earthquakes and volcanoes, the Japanese have
evolved a view of the world: a cooperative, stoic, almost magical way
of thinking. Get along, work hard, and never quite see the things that
can bring you pain. Against the tyranny of nature, of feudal lords, of
wartime hysteria, the charm works equally well.

And so my parents gave me an American name and hoped that I   22
could pass. They nourished me with the American dream: Opportunity, Will, Transformation.

When I was four and my sister was eight, Misa regularly used me   23
as a comic foil. She would bring her playmates home from school and
query me as I sat amidst the milk bottles on the front steps.

"What do you want to be when you grow up?" she would say. She   24
would nudge her audience into attentiveness.

"A mother kitty cat!" I would enthuse. Our cat had just delivered   25
her first litter of kittens and I was enchanted by the rasping tongue and
soft mewings of motherhood.

"And what makes you think you can become a cat?" Misa would   26
prompt, gesturing to her howling friends—wait for this; it gets better
yet.

"This is America," I stoutly would declare. "I can grow up to be   27
anything I want!"

My faith was unshakable. I believed. Opportunity. Will. Transfor-   28
mation.

When we lived in Albany, I always was the teachers' pet. "So tiny,   29
so precocious, so prettily dressed!" They thought I was a living doll
and this was fine with me.

My father knew that the effusive praise would die. He had been   30
through this with my sister. After five years of being a perfect darling,
Misa had reached the age where students were tracked by ability. Then,
the anger started. Misa had tested into the advanced track. It was impossible, the community declared. Misa was forbidden entry into advanced classes as long as there were white children being placed below
her. In her defense, before an angry rabble, my father made a presentation to the Board of Education.

But I was too young to know of this. I knew only that my teachers   31
praised and petted me. They took me to other classes as an example.
"Watch now, as Lydia demonstrates attentive behavior," they would

croon as I was led to an empty desk at the head of the class. I had a routine. I would sit carefully, spreading my petticoated skirt neatly beneath me. I would pull my chair close to the desk, crossing my swinging legs at my snowy white anklets. I would fold my hands carefully on the desk before me and stare pensively at the blackboard.

32   This routine won me few friends. The sixth-grade boys threw rocks at me. They danced around me in a tight circle, pulling at the corners of their eyes. "Ching Chong Chinaman," they chanted. But teachers loved me. When I was in first grade, a third-grade teacher went weeping to the principal. She begged to have me skipped. She was leaving to get married and wanted her turn with the dolly.

33   When we moved, the greatest shock was the knowledge that I had lost my charm. From the first, my teacher failed to notice me. But to me, it did not matter. I was in love. I watched her moods, her needs, her small vanities. I was determined to ingratiate.

34   Miss Hempstead was a shimmering vision with a small upturned nose and eyes that were kewpie doll blue. Slender as a sylph, she tripped around the classroom, all saucy in her high-heeled shoes. Whenever I looked at Miss Hempstead, I pitied the Albany teachers whom, formerly, I had adored. Poor old Miss Rosenberg. With a shiver of distaste, I recalled her loose fleshy arms, her mottled hands, the scent of lavender as she crushed me to her heavy breasts.

35   Miss Hempstead had a pet of her own. Her name was Linda Sherlock. I watched Linda closely and plotted Miss Hempstead's courtship. The key was the piano. Miss Hempstead played the piano. She fancied herself a musical star. She sang songs from Broadway revues and shaped her students' reactions. "Getting to know you," she would sing. We would smile at her in a staged manner and position ourselves obediently at her feet.

36   Miss Hempstead was famous for her ability to soothe. Each day at rest time, she played the piano and sang soporific songs. Linda Sherlock was the only child who succumbed. Routinely, Linda's head would bend and nod until she crumpled gracefully onto her folded arms. A tousled strand of blonde hair would fall across her forehead. Miss Hempstead would end her song, would gently lower the keyboard cover. She would turn toward the restive eyes of the class. "Isn't she sweetness itself!" Miss Hempstead would declare. It made me want to vomit.

37   I was growing weary. My studiousness, my attentiveness, my fastidious grooming and pert poise: all were failing me. I changed my tactics. I became a problem. Miss Hempstead sent me home with nasty notes in sealed envelopes: Lydia is a slow child, a noisy child, her presence is disruptive. My mother looked at me with surprise, "*Nani desu*

ka? Are you having problems with your teacher?" But I was tenacious. I pushed harder and harder, firmly caught in the obsessive need of the scorned.

One day I snapped. As Miss Hempstead began to sing her 38 wretched lullabies, my head dropped to the desk with a powerful CRACK! It lolled there, briefly, then rolled toward the edge with a momentum that sent my entire body catapulting to the floor. Miss Hempstead's spine stretched slightly, like a cat that senses danger. Otherwise, she paid no heed. The linoleum floor was smooth and cool. It emitted a faint pleasant odor: a mixture of chalk dust and wax.

I began to snore heavily. The class sat electrified, There would be 39 no drowsing today. The music went on and on. Finally, one boy could not stand it. "Miss Hempstead," he probed plaintively, "Lydia has fallen asleep on the floor!" Miss Hempstead did not turn. Her playing grew slightly strident but she did not falter.

I lay on the floor through rest time. I lay on the floor through math 40 drill. I lay on the floor while my classmates scraped around me, pushing their sturdy little wooden desks into the configuration for reading circle. It was not until penmanship practice that I finally stretched and stirred. I rose like Sleeping Beauty and slipped back to my seat. I smiled enigmatically. A spell had been broken. I never again had a crush on a teacher.

✦ Questions for Discussion and Writing

1. What underlying cultural assumptions from the parents' perspective should determine the choice of a name for a child?

2. How does Minatoya's description of the relocation of Japanese into internment camps during World War II and their lives in these camps provide insight into the forces that led to her parents deciding to name her Lydia?

3. How does her attitude toward her name differ from the expectations of her parents?

4. How does Lydia's "transformation" involve liberating herself from the role into which she had been cast as teacher's pet? What does freeing herself from this role signify?

5. Describe the circumstances underlying the choice of your name. Do you like your given name, or do you prefer to be called by a nickname?

6. Have you ever rebelled, either negatively or positively, against a role into which you had been cast? Tell what happened.

Mary Crow Dog and
Richard Erdoes

Civilize Them with a Stick

◆

Mary Crow Dog (who later took the name Mary Brave Bird) was born in 1956 and grew up on a South Dakota reservation in a one-room cabin without running water or electricity. She joined the new movement of tribal pride sweeping Native American communities in the 1960s and 1970s and was at the siege of Wounded Knee, South Dakota, in 1973. She married the American Indian Movement (AIM) leader Leonard Crow Dog, the movement's chief medicine man. Her powerful autobiography Lakota Woman, *written with Richard Erdoes, one of America's leading writers on Native American affairs and the author of eleven books, became a national bestseller and won the American Book Award for 1991. In it she describes what it was like to grow up a Sioux in a white-dominated society. Her second book,* Ohitka Woman *(1993), also written with Richard Erdoes, continues the story of a woman whose struggle for a sense of self and freedom is a testament to her will and spirit. In "Civilize Them with a Stick," from* Lakota Woman, *the author recounts her personal struggle as a young student at a boarding school run by the Bureau of Indian Affairs.*

> *...Gathered from the cabin, the wickiup, and the tepee,*
> *partly by cajolery and partly by threats,*
> *partly by bribery and partly by force,*
> *they are induced to leave their kindred*
> *to enter these schools and take upon themselves*
> *the outward appearance of civilized life.*
>   *—Annual report of the Department of Interior, 1901*

1 It is almost impossible to explain to a sympathetic white person what a typical old Indian boarding school was like; how it affected the Indian child suddenly dumped into it like a small creature from another world, helpless, defenseless, bewildered, trying desperately and instinctively to survive and sometimes not surviving at all. I think such children were like the victims of Nazi concentration camps trying to tell average, middle-class Americans what their experience had been like. Even now, when these schools are much improved, when the buildings are new, all gleaming steel and glass, the food tolerable, the teachers well trained and well intentioned, even trained in child psychology—

unfortunately the psychology of white children, which is different from ours—the shock to the child upon arrival is still tremendous. Some just seem to shrivel up, don't speak for days on end, and have an empty look in their eyes. I know of an eleven-year-old on another reservation who hanged herself, and in our school, while I was there, a girl jumped out of the window, trying to kill herself to escape an unbearable situation. That first shock is always there....

The mission school at St. Francis was a curse for our family for gen-   2
erations. My grandmother went there, then my mother, then my sisters and I. At one time or other every one of us tried to run away. Grandma told me once about the bad times she had experienced at St. Francis. In those days they let students go home only for one week every year. Two days were used up for transportation, which meant spending just five days out of three hundred and sixty-five with her family. And that was an improvement. Before grandma's time, on many reservations they did not let the students go home at all until they had finished school. Anybody who disobeyed the nuns was severely punished. The building in which my grandmother stayed had three floors, for girls only. Way up in the attic were little cells, about five by five by ten feet. One time she was in church and instead of praying she was playing jacks. As punishment they took her to one of those little cubicles where she stayed in darkness because the windows had been boarded up. They left her there for a whole week with only bread and water for nourishment. After she came out she promptly ran away, together with three other girls. They were found and brought back. The nuns stripped them naked and whipped them. They used a horse buggy whip on my grandmother. Then she was put back into the attic—for two weeks.

My mother had much the same experiences but never wanted to   3
talk about them, and then there I was, in the same place. The school is now run by the BIA—the Bureau of Indian Affairs—but only since about fifteen years ago. When I was there, during the 1960s, it was still run by the Church. The Jesuit fathers ran the boys' wing and the Sisters of the Sacred Heart ran us—with the help of the strap. Nothing had changed since my grandmother's days. I have been told recently that even in the '70s they were still beating children at that school. All I got out of school was being taught how to pray. I learned quickly that I would be beaten if I failed in my devotions or, God forbid, prayed the wrong way, especially prayed in Indian to Wakan Tanka, the Indian Creator.

The girls' wing was built like an F and was run like a penal institu-   4
tion. Every morning at five o'clock the sisters would come into our large dormitory to wake us up, and immediately we had to kneel down at the sides of our beds and recite the prayers. At six o'clock we were herded into the church for more of the same. I did not take kindly to the

discipline and to marching by the clock, left-right, left-right. I was never one to like being forced to do something. I do something because I feel like doing it. I felt this way always, as far as I can remember, and my sister Barbara felt the same way. An old medicine man once told me: "Us Lakotas are not like dogs who can be trained, who can be beaten and keep on wagging their tails, licking the hand that whipped them. We are like cats, little cats, big cats, wildcats, bobcats, mountain lions. It doesn't matter what kind, but cats who can't be tamed, who scratch if you step on their tails." But I was only a kitten and my claws were still small.

5   Barbara was still in the school when I arrived and during my first year or two she could still protect me a little bit. When Barb was a seventh-grader she ran away together with five other girls, early in the morning before sunrise. They brought them back in the evening. The girls had to wait for two hours in front of the mother superior's office. They were hungry and cold, frozen through. It was wintertime and they had been running the whole day without food, trying to make good their escape. The mother superior asked each girl, "Would you do this again?" She told them that as punishment they would not be allowed to visit home for a month and that she'd keep them busy on work details until the skin on their knees and elbows had worn off. At the end of her speech she told each girl, "Get up from this chair and lean over it." She then lifted the girls' skirts and pulled down their underpants. Not little girls either, but teenagers. She had a leather strap about a foot long and four inches wide fastened to a stick, and beat the girls, one after another, until they cried. Barb did not give her that satisfaction but just clenched her teeth. There was one girl, Barb told me, the nun kept on beating and beating until her arm got tired.

6   I did not escape my share of the strap. Once, when I was thirteen years old, I refused to go to Mass. I did not want to go to church because I did not feel well. A nun grabbed me by the hair, dragged me upstairs, made me stoop over, pulled my dress up (we were not allowed at the time to wear jeans), pulled my panties down, and gave me what they called "swats"—twenty-five swats with a board around which Scotch tape had been wound. She hurt me badly.

7   My classroom was right next to the principal's office and almost every day I could hear him swatting the boys. Beating was the common punishment for not doing one's homework, or for being late to school. It had such a bad effect upon me that I hated and mistrusted every white person on sight, because I met only one kind. It was not until much later that I met sincere white people I could relate to and be friends with. Racism breeds racism in reverse.

8   The routine at St. Francis was dreary. Six A.M., kneeling in church for an hour or so; seven o'clock, breakfast; eight o'clock, scrub the floor, peel spuds, make classes. We had to mop the dining room twice every

day and scrub the tables. If you were caught taking a rest, doodling on the bench with a fingernail or knife, or just rapping, the nun would come up with a dish towel and just slap it across your face, saying, "You're not supposed to be talking, you're supposed to be working!" Monday mornings we had cornmeal mush, Tuesday oatmeal, Wednesday rice and raisins, Thursday cornflakes, and Friday all the leftovers mixed together or sometimes fish. Frequently the food had bugs or rocks in it. We were eating hot dogs that were weeks old, while the nuns were dining on ham, whipped potatoes, sweet peas, and cranberry sauce. In winter our dorm was icy cold while the nuns' rooms were always warm.

I have seen little girls arrive at the school, first-graders, just fresh 9
from home and totally unprepared for what awaited them, little girls with pretty braids, and the first thing the nuns did was chop their hair off and tie up what was left behind their ears. Next they would dump the children into tubs of alcohol, a sort of rubbing alcohol, "to get the germs off." Many of the nuns were German immigrants, some from Bavaria, so that we sometimes speculated whether Bavaria was some sort of Dracula country inhabited by monsters. For the sake of objectivity I ought to mention that two of the German fathers were great linguists and that the only Lakota-English dictionaries and grammars which are worth anything were put together by them.

At night some of the girls would huddle in bed together for com- 10
fort and reassurance. Then the nun in charge of the dorm would come in and say, "What are the two of you doing in bed together? I smell evil in this room. You girls are evil incarnate. You are sinning. You are going to hell and burn forever. You can act that way in the devil's frying pan." She would get them out of bed in the middle of the night, making them kneel and pray until morning. We had not the slightest idea what it was all about. At home we slept two and three in a bed for animal warmth and a feeling of security.

The nuns and the girls in the two top grades were constantly bat- 11
tling it out physically with fists, nails, and hair-pulling. I myself was growing from a kitten into an undersized cat. My claws were getting bigger and were itching for action. About 1969 or 1970 a strange young white girl appeared on the reservation. She looked about eighteen or twenty years old. She was pretty and had long, blond hair down to her waist, patched jeans, boots, and a backpack. She was different from any other white person we had met before. I think her name was Wise. I do not know how she managed to overcome our reluctance and distrust, getting us into a corner, making us listen to her, asking us how we were treated. She told us that she was from New York. She was the first real hippie or Yippie we had come across. She told us of people called the Black Panthers, Young Lords, and Weathermen. She said, "Black people are getting it on. Indians are getting it on in St. Paul and California.

How about you?" She also said, "Why don't you put out an underground paper, mimeograph it. It's easy. Tell it like it is. Let it all hang
out." She spoke a strange lingo but we caught on fast.

12   Charlene Left Hand Bull and Gina One Star were two full-blood
girls I used to hang out with. We did everything together. They were
willing to join me in a Sioux uprising. We put together a newspaper
which we called the *Red Panther*. In it we wrote how bad the school
was, what kind of slop we had to eat—slimy, rotten, blackened potatoes for two weeks—the way we were beaten. I think I was the one who
wrote the worst article about our principal of the moment, Father
Keeler. I put all my anger and venom into it. I called him a goddam
wasičun son of a bitch. I wrote that he knew nothing about Indians and
should go back to where he came from, teaching white children whom
he could relate to. I wrote that we knew which priests slept with which
nuns and that all they ever could think about was filling their bellies
and buying a new car. It was the kind of writing which foamed at the
mouth, but which also lifted a great deal of weight from one's soul.

13   On Saint Patrick's Day, when everybody was at the big powwow,
we distributed our newspapers. We put them on windshields and bulletin boards, in desks and pews, in dorms and toilets. But someone saw
us and snitched on us. The shit hit the fan. The three of us were taken
before a board meeting. Our parents, in my case my mother, had to
come. They were told that ours was a most serious matter, the worst
thing that had ever happened in the school's long history. One of the
nuns told my mother, "Your daughter really needs to be talked to."
"What's wrong with my daughter?" my mother asked. She was given
one of our *Red Panther* newspapers. The nun pointed out its name to
her and then my piece, waiting for mom's reaction. After a while she
asked, "Well, what have you got to say to this? What do you think?"

14   My mother said, "Well, when I went to school here, some years
back, I was treated a lot worse then these kids are. I really can't see how
they can have any complaints, because we was treated a lot stricter. We
could not even wear skirts halfway up our knees. These girls have it
made. But you should forgive them because they are young. And it's
supposed to be a free country, free speech and all that. I don't believe
what they done is wrong." So all I got out of it was scrubbing six flights
of stairs on my hands and knees, every day. And no boy-side privileges.

15   The boys and girls were still pretty much separated. The only time
one could meet a member of the opposite sex was during free time, between four and five-thirty, in the study hall or on benches or the volley-
ball court outside, and that was strictly supervised. One day Charlene
and I went over to the boys' side. We were on the ball team and they
had to let us practice. We played three extra minutes, only three minutes more than we were supposed to. Here was the nuns' opportunity
for revenge. We got twenty-five swats. I told Charlene, "We are getting

too old to have our bare asses whipped that way. We are old enough to have babies. Enough of this shit. Next time we fight back." Charlene only said, "Hoka-hay!"

We had to take showers every evening. One little girl did not want   16
to take her panties off and one of the nuns told her, "You take those underpants off—or else!" But the child was ashamed to do it. The nun was getting her swat to threaten the girl. I went up to the sister, pushed her veil off, and knocked her down. I told her that if she wanted to hit a little girl she should pick on me, pick one her own size. She got herself transferred out of the dorm a week later.

In a school like this there is always a lot of favoritism. At St. Francis   17
it was strongly tinged with racism. Girls who were near-white, who came from what the nuns called "nice families," got preferential treatment. They waited on the faculty and got to eat ham or eggs and bacon in the morning. They got the easy jobs while the skins, who did not have the right kind of background—myself among them—always wound up in the laundry room sorting out ten bushel baskets of dirty boys' socks every day. Or we wound up scrubbing the floors and doing all the dishes. The school therefore fostered fights and antagonism between whites and breeds, and between breeds and skins. At one time Charlene and I had to iron all the robes and vestments the priests wore when saying Mass. We had to fold them up and put them into a chest in the back of the church. In a corner, looking over our shoulders, was a statue of the crucified Savior, all bloody and beaten up. Charlene looked up and said, "Look at that poor Indian. The pigs sure worked him over." That was the closest I ever came to seeing Jesus.

I was held up as a bad example and didn't mind. I was old enough   18
to have a boyfriend and promptly got one. At the school we had an hour and a half for ourselves. Between the boys' and the girls' wings were some benches where one could sit. My boyfriend and I used to go there just to hold hands and talk. The nuns were very uptight about any boy-girl stuff. They had an exaggerated fear of anything having even the faintest connection with sex. One day in religion class, an all-girl class, Sister Bernard singled me out for some remarks, pointing me out as a bad example, an example that should be shown. She said that I was too free with my body. That I was holding hands which meant that I was not a good example to follow. She also said that I wore unchaste dresses, skirts which were too short, too suggestive, shorter than regulations permitted, and for that I would be punished. She dressed me down before the whole class, carrying on and on about my unchastity.

I stood up and told her, "You shouldn't say any of those things,   19
miss. You people are a lot worse than us Indians. I know all about you, because my grandmother and my aunt told me about you. Maybe twelve, thirteen years ago you had a water stoppage here in St. Francis. No water could get through the pipes. There are water lines right under

the mission, underground tunnels and passages where in my grand-mother's time only the nuns and priests could go, which were off-limits to everybody else. When the water backed up they had to go through all the water lines and clean them out. And in those huge pipes they found the bodies of newborn babies. And they were white babies. They weren't Indian babies. At least when our girls have babies, they don't do away with them that way, like flushing them down the toilet, almost.

20   "And that priest they sent here from Holy Rosary in Pine Ridge be-cause he molested a little girl. You couldn't think of anything better than dump him on us. All he does is watch young women and girls with that funny smile on his face. Why don't you point him out for an example?"

21   Charlene and I worked on the school newspaper. After all we had some practice. Every day we went down to Publications. One of the priests acted as the photographer, doing the enlarging and developing. He smelled of chemicals which had stained his hands yellow. One day he invited Charlene into the darkroom. He was going to teach her de-veloping. She was developed already. She was a big girl compared to him, taller too. Charlene was nicely built, not fat, just rounded. No sharp edges anywhere. All of a sudden she rushed out of the dark-room, yelling to me, "Let's get out of here! He's trying to feel me up. That priest is nasty." So there was this too to contend with—sexual ha-rassment. We complained to the student body. The nuns said we just had a dirty mind.

22   We got a new priest in English. During one of his first classes he asked one of the boys a certain question. The boy was shy. He spoke poor English, but he had the right answer. The priest told him, "You did not say it right. Correct yourself. Say it over again." The boy got flustered and stammered. He could hardly get out a word. But the priest kept after him: "Didn't you hear? I told you to do the whole thing over. Get it right this time." He kept on and on.

23   I stood up and said, "Father, don't be doing that. If you go into an Indian's home and try to talk Indian, they might laugh at you and say, 'Do it over correctly. Get it right this time!'"

24   He shouted at me, "Mary, you stay after class. Sit down right now!"

25   I stayed after class, until after the bell. He told me, "Get over here!"

26   He grabbed me by the arm, pushing me against the blackboard, shouting, "Why are you always mocking us? You have no reason to do this."

27   I said, "Sure I do. You were making fun of him. You embarrassed him. He needs strengthening, not weakening. You hurt him. I did not hurt you."

28   He twisted my arm and pushed real hard. I turned around and hit him in the face, giving him a bloody nose. After that I ran out of the room, slamming the door behind me. He and I went to Sister Bernard's office. I told her, "Today I quit school. I'm not taking any more of this,

none of this shit anymore. None of this treatment. Better give me my diploma. I can't waste any more time on you people."

Sister Bernard looked at me for a long, long time. She said, "All right, Mary Ellen, go home today. Come back in a few days and get your diploma." And that was that. Oddly enough, that priest turned out okay. He taught a class in grammar, orthography, composition, things like that. I think he wanted more respect in class. He was still young and unsure of himself. But I was in there too long. I didn't feel like hearing it. Later he became a good friend of the Indians, a personal friend of myself and my husband. He stood up for us during Wounded Knee and after. He stood up to his superiors, stuck his neck way out, became a real people's priest. He even learned our language. He died prematurely of cancer. It is not only the good Indians who die young, but the good whites, too. It is the timid ones who know how to take care of themselves who grow old. I am still grateful to that priest for what he did for us later and for the quarrel he picked with me—or did I pick it with him?—because it ended a situation which had become unendurable for me. The day of my fight with him was my last day in school.

◆ Questions for Discussion and Writing

1. What aspects of life at the government boarding school most clearly illustrate the government's desire to transform Native Americans?

2. How did Mary Crow Dog react to the experiences she endured at the government-run school?

3. What historical insight did the experiences of Mary Crow Dog's mother and grandmother add to those of Mary Crow Dog herself?

4. Why was the underground newspaper incident a crucial one for Mary Crow Dog?

5. What experiences have you had that made you aware of institutionalized racism?

Connections

1. Compare Helen Keller and Frederick Douglass in terms of their motivations and methods in overcoming obstacles to self-education.

2. Evaluate the teaching techniques described by Mark Salzman with those of Annie Sullivan, as related by Helen Keller.

3. Contrast the differences in cultural stereotyping that Lydia Minatoya experienced as an Asian American with the treatment Mary Crow Dog received as a Native American.

4. What common character traits emerge from accounts by Helen Keller, Frederick Douglass, Christy Brown ("The Letter 'A'," Chapter 8) and Sucheng Chan ("You're Short, Besides!" Chapter 8) that enabled each one to overcome obstacles to getting an education?

5. What insights into the importance of achievement for African Americans, over the last century, are provided by Frederick Douglass, Maya Angelou ("Liked for Myself," Chapter 8) and Jill Nelson ("Number One!" Chapter 1)?

6. Compare the teaching techniques Annie Sullivan used with Helen Keller to those employed by George Gurdjieff to enlighten Fritz Peters ("Gurdjieff Remembered," Chapter 2).

7. How do the accounts by Lydia Minatoya and Amy Tan ("Two Kinds," Chapter 12) offer insight into the kinds of pressures to which Asian American students are subjected?

8. What similarities underlie Mary Crow Dog's account of life as a Native American and Rigoberta Menchú's depiction of Quiché Indian life in Guatemala ("Things Have Happened to Me as in a Movie," Chapter 10)?

7

Our Working Lives

◆────────────◆

It's true, hard work never killed anybody,
but I figure, why take the chance?

—Ronald Reagan, Speech, Annual Gridiron Dinner, April 22, 1987

Work is life, you know, and without it,
there is nothing but fear and insecurity.

—John Lennon, *Twenty-four Hours,* December 15, 1969, BBC

The way we identify ourselves in terms of the work we do is far-reaching. Frequently, the first question we ask when we meet someone is, "What do you do?" Through work, we define ourselves and others; yet cultural values also play a part in influencing how we feel about the work we do. In addition to providing a means to live, work has an important psychological meaning. Some societies value work more than leisure; in other cultures, the reverse is true, and work is viewed as something you do just to provide the necessities of life. In the United States, what you do to make a living is often intertwined with your sense of identity and self-esteem.

Every society is also capable of being characterized in terms of social class. Although the principles by which class is identified vary widely—from the amount of money you earn in the United States to the kind of accent with which you speak in England to the religious caste you are born into in India—class considerations set boundaries around individuals that affect opportunities and possibilities.

For many reasons, conflicts based on inequalities of social class are often enmeshed with those of race. Minorities usually receive the least amount of education, have less political clout, earn the least income, and find work in occupations considered menial with no possibility of advancement. The writers in this chapter explore many of the less obvious connections between work, social class, and the control people exercise over their lives.

Lesley Hazleton tells how she met the physical and psychological demands of being an apprentice auto mechanic in "Confessions of a Fast Woman." Nancy Bazelon Goldstone recounts, in "A Trader in London," what it is like to be a female stockbroker in the world of high finance. Larry Brown, in "On Fire," describes a typical day and clarifies why fire-fighting is such a demanding profession. Margaret Sanger, in "The Turbid Ebb and Flow of Misery," describes how the experiences she had as a nurse led her to become an activist, disseminating birth-control information at the turn of the century.

Lesley Hazleton

Confessions of a Fast Woman

Lesley Hazleton was born in 1945 in Reading, England, received a B.A. in 1966 from Manchester University, and an M.A. in 1971 from the Hebrew University in Jerusalem. She immigrated to the United States in 1979. She has worked as a feature writer for the Jerusalem Post, *1968–1973, and as a reporter for* Time-Life, Inc., *Jerusalem, 1973–1976. She has been a distinguished writer in residence at Pacific Lutheran University, Tacoma, Washington, 1986, and has taught creative nonfiction writing at Pennsylvania State University, University Park, 1989. Her writings include* Israeli Women *(1978) and* Where Mountains Roar: A Personal Report from the Sinai and Negev Desert *(1980). Hazleton's dramatic reporting from the Middle East has been published in the award-winning* Jerusalem, Jerusalem *(1986). She has also written* England, Bloody England *(1989) and* Confessions of a Fast Woman *(1992). Since 1989, she has written the car column for* Lear's *magazine and has also written about cars and driving for* The New York Times, Connoisseur, Penthouse, *and* Newsday. *"Confessions of a Fast Woman," from her 1992 book of that name, tells how her lifelong passion for racing survived a stint working as an auto mechanic in upstate Vermont.*

I loved working at the sink. Harvey thought this was perverse of me. He was probably right. It was one of the dirtiest jobs in the shop.

The sink was a neatly self-enclosed system: a steel tub set atop a barrel containing parts cleaner, a small pump sucking the cleaner up from the barrel into a tube with a thick steel brush at the end, and a filter to clean the used fluid before it drained back into the barrel to be used again.

Working there, I'd stand with my back to everything else in the shop, concentrated entirely on the mass of gunked parts before me. The gunk was thick, black. The parts were so filthy they seemed almost anonymous, just so many interchangeable relics of the mechanical age. Even thinking of cleaning them at first seemed pointless.

But leave something to soak in that sink for a while, then come back to it and start scrubbing, and a kind of magic happened. What had been anonymous began to reveal form and personality. Vague shapes achieved particularity.

Black paled, gleamed here and there, turned slowly to silver. An ancient alchemy took place right under my hands as I hosed and scrubbed.

235

Years of baked grease and oil and road dirt gave way to the corrosiveness of the parts cleaner, and as I worked, it seemed that here, under my very hands, I was rediscovering the original form, the bright gleaming essence of each part. Old melted gaskets disappeared under the brush. Flywheel teeth became sharp and effective. Clutch plates became intricate pieces of sculpture. I had a distinct sense of creating each part anew, of restoring its form and function.

6   And all the time, of course, I was breathing in the fumes of the parts cleaner, so that I am still not sure if the work itself was really that satisfying, or if I was simply so high that it seemed that way.

7   All the cleaners began to smell good—a seductive, chemical smell that seemed to enter my head, clear my sinuses, clean up all the synapses of my brain. There was the 5-56, so much like dry-cleaning fluid that I sometimes thought if I just stood in the path of its fumes, it would clean the clothes right on me. Oddly, I'd always hated that smell before. Then there was the Carb Clean, for gummed-up carbs; the Brakleen brakes cleaner, each can with a thin red straw laid horizontally across its black cap like the headgear of a Japanese geisha; and the Gunk—a registered trademark name for heavy-duty engine cleaner.

8   I had no idea just how addictive the fumes were until a few weeks into my apprenticeship, on our Monday off. I was driving past another repair shop that was open on Mondays. The windows of my car were wide open, and as I went by, I recognized the smells of parts cleaner, gasoline, lubricants—all the acids and oils with which I now worked five days a week. I slowed way down, breathed in deep, and was suffused with an immense sense of well-being.

9   After a month, the shop and the smells and the work were in my dreams. They were good dreams, but I'd wake with the fumes still in my nostrils, wondering how smells from a dream could spill over into the first moments of waking. Was the sense of smell independent of reality? Was my brain so addicted that it could create the smell by itself, without any external stimulus?

10   No matter how seductive the fumes, however, there was no doubt as to the corrosiveness of the parts cleaner: it turned my tanned hands a whitish hue and made the skin parchment dry. I began to use rubber gloves when working at the sink, but even then the chemicals seemed to work their way through the rubber, and my hands still paled.

11   Meanwhile, the blackened asbestos dust from the brake pads was just plain hazardous. It was caked onto the calipers and the whole of the brake assembly. Cleaning it out demanded a screwdriver and a rag and copious amounts of Brakleen. It was close-up work, so that however careful I was, I still inhaled the dust.

12   You take all the precautions you can in a repair shop. You keep as many doors and windows open as possible. You keep fans going. You back out cars and bikes to start them up, or if you have to start them in-

side, you attach a hose to the exhaust pipe and run the fumes outside. You could, of course, wear a mask, but few mechanics do. Most know they should, but the masks are hot and stuffy and they get in the way. And besides, the truth is that most mechanics do not worry about fumes. They have bigger things to worry about: a jack or a hoist giving way, a fire, a loose part spinning off. Auto mechanics is not a safe profession.

Despite all the protestations of writers and researchers that intellectual work is hard and exhausting, physical work is harder. Like anyone who's done it day in and day out, I now know this in my bones. 13

For years, I argued that intellectual work was exhausting, as indeed it can be. After a few hours at the typewriter, there is little I can do for a while. All my energy has been consumed, poured onto the page. Sometimes I do some physical work for a change—scythe an overgrown garden, for instance, or clean the oven. In such circumstances, physical work seems a pleasure and a relief, something that produces a healthy kind of exhaustion instead of the enervating overload of the mind that I am escaping. 14

This kind of short-term excursion into physical work can indeed make it seem attractive. But when you do it for a living, it exacts a heavy toll. The long-term effects of fumes and asbestos dust working their way into the body's cells are one thing, but the short term can be riskier still. With all due respect to the physical strain on hands, eyes, back, and brain from working at a keyboard all day, in physical work you can literally break your back. 15

I was lucky. I only sprained mine. 16

The culprit was a Datsun 240Z. It arrived on a truck with a note that read, "It went to Woodstock, and while there, the gears went." Just that, and a signature. 17

It hadn't been cruising the idyllic scenery of Woodstock. It had been drag racing. The owners had put a six-cylinder 260 engine into it, with triple carbs and a psi gauge. There'd been a big pop, it seemed, and then—nothing. No motion. 18

"We'll have to pull out the transmission and replace it," said Carl. 19

I was delighted. The heavier the work—the more it got down to the basics, into the actual drive mechanisms—the happier I was because the more I'd learn. Better still, if we had to replace the transmission, I could take the broken one apart. I already knew from the exploded diagrams in my textbook that there's nothing like taking things apart to understand how they work. Putting them back together again, I had still to discover, is yet another level of understanding. 20

The Z-car rode so low to the ground that we had to jack it up just to get the arms of the hydraulic lift underneath it. Harvey removed the bolt at the bottom of the transmission case so we could drain the trans- 21 mission fluid—foul-smelling stuff—and found a small chunk of metal sitting on top of the bolt. "Bad sign," he said. "Something's come loose and ripped through the gears."

22   The next stage was to get the exhaust system off. That should have been simple enough, but there was so much gunk and rust that even after we'd loosened all the bolts, nothing moved. So Harvey stood up front and yanked, and I stood toward the back, pulling and yanking at the pipe above my head.

23   I felt something go inside me. Somewhere in my abdomen, it seemed. But I was focused on that exhaust pipe, eyes half-closed against flecks of grit and rust, and paid no attention. Harvey finally managed to loosen the front end, then we swapped places, me steadying as he pulled, and finally, lo and behold, the pipe slid off. We disconnected the fuel and oil lines, and then faced the really tough part.

24   When you're deeply involved in hard work, you simply don't notice pain. By the time we got the transmission case down from its mountings and into the yard, and then dismantled the clutch, it was late afternoon, and it was clear that this was going to be a long, drawn-out job. The drive plate and flywheel were so badly worn that they too would have to be replaced.

25   I went home that night exhausted. That was nothing unusual. Most evenings I'd flop down in an armchair with a beer in one hand, and find myself unable to move. It was the kind of deep exhaustion that comes only from hard physical work, the kind that you can feel in every muscle of your body, that seems to reach into your bones and sit there, making them feel both incredibly heavy and weightless at the same time. There is a strange kind of floating feeling to this exhaustion, yet at the same time you are convinced that you must weigh twice what you usually weigh.

26   If someone had shouted "Fire!" right then, I'd have nodded, said "Fine," and not moved an inch.

27   This stage of exhaustion would usually last a good half hour or so, and in that half hour, I'd hold my hands up in front of my face and wonder where all those cuts and burns and scrapes had come from. From the repair shop, obviously, but what car, what movement, what moment? I never knew. Cuts and burns and scrapes and other minor injuries were just part of the job, so much so that I never noticed them at the time. Only later, in another place and time, in a comfortable armchair as the sun was setting, did they begin to seem remarkable. And then I'd feel an odd pride in them. They were proof of my work, small badges of my apprenticeship.

28   That Z-car had been a tougher job than most. We'd been working on it nearly the whole of the ten-hour day, and now, as I sat still, I realized my abdomen was really hurting, and that the pain was spreading to my back. A pulled muscle, I thought. We had three days off now for the Fourth of July weekend, and I was glad: my body needed it.

The next morning, I picked up a loaded wheelbarrow of split wood, turned it to the right, and could almost swear that I heard something go pop in my lower back, just like the gears of that Z-car. For the first time in my life, I understood what crippling pain was. By the time I got to a chiropractor in Barre, the only one around who'd see me on a holiday weekend, I couldn't walk without a crutch. 29

Half an hour later, I walked out carrying the crutch—still in pain, but mobile. The chiro, young and gentle, merely smiled tolerantly when I compared him to Christ. 30

"This back has forty-eight hours to heal," I told him. 31

"It will probably take four or five weeks," he said. 32

I shook my head. "It can't," I said. "I've got to go to work." 33

He studied my face. "Come on in tomorrow and the next day," he said, "and we'll see what we can do." 34

That included the Fourth of July itself. Rob Borowske became more and more Christ-like in my mind. Forty-eight hours of cold compresses, gentle stretching, electrical stimulation, aspirin, and chiropractic adjustments did not make for the happiest of weekends, but on the morning of July 5, I was there at Just Imports, a compress strapped to my lower back, cautiously mobile. 35

It wasn't macho that made me so determined. Partly it was the awareness that if I lay in bed and played invalid, my back would "freeze" and take far longer to heal. But more than that, it was the knowledge that Harvey and Bud would have to literally break their backs before they'd stay away from work. A mere "subluxation" simply did not rank. Not alongside what Harvey had been through. 36

The back healed quickly. Between Rob's four or five weeks and my forty-eight hours, it compromised on two weeks, although by the middle of the first week I was working as I had been. Being on my feet all day helped. Besides, I had to take apart that transmission case, discovering in the process that Harvey had been right: ball bearings had come loose and torn through the gears. No wonder nothing would move. 37

Harvey asked after the back a couple of times, but after that it was business as usual. Neither he nor Bud nor Carl thought it at all odd that I should turn up for work. Injuries were just part of the job. My back, the left foot I bruised badly when I moved a motorcycle the wrong way, the concussion I'd get a couple of weeks later when I'd stand up and hit my head on the strut of the hydraulic lift ("Every apprentice has to do it at least once," said Harvey)—these were just par for the course. As one injury healed and another replaced it, I began to think of them as rites of passage: stages in my evolution as an apprentice. 38

✦ *Questions for Discussion and Writing*

1. Describe the tasks Hazleton confronted in her everyday work as an auto mechanic.

2. What explains her unwillingness to let her back injury incapacitate her?

3. In your opinion, what does being an apprentice in an auto repair shop mean to her? What satisfactions does she seem to be getting from it?

4. Compare the demands of hard physical work with the stresses of hard intellectual work. Which did you find more exhausting and why?

5. Have you ever had a job where you performed work traditionally associated with the opposite gender? Did you find it to be a pleasant or unpleasant experience?

Nancy Bazelon Goldstone

A Trader in London

---◆---

Nancy Bazelon Goldstone is a financial analyst and stockbroker. Her essay, "A Trader in London," originally appeared in the "Hers" Column of The New York Times Magazine *(1987). In it she reveals her battle with sexual stereotyping and male prejudices in the world of high finance in New York City and London.*

1 At the age of 27 I became the head foreign-exchange options trader at a major commercial bank in New York. I managed hundreds of millions of dollars' worth of options. I ran offices in New York and London. It was a powerful and demanding position.

2 Few women have had this experience, so I am often asked what it was like to work in a bank trading room on Wall Street. I like to tell the following story:

3 It was a cold day in early February, almost a year to the day since I had started my trading career. We'd had an unusually hectic morning, and I was sitting at my desk, frantically trying to calculate the effect of the morning's trades on the overall position. This had to be done quickly and accurately.

4 I was lost in concentration when suddenly I noticed that there was something wrong. It took me a second or two to realize what was the matter. The room had gone completely quiet.

5 During the entire year I had been trading, I had never experienced so complete a silence. Instinctively, I glanced at the Reuters screen. The currency prices had remained unchanged. Whatever was causing the sudden calm had not yet been acted on in the market.

6 I got to my feet and saw at once that most of the traders in the room were huddled around the spot foreign-exchange desk. This is the place where the latest information comes across a Telerate machine. There is also a television set there so that the traders can listen to important news conferences or bulletins.

7 I swore to myself. What could it be? Something so important that the market hadn't had the time to digest the full implications of the information. I ran over the spot desk, praying silently that it wasn't an assassination.

8 "What is it?" I cried.

9 Surprised by my intensity, several of the traders turned toward me. Through the opening I saw the cause of the trouble.

241

10   The "swimsuit issue" of Sports Illustrated had arrived.

11   Trading is a profession dominated almost exclusively by men. It's not that I was ever discriminated against. It's just that the atmosphere, outlook and energy of every trading room I've ever been in is distinctly and overtly male. Raunchy jokes are the order of the day—the dirtier, the better. The first half-hour of every morning is spent discussing the previous night's exploits, real or imagined, in vivid detail. I've seen competent, professional traders turned to jelly by the entrance of some-one's teen-age daughter. Sometimes this took a little getting used to.

12   For example, in December '85 I proposed to expand my New York operation to London. The bank already had a trading room there deal-ing in foreign currencies and Eurodollars. It was simply a matter of set-ting up a desk to trade options and hiring some people locally. Senior management approved my plan, and just before Christmas I flew over to make arrangements for the addition of my group.

13   By this time I was used to walking into a trading room, so I knew what to expect. A sea of white shirts and blue ties surrounded by a pale gray cloud of cigarette smoke. The only other woman in the room was a secretary whose duties included serving tea in the afternoon.

14   Although the office had been notified of my visit, it appeared that they were not quite as prepared for me as I was for them. The branch manager's eyes widened slightly when I introduced myself. Surely, I wasn't the woman who was heading up the options unit? I'm afraid I was. He was expecting someone, well, older. I could almost read his thoughts. How could a young woman, wearing lipstick and high heels, possibly be the head of a trading unit that included a staff in New York and the responsibility for a billion-dollar portfolio? It's not that he meant to be rude, you understand. It's just that it was beyond his level of comprehension.

15   My meeting included an inspection of the premises. After the ini-tial shock, the branch manager was exceedingly polite and made a point of introducing me to all of the traders on his staff. They were, to a man, young and friendly, and from their accents I could tell that they were members of the British working class. Just a nice, normal, every-day bunch of guys. The kind who like to drink beer in the pubs after work. Although they were very hospitable, it was clear that they viewed my presence as a kind of joke.

16   In the spirit of Christmas, the office was decorated with a tree, and there were tinsel and red ribbons scattered about. A bulletin board was overrun with Christmas cards and pictures of naked women.

17   Pictures of naked women?

I'm sure if they'd given the matter any thought, they would have been embarrassed and taken the photographs down prior to my visit. But the pictures had apparently been around for so long that the traders no longer noticed them. Just part of an environment designed to keep them happy and comfortable at their work. 18

I felt kind of sorry for those guys actually. I knew I was about to do something that would change their lives. 19

I needed a trader in London. 20

I was going to hire a woman. 21

✦ Questions for Discussion and Writing

1. How does the way in which Goldstone sets up her narrative intensify suspense?

2. How does the cause of the unusual silence in the stockbrokers' offices illustrate her thesis?

3. How does Goldstone present herself? Does her use of language add to this impression? How does the contrast between Goldstone and other women add to this characterization?

4. Reflect on your personal experience in a part-time or full-time job that took place over several weeks or months. Write an essay in which you evaluate or interpret that experience and its significance in changing your attitudes towards the value of work.

5. What sexual stereotypes have you encountered in any job you have held? Describe the circumstances.

6. Goldstone is very conscious of the impression she makes. In your journal, write a brief description of yourself from the perspective of the receptionist, secretary, or interviewer in an office where you are applying for a job.

Larry Brown

On Fire

◆───────◆

Larry Brown was born and raised in Oxford, Mississippi, and was a Marine during the Viet Nam War. He joined the Oxford Fire Department in 1973, where he worked until 1990, when he retired with the rank of captain. His works of fiction include Facing the Music *(1984) and* Joe, *which won the 1992 Southern Book Circle Award for Fiction. "On Fire" is drawn from his 1994 autobiography of the same name.*

1   I was cooking some ribs one evening and drinking a beer, taking life easy on a Saturday afternoon. The ribs were par-boiling in some water, getting tender, and about dark I was going to put them over a fire on the grill, slap some barbecue sauce on them, cook my family a little feast. Maybe we were going to watch a movie, too, I don't know. That's one of our big things: cook something on the grill outside and then watch a good movie while we're eating, then kind of just fall out all over the living room to finish watching it, then sometimes even watch another one. I usually have several cold beers while I'm doing that. The ribs were going to cook for a couple of hours and I had plenty of beer.

2   The phone rang and my plans got changed. It was the dispatcher at Station No. 1, and he said we had a fire at the Law School at Ole Miss, and all hands were being called in. It was what we call a Code Red.

3   I cut off the ribs but I did take my beer. I thought if the fire wasn't too bad, a beer would be pretty good on the way back. I drove my little truck at what is an abnormal speed for me, about sixty-five. I live about ten miles from Oxford so it didn't take long to get there.

4   You never know what to expect except that if it's bad you can certainly expect to be dirty and exhausted and possibly coughing or throwing up or maybe even burned, your ears singed a little before it's over. I knew the building but I'd only been in the bottom of it once, and in the library once, and that was on the second floor. The fire we had that night was on the fifth, top floor.

5   I stopped by Station No. 1 and got my turnouts, pulling my pickup right into the truck bay where a lot of leather boots were lying, where my partners had kicked them off and left them. The turnout pants stand on low shelves, folded down with the rubber boots already inside them, so that all you have to do is step into them and pull the pants up, snap them shut, grab your coat and helmet, climb on the

truck and roll out the door. Every piece of equipment in the house was gone, our big diesel pumper, the van, and the ladder truck that could reach ten stories high. The dispatcher came out for a second and said we had a working fire but they didn't know how bad it was yet. I drove fast through town, knowing where all the cops were.

The ladder truck was being set up when I pulled into the parking lot. There was a little smoke showing from the top of the building. I could see our boys in full gear down on their knees putting airpacks on. I put my turnouts on, got my gloves in one hand and my helmet in the other, and ran to report to the assistant chief in charge that I was there and ready for my assignment. Off-duty people were arriving all around me. They'd called everybody in.

The structure was a five-story building with a concrete exterior, lined with windows about seven or eight feet long and about five and a half feet tall. None of the windows were designed to open, had no hinges or handles, and the glass was tempered, somewhere between a quarter and a half inch thick. There was no outside egress to the building except through the first and top floors. It was not equipped with a sprinkler system, since it was considered to be a fireproof building, but it did have a wet standpipe system with those little piss-ant hoses.

I found out that the alarm inside the building had been going for quite a while, but people had simply ignored it. Kept walking around in there, conducting their whatever. I was told to put on an airpack and climb the stairwell with some other firefighters to the top floor and descend into the building to try and locate the fire. I donned my apparatus, found my partners, and we started up. We all had flashlights.

The rig weighs between thirty and forty pounds. It will give you about twenty minutes of air if you're lying flat on your back breathing through the respirator; that's if you're not exerting yourself. When five minutes of air is left, a little bell mounted on the tank will start ringing, loud and insistently, driven by the declining air pressure. With experience you learn to leave the mask off until you're ready to enter your dangerous atmosphere. They work just like a diver's rig, but the mask and mouthpiece are all molded together, so that the mask covers your whole face. They're called SCBA, self-contained breathing apparatus. You can enter a poisonous atmosphere, live in a superheated temperature if the rest of your body can stand it. The main purpose is to prevent the firefighter from breathing smoke.

We were already a little winded by the time we got to the top floor. As soon as we stepped into the hall, we were enveloped in heavy black smoke. It was bad enough to put the masks on. An initial search revealed nothing but more smoke and nearly zero visibility. Things were much worse than they appeared from outside, certainly. I got worried when I saw that it was impossible to see my partners' flashlight beams if they were over three or four feet away. I got everybody back together and told them to go back outside. I didn't want anybody getting separated from the group and getting lost in the smoke. We hadn't had time to bring in any safety lines or anything like that yet. It was still very early. No tactical decisions had been made. We went back down for fresh tanks and more men. I knew by then I wouldn't be getting back to those ribs any time soon.

11   I reported what we'd found up there: bad conditions, heavy smoke, zero visibility, no flame found yet. The ladder was operating by then and more off-duty people had arrived. Most of the people on my shift were there, including my boss, who took charge of the ladder. My two duty partners were there, getting their turnouts on, getting ready to go up. I got another tank and climbed on the ladder platform and caught a ride to the roof. There was a wide ledge, maybe twelve feet or so, outside the fifth floor. The captain of the shift on duty got off on the ledge and the rest of us went on to the roof. My boss let us off and went back down for more men and equipment. His steady, up-and-down trips, five stories high, ferrying people and supplies, would go on unceasingly for the next few hours.

12   The fire needed to be ventilated—that is, an opening of some sort made in the building to let the buildup of heat and smoke out, to improve visibility conditions so the fire could be located and attacked. It was a long time before that happened.

13   We started another search of the fifth floor. We appeared to be in a hall that was built in a large rectangle with numerous doors that opened into offices. What we didn't know was that the fire was in the very center of the building, in a lounge area that had only two doors. We wasted an enormous amount of time checking for fire in the outlying offices, working by feel and touch in a place that was solid black to the eye, a place growing uncomfortably hot. We had a bad fire, it was rapidly worsening, and we didn't have it located, although we were searching as diligently as we could. Bells started ringing on the tanks, and I realized that it might be possible for some of us to become disoriented in the smoke, run out of air, and have to pull the mask off, and maybe never make it back to safety and fresh air. We went back outside to count heads and then we climbed on up to the roof.

14   An entry saw with a gasoline engine had been sent up in case we decided to cut a hole in the roof, but the roof was constructed of gravel over tar paper over concrete. Something else had to be done, something quick. The smoke had to be let out of the building right away, before a bad fire got any worse, before the heat intensified any more. The only thing we saw was the windows.

15   More people had come up, along with hoses and nozzles and ropes and more airpacks. I went over to the ladder and told my boss about the conditions, that it was evidently a bad fire and getting worse, and

that we were going to have to break some windows on the fifth floor. He listened and nodded, and went down for tools.

I don't know what all happened then. Adrenaline. The next major 16 event was the arrival via the ladder of two men with a fire ax and a heavy pry bar. I got back on the ladder platform and went with them down to the fifth-floor ledge and we walked to the corner window, a huge pane of dark glass that looked very expensive. Hundreds of people were standing below on the ground. Red and blue lights were flashing everywhere down there. The ladder was running at a high throttle, and hoses had been laid from the pumpers to the building so that we could boost the water pressure inside the standpipe system. I took a deep breath and swung the heavy pry bar as hard as I could at the window. It bounced off.

I braced my feet, tightened my helmet strap, turned the point of the 17 tool to the glass and tried my best to shatter it. It bounced off.

I'm no ball player, never have been. But I brought the heavy bar 18 around from behind my back with both hands gripping it like a baseball bat and delivered all the weight of it to the center of the window and it caved in in large jagged pieces. We were immediately engulfed in a roar of dense black smoke that barreled out over us so heavily that we had to move out of it and go on to the next window. People on the ground were yelling.

We eventually broke nine windows in a row all down that side of 19 the fifth floor, walking down the ledge, swinging the pry bar in, knocking the sharp edges of glass out of the casement. More men were delivered to the ledge and we established our entry and exit route: through a window halfway down the side, step down into a nicely upholstered Law School dean's desk chair, walk across his desk and papers, drop onto the floor, try to find the fire. I think we knocked a lot of things over. A forward command post was set up on the ledge, and the captain relayed his orders for men and equipment via walkie-talkie back to the assistant chief, who directed the ground operations from the parking lot.

That trip I went in without a mask, because the smoke was lifting a 20 little, even though the temperature seemed to have increased. I knew that was because the fire was getting a fresh supply of oxygen, but that's something you have to deal with when you ventilate. If you can go on in and make your stop, it doesn't make a shit.

Our pumpers were feeding the standpipe system, and we got the 21 little piss-ant hose off the rack and stretched out the line. We thought the fire was right in front of us, and we were going to crawl our way up to it and find it and fight it. But we couldn't get the valve turned on. We tried and tried and even hammered on it with spanner wrenches, but we couldn't get it to open. We sent somebody out for a pipe wrench and then got it turned on, but blew the hose completely out of the coupling from the tremendous pressure our pump operators were sending through the pipe.

22   It took a little while to shut it off, take off the burst hose, and put our own nozzles and hose on it. But when we had that done, we put on fresh tanks and went down the hall in a group, close to the floor. We knew where it was now, back there in that lounge.

23   The air was burning our ears, even down that low. All of us crawling and sliding in the water, going inside a door where the thing was feeding and getting bigger. That is a special place to be in, with men in a burning building, where you can only barely hear one another talking behind the masks, where the glow of the fire makes a light on the masks around you, where you are all panting and pulling on the hose and trying to be as small and concentrated as possible, trying to do the job. Sometimes you reach a stage of near exhaustion after only a few minutes.

24   All we could see was a hellish red light in front of us somewhere. But we could hear the damn thing. Everything around us was charred, the water we were crawling in was black and hot, and the only smell was that of heavy smoke. My partners had the nozzle and I had my hand on their shoulders and we were inching forward, spraying water. We slipped on the tiles until we got to the carpet and then we pushed close to the fire, to that awful heat, until it came through our turnouts and our gloves and into our knees where we knelt in the hot water. Another bell started ringing and I hollered for whoever it was to get out. Somebody left and somebody came in on the line to replace him. We kept pushing forward, yelling, urging each other on.

25   You have to meet the thing is what it is. You have to do something in your life that is honorable and not cowardly if you are able to live in peace with yourself, and for the firefighter it is fire. It has to be faced and defeated so that you prove to yourself that you meet the measure of the job. You cannot turn your back on it, as much as you would like to be in cooler air, as much as you would like to breathe it. You have to stay huddled with the men you are with.

26   We whipped that fire's ass. It fought back, leaping and dodging the water, but we kept the nozzle open and on fog and rotated it in a counterclockwise manner due to the rotation and curvature of the earth, and the water was dispersed into tiny droplets by the turbojet nozzle. The droplets were converted into steam by the heat of the fire and steam is what put the fire out.

27   We pulled back for a breather and more people came in to mop up small fires and start salvage and overhaul.

28   In the Law School dean's office I saw my partners with sootstreaked faces, exhausted beer-drinking buddies with their coats open, lying on shards of glass in the floor with cigarettes in their hands. There was an unbelievable amount of talking and confusion. I lit my own cigarette,

went back across the man's nice desk and out on the ledge, and told them we'd knocked it down.

It isn't until later that the real exhaustion sets in. They sent up some cold Gatorade that was delivered while the overhaul went on, while more men, fresh men, came up, while they ferried empty air tanks back and forth to Station One for refilling at the compressor, while men worked at the station filling the tanks, while the pump operators watched the gauges and engine temperatures, while the people in charge oversaw everything from outside and talked on their walkie-talkies, while the dispatcher manned the radio, while my boss carried the platform of the ladder up and down, over and over.

I sat down on the floor and smoked a cigarette and drank some Gatorade. We all looked at each other and just shook our heads.

Later we were told that it looked like a black tornado had come out of the building when we broke the first window, and that a man from the university's physical plant department had started tearing at his hair when we started breaking the windows because they cost $1,500 apiece.

Well, yeah. But it got the smoke out. Their fireproof building didn't burn down. And we were all still alive when it was over.

✦ Questions for Discussion and Writing

1. What specific details and facts concerning firemen's gear and the circumstances of actual firefighting made you realize the extraordinary demands made upon firefighters?

2. How does Brown characterize the gap between the public perception of volunteer firemen and his actual experiences? To what extent is Brown's narrative designed to change the reader's perception of volunteer firemen?

3. How does the recurrent image of breaking more windows in the dean's office symbolize the difference between society's perspective on firefighters and the actual challenges and dangers they face?

4. Describe an experience in which you became aware that a person you knew only through his or her role at work had a "real" life outside the workplace.

5. Have you ever been a volunteer? Describe your experiences and the differences between society's perception and your personal view, based on your experience.

Margaret Sanger

The Turbid Ebb and
Flow of Misery*

◆

*Margaret Sanger (1883–1966), who began her career as a nurse, was an
early advocate for the dissemination of birth-control information in America. In "The Turbid Ebb and Flow of Misery," from* The Autobiography
of Margaret Sanger *(1938), she describes the horrendous circumstances
and ignorance about sexual matters that compelled her to fight for the
rights of poor women. She organized the first conference on birth control
in America and wrote numerous books and articles on the subject
throughout her life.*

> Every night and every morn
> Some to misery are born.
> Every morn and every night
> Some are born to sweet delight.
> Some are born to sweet delight,
> Some are born to endless night.
>
> —William Blake

1 　　During these years [about 1912] in New York trained nurses were
in great demand. Few people wanted to enter hospitals; they were
afraid they might be "practiced" upon, and consented to go only in
desperate emergencies. Sentiment was especially vehement in the matter of having babies. A woman's own bedroom, no matter how incon-
veniently arranged, was the usual place for her lying-in. I was not
sufficiently free from domestic duties to be a general nurse, but I could
ordinarily manage obstetrical cases because I was notified far enough
ahead to plan my schedule. And after serving my two weeks I could
get home again.

2 　　Sometimes I was summoned to small apartments occupied by
young clerks, insurance salesmen, or lawyers, just starting out, most of
them under thirty and whose wives were having their first or second
baby. They were always eager to know the best and latest method in in-

---

*Chapter 7 of *An Autobiography* (1938). Sanger has taken her chapter title from a line in
Matthew Arnold's poem "Dover Beach." [Editor's note.]

fant care and feeding. In particular, Jewish patients, whose lives centered around the family, welcomed advice and followed it implicitly.

But more and more my calls began to come from the Lower East 3
Side, as though I were being magnetically drawn there by some force outside my control. I hated the wretchedness and hopelessness of the poor, and never experienced that satisfaction in working among them that so many noble women have found. My concern for my patients was now quite different from my earlier hospital attitude. I could see that much was wrong with them which did not appear in the physiological or medical diagnosis. A woman in childbirth was not merely a woman in childbirth. My expanded outlook included a view of her background, her potentialities as a human being, the kind of children she was bearing, and what was going to happen to them.

The wives of small shopkeepers were my most frequent cases, but I 4
had carpenters, truck drivers, dishwashers, and pushcart vendors. I admired intensely the consideration most of these people had for their own. Money to pay doctor and nurse had been carefully saved months in advance—parents-in-law, grandfathers, grandmothers, all contributing.

As soon as the neighbors learned that a nurse was in the building 5
they came in a friendly way to visit, often carrying fruit, jellies, or gefüllter fish made after a cherished recipe. It was infinitely pathetic to me that they, so poor themselves, should bring me food. Later they drifted in again with the excuse of getting the plate, and sat down for a nice talk; there was no hurry. Always back of the little gift was the question, "I am pregnant (or my daughter, or my sister is). Tell me something to keep from having another baby. We cannot afford another yet."

I tried to explain the only two methods I had ever heard of among 6
the middle classes, both of which were invariably brushed aside as unacceptable. They were of no certain avail to the wife because they placed the burden of responsibility solely upon the husband—a burden which he seldom assumed. What she was seeking was self-protection she could herself use, and there was none.

Below this stratum of society was one in truly desperate circum- 7
stances. The men were sullen and unskilled, picking up odd jobs now and then, but more often unemployed, lounging in and out of the house at all hours of the day and night. The women seemed to slink on their way to market and were without neighborliness.

These submerged, untouched classes were beyond the scope of or- 8
ganized charity or religion. No labor union, no church, not even the Salvation Army reached them. They were apprehensive of everyone and rejected help of any kind, ordering all intruders to keep out; both birth and death they considered their own business. Social agents, who were just beginning to appear, were profoundly mistrusted because they pried into homes and lives, asking questions about wages, how many were in the family, had any of them ever been in jail. Often two or

three had been there or were now under suspicion of prostitution, shoplifting, purse snatching, petty thievery, and, in consequence, passed furtively by the big blue uniforms on the corner.

9   The utmost depression came over me as I approached this surreptitious region. Below Fourteenth Street I seemed to be breathing a different air, to be in another world and country where the people had habits and customs alien to anything I had ever heard about.

10   There were then approximately ten thousand apartments in New York into which no sun ray penetrated directly; such windows as they had opened only on a narrow court from which rose fetid odors. It was seldom cleaned, though garbage and refuse often went down into it. All these dwellings were pervaded by the foul breath of poverty, that moldy, indefinable, indescribable smell which cannot be fumigated out, sickening to me but apparently unnoticed by those who lived there. When I set to work with antiseptics, their pungent sting, at least temporarily, obscured the stench.

11   I remember one confinement case to which I was called by the doctor of an insurance company. I climbed up the five flights and entered the airless rooms, but the baby had come with too great speed. A boy of ten had been the only assistant. Five flights was a long way; he had wrapped the placenta in a piece of newspaper and dropped it out the window into the court.

12   Many families took in "boarders," as they were termed, whose small contributions paid the rent. These derelicts, wanderers, alternately working and drinking, were crowded in with the children; a single room sometimes held as many as six sleepers. Little girls were accustomed to dressing and undressing in front of the men, and were often violated, occasionally by their own fathers or brothers, before they reached the age of puberty.

13   Pregnancy was a chronic condition among the women of this class. Suggestions as to what to do for a girl who was "in trouble" or a married woman who was "caught" passed from mouth to mouth—herb teas, turpentine, steaming, rolling downstairs, inserting slippery elm, knitting needles, shoe-hooks. When they had word of a new remedy they hurried to the drugstore, and if the clerk were inclined to be friendly he might say, "Oh, that won't help you, but here's something that may." The younger druggists usually refused to give advice because, if it were to be known, they would come under the law; midwives were even more fearful. The doomed women implored me to reveal the "secret" rich people had, offering to pay me extra to tell them; many really believed I was holding back information for money. They asked everybody and tried anything, but nothing did them any good. On Saturday nights I have seen groups of from fifty to one hundred with their shawls over their heads waiting outside the office of a five-dollar abortionist.

Each time I returned to this district, which was becoming a recur- 14
rent nightmare, I used to hear that Mrs. Cohen "had been carried to a
hospital, but had never come back," or that Mrs. Kelly "had sent the
children to a neighbor and had put her head into the gas oven." Day after day such tales were poured into my ears—a baby born dead, great
relief—the death of an older child, sorrow but again relief of a sort—the
story told a thousand times of death from abortion and children going
into institutions. I shuddered with horror as I listened to the details and
studied the reasons back of them—destitution linked with excessive
childbearing. The waste of life seemed utterly senseless. One by one
worried, sad, pensive, and aging faces marshaled themselves before
me in my dreams, sometimes appealingly, sometimes accusingly.

These were not merely "unfortunate conditions among the poor" 15
such as we read about. I knew the women personally. They were living,
breathing, human beings, with hopes, fears, and aspirations like my
own, yet their weary, misshapen bodies, "always ailing, never failing,"
were destined to be thrown on the scrap heap before they were thirty-
five. I could not escape from the facts of their wretchedness; neither
was I able to see any way out. My own cozy and comfortable family existence was becoming a reproach to me.

Then one stifling mid-July day of 1912 I was summoned to a Grand 16
Street tenement. My patient was a small, slight Russian Jewess, about
twenty-eight years old, of the special cast of feature to which suffering
lends a madonna-like expression. The cramped three-room apartment
was in a sorry state of turmoil. Jake Sachs, a truck driver scarcely older
than his wife, had come home to find the three children crying and her
unconscious from the effects of a self-induced abortion. He had called
the nearest doctor, who in turn had sent for me. Jake's earnings were
trifling, and most of them had gone to keep the none-too-strong children clean and properly fed. But his wife's ingenuity had helped them
to save a little, and this he was glad to spend on a nurse rather than
have her go to a hospital.

The doctor and I settled ourselves to the task of fighting the septi- 17
cemia. Never had I worked so fast, never so concentratedly. The sultry
days and nights were melted into a torpid inferno. It did not seem possible there could be such heat, and every bit of food, ice, and drugs had
to be carried up three flights of stairs.

Jake was more kind and thoughtful than many of the husbands I 18
had encountered. He loved his children, and had always helped his
wife wash and dress them. He had brought water up and carried garbage down before he left in the morning, and did as much as he could
for me while he anxiously watched her progress.

After a fortnight Mrs. Sachs' recovery was in sight. Neighbors, or- 19
dinarily fatalistic as to the results of abortion, were genuinely pleased
that she had survived. She smiled wanly at all who came to see her and

thanked them gently, but she could not respond to their hearty congrat-
ulations. She appeared to be more despondent and anxious than she
should have been, and spent too much time in meditation.

20   At the end of three weeks, as I was preparing to leave the fragile
patient to take up her difficult life once more, she finally voiced her
fears, "Another baby will finish me, I suppose?"

21   "It's too early to talk about that," I temporized.

22   But when the doctor came to make his last call, I drew him aside.
"Mrs. Sachs is terribly worried about having another baby."

23   "She well may be," replied the doctor, and then he stood before her
and said, "Any more such capers, young woman, and there'll be no
need to send for me."

24   "I know, doctor," she replied timidly, "but," and she hesitated as
though it took all her courage to say it, "what can I do to prevent it?"

25   The doctor was a kindly man, and he had worked hard to save her,
but such incidents had become so familiar to him that he had long since
lost whatever delicacy he might once have had. He laughed good-na-
turedly. "You want to have your cake and eat it too, do you? Well, it
can't be done."

26   Then picking up his hat and bag to depart he said, "Tell Jake to
sleep on the roof."

27   I glanced quickly at Mrs. Sachs. Even through my sudden tears I
could see stamped on her face an expression of absolute despair, We
simply looked at each other, saying no word until the door had closed
behind the doctor. Then she lifted her thin, blue-veined hands and
clasped them beseechingly. "He can't understand. He's only a man. But
you do, don't you? Please tell me the secret, and I'll never breathe it to
a soul. *Please!*"

28   What was I to do? I could not speak the conventionally comforting
phrases which would be of no comfort. Instead, I made her as physically easy as I could and promised to come back in a few days to talk
with her again. A little later, when she slept, I tiptoed away.

29   Night after night the wistful image of Mrs. Sachs appeared before
me. I made all sorts of excuses to myself for not going back. I was busy
on other cases; I really did not know what to say to her or how to convince her of my own ignorance; I was helpless to avert such monstrous
atrocities. Time rolled by and I did nothing.

30   The telephone rang one evening three months later, and Jake Sachs'
agitated voice begged me to come at once; his wife was sick again and
from the same cause. For a wild moment I thought of sending someone
else, but actually, of course, I hurried into my uniform, caught up my
bag, and started out. All the way I longed for a subway wreck, an explosion, anything to keep me from having to enter that home again. But
nothing happened, even to delay me. I turned into the dingy doorway

and climbed the familiar stairs once more. The children were there, young little things.

Mrs. Sachs was in a coma and died within ten minutes. I folded her still hands across her breast, remembering how they had pleaded with me, begging so humbly for the knowledge which was her right. I drew a sheet over her pallid face. Jake was sobbing, running his hands through his hair and pulling it out like an insane person. Over and over again he wailed, "My God! My God! My God!"   31

I left him pacing desperately back and forth, and for hours I myself walked and walked and walked through the hushed streets. When I finally arrived home and let myself quietly in, all the household was sleeping. I looked out my window and down upon the dimly lighted city. Its pains and griefs crowded in upon me, a moving picture rolled before my eyes with photographic clearness: women writhing in travail to bring forth little babies; the babies themselves naked and hungry, wrapped in newspapers to keep them from the cold; six-year-old children with pinched, pale, wrinkled faces, old in concentrated wretchedness, pushed into gray and fetid cellars, crouching on stone floors, their small scrawny hands scuttling through rags, making lamp shades, artificial flowers; white coffins, black coffins, coffins, coffins interminably passing in never-ending succession. The scenes piled one upon another on another. I could bear it no longer.   32

As I stood there the darkness faded. The sun came up and threw its reflection over the house tops. It was the dawn of a new day in my life also. The doubt and questioning, the experimenting and trying, were now to be put behind me. I knew I could not go back merely to keeping people alive.   33

I went to bed, knowing that no matter what it might cost, I was finished with palliatives and superficial cures; I was resolved to seek out the root of evil, to do something to change the destiny of mothers whose miseries were vast as the sky.   34

✦ Questions for Discussion and Writing

1. From Sanger's perspective, based on her experiences on New York City's Lower East Side, what characteristics establish clear boundaries between social classes in terms of access to resources and information?

2. How does Sanger's account reflect her personal crisis regarding activism in dissemination of birth-control information?

3. What function is served by the example of Mrs. Sachs? Why did this episode prove to be such a decisive turning point for Sanger?

4. In what way is Sanger's account a sophisticated sociological analysis whose generalizations, based on her experiences and taken together with statistical data and reports of others, make her thesis more persuasive?

5. Describe an episode that was a turning point in your life in terms of becoming active in a way you were not before. Structure your account in a way that allows your readers to feel your growing commitment to this new course of action.

Connections

1. Compare the experiences of Lesley Hazleton with those of Nancy Bazelon Goldstone as women working in what are usually male-dominated environments.

2. How do considerations of social class enter the accounts by Lesley Hazleton and Larry Brown?

3. How do the accounts by Lesley Hazleton and Margaret Sanger, taken together, provide a social history of the choices that have opened to women over the past hundred years?

4. What role does the need for distinctive achievement play in accounts by Lesley Hazleton, Nancy Bazelon Goldstone, and Jill Nelson ("Number One!" Chapter 1)?

5. What typical effects of poverty are depicted by Margaret Sanger, Jo Goodwin Parker ("What Is Poverty?" Chapter 10) and Luis Alberto Urrea ("My Story," Chapter 2)?

8

Self-Acceptance

◆

All men should strive to learn before they die what they are running from, and to, and why.

—James Thurber, "The Shore and the Sea,"
Further Fables for Our Time, 1956

To have that sense of one's intrinsic worth which constitutes self-respect is potentially to have everything: the ability to discriminate, to love, and to remain indifferent.

—Joan Didion, "On Self-Respect,"
Slouching Towards Bethlehem, 1968

The selections in this chapter are among the most dramatic and challenging in the entire book. Each shows a writer coming to terms with difficult life circumstances or coping with limitations that are hereditary, personal or cultural. Even those entries that strike us as too personal, too revealing or too self-involved offer a valuable window through which to study the writer's art. In reading these works, we become witness to the private dialogues of writers who do not edit out, tone down, or falsify their personal experiences. Autobiography offers a unique way through which writers can define themselves as individuals distinct from the negative self-images fostered by societal or cultural stereotyping. To do this, writers must come to terms with painful memories, unearth secrets, demystify the past, and admit to what was hidden or repressed. The process of writing about these experiences often serves as a catharsis.

"In Bed" reflects Joan Didion's lifelong struggle with migraine headaches. The supposed advantages of physical fitness come under Mike Royko's skeptical scrutiny in "Farewell to Fitness." The difficulties of not being part of white mainstream society are humorously portrayed by Itabari Njeri in "Hair Piece." In "The Letter 'A'" Christy Brown reveals a story of extraordinary courage in the face of supreme adversity. Sucheng Chan in "You're Short, Besides!" displays a remarkable ability to get beyond her infirmities with grace and good humor. In "Liked for Myself" Maya Angelou remembers the moment when special attention from a respected adult gave her much needed self-esteem.

Joan Didion

In Bed

◆

Joan Didion, born in 1934 in Sacramento, California, is a sixth-genera-tion Californian. After graduating from the University of California at Berkeley, she worked as a feature editor at Vogue *magazine. Her pub-lished work includes novels such as* Play It as It Lays *(1971);* A Book of Common Prayer *(1977), and* Democracy *(1984); two collections of es-says,* Slouching Towards Bethlehem *(1968) and* The White Album *(1979), from which "In Bed" is taken; a book-length account of her experi-ences as a reporter, entitled* Salvador *(1983); and an in-depth account of Dade County, Florida, titled* Miami *(1987). In the following essay, Didi-on tells how she learned to cope with migraine headaches.*

1   Three, four, sometimes five times a month, I spend the day in bed with a migraine headache, insensible to the world around me. Almost every day of every month, between these attacks, I feel the sudden irra-tional irritation and flush of blood into the cerebral arteries which tell me that migraine is on its way, and I take certain drugs to avert its ar-rival. If I did not take the drugs, I would be able to function perhaps one day in four. The physiological error called migraine is, in brief, central to the given of my life. When I was 15, 16, even 25, I used to think that I could rid myself of this error by simply denying it, character over chemistry. "Do you have headaches *sometimes? frequently? never?*" the application forms would demand. "Check one." Wary of the trap, wanting whatever it was that the successful circumnavigation of that particular form could bring (a job, a scholarship, the respect of mankind and the grace of God), I would check one. "*Sometimes,*" I would lie. That in fact I spent one or two days a week almost unconscious with pain seemed a shameful secret, evidence not merely of some chemical inferi-ority but of all my bad attitudes, unpleasant tempers, wrongthink.

2   For I had no brain tumor, no eyestrain, no high blood pressure, nothing wrong with me at all: I simply had migraine headaches, and migraine headaches were, as everyone who did not have them knew, imaginary. I fought migraine then, ignored the warnings it sent, went to school and later to work in spite of it, sat through lectures in Middle English and presentations to advertisers with involuntary tears run-ning down the right side of my face, threw up in washrooms, stumbled home by instinct, emptied ice trays onto my bed and tried to freeze the

pain in my right temple, wished only for a neurosurgeon who would do a lobotomy on house call, and cursed my imagination.

It was a long time before I began thinking mechanistically enough   3
to accept migraine for what it was: something with which I would be living, the way some people live with diabetes. Migraine is something more than the fancy of a neurotic imagination. It is an essentially hereditary complex of symptoms, the most frequently noted but by no means the most unpleasant of which is a vascular headache of blinding severity, suffered by a surprising number of women, a fair number of men (Thomas Jefferson had migraine, and so did Ulysses S. Grant, the day he accepted Lee's surrender), and by some unfortunate children as young as two years old. (I had my first when I was eight. It came on during a fire drill at the Columbia School in Colorado Springs, Colorado. I was taken first home and then to the infirmary at Peterson Field, where my father was stationed. The Air Corps doctor prescribed an enema.) Almost anything can trigger a specific attack of migraine: stress, allergy, fatigue, an abrupt change in barometric pressure, a contretemps over a parking ticket. A flashing light. A fire drill. One inherits, of course, only the predisposition. In other words I spent yesterday in bed with a headache not merely because of my bad attitudes, unpleasant tempers and wrongthink, but because both my grandmothers had migraine, my father has migraine and my mother has migraine.

No one knows precisely what it is that is inherited. The chemistry   4
of migraine, however, seems to have some connection with the nerve hormone named serotonin, which is naturally present in the brain. The amount of serotonin in the blood falls sharply at the the onset of migraine, and one migraine drug, methysergide, or Sansert, seems to have some effect on serotonin. Methysergide is a derivative of lysergic acid (in fact Sandoz Pharmaceuticals first synthesized LSD-25 while looking for a migraine cure), and its use is hemmed about with so many contraindications and side effects that most doctors prescribe it only in the most incapacitating cases. Methysergide, when it is prescribed, is taken daily, as a preventive; another preventive which works for some people is old-fashioned ergotamine tartrate, which helps to constrict the swelling blood vessels during the "aura," the period which in most cases precedes the actual headache.

Once an attack is under way, however, no drug touches it. Migraine   5
gives some people mild hallucinations, temporarily blinds others, shows up not only as a headache but as a gastrointestinal disturbance, a painful sensitivity to all sensory stimuli, an abrupt overpowering fatigue, a strokelike aphasia, and a crippling inability to make even the most routine connections. When I am in a migraine aura (for some people the aura lasts fifteen minutes, for others several hours), I will drive through red lights, lose the house keys, spill whatever I am holding, lose the ability to focus my eyes or frame coherent sentences, and generally

give the appearance of being on drugs, or drunk. The actual headache, when it comes, brings with it chills, sweating, nausea, a debility that seems to stretch the very limits of endurance. That no one dies of migraine seems, to someone deep into an attack, an ambiguous blessing.

6   My husband also has migraine, which is unfortunate for him but fortunate for me: perhaps nothing so tends to prolong an attack as the accusing eye of someone who has never had a headache. "Why not take a couple of aspirin," the unafflicted will say from the doorway, or "I'd have a headache, too, spending a beautiful day like this inside with all the shades drawn." All of us who have migraine suffer not only from the attacks themselves but from this common conviction that we are perversely refusing to cure ourselves by taking a couple of aspirin, that we are making ourselves sick, that we "bring it on ourselves." And in the most immediate sense, the sense of why we have a headache this Tuesday and not last Thursday, of course we often do. There certainly is what doctors call a "migraine personality," and that personality tends to be ambitious, inward, intolerant of error, rather rigidly organized, perfectionist. "You don't look like a migraine personality," a doctor once said to me. "Your hair's messy. But I suppose you're a compulsive housekeeper." Actually my house is kept even more negligently than my hair, but the doctor was right nonetheless: perfectionism can also take the form of spending most of a week writing and rewriting and not writing a single paragraph.

7   But not all perfectionists have migraine, and not all migrainous people have migraine personalities. We do not escape heredity. I have tried in most of the available ways to escape my own migrainous heredity (at one point I learned to give myself two daily injections of histamine with a hypodermic needle, even though the needle so frightened me that I had to close my eyes when I did it), but I still have migraine. And I have learned now to live with it, learned when to expect it, how to outwit it, even how to regard it, when it does come, as more friend than lodger. We have reached a certain understanding, my migraine and I. It never comes when I am in real trouble. Tell me that my house is burned down, my husband has left me, that there is gunfighting in the streets and panic in the banks, and I will not respond by getting a headache. It comes instead when I am fighting not an open guerrilla war with my own life, during weeks of small household confusions, lost laundry, unhappy help, canceled appointments, on days when the telephone rings too much and I get no work done and the wind is coming up. On days like that my friend comes uninvited.

8   And once it comes, now that I am wise in its ways, I no longer fight it. I lie down and let it happen. At first every small apprehension is magnified, every anxiety a pounding terror. Then the pain comes, and I concentrate only on that. Right there is the usefulness of migraine, there in that imposed yoga, the concentration on the pain. For when the

pain recedes, ten or twelve hours later, everything goes with it, all the hidden resentments, all the vain anxieties. The migraine has acted as a circuit breaker, and the fuses have emerged intact. There is a pleasant convalescent euphoria. I open the windows and feel the air, eat gratefully, sleep well. I notice the particular nature of a flower in a glass on the stair landing. I count my blessings.

1968

✦ *Questions for Discussion and Writing*

1. What techniques does Didion use to convey to the reader how the life-altering consequences of migraine headaches incapacitate her?

2. Evaluate the means Didion uses to provide the historical, medical, and psychological context in which migraine headaches should be understood.

3. How has Didion learned to cope with her migraine headaches? Has she discovered any positive effects of her affliction?

4. Describe a personal health problem you have that is directly linked to your personality. How have you learned to cope with it? Have you discovered any positive effects of this affliction?

Mike Royko

Farewell to Fitness

———————◆———————

Mike Royko is a nationally known columnist who writes for the Chicago Tribune. *He is the author of* Boss *(1971), a biography of Chicago's former mayor, Richard Daley. A collection of Royko's columns has appeared in* Like I Was Sayin' *(1984). "Farewell to Fitness," a witty indictment of our society's obsession with physical fitness, first appeared in his column in 1980.*

1   At least once a week, the office jock will stop me in the hall, bounce on the balls of his feet, plant his hands on his hips, flex his pectoral muscles and say: "How about it? I'll reserve a racquetball court. You can start working off some of that...." And he'll jab a finger deep into my midsection.

2   It's been going on for months, but I've always had an excuse: "Next week, I've got a cold." "Next week, my back is sore." "Next week, I've got a pulled hamstring." "Next week, after the holidays."

3   But this is it. No more excuses. I made one New Year's resolution, which is that I will tell him the truth. And the truth is that I don't want to play racquetball or handball or tennis, or jog, or pump Nautilus machines, or do push-ups or sit-ups or isometrics, or ride a stationary bicycle, or pull on a rowing machine, or hit a softball, or run up a flight of steps, or engage in any other form of exercise more strenuous than rolling out of bed.

4   This may be unpatriotic, and it is surely out of step with our muscle-flexing times, but I am renouncing the physical-fitness craze.

5   Oh, I was part of it. Maybe not as fanatically as some. But about 15 years ago, when I was 32, someone talked me into taking up handball, the most punishing court game there is.

6   From then on it was four or five times a week—up at 6 A.M., on the handball court at 7, run, grunt, sweat, pant until 8:30, then in the office at 9. And I'd go around bouncing on the balls of my feet, flexing my pectoral muscles, poking friends in their soft guts, saying: "How about working some of that off? I'll reserve a court," and being obnoxious.

7   This went on for years. And for what? I'll tell you what it led to: I stopped eating pork shanks, that's what. It was inevitable. When you join the physical-fitness craze, you have to stop eating wonderful things like pork shanks because they are full of cholesterol. And you have to

give up eggs benedict, smoked liverwurst, Italian sausage, butter-pecan ice cream, Polish sausage, goose-liver pate, Sara Lee cheesecake, Twinkies, potato chips, salami-and-Swiss-cheese sandwiches, double cheeseburgers with fries, Christian Brothers brandy with a Beck's chaser, and everything else that tastes good.

Instead, I ate broiled skinless chicken, broiled whitefish, grapefruit, 8 steamed broccoli, steamed spinach, unbuttered toast, yogurt, eggplant, an apple for dessert and Perrier water to wash it down. Blahhhhh!

You do this for years, and what is your reward for panting and 9 sweating around a handball-racquetball court, and eating yogurt and the skinned flesh of a dead chicken?

—You can take your pulse and find that it is slow. So what? Am I a 10 clock?

—You buy pants with a narrower waistline. Big deal. The pants 11 don't cost less than the ones with a big waistline.

—You get to admire yourself in the bathroom mirror for about 10 12 seconds a day after taking a shower. It takes five seconds to look at your flat stomach from the front, and five more seconds to look at your flat stomach from the side. If you're a real creep of a narcissist, you can add another 10 seconds for looking at your small behind with a mirror. That's it. 13

Wait, I forgot something. You will live longer. I know that because 14 my doctor told me so every time I took a physical. My fitness-conscious doctor was very slender—especially the last time I saw him, which was at his wake.

But I still believe him. Running around a handball court or logging 15 five miles a day, eating yogurt and guzzling Perrier will make you live longer.

So you live longer. Have you been in a typical nursing home lately? 16 Have you walked around the low-rent neighborhoods where the geezers try to survive on Social Security?

If you think living longer is rough now, wait until the 1990s, when 17 today's Me Generation potheads and coke sniffers begin taking care of the elderly (today's middle-aged joggers). It'll be: "Just take this little happy pill, gramps, and you'll wake up in heaven."

It's not worth giving up pork shanks and Sara Lee cheesecake. 18

Nor is it the way to age gracefully. Look around at all those middle- 19 aged jogging chicken-eaters. Half of them tape hairpieces to their heads. That's what comes from having a flat stomach. You start thinking that you should also have hair. And after that comes a facelift. And that leads to jumping around a disco floor, pinching an airline stewardess and other bizarre behavior.

I prefer to age gracefully, the way men did when I was a boy. The 20 only time a man over 40 ran was when the cops caught him burglarizing a warehouse. The idea of exercise was to walk to and from the corner tavern, mostly to. A well-rounded health-food diet included pork shanks, dumplings, Jim Beam and a beer chaser.

21   Anyone who was skinny was suspected of having TB or an ulcer. A fine figure of a man was one who could look down and not see his knees, his feet or anything else in that vicinity. What do you have to look for, anyway? You ought to know if anything is missing.

22   A few years ago I was in Bavaria, and I went to a German beer hall. It was a beautiful sight. Everybody was popping sausages and pork shanks and draining quart-sized steins of thick beer. Every so often they'd thump their magnificent bellies and smile happily at the booming sound that they made.

23   Compare that to the finish line of a marathon, with all those emaciated runners sprawled on the grass, tongues hanging out, wheezing, moaning, writhing, throwing up.

24   If that is the way to happiness and a long life, pass me the cheesecake.

25   May you get a hernia, Arnold Schwarzenegger. And here's to you, Orson Welles.

✦ Questions for Discussion and Writing

1. What part does one-upmanship play in explaining why people seem to have a need to get others involved in physical fitness activities?

2. How does Royko undercut the advantages that supposedly derive from physical fitness and anticipate and reply to objections that might be forthcoming?

3. In which examples does Royko use exaggeration and humor to get his points across?

4. Does Royko's characterization of the excessively physically fit match your own observations? Describe someone you know who is like Royko's co-worker.

5. Did you find Royko's argument persuasive? Do you agree or disagree with his indictment of prevalent cultural values? To what extent would this article influence your decision to embark on or to cease a regimen of physical fitness?

Itabari Njeri

Hair Piece

◆

Itabari Njeri graduated from Boston University and the Columbia University Graduate School of Journalism. She has worked as a reporter and producer for National Public Radio in Boston, as an arts critic and essayist for the Miami Herald, *and is currently a reporter for the* Los Angeles Times. *She has received numerous fellowships and awards including the Associated Press Award for Feature Writing and the National Association for Black Journalists Award. Njeri won the 1990 American Book Award for* Every Goodbye Ain't Gone, *from which "Hair Piece" is taken. This engaging and witty account of the difficulties black women face in finding hairdressers poignantly evokes the panorama of obstacles that have been put in the way of black women for the past four hundred years.*

The king of curls in Opa-Locka, Florida, has no first name. He's just 1
Mr. Vance. My hairdresser in Atlanta has no last name. He's just Kamal.
In Miami, it's Raul. In New York, it's Mr. Joseph. This new breed of
haute coiffeur was driving me mad.

"Hello, Mr. Vance, I'm a friend of Sujay's. I think she mentioned I'd 2
be calling."
Silence. 3
"I'd like to make an appointment for a cold wave. Could you see 4
me sometime next—"
"You'll have to come in for a consultation first," said a preoccupied 5
voice.
"I see. Well, when can I have an appointment for a consultation?" 6
"I can do nothing until we consult." 7
"But you don't understand. I have a very busy schedule. If I have 8
to take time off to get my hair done, I need to plan in advance, so—"
"You'll have to come in for a consultation." 9
The *b's* in "bu-but" were exploding on my lips when he hung up. 10
"That's why I do my own hair," said Norma, standing over me 11
laughing. There was a bald spot in the middle of her pageboy. "You had
a call from the city manager's office while you were on the phone. And
I have a doctor from the National Institute of Drug Abuse on hold for
you now."

12   "Thanks. Let me call the city manager. Take a message from the NIDA guy, please."

13   I made the call, then walked to Norma's desk. On the way, I looked around the newsroom. I didn't see a single hairstyle that I liked on a black woman. Pageboys in 1981. Miami, what a backwater.

14   "What did the guy from NIDA want?"

15   "You can interview him the end of the week in Washington for your cocaine story."

16   "Great," I growled, one hand on my hip, the other trying to sculpt the hair at the back of my head into place.

17   "Your hair looks fine to me," Norma said. I was standing over her now. I had a direct view of the few wisps of hair covering a shiny, two-by-three-inch patch of scalp.

18   "I resent having to search from here to East Jablip for a competent hairdresser. You should, too. Don't you remember what black beauty salons were like twenty years ago?"

19   "No."

20   "How old are you?"

21   "Twenty-six," she said. "And you ain't much older."

22   "I'm trying to place this in some historical and cultural perspective for you."

23   "Really?" she said, her lips pursed, her eyebrows raised.

24   "Never mind," I said, and walked back to my desk. But I remembered.

25   They were where my grandmother bet a quarter every day on the numbers, sometimes more when she'd had a dream. "Here's a dollar, I dreamt seven-four-two last night. Play a combination." They were where *Let's Make a Deal* took on new meaning: hot goods peddled at record speeds to the music of police sirens. I once got a Borgana jacket, a pair of real leather gloves and a rabbit hat for twenty-five dollars. Had I been flush that day at Frankie's Harlem salon, I could have had a color TV and stereo for a hundred dollars.

26   But I liked my first beautician best. Her name was Mrs. Lane. She was our landlady, too, and ran a discreet salon on the ground floor of her Brooklyn row house. If hot goods were peddled there, it was done with the greatest subtlety. Or maybe my head was just in the shampoo bowl when they came. After my wash, Mrs. Lane would put me under the dryer, press my hair, then send me upstairs to our apartment for dinner. That gave her time to work on another head. When I heard a knock on the kitchen pipes, I'd go back down for a curl. I miss that.

27   "Mr. Vance? This is Itabari Njeri. I spoke to you a few weeks ago."

28   "Yes, I thought you would have been in by now."

"Well, it's my schedule. It's difficult for me to take time off for a   29
consultation without some guarantee that you'll see me. At least give
me an appointment that can be broken."

"As I explained to you, we can do nothing until we consult."   30

"If I come in for a consultation and you decide to do my hair, will   31
you confer with my previous hairdresser?"

"That's not necessary."   32

"It's taken many trials and much error for hairdressers to find what   33
works on my hair. My previous hairdresser knows all this. He can save
us both a lot of grief."

"Then go back to your hairdresser if you like him so much."   34

"But he's in Atlanta."   35

"Then you have a problem."   36

I felt a migraine coming on.   37

Anne, the reporter next to me, leaned over the top of her video dis-   38
play terminal. "Itabari, why are you putting yourself through all these
changes over a hairdresser?"

I looked at her freckled face and blond hair for a moment in silence.   39
Then slowly I said, "Most white hairdressers don't know how to handle black hair unless they chemically straighten it first. I don't want my
hair straightened. And a lot of black hairdressers, who use all sorts of
chemicals for a variety of hairstyles, don't really know what they are
doing. But the ones who do all seem to be a pain in the ass."

"Oh," she said, her head cocked like a dog's. I dropped it.   40

But even among the talented bastards, it was hard to know whom   41
to trust. One stylist's concoctions left me almost bald, and I swore the
next time that happened I'd sue.

But there was not going to be a next time, I told myself. Myself told   42
me there was. I was having trouble sleeping at night. I began dreaming
about baldness. There I was in a wig, on a date. My passionate companion clasped the back of my neck with his left hand and kissed me full
on the mouth. The fingers of his right hand stroked my temple. And as
he kissed me harder and pulled at my tongue with his teeth, his hand
slipped under the wig's elastic band and his fingers became enmeshed
in the netting.

Sujay swore by Mr. Vance. He had saved her troubled curls; maybe   43
he could help me. After all, he had more than a salon. His business card
said: "The Famous Mr. Vance's Professional Unisex Hair *Clinic* Salon.
The hair clinic that embraces science, technology and you."

"How do you do, Mr. Vance. I'm Itabari Njeri. As you may recall, I'm   44
the woman you gave such a hard way to go on the telephone yesterday."

45   "Oh," he said, surprised by the sight of me. I had dressed for the occasion. I wore a sun-yellow tunic made of Indian cotton with matching jodhpur pants. The tunic was cinched at the waist by a cummerbund cut from the same cloth. The sash gathered the starched tunic's skirt and caused it to puff and stay like an air-filled shell. The wide sleeves billowed when I moved. Any moment, I could be airborne. I was a brilliant butterfly. "Please have a seat," he said.

46   I patiently sat reading the signs in his small but attractive salon: No Check, No Credit, No Kids. There are two sides to every story. But I don't have time to hear yours.

47   This is the salon that embraces you?

48   "Now, tell me about some of the concerns you mentioned on the phone."

49   Butter wouldn't melt in his mouth. I relaxed, too.

50   I told him my troubles with past beauticians. "I'm determined to be more careful this time," I said.

51   "I feel sorry for you," he said. "You are a very unhappy woman. You don't trust people. No wonder your hair fell out."

52   "Look, I don't need a dime-store shrink. Are you trying to tell me it was my fault? It was the hairdresser's fault."

53   "That is speculation. We deal in facts here."

54   "Oh yeah? Well, when I went to the hairdresser, I had a full head of hair. A week later, my hair was in the sink."

55   "I wish you were as concerned about the other things I see wrong with you as you are about your hair," he said, staring at the enlarged pores on my nose and the pimple on my chin.

56   I wanted to deck him.

57   "Have you tried vitamins?" he asked.

58   "Look," I said, my voice spiraling toward hysteria, "I just worked a seventy-hour week at the paper, I can't find a decent apartment because people won't let me in the door once they see my black face, I got an editor who thinks that Jews and Italians are a separate race of people, and I can't get a bottle of my regular shampoo because the company doesn't ship as far south as Miami. You bet I look bad."

59   He smiled beatifically. "You are very attractive. You seem to be an intelligent woman. I want you to be satisfied."

60   He gave me a special shampoo and conditioner to use for a week before he did my hair.

61   "Mr. Vance, this is Itabari Njeri. That stuff you gave me left my hair bone dry and it's breaking."

62   "Yes. That'll be fine."

63   "What do you mean that'll be fine?"

64   "You must trust me. You have such a lovely voice."

"Thanks. But my hair is so dry it's breaking off." 65

"Yes, that's just the way I want it." 66

I wanted to cry. These pretentious shaft artists had forgotten their 67
roots. Then I thought about Kamal. His shop was one of the few high-
fashion salons that retained the warmth I remembered as a child. But
he was in Atlanta.

I remembered Raul. A black woman had mentioned him to me be- 68
fore she left the paper and Miami. "In a pinch," she told me, "try Raul."

He was courtly and courteous. Unlike Mr. Vance, he consulted with 69
Kamal by telephone and gave him his credentials. Things seemed to be
going well. Raul handed me the phone.

"Don't let that man touch your hair," Kamal screamed. "I'm com- 70
ing down there on the first thing smoking. He wants to put sodium hy-
droxide on your hair—lye. He wants to relax your hair, then put in a
cold wave. You don't need that. Your hair will fall out again. I won't be
responsible if you let anyone touch your hair. I'm coming down there
this weekend to do it myself."

"That's not practical," I said. "It'll cost three hundred dollars just to 71
fly you here and back and another sixty bucks to get my hair done. I
can't afford that."

Besides, Kamal could mean trouble. The last time his fingers mas- 72
saged my scalp it was a clandestine affair, carried out about midnight at
the house of my girlfriend. He had just been sprung from jail for non-sup-
port of three kids and two ex-wives, one of whom he had married twice.

"No, Kamal, you'll have a horde of women thinking there's some- 73
thing going on between us."

"Noooooo, Itabareeeee, I'm straight now. I need a short trip to cool 74
out anyway."

"Why do I feel you don't do this for everybody?" I told him I'd 75
think about it.

I looked in the mirror. Nothing was wrong with my hair, I rea- 76
soned. I looked at *Essence*. I looked at the model on the cover. I looked
in the mirror. I picked up the phone.

I called every kinky-headed, curly-haired Hispanic and African- 77
American in the newsroom. I knew I wasn't the only woman who
couldn't get the cut or curl she wanted from any hairdresser in town.

Within an hour, it was agreed. Five of us would fly him in and pay 78
sixty dollars apiece.

Saturday night, nine-ten P.M., I went to pick up Kamal at the airport. 79

Nine-thirty P.M. No Kamal. How could I forget about old unde- 80
pendable? This is the man who would arrive three hours late for my
appointment after I'd driven 144 miles from Greenville, South Carolina, to Atlanta just to have him do my hair.

Nine forty-five P.M. I call Atlanta. 81

82   "Itabareeeee, I'll be there. I tried to call you."

83   "You didn't try to call me, you jive so-and-so. 'Cause I've been
home all afternoon, cleaning, cooking, preparing for you. You've got
two cold waves; one Afro cut; one wash, shape and trim and a potential
permanent stirring restlessly in my living room."

84   "I'll be there, Itabari."

85   "Yeah, well you can call me from the airport when your feet touch
Miami soil. Then I'll come and get you."

86   I went home and played my stress-reduction tape.

87   At eight-fifteen the next morning, the phone rang.

88   "I'm here." The voice was full of gravel.

89   "Who is this?"

90   "Kamal."

91   "I don't believe it."

92   "I told you you could count on me."

93   One of the other desperate heads, who lived close to the airport,
went to get him while I whipped up the quiches and spiked the juices.
The *Miami Herald* photographer arrived. My problem had become a sociological epic: the hairy plight of the black woman.

94   By day's end, our coifs were cover girl perfect.

95   Two months later we did it again; Kamal was two days late that
time. During the fourth episode, Kamal called three days late to say he
was "on his way." He didn't show. Not even vanity could compel me to
maintain this shuttle beauty service. I called his Atlanta shop. I learned
he was in a drug treatment program for cocaine addiction.

96   The long waits. The sudden disappearances from his salon. All Kamal's erratic behavior over the years became clear.

97   What was I going to do about my hair now?

98   A braider named Mashariki, who'd read the article about my search
for a beautician, called me. She was considered one of the best African-
hair sculptors in the country, she said. Perhaps I'd like to do a story
about her, she said. I told her I'd be glad to stop by her salon one day.

99   "Have you read *Four Hundred Years Without a Comb?*" she asked the
day I visited her shop.

100   "No. I'm not familiar with that one."

101   "Well, I thought you might like a copy after reading about all the
problems you've had with your hair. Black people have a terrible preoccupation with hair because of our four hundred years without a
comb," she explained.

102   "I'm not sure I understand."

103   "We didn't have a comb. We couldn't comb our hair with European
combs so we were poorly groomed and self-conscious about our hair.
That's why we resorted to all sorts of things to make us look better. Ba-

con fat to make it lie down—we didn't have anything else. Rags to cover it up. All because we didn't have a comb."

"You mean an Afro pick?"   104

"Yes," she said.   105

"Well, we've got the comb now."   106

"But we haven't changed our behavior. As a braider, I'm trying to   107
get black women to give up these harsh chemicals and go back to natural hairstyles," she said.

I like braids, I told her. For the past thirteen years, when my hair   108
wasn't in an Afro, it had been cornrowed. But I got tired of both styles.
Besides, I told her, "the cornrows were tight. They either gave me a
headache or made my head itch."

"Ohhhh," she cooed, "then you'd love the individual braids. No   109
tension on the scalp. Great styling versatility."

"How much is it?" I asked.   110

"Four hundred dollars."   111

"What!"   112

"Oh, it takes a great deal of skill and time. It's an art. I take credit   113
cards. And if you don't have cash, I'm not locked into this capitalist
system. We can barter. Or, you can give me something as collateral. Do
you have any jewelry or African art?"

"Well," I said, watching her braid as we talked—she did do beauti-   114
ful work, "I have some Makonde statues I brought back from Tanzania."

"I'd love to see those," she said.   115

I noticed she had several pieces of beautiful African art in the shop   116
already. I wondered if one ever got one's "collateral" back from her.

"No," I said, musing, "I wouldn't want to put up my African art as   117
collateral."

"What else do you have?"   118

"I've got that famous photograph of Billie Holiday at her last re-   119
cording session, shot by Milt Hinton."

"I'd love to see that," she said eagerly.   120

I gave in eventually, but I never put up any of my art as collateral.   121

The price of a good braider has dropped since then. The one I have   122
in Los Angeles now is reliable and reasonably priced. She works out of
her home—I like that. And when we take breaks—braiding is an all-
day affair—we make an indoor picnic out of it. It reminds me a little of
the old days and Mrs. Lane.

You can't get hot goods at my braider's house, but she makes up   123
for it with great stories. Like the one about her friend who checks insurance claims. One claim was for a lady who'd been rushed to the emergency room to have a potato removed. The woman told the doctor
she'd been in her garden that night digging up potatoes and fell on one.

The potatoectomy—from the woman's most intimate bodily orifice—went unchallenged by the insurance company. Even though the raw tuber was completely peeled when retrieved.

124   I never heard anything that good in Mrs. Lane's shop.

✦ Questions for Discussion and Writing

1. How would you characterize Njeri's personality, her job, and the kind of image she would like to project? Why is having a satisfactory hairdresser so important to her?

2. Compare and contrast the kinds of relationships the narrator has had with two of her past hairdressers, Kamal and Mr. Vance.

3. Describe the narrator's relationship with the African hair sculptor Mashariki.

4. How do the different hair styles the narrator goes through show a movement towards an authentic affirmation of her African American heritage?

5. Do you see any significance in the fact that the narrator's first hairdresser was a woman (Mrs. Lane), her hairdressers along the way were all men, and that she is now happy with a woman hairdresser once again, in modern-day circumstances quite reminiscent of those in Mrs. Lane's house? What does this tell you about the narrator?

6. Discuss the significance of the essay's title and all its possible ramifications. Why would hair be such an accurate image to reflect the progress made by an entire generation and the change in society's attitudes? How would you characterize these changes?

7. Describe a person in the context of where you met him or her that makes it clear why you will always associate this person with this particular place, as Njeri does with Mrs. Lane's.

Christy Brown

The Letter "A"

◆───────────◆

*Christy Brown (1932–1981) was born in Dublin, the tenth child in a fami-
ly of twenty-two. Brown was diagnosed as having cerebral palsy and as being hopelessly retarded. An intense personal struggle and the loving
attention and faith of his mother resulted in a surprising degree of rehabili-
tation. Brown's autobiography,* My Left Foot *(1954), describing his struggle to overcome his massive handicap, was the basis for the 1989 Academy
Award-winning film. Brown is also the author of an internationally acclaimed novel,* Down All the Days *(1970). "The Letter 'A'," from his autobiography, describes the crucial moment when he first communicated
signs of awareness and intelligence.*

I was born in the Rotunda Hospital,[1] on June 5th, 1932. There were
nine children before me and twelve after me, so I myself belong to the
middle group. Out of this total of twenty-two, seventeen lived, but four
died in infancy, leaving thirteen still to hold the family fort.

Mine was a difficult birth, I am told. Both mother and son almost
died. A whole army of relations queued up outside the hospital until
the small hours of the morning, waiting for news and praying furiously
that it would be good.

After my birth Mother was sent to recuperate for some weeks and I
was kept in the hospital while she was away. I remained there for some
time, without name, for I wasn't baptized until my mother was well
enough to bring me to church.

It was Mother who first saw that there was something wrong with
me. I was about four months old at the time. She noticed that my head
had a habit of failing backward whenever she tried to feed me. She attempted to correct this by placing her hand on the back of my neck to
keep it steady. But when she took it away, back it would drop again.
That was the first warning sign. Then she became aware of other de-
fects as I got older. She saw that my hands were clenched nearly all of
the time and were inclined to twine behind my back; my mouth
couldn't grasp the teat of the bottle because even at that early age my
jaws would either lock together tightly, so that it was impossible for her
to open them, or they would suddenly become limp and fall loose,
dragging my whole mouth to one side. At six months I could not sit up

---

[1]*Rotunda Hospital,* a hospital in Dublin, Ireland.

without having a mountain of pillows around me. At twelve months it was the same.

5   Very worried by this, Mother told my father her fears, and they decided to seek medical advice without any further delay. I was a little over a year old when they began to take me to hospitals and clinics, convinced that there was something definitely wrong with me, something which they could not understand or name, but which was very real and disturbing.

6   Almost every doctor who saw and examined me labeled me a very interesting but also a hopeless case. Many told Mother very gently that I was mentally defective and would remain so. That was a hard blow to a young mother who had already reared five healthy children. The doctors were so very sure of themselves that Mother's faith in me seemed almost an impertinence. They assured her that nothing could be done for me.

7   She refused to accept this truth, the inevitable truth—as it then seemed—that I was beyond cure, beyond saving, even beyond hope. She could not and would not believe that I was an imbecile, as the doctors told her. She had nothing in the world to go by, not a scrap of evidence to support her conviction that, though my body was crippled, my mind was not. In spite of all the doctors and specialists told her, she would not agree. I don't believe she knew why—she just knew, without feeling the smallest shade of doubt.

8   Finding that the doctors could not help in any way beyond telling her not to place her trust in me, or, in other words, to forget I was a human creature, rather to regard me as just something to be fed and washed and then put away again, Mother decided there and then to take matters into her own hands. I was *her* child, and therefore part of the family. No matter how dull and incapable I might grow up to be, she was determined to treat me on the same plane as the others, and not as the "queer one" in the back room who was never spoken of when there were visitors present.

9   That was a momentous decision as far as my future life was concerned. It meant that I would always have my mother on my side to help me fight all the battles that were to come, and to inspire me with new strength when I was almost beaten. But it wasn't easy for her because now the relatives and friends had decided otherwise. They contended that I should be taken kindly, sympathetically, but not seriously. That would be a mistake. "For your own sake," they told her, "don't look to this boy as you would to the others; it would only break your heart in the end." Luckily for me, Mother and Father held out against the lot of them. But Mother wasn't content just to say that I was not an idiot: she set out to prove it, not because of any rigid sense of duty, but out of love. That is why she was so successful.

At this time she had the five other children to look after besides the 10
"difficult one," though as yet it was not by any means a full house.
They were my brothers, Jim, Tony, and Paddy, and my two sisters, Lily
and Mona, all of them very young, just a year or so between each of
them, so that they were almost exactly like steps of stairs.

Four years rolled by and I was now five, and still as helpless as a 11
newly born baby. While my father was out at bricklaying, earning our
bread and butter for us, Mother was slowly, patiently pulling down the
wall, brick by brick, that seemed to thrust itself between me and the
other children, slowly, patiently penetrating beyond the thick curtain
that hung over my mind, separating it from theirs. It was hard, heart-
breaking work, for often all she got from me in return was a vague smile
and perhaps a faint gurgle. I could not speak or even mumble, nor could
I sit up without support on my own, let alone take steps. But I wasn't inert or motionless. I seemed, indeed, to be convulsed with movement,
wild, stiff, snakelike movement that never left me, except in sleep. My
fingers twisted and twitched continually, my arms twined backwards
and would often shoot out suddenly this way and that, and my head
lolled and sagged sideways. I was a queer, crooked little fellow.

Mother tells me how one day she had been sitting with me for 12
hours in an upstairs room, showing me pictures out of a great big storybook that I had got from Santa Claus last Christmas and telling me
the names of the different animals and flowers that were in them, trying without success to get me to repeat them. This had gone on for
hours while she talked and laughed with me. Then at the end of it she
leaned over me and said gently into my ear:

"Did you like it, Chris? Did you like the bears and the monkeys 13
and all the lovely flowers? Nod your head for yes, like a good boy."

But I could make no sign that I had understood her. Her face was 14
bent over mine hopefully. Suddenly, involuntarily, my queer hand
reached up and grasped one of the dark curls that fell in a thick cluster
about her neck. Gently she loosened the clenched fingers, though some
dark strands were still clutched between them.

Then she turned away from my curious stare and left the room, 15
crying. The door closed behind her. It all seemed hopeless. It looked as
though there was some justification for my relatives' contention that I
was an idiot and beyond help.

They now spoke of an institution. 16

"Never!" said my mother almost fiercely, when this was suggested 17
to her. "I know my boy is not an idiot; it is his body that is shattered,
not his mind. I'm sure of that."

Sure? Yet inwardly, she prayed God would give her some proof of 18
her faith. She knew it was one thing to believe but quite another thing
to prove.

19   I was now five, and still I showed no real sign of intelligence. I showed no apparent interest in things except with my toes—more especially those of my left foot. Although my natural habits were clean, I could not aid myself, but in this respect my father took care of me. I used to lie on my back all the time in the kitchen or, on bright warm days, out in the garden, a little bundle of crooked muscles and twisted nerves, surrounded by a family that loved me and hoped for me and that made me part of their own warmth and humanity. I was lonely, imprisoned in a world of my own, unable to communicate with others, cut off, separated from them as though a glass wall stood between my existence and theirs, thrusting me beyond the sphere of their lives and activities. I longed to run about and play with the rest, but I was unable to break loose from my bondage.

20   Then, suddenly, it happened! In a moment everything was changed, my future life molded into a definite shape, my mother's faith in me rewarded, and her secret fear changed into open triumph.

21   It happened so quickly, so simply after all the years of waiting and uncertainty, that I can see and feel the whole scene as if it had happened last week. It was the afternoon of a cold, gray December day. The streets outside glistened with snow, the white sparkling flakes stuck and melted on the windowpanes and hung on the boughs of the trees like molten silver. The wind howled dismally, whipping up little whirling columns of snow that rose and fell at every fresh gust. And over all, the dull, murky sky stretched like a dark canopy, a vast infinity of grayness.

22   Inside, all the family were gathered round the big kitchen fire that lit up the little room with a warm glow and made giant shadows dance on the walls and ceiling.

23   In a corner Mona and Paddy were sitting, huddled together, a few torn school primers before them. They were writing down little sums onto an old chipped slate, using a bright piece of yellow chalk. I was close to them, propped up by a few pillows against the wall, watching.

24   It was the chalk that attracted me so much. It was a long, slender stick of vivid yellow. I had never seen anything like it before, and it showed up so well against the black surface of the slate that I was fascinated by it as much as if it had been a stick of gold.

25   Suddenly, I wanted desperately to do what my sister was doing. Then—without thinking or knowing exactly what I was doing, I reached out and took the stick of chalk out of my sister's hand—with my left foot.

26   I do not know why I used my left foot to do this. It is a puzzle to many people as well as to myself, for, although I had displayed a curious interest in my toes at an early age, I had never attempted before this to use either of my feet in any way. They could have been as useless to me as were my hands. That day, however, my left foot, apparently by

its own volition, reached out and very impolitely took the chalk out of my sister's hand.

I held it tightly between my toes, and, acting on an impulse, made 27 a wild sort of scribble with it on the slate. Next moment I stopped, a bit dazed, surprised, looking down at the stick of yellow chalk stuck between my toes, not knowing what to do with it next, hardly knowing how it got there. Then I looked up and became aware that everyone had stopped talking and was staring at me silently. Nobody stirred, Mona, her black curls framing her chubby little face, stared at me with great big eyes and open mouth. Across the open hearth, his face lit by flames, sat my father, leaning forward, hands outspread on his knees, his shoulders tense. I felt the sweat break out on my forehead.

My mother came in from the pantry with a steaming pot in her 28 hand. She stopped midway between the table and the fire, feeling the tension flowing through the room. She followed their stare and saw me in the corner. Her eyes looked from my face down to my foot, with the chalk gripped between my toes. She put down the pot.

Then she crossed over to me and knelt down beside me, as she had 29 done so many times before.

"I'll show you what to do with it, Chris," she said, very slowly and 30 in a queer, choked way, her face flushed as if with some inner excitement.

Taking another piece of chalk from Mona, she hesitated, then very 31 deliberately drew, on the floor in front of me, *the single letter "A."*

"Copy that," she said, looking steadily at me. "Copy it, Christy." 32

I couldn't. 33

I looked about me, looked around at the faces that were turned to- 34 wards me, tense, excited faces that were at that moment frozen, immobile, eager, waiting for a miracle in their midst.

The stillness was profound. The room was full of flame and 35 shadow that danced before my eyes and lulled my taut nerves into a sort of waking sleep. I could hear the sound of the water tap dripping in the pantry, the loud ticking of the clock on the mantel shelf, and the soft hiss and crackle of the logs on the open hearth.

I tried again. I put out my foot and made a wild jerking stab with 36 the chalk which produced a very crooked line and nothing more. Mother held the slate steady for me.

"Try again, Chris," she whispered in my ear. "Again." 37

I did. I stiffened my body and put my left foot out again, for the 38 third time. I drew one side of the letter. I drew half the other side. Then the stick of chalk broke and I was left with a stump. I wanted to fling it away and give up. Then I felt my mother's hand on my shoulder. I tried once more. Out went my foot. I shook, I sweated and strained every muscle. My hands were so tightly clenched that my fingernails bit into the flesh. I set my teeth so hard that I nearly pierced my lower lip. Everything in the room swam till the faces around me were mere

patches of white. But—I drew it—*the letter "A."* There it was on the
floor before me. Shaky, with awkward, wobbly sides and a very uneven
center line. But it was the letter "A." I looked up. I saw my mother's
face for a moment, tears on her cheeks. Then my father stooped and
hoisted me onto his shoulder.

39   I had done it! It had started—the thing that was to give my mind its
chance of expressing itself. True, I couldn't speak with my lips. But now
I would speak through something more lasting than spoken words—
written words.

40   That one letter, scrawled on the floor with a broken bit of yellow
chalk gripped between my toes, was my road to a new world, my key
to mental freedom. It was to provide a source of relaxation to the tense,
taut thing that was I, which panted for expression behind a twisted
mouth.

✦ Questions for Discussion and Writing

1. What did Christy's mother hope to achieve by showing him pictures of
   animals and flowers? How did her friends and relatives react to her
   decision to treat Christy as if he were capable of mental development?
   How would Christy's day-to-day treatment have differed if his mother
   had not treated him as a member of the family?

2. What is the reason the narrative shifts from Christy's mother's perspective to Christy's recollection of the day he was able to form the letter "A" with his left foot?

3. From the point of view of Christy's mother, father, and siblings, how
   did they know that his forming the letter "A" was a sign of intelligence
   and not merely an imitative gesture?

4. How does the conclusion of this account suggest that this moment had
   deeper meaning for Christy than it did even for his family? What did
   this achievement mean to him?

5. On any given day, how do you think Christy would have been treated
   if his mother had not made the decision to treat him as a member of
   the family? Write a brief account analyzing why, over a period of time,
   the difference in the way he was treated might have been capable of
   producing the unexpected development Christy describes. Include everyday events, such as meals, visits from friends, and so on, in your
   account.

Sucheng Chan

You're Short, Besides!

◆

*Sucheng Chan graduated from Swarthmore College in 1963 and received
an M.A. from the University of Hawaii in 1965. She earned a Ph.D. from
the University of California at Berkeley in 1973, where she subsequently
taught for a decade. She is currently professor of history and chair of
Asian American Studies at the University of California at Santa Barbara.
Her works include* Quiet Odyssey: A Pioneer Korean Woman in
America *(1990) and the award-winning* The Asian Americans: An In-
terpretive History *(1991). "You're Short, Besides!" first appeared in*
Making Waves: An Anthology of Writing By and About Asian
American Women *(1989).*

When asked to write about being a physically handicapped Asian   1
American woman, I considered it an insult. After all, my accomplish-
ments are many, yet I was not asked to write about any of them. Is being handicapped the most salient feature about me? The fact that it
might be in the eyes of others made me decide to write the essay as requested. I realized that the way I think about myself may differ considerably from the way others perceive me. And maybe that's what being
physically handicapped is all about.

I was stricken simultaneously with pneumonia and polio at the age   2
of four. Uncertain whether I had polio of the lungs, seven of the eight
doctors who attended me—all practitioners of Western medicine—told
my parents they should not feel optimistic about my survival. A Chinese fortune teller my mother consulted also gave a grim prognosis, but
for an entirely different reason: I had been stricken because my name
was offensive to the gods. My grandmother had named me "grandchild
of wisdom," a name that the fortune teller said was too presumptuous
for a girl. So he advised my parents to change my name to "chaste virgin." All these pessimistic predictions notwithstanding, I hung onto
life, if only by a thread. For three years, my body was periodically
pierced with electric shocks as the muscles of my legs atrophied. Before
my illness, I had been an active, rambunctious, precocious, and very curious child. Being confined to bed was thus a mental agony as great as
my physical pain. Living in war-torn China, I received little medical attention; physical therapy was unheard of. But I was determined to
walk. So one day, when I was six or seven, I instructed my mother to set
up two rows of chairs to face each other so that I could use them as I

281

would parallel bars. I attempted to walk by holding my body up and moving it forward with my arms while dragging my legs along behind. Each time I fell, my mother gasped, but I badgered her until she let me try again. After four nonambulatory years, I finally walked once more by pressing my hands against my thighs so my knees wouldn't buckle.

3   My father had been away from home during most of those years because of the war. When he returned, I had to confront the guilt he felt about my condition. In many East Asian cultures, there is a strong folk belief that a person's physical state in this life is a reflection of how morally or sinfully he or she lived in previous lives. Furthermore, because of the tendency to view the family as a single unit, it is believed that the fate of one member can be caused by the behavior of another. Some of my father's relatives told him that my illness had doubtless been caused by the wild carousing he did in his youth. A well-meaning but somewhat simple man, my father believed them.

4   Throughout my childhood, he sometimes apologized to me for having to suffer retribution for his former bad behavior. This upset me; it was bad enough that I had to deal with the anguish of not being able to walk, but to have to assuage his guilt as well was a real burden! In other ways, my father was very good to me. He took me out often, carrying me on his shoulders or back, to give me fresh air and sunshine. He did this until I was too large and heavy for him to carry. And ever since I can remember, he has told me that I am pretty.

5   After getting over her anxieties about my constant falls, my mother decided to send me to school. I had already learned to read some words of Chinese at the age of three by asking my parents to teach me the sounds and meaning of various characters in the daily newspaper. But between the ages of four and eight, I received no education since just staying alive was a full-time job. Much to her chagrin, my mother found no school in Shanghai, where we lived at the time, which would accept me as a student. Finally, as a last resort, she approached the American School, which agreed to enroll me only if my family kept an *amah* (a servant who takes care of children) by my side at all times. The tuition at the school was twenty U.S. dollars per month—a huge sum of money during those years of runaway inflation in China—and payable only in U.S. dollars. My family afforded the high cost of tuition and the expense of employing a full-time *amah* for less than a year.

6   We left China as the Communist forces swept across the country in victory. We found an apartment in Hong Kong across the street from a school run by Seventh-Day Adventists. By that time I could walk a little, so the principal was persuaded to accept me. An *amah* now had to take care of me only during recess when my classmates might easily knock me over as they ran about the playground.

7   After a year and a half in Hong Kong, we moved to Malaysia, where my father's family had lived for four generations. There I

learned to swim in the lovely warm waters of the tropics and fell in love with the sea. On land I was a cripple; in the ocean I could move with the grace of a fish. I liked the freedom of being in the water so much that many years later, when I was a graduate student in Hawaii, I became greatly enamored with a man just because he called me a "Polynesian water nymph."

As my overall health improved, my mother became less anxious   8
about all aspects of my life. She did everything possible to enable me to lead as normal a life as possible. I remember how once some of her colleagues in the high school where she taught criticized her for letting me wear short skirts. They felt my legs should not be exposed to public view. My mother's response was, "All girls her age wear short skirts, so why shouldn't she?"

The years in Malaysia were the happiest of my childhood, even   9
though I was constantly fending off children who ran after me calling, "*Baikah! Baikah!*" ("Cripple! Cripple!" in the Hokkien dialect commonly spoken in Malaysia). The taunts of children mattered little because I was a star pupil. I won one award after another for general scholarship as well as for art and public speaking. Whenever the school had important visitors my teacher always called on me to recite in front of the class.

A significant event that marked me indelibly occurred when I was   10
twelve. That year my school held a music recital and I was one of the students chosen to play the piano. I managed to get up the steps to the stage without any problem, but as I walked across the stage, I fell. Out of the audience, a voice said loudly and clearly, "Ayah! A *baikah* shouldn't be allowed to perform in public." I got up before anyone could get on stage to help me and, with tears streaming uncontrollably down my face, I rushed to the piano and began to play. Beethoven's "Für Elise" had never been played so fiendishly fast before or since, but I managed to finish the whole piece. That I managed to do so made me feel really strong. I never again feared ridicule.

In later years I was reminded of this experience from time to time.   11
During my fourth year as an assistant professor at the University of California at Berkeley, I won a distinguished teaching award. Some weeks later I ran into a former professor who congratulated me enthusiastically. But I said to him, "You know what? I became a distinguished teacher by *limping* across the stage of Dwinelle 155!" (Dwinelle 155 is a large, cold, classroom that most colleagues of mine hate to teach in.) I was rude not because I lacked graciousness but because this man, who had told me that my dissertation was the finest piece of work he had read in fifteen years, had nevertheless advised me to eschew a teaching career.

"Why?" I asked.   12

"Your leg..." he responded.   13

"What about my leg?" I said, puzzled.   14

15   "Well, how would you feel standing in front of a large lecture class?"

16   "If it makes any difference, I want you to know I've won a number of speech contests in my life, and I am not the least bit self-conscious about speaking in front of large audiences. . . . Look, why don't you write me a letter of recommendation to tell people how brilliant I am, and let *me* worry about my leg!"

17   This incident is worth recounting only because it illustrates a dilemma that handicapped persons face frequently: those who care about us sometimes get so protective that they unwittingly limit our growth. This former professor of mine had been one of my greatest supporters for two decades. Time after time, he had written glowing letters of recommendation on my behalf. He had spoken as he did because he thought he had my best interest at heart; he thought that if I got a desk job rather than one that required me to be a visible, public person, I would be spared the misery of being stared at.

18   Americans, for the most part, do not believe as Asians do that physically handicapped persons are morally flawed. But they are equally inept at interacting with those of us who are not able-bodied. Cultural differences in the perception and treatment of handicapped people are most clearly expressed by adults. Children, regardless of where they are, tend to be openly curious about people who do not look "normal." Adults in Asia have no hesitation in asking visibly handicapped people what is wrong with them, often expressing their sympathy with looks of pity, whereas adults in the United States try desperately to be polite by pretending not to notice.

19   One interesting response I often elicited from people in Asia but have never encountered in America is the attempt to link my physical condition to the state of my soul. Many a time while living and traveling in Asia people would ask me what religion I belonged to. I would tell them that my mother is a devout Buddhist, that my father was baptized a Catholic but has never practiced Catholicism, and that I am an agnostic. Upon hearing this, people would try strenuously to convert me to their religion so that whichever God they believed in could bless me. If I would only attend this church or that temple regularly, they urged, I would surely get cured. Catholics and Buddhists alike have pressed religious medallions into my palm, telling me if I would wear these, the relevant deity or saint would make me well. Once while visiting the tomb of Muhammad Ali Jinnah in Karachi, Pakistan, an old Muslim, after finishing his evening prayers, spotted me, gestured toward my legs, raised his arms heavenward, and began a new round of prayers, apparently on my behalf.

20   In the United States adults who try to act "civilized" toward handicapped people by pretending they don't notice anything unusual sometimes end up ignoring handicapped people completely. In the first few months I lived in this country, I was struck by the fact that when-

ever children asked me what was the matter with my leg, their adult companions would hurriedly shush them up, furtively look at me, mumble apologies, and rush their children away. After a few months of such encounters, I decided it was my responsibility to educate these people. So I would say to the flustered adults, "It's okay, let the kid ask." Turning to the child, I would say, "When I was a little girl, no bigger than you are, I became sick with something called polio. The muscles of my leg shrank up and I couldn't walk very well. You're much luckier than I am because now you can get a vaccine to make sure you never get my disease. So don't cry when your mommy takes you to get a polio vaccine, okay?" Some adults and their little companions I talked to this way were glad to be rescued from embarrassment; others thought I was strange.

Americans have another way of covering up their uneasiness: they   21
become jovially patronizing. Sometimes when people spot my crutch, they ask if I've had a skiing accident. When I answer that unfortunately it is something less glamorous than that they say, "I bet you could ski if you put your mind to it!" Alternately, at parties where people dance, men who ask me to dance with them get almost belligerent when I decline their invitation. They say, "Of course you can dance if you *want* to!" Some have given me pep talks about how if I would only develop the right mental attitude, I would have more fun in life.

Different cultural attitudes toward handicapped persons came out   22
clearly during my wedding. My father-in-law, as solid a representative of middle America as could be found, had no qualms about objecting to the marriage on racial grounds, but he could bring himself to comment on my handicap only indirectly. He wondered why his son, who had dated numerous high school and college beauty queens, couldn't marry one of them instead of me. My mother-in-law, a devout Christian, did not share her husband's prejudices, but she worried aloud about whether I could have children. Some Chinese friends of my parents, on the other hand, said that I was lucky to have found such a noble man, one who would marry me despite my handicap. I, for my part, appeared in church in a white lace wedding dress I had designed and made myself—a miniskirt!

How Asian Americans treat me with respect to my handicap tells   23
me a great deal about their degree of acculturation. Recent immigrants behave just like Asians in Asia; those who have been here longer or who grew up in the United States behave more like their white counterparts. I have not encountered any distinctly Asian American pattern of response. What makes the experience of Asian American handicapped people unique is the duality of responses we elicit.

Regardless of racial or cultural background, most handicapped   24
people have to learn to find a balance between the desire to attain physical independence and the need to take care of ourselves by not overtax-

ing our bodies. In my case, I've had to learn to accept the fact that leading an active life has its price. Between the ages of eight and eighteen, I walked without using crutches or braces but the effort caused my right leg to become badly misaligned. Soon after I came to the United States, I had a series of operations to straighten out the bones of my right leg; afterwards though my leg looked straighter and presumably better, I could no longer walk on my own. Initially my doctors fitted me with a brace, but I found wearing one cumbersome and soon gave it up. I could move around much more easily—and more important, faster— by using one crutch. One orthopedist after another warned me that using a single crutch was a bad practice. They were right. Over the years my spine developed a double-S curve and for the last twenty years I have suffered from severe, chronic back pains, which neither conventional physical therapy nor a lighter work load can eliminate.

25   The only thing that helps my backaches is a good massage, but the soothing effect lasts no more than a day or two. Massages are expensive, especially when one needs them three times a week. So I found a job that pays better, but at which I have to work longer hours, consequently increasing the physical strain on my body—a sort of vicious circle. When I was in my thirties, my doctors told me that if I kept leading the strenuous life I did, I would be in a wheelchair by the time I was forty. They were right on target: I bought myself a wheelchair when I was forty-one. But being the incorrigible character that I am, I use it only when I am *not* in a hurry!

26   It is a good thing, however, that I am too busy to think much about my handicap or my backaches because pain can physically debilitate as well as cause depression. And there are days when my spirits get rather low. What has helped me is realizing that being handicapped is akin to growing old at an accelerated rate. The contradiction I experience is that often my mind races along as though I'm only twenty while my body feels about sixty. But fifteen or twenty years hence, unlike my peers who will have to cope with aging for the first time, I shall be full of cheer because I will have already fought, and I hope won, that battle long ago.

27   Beyond learning how to be physically independent and, for some of us, living with chronic pain or other kinds of discomfort, the most difficult thing a handicapped person has to deal with, especially during puberty and early adulthood, is relating to potential sexual partners. Because American culture places so much emphasis on physical attractiveness, a person with a shriveled limb, or a tilt to the head, or the inability to speak clearly, experiences great uncertainty—indeed trauma—when interacting with someone to whom he or she is attracted. My problem was that I was not only physically handicapped, small, and short, but worse, I also wore glasses and was smarter than all the boys I knew! Alas, an insurmountable combination. Yet some-

how I have managed to have intimate relationships, all of them with extraordinary men. Not surprisingly, there have also been countless men who broke my heart—men who enjoyed my company "as a friend," but who never found the courage to date or make love with me, although I am sure my experience in this regard is no different from that of many able-bodied persons.

The day came when my backaches got in the way of having an active sex life. Surprisingly that development was liberating because I stopped worrying about being attractive to men. No matter how headstrong I had been, I, like most women of my generation, had had the desire to be alluring to men ingrained into me. And that longing had always worked like a brake on my behavior. When what men think of me ceased to be compelling, I gained greater freedom to be myself.   28

I've often wondered if I would have been a different person had I not been physically handicapped. I really don't know, though there is no question that being handicapped has marked me. But at the same time I usually do not *feel* handicapped—and consequently, I do not *act* handicapped. People are therefore less likely to treat me as a handicapped person. There is no doubt, however, that the lives of my parents, sister, husband, other family members, and some close friends have been affected by my physical condition. They have had to learn not to hide me away at home, not to feel embarrassed by how I look or react to people who say silly things to me, and not to resent me for the extra demands my condition makes on them. Perhaps the hardest thing for those who live with handicapped people is to know when and how to offer help. There are no guidelines applicable to all situations. My advice is, when in doubt, ask, but ask in a way that does not smack of pity or embarrassment. Most important, please don't talk to us as though we are children.   29

So, has being physically handicapped been a handicap? It all depends on one's attitude. Some years ago, I told a friend that I had once said to an affirmative action compliance officer (somewhat sardonically since I do not believe in the head count approach to affirmative action) that the institution which employs me is triply lucky because it can count me as non-white, female and handicapped. He responded, "Why don't you tell them to count you four times?... Remember, you're short, besides!"   30

✦ Questions for Discussion and Writing

1. What insight into cross-cultural perceptions of disabilities do you get from Chan's account? Specifically, how do Asian perceptions of disabilities differ from those in America?

2. To what extent did Chan have to overcome the well-meaning advice of family and friends and discount their perception of her diminished potential?

3. Chan has very individualistic views; that is, she is an agnostic, does not believe in affirmative action, is uninhibited about sex, and has an unusual attitude towards the accelerating nature of her handicap. Which of her responses towards events made you aware of this?

4. Do you know anyone who has a disability or ailment as well as a sense of irony and detachment such as Chan displays toward her handicap? Write a short account of the way in which this attitude enables the person to cope with circumstances that might destroy someone else.

5. If you have ever been temporarily physically incapacitated, or if you have a disability, write an essay that will help your readers to understand your plight as well as the overt and subtle aspects of discrimination.

Maya Angelou

Liked for Myself

◆

Maya Angelou was born in 1928 in St. Louis, Missouri, and attended public schools in Arkansas and California. In her widely varied career she has been a streetcar conductor, successful singer, actress, and teacher. She is the author of several volumes of poetry and ten plays for stage, screen, and television; but she is best known for her autobiography, a work still in progress (five volumes of which have been published). "Liked for Myself" originally appeared in the first volume of this autobiography, I Know Why the Caged Bird Sings *(1970).*

For nearly a year, I sopped around the house, the Store, the school and the church, like an old biscuit, dirty and inedible. Then I met, or rather got to know, the lady who threw me my first life line. 1

Mrs. Bertha Flowers was the aristocrat of Black Stamps. She had the grace of control to appear warm in the coldest weather, and on the Arkansas summer days it seemed she had a private breeze which swirled around, cooling her. She was thin without the taut look of wiry people, and her printed voile dresses and flowered hats were as right for her as denim overalls for a farmer. She was our side's answer to the richest white woman in town. 2

Her skin was a rich black that would have peeled like a plum if snagged, but then no one would have thought of getting close enough to Mrs. Flowers to ruffle her dress, let alone snag her skin. She didn't encourage familiarity. She wore gloves too. 3

I don't think I ever saw Mrs. Flowers laugh, but she smiled often. A slow widening of her thin black lips to show even, small white teeth, then the slow effortless closing. When she chose to smile on me, I always wanted to thank her. The action was so graceful and inclusively benign. 4

She was one of the few gentlewomen I have ever known, and has remained throughout my life the measure of what a human being can be.... 5

One summer afternoon, sweet-milk fresh in my memory, she stopped at the Store to buy provisions. Another Negro woman of her health and age would have been expected to carry the paper sacks home in one hand, but Momma said, "Sister Flowers, I'll send Bailey up to your house with these things." 6

She smiled that slow dragging smile, "Thank you, Mrs. Henderson. I'd prefer Marguerite, though." My name was beautiful when she said 7 it. "I've been meaning to talk to her, anyway." They gave each other age-group looks. . . .

8   There was a little path beside the rocky road, and Mrs. Flowers walked in front swinging her arms and picking her way over the stones.

9   She said, without turning her head, to me, "I hear you're doing very good school work, Marguerite, but that it's all written. The teachers report that they have trouble getting you to talk in class." We passed the triangular farm on our left and the path widened to allow us to walk together. I hung back in the separate unasked and unanswerable questions.

10   "Come and walk along with me, Marguerite." I couldn't have refused even if I wanted to. She pronounced my name so nicely. Or more correctly, she spoke each word with such clarity that I was certain a foreigner who didn't understand English could have understood her.

11   "Now no one is going to make you talk—possibly no one can. But bear in mind, language is man's way of communicating with his fellow man and it is language alone which separates him from the lower animals." That was a totally new idea to me, and I would need time to think about it.

12   "Your grandmother says you read a lot. Every chance you get. That's good, but not good enough. Words mean more than what is set down on paper. It takes the human voice to infuse them with the shades of deeper meaning."

13   I memorized the part about the human voice infusing words. It seemed so valid and poetic.

14   She said she was going to give me some books and that I not only must read them, I must read them aloud. She suggested that I try to make a sentence sound in as many different ways as possible.

15   "I'll accept no excuse if you return a book to me that has been badly handled." My imagination boggled at the punishment I would deserve if in fact I did abuse a book of Mrs. Flowers'. Death would be too kind and brief.

16   The odors in the house surprised me. Somehow I had never connected Mrs. Flowers with food or eating or any other common experience of common people. There must have been an outhouse, too, but my mind never recorded it.

17   The sweet scent of vanilla had met us as she opened the door.

18   "I made tea cookies this morning. You see, I had planned to invite you for cookies and lemonade so we could have this little chat. The lemonade is in the icebox."

19   It followed that Mrs. Flowers would have ice on an ordinary day, when most families in our town bought ice late on Saturdays only a few times during the summer to be used in the wooden ice-cream freezers.

She took the bags from me and disappeared through the kitchen   20
door. I looked around the room that I had never in my wildest fantasies
imagined I would see. Browned photographs leered or threatened from
the walls and the white, freshly done curtains pushed against themselves and against the wind. I wanted to gobble up the room entire and
take it to Bailey, who would help me analyze and enjoy it.

"Have a seat, Marguerite. Over there by the table." She carried a   21
platter covered with a tea towel. Although she warned that she hadn't
tried her hand at baking sweets for some time, I was certain that like
everything else about her the cookies would be perfect.

They were flat round wafers, slightly browned on the edges and   22
butter-yellow in the center. With the cold lemonade they were sufficient
for childhood's lifelong diet. Remembering my manners, I took nice little lady-like bites off the edges. She said she had made them expressly
for me and that she had a few in the kitchen that I could take home to
my brother. So I jammed one whole cake in my mouth and the rough
crumbs scratched the insides of my jaws, and if I hadn't had to swallow, it would have been a dream come true.

As I ate she began the first of what we later called "my lessons in   23
living." She said that I must always be intolerant of ignorance but understanding of illiteracy. That some people, unable to go to school,
were more educated and even more intelligent than college professors.
She encouraged me to listen carefully to what country people called
mother wit. That in those homely sayings was couched the collective
wisdom of generations.

When I finished the cookies she brushed off the table and brought   24
a thick, small book from the bookcase. I had read *A Tale of Two Cities*
and found it up to my standards as a romantic novel. She opened the
first page and I heard poetry for the first time in my life.

"It was the best of times and the worst of times..." Her voice slid   25
in and curved down through and over the words. She was nearly singing. I wanted to look at the pages. Were they the same that I had read?
Or were there notes, music, lined on the pages, as in a hymn book? Her
sounds began cascading gently. I knew from listening to a thousand
preachers that she was nearing the end of her reading, and I hadn't really heard, heard to understand, a single word.

"How do you like that?"   26

It occurred to me that she expected a response. The sweet vanilla   27
flavor was still on my tongue and her reading was a wonder in my
ears. I had to speak.

I said, "Yes, ma'am." It was the least I could do, but it was the most   28
also.

"There's one more thing. Take this book of poems and memorize   29
one for me. Next time you pay me a visit, I want you to recite."

30   I have tried often to search behind the sophistication of years for
the enchantment I so easily found in those gifts. The essence escapes
but its aura remains. To be allowed, no, invited, into the private lives of
strangers, and to share their joys and fears, was a chance to exchange
the Southern bitter wormwood for a cup of mead with Beowulf or a hot
cup of tea and milk with Oliver Twist. When I said aloud, "It is a far, far
better thing that I do, than I have ever done..." tears of love filled my
eyes at my selfishness.

31   On that first day, I ran down the hill and into the road (few cars
ever came along it) and had the good sense to stop running before I
reached the Store.

32   I was liked, and what a difference it made. I was respected not as
Mrs. Henderson's grandchild or Bailey's sister but for just being
Marguerite Johnson.

33   Childhood's logic never asks to be proved (all conclusions are absolute). I didn't question why Mrs. Flowers had singled me out for attention, nor did it occur to me that Momma might have asked her to
give me a little talking to. All I cared about was that she had made tea
cookies for *me* and read to *me* from her favorite book. It was enough to
prove that she liked me.

✦ Questions for Discussion and Writing

1. How did Bertha Flowers's treatment help Marguerite gain self-esteem?

2. What insights about attitudes towards race, at the time, does Angelou's account provide?

3. What do you think Angelou means by "Mother Wit"? How does it differ from formal education?

4. Write about a significant experience in which your relationship with
   someone much younger or older resulted in greater self-acceptance for
   you or the other person.

5. Describe how someone you know well, who initially had low self-esteem, gained self-confidence. What were the circumstances responsible for this? In your character sketch, describe how you know this
   person, share important memories that make clear how that person
   changed, and give reasons for this change.

6. Angelou's narrative recalls her conversations with Mrs. Flowers. Using your journal/diary you might consider writing a dialogue in
   which you converse with someone who is no longer in your life, using
   the opportunity to get in touch with your true feelings towards this
   person. Project what the other person is saying in your dialogue.

Connections

1. What connections can you discover between the accounts of Joan Didion and Sucheng Chan in terms of how each writer learned to cope with impairments?

2. What kinds of humorous techniques do Mike Royko and Itabari Njeri use to satirize aspects of contemporary society?

3. In what way do the accounts of Itabari Njeri and Maya Angelou focus on the theme of minority status and self-esteem?

4. What societal stereotypes did Christy Brown and Sucheng Chan have to overcome simply to be perceived as human beings?

5. How do the accounts by Mike Royko and Kim Chernin ("The Flesh and the Devil," Chapter 3) present different sides of the same coin?

6. In your view, are social or personal considerations more important in explaining Itabari Njeri's and Nora Ephron's ("A Few Words About Breasts," Chapter 5) concern about the way they look?

7. What differences in cross-cultural expectations are explored in the accounts by Sucheng Chan and Le Ly Hayslip ("Yearning to Breathe Free," Chapter 9)?

8. How was Maya Angelou's life influenced by Mrs. Flowers and Jill Nelson's ("Number One!" Chapter 1) by her father?

9

Finding One's Place

---◆---

One's destination is never a place, but rather a new way of looking at things.

—Henry Miller, "The Oranges of the Millennium,"
Big Sur and the Oranges of Hieronymus Bosch (1957)

Selections in this chapter draw from several traditions, including nature writing, the journals of travelers and explorers, and the reflections of immigrants and exiles. A common element of these works is the need to redefine oneself in an unfamiliar environment.

The journals kept by explorers are particularly interesting, and the many detailed observations they contain suggest that the faculty of seeing things as they are is a virtue in itself. Some writers respond to landscapes with deeply felt meditations on values, ideals, and attitudes. Others use locations to symbolize social and cultural forces. Yet, in all cases, the look, sound, touch, and feel of the environment is paramount in communicating the author's observations and reflections.

Several works in this chapter explore the needs of those who have left home, whether as refugees, immigrants, or travelers, and must make sense of their lives in a new place. The jarring, intense, and often painful emotional experience of having to redefine oneself in a strange land, of trying to reconcile conflicting cultural values, forces immigrants to surrender all ideas of safety, the comfort of familiar surroundings, and a common language.

The journal entries by the explorers Meriwether Lewis and William Clark provide a wealth of observations recorded as they made their way along the Missouri River toward the Pacific Ocean. "The Flood," a firsthand account by Sir Leonard Woolley, the archeologist who discovered the ancient city of Ur, lets us observe the methods he used to solve one of the world's oldest riddles. A founder of the conservation movement, Aldo Leopold, in "Thinking Like a Mountain," describes his discovery of the important role wolves play in maintaining the wilderness. In "Niagara Falls" William Zinsser seeks to uncover the source of America's fascination with this natural wonder. The cross-cultural challenges Le Ly Hayslip faced in emigrating to the United States are related in "Yearning to Breathe Free."

Meriwether Lewis and William Clark

The Journals of Lewis and Clark

———————◆———————

Meriwether Lewis (1774–1809) was born in Virginia and served as President Jefferson's private secretary from 1801–1803. Lewis selected, with Jefferson's approval, fellow Virginian and Indian agent William Clark to join him in leading an expedition designed to open the vast American wilderness to westward expansion, for which Congress appropriated $2,500. Meriwether Lewis and William Clark were instructed by President Thomas Jefferson to lead an expedition up the Missouri River, which departed in May 1804, to find an accessible route to the Pacific Ocean and to explore the newly acquired Louisiana territory. They were further ordered to keep careful, detailed journals on their discoveries and observations of numerous Indian tribes, plants, animals, and possible routes to the Pacific Ocean. As a precaution, both men kept separate journals in the event that one might be lost or destroyed. Their efforts appeared in combined form in the eight-volume publication Original Journals of the Lewis and Clark Expedition. *The following excerpts are drawn from this work.*

To Meriwether Lewis:

1   The object of your mission is to explore the Missouri River, as, by its course and communication with the waters of the Pacific Ocean, may offer the most direct and practicable water-communication across the continent for the purpose of commerce.

2   Beginning at the mouth of the Missouri, you will take observations of latitude and longitude, at all remarkable points on the river. Your observations are to be taken with great pains and accuracy. Several copies of these should be made at leisure times.

3   Objects worthy of notice will be: the soil and face of the country, the animals, the mineral productions of every kind, and the climate.

4   You will make yourself acquainted with the names of the [Indian] nations and their numbers; the extent of their possessions; their relations with other tribes or nations; their language and traditions.

5   In all your intercourse with natives, treat them in the most friendly and conciliatory manner which their own conduct will admit. If a supe-

rior force should be arrayed against your further passage, and inflexibly determined to arrest it, you must return. In the loss of yourselves we should also lose the information you will have acquired. To your own discretion, therefore, must be left the degree of danger you may risk, and the point at which you should decline; we wish you to err on the side of your safety, and to bring back your party safe.

To provide, on the accident of your death, and the consequent danger to your party, and total failure of the enterprise, you are authorized to name the person who shall succeed to the command on your decease. 6

Given under my hand at the City of Washington, this twentieth day of June, 1803. 7

Thomas Jefferson
President of the United States of America

June 27, 1804. We remained two days at the mouth of the Kansas River, during which we made the necessary observations and repaired the boat. On the banks of the Kansas reside the Indians of the same name, consisting of two villages and amounting to about 300 men. 8

July 4, 1804. The morning was announced by the discharge of one shot from our bow piece. Joseph Fields got bitten by a snake, and was quickly doctored with bark and gunpowder by Captain Lewis. We passed a creek 12 yards wide and this being the Fourth of July, the day of independence of the United States, we called it Fourth of July 1804 Creek. 9

July 7, 1804. The rapidity of the water obliged us to draw the boat along with ropes. We made 14 miles and halted. Saw a number of young swans. Killed a wolf. Another of our men had a stroke of the sun. He was bled, and took a preparation of niter, which relieved him considerably. 10

July 12, 1804. Tried a man for sleeping on his post, and inspected the arms, ammunition, etc. of the party. Found all complete. Took some lunar observations. Three deer killed today. 11

July 22–26, 1804. Our camp is by observation in latitude 41° 3' 11". We stayed here several days, during which we dried our provisions, made new oars, and prepared our dispatches and maps of the country we had passed, for the President of the United States. The present season is that in which the Indians go out on the prairies to hunt the buf- 12 falo. Five beaver caught near the camp, the flesh of which we made use of.

13   *July 30, 1804.* Walked a short distance. This prairie is covered with grass 10 or 12 inches in height. Soil is of good quality. The most beautiful prospect of the river, up and down, which we ever beheld.

14   *August 1–2, 1804.* We waited with much anxiety the return of our messenger to the Ottoes. Our apprehensions relieved by the arrival of a party of 14 Indians. We sent them some roasted meat, pork, flour, and meal. In return they made us a present of watermelons.

15   *August 3, 1804.* This morning the Indians, with their six chiefs, were all assembled under an awning formed with a mainsail. A speech was made announcing to them the change in the government from French to American, our promise of protection, and advice as to their future conduct. All six chiefs replied to our speech, each in his turn, according to rank. They expressed their joy at the change of government, their hopes that we would recommend them to their Great Father (the President), that they might obtain trade. They wanted arms as well for hunting as for defense. We proceeded to distribute our presents. To the six chiefs we gave medals according to their rank. Each of these medals was accompanied by a present of paint, garters, and cloth ornaments of dress, a canister of powder, a bottle of whiskey, and a few presents to the whole, which appeared to make them perfectly satisfied. The airgun was fired, and astonished them greatly. The incident just related induced us to give to this place the name of Council Bluffs; the situation of it is exceedingly favorable for a fort and trading factory. It is central to the chief resorts of the Indians. The ceremonies being concluded, we set sail in the afternoon. Mosquitoes very troublesome.

✦ *Questions for Discussion and Writing*

1. What were the purpose and objectives of the expedition as outlined by President Thomas Jefferson? How well did Lewis and Clark carry out President Jefferson's instructions?

2. What do the journals tell you about Lewis as the leader of the expedition?

3. Of the many observations and discoveries recorded by Lewis and Clark, which struck you as the most significant, and why?

4. Have you ever participated in an expedition or an extended hike, nature walk, etc.? How was it organized, and what did you notice along the way?

5. If you were an archeologist in the distant future who came across items that you had never seen before, what would you think was the purpose or function of any of the following: popcorn maker, vacuum cleaner, television, microwave, VCR, electric can opener, and electric knife sharpener? Describe one of these, or any other common household appliance, as if you were seeing it for the first time.

Sir Leonard Woolley

The Flood

◆

Sir Leonard Woolley (1880–1960) was born in London, England. He was educated at New College, Oxford, and was an assistant to Sir Arthur Evans at the Ashmolean Museum in 1905. After a period of field work in the Near East, Woolley was appointed as director of the British Museum expedition to Carchemish in 1912. He was accompanied there by T. E. Lawrence (better known as "Lawrence of Arabia"), with whom he coauthored The Wilderness of Zin *(1915), an account of their discoveries. After directing a joint expedition of the British Museum and the Museum of the University of Pennsylvania, Woolley, in 1926, discovered and excavated the royal tombs at Ur, whose treasures invited comparisons with the discoveries by Schliemann (at Mycenae) and those of Carter and Lord Carnarvon (of Tutankhamen's Tomb). Woolley's excavations at Ur revealed the existence and importance of Sumerian culture in Mesopotamia. His remarkably clear and readable accounts of his archaeological discoveries were published in* Ur of the Chaldees *(1929),* The Sumerians *(1930), and* Excavations at Ur: A Record of Twelve Years' Work *(1954). In "The Flood," from* Myth or Legend *(1968), Woolley describes the ingenious method he used to solve the age-old problem of proving the authenticity of the Biblical flood.*

1   There can be few stories more familiar to us than that of the Flood. The word "antediluvian" has passed into common speech, and Noah's Ark is still one of the favourite toys of the children's nursery.

2   The Book of Genesis tells us how the wickedness of man was such that God repented Him that He had made man upon the earth, and decided to destroy all flesh; but Noah, being the one righteous man, found grace in the eyes of the Lord. So Noah was bidden by God to build an ark, and in due time he and all his family went in, with all the beasts and the fowls of the air, going in two by two; and the doors of the ark were shut and the rain was upon the earth for forty days and forty nights, and the floods prevailed exceedingly and the earth was covered, and all flesh that moved upon the earth died, and Noah only remained alive and they that were with him in the ark. And then the floods abated. Noah sent out a raven and a dove, and at last the dove brought him back an olive leaf, proof that the dry land had appeared. And they all went forth out of the ark, and Noah built an altar and offered sacrifice, and the Lord smelt a sweet savour and promised that

never again would He smite everything living, as He had done; and God set His bow in the clouds as a token of the covenant that there should not any more be a flood to destroy the earth.

For many centuries, indeed until only a few generations ago, the story of Noah was accepted as an historical fact; it was part of the Bible, it was the inspired Word of God, and therefore every word of it must be true. To deny the story was to deny the Christian faith.

3

Then two things happened. On the one hand scholars, examining the Hebrew text of Genesis, discovered that it was a composite narrative. There had been two versions of the Flood story which differed in certain small respects, and these two had been skillfully combined into one by the Jewish scribes four or five hundred years before the time of Christ, when they edited the sacred books of their people and gave to them the form which they had to-day. That discovery shook the faith of many old-fashioned believers, or was indignantly denied by them; they said that it was an attack on the Divine Word. Really, of course, it was nothing of the sort. Genesis is an historical book, and the writer of history does not weave the matter out of his imagination; he consults older authorities of every sort and quotes them as freely and as often as may be. The older the authorities are, and the more his account embodies theirs, the more reason we have to trust what he writes; if it be insisted that his writings are divinely inspired, the answer is that 'inspiration' consists not in dispensing with original sources but in making the right use of them. The alarm felt by the orthodox when confronted with the discoveries of scholarship was a false alarm.

4

The second shock came when from the ruins of the ancient cities of Mesopotamia archaeologists unearthed clay tablets on which was written another version of the Flood story—the Sumerian version. According to that, mankind had grown wicked and the gods in council decided to destroy the human race which they had made. But one of the gods happened to be a good friend of one mortal man, so he went down and warned him of what was to happen and counselled him to build an ark. And the man did so; and he took on board all his family, and his domestic animals, and shut the door, and the rain fell and the floods rose and covered all the earth. At last the storms abated and the ark ran aground, and the man sent out a dove and a swallow and a raven, and finally came forth from the ark and built an altar and did sacrifice, and the gods (who had had no food since the Flood started and were terribly hungry) "came round the altar like flies," and the rainbow is set in the clouds as a warrant that never again will the gods destroy all men by water.

5

It is clear that this is the same story as we have in Genesis. But the Sumerian account was actually written before the time of Moses (whom some people had, without reason, thought to be the author of Genesis), and not only that, but before the time of Abraham. There-

6

fore the Flood story was not by origin a Hebrew story at all but had
been taken over by the Hebrews from the idolatrous folk of Babylo-
nia; it was a pagan legend, so why should we for a moment suppose
that it was true? All sorts of attempts were made to show that the Bible story was independent, or was the older of the two, but all the attempts were in vain, and to some it seemed as if the battle for the Old
Testament had been lost.

7   Once more, it was a false alarm. Nobody had ever supposed that
the Flood had affected only the Hebrew people; other people had suffered by it, and a disaster of such magnitude was bound to be remembered in their traditions; in so far as the Sumerian legend was closer in
time to the event, it might be said to strengthen rather than to weaken
the case for the Biblical version. But it could well be asked, "Why
should we believe a Sumerian legend which is, on the face of it, a fantastic piece of pagan mythology?" It is perfectly true that the Sumerian
Flood story is a religious poem. It reflects the religious beliefs of a pagan people just as the biblical story reflects the religious beliefs of the
Hebrews; and we cannot accept the Sumerian religion as true. Also, it is
a poem, and everybody knows what poets are! Shakespeare certainly
did:

8   The poet's eye, in a fine frenzy rolling,
             Doth glance from heaven to earth, from earth to heaven,
             And, as imagination bodies forth
             The forms of things unknown, the poet's pen
             Turns them to shapes, and gives to airy nothing
             A local habitation and a name.

9   But the legend does not stand alone. Sober Sumerian historians
wrote down a sort of skeleton of their country's history in the form of a
list of its kings (like our "William I, 1066," and all that); starting at the
very beginning there is a series of perhaps fabulous rulers, and, they
say, "Then came the Flood. And after the Flood kingship again descended from heaven"; and they speak of a dynasty of kings who established themselves in the city of Kish, and next of a dynasty whose
capital was Erech. Here, at least, we are upon historic ground, for archaeological excavation in modern times has recovered the material
civilization of those ancient days when Erech was indeed the chief city
of Mesopotamia. The old historians were sure that not long before
these days the course of their country's history had been interrupted by
a great flood. If they were right, it does not, of course, mean that the
Flood legend is correct in all its details, but it does at least give it a basis
of fact.

10   In the year 1929, when we had been digging at Ur the famous
"royal graves" with their extraordinary treasures, which can be dated
to something like 2800 B.C., I determined to test still lower levels so as to

get an idea of what might be found by digging yet deeper. We sank a small shaft below the stratum of soil in which the graves lay, and went down through the mixed rubbish that is characteristic of an old inhabited site—a mixture of decomposed mud-brick, ashes and broken pottery, very much like what we had been finding higher up. Then suddenly it all stopped: there were no more potsherds, no ashes, only clean, water-laid mud, and the workman in the shaft told me that he had reached virgin soil; there was nothing more to be found, and he had better go elsewhere.

I got down and looked at the evidence and agreed with him; but then I took my levels and found that "virgin soil" was not nearly as deep down as I expected. That upset a favourite theory or mine, and I hate having my theories upset except on the very best of evidence, so I told him to get back and go on digging. Most unwillingly he did so, turning up nothing but clean soil that contained no sign of human activity; he worked down through eight feet of it and then, suddenly, flint implements appeared and sherds of painted pottery which, we were fairly sure, was the earliest pottery made in southern Mesopotamia. I was convinced of what it meant, but I wanted to see whether others would arrive at the same conclusion. I brought up two of my staff and, after pointing out the facts, asked for their conclusions. They did not know what to say. My wife came along and looked and was asked the same question, and she turned away, remarking quite casually, "Well, of course it's the Flood." 11

So it was. But one could scarcely argue for the Deluge on the strength of a shaft a yard square; so the next season I marked out on the low ground where the graves had been a rectangle some seventy-five feet by sixty, and there dug a huge pit which went down, in the end, for sixty-four feet. The level at which we started had been the ground surface about 2600 B.C. Almost immediately we came on the ruins of houses slightly older than that; we cleared them away and found more houses below them. In the first twenty feet we dug through no fewer than eight sets of houses, each of which had been built over the ruins of the age before. Then the house ruins stopped and we were digging through a solid mass of potsherds wherein, at different levels, were the kilns in which the pots had been fired; the sherds represented those pots which went wrong in the firing and, having no commercial value, had been smashed by the potter and the bits left lying until they were so heaped up that the kilns were buried and new kilns had to be built. It was a vase factory which was running for so long a time that by the stratified sherds we could trace the course of history: near the bottom came the wares in use when Erech was the royal city, and at the very bottom was the painted ware of the lands's earliest immigrants. And then came the clean, water-laid mud, eleven feet of it, mud which on analysis proved to be the silt brought down by the River Euphrates 12

from its upper reaches hundreds of miles away; and under the silt, based on what really was virgin soil, the ruins of the houses that had been overwhelmed by the flood and buried deep beneath the mud carried by its waters.

13   This was the evidence we needed: a flood of magnitude unparalleled in any later phase of Mesopotamian history; and since, as the pottery proved, it had taken place some little while before the time of the Erech dynasty, this was the Flood of the Sumerian king-lists and that of the Sumerian legend and that of Genesis.

14   We have proved that the Flood really happened; but that does not mean that all the details of the Flood legend are true—we did not find Noah and we did not find his ark! But take a few details. The Sumerian version says (this is not mentioned in Genesis) that antediluvian man lived in huts made of reeds; under the Flood deposit we found the wreckage of reed huts. Noah built his ark of light wood and bitumen. Just on top of the Flood deposit we found a big lump of bitumen, bearing the imprint of the basket in which it had been carried, just as I have myself seen the crude bitumen from the pits of Hit on the middle Euphrates being put in baskets for export downstream. I reckoned that to throw up an eleven-foot pile of silt against the mound on which the primitive town of Ur stood the water would have to be at least twenty-five feet deep; the account in Genesis says that the depth of the flood water was fifteen cubits, which is roughly twenty-six feet. "Twenty-six feet?" you may say; "that's not much of a flood!" Lower Mesopotamia is so flat and low-lying that a flood having that depth at Ur would spread over an area 300 miles long and 100 miles wide.

15   Noah's Flood was not a universal deluge; it was a vast flood in the valley of the Rivers Tigris and Euphrates. It drowned the whole of the habitable land between the eastern and the western deserts; for the people who lived there that was all the world. It wiped out the villages and exterminated their inhabitants, and although some of the towns set upon mounds survived, it was but a scanty and dispirited remnant of the nation that watched the waters recede at last. No wonder that they saw in this disaster the gods' punishment of a sinful generation and described it as such in a great religious poem; and if, as may well have been the case, one household managed to escape by boat from the drowned lowlands, the head of that house would naturally be made the hero of the saga.

✦ Questions for Discussion and Writing

1. What discoveries in the fields of Biblical scholarship and Sumerian archeology raised questions about the literal truth of the flood story? How does Woolley make use of information gleaned from fables and legends to guide his investigation?

2. Why was the find of the rubble of a pottery kiln significant? What did testing of the silt disclose? Why was the discovery of bitumen another piece of confirming evidence?

3. What problem confronted Woolley when he was well into the archeological excavations in 1929 at the ancient city of Ur?

4. How does Woolley's use of the first person singular allow the readers to share his ingenious problem-solving processes?

5. In your own words, state why Woolley concludes that the Biblical flood was not a universal deluge, as previously believed. How persuasive do you find Woolley's interpretation of the evidence his investigation disclosed? Has this research changed the way you look at the story of Noah and the flood, as related in the Book of Genesis, Chapters 6–8?

6. Imagine that you are sitting across the street from a building that is to be demolished and replaced. Describe the kind of building you would design to put in its place—its function, appearance, and uses.

Aldo Leopold

Thinking Like a Mountain

◆

Aldo Leopold (1876–1944) was a conservationist, forester, writer, and teacher who devoted himself to wilderness preservation and wildlife management. Through his efforts, the first protected wilderness area, located in Gila National Forest in New Mexico, was established. Leopold was instrumental in founding the Wilderness Society in 1934. He was posthumously honored in 1978 with the John Burroughs Medal in recognition of a lifetime of work in conservation. "Thinking Like a Mountain," drawn from his classic work A Sand County Almanac *(1949), reveals an exceptionally subtle appreciation of the interplay between animals and the environment.*

1   A deep chesty bawl echoes from rimrock to rimrock, rolls down the mountain, and fades into the far blackness of the night. It is an outburst of wild defiant sorrow, and of contempt for all the adversities of the world.

2   Every living thing (and perhaps many a dead one as well) pays heed to that call. To the deer it is a reminder of the way of all flesh, to the pine a forecast of midnight scuffles and of blood upon the snow, to the coyote a promise of gleanings to come, to the cowman a threat of red ink at the bank, to the bunter a challenge of fang against bullet. Yet behind these obvious and immediate hopes and fears there lies a deeper meaning, known only to the mountain itself. Only the mountain has lived long enough to listen objectively to the howl of a wolf.

3   Those unable to decipher the hidden meaning know nevertheless that it is there, for it is felt in all wolf country, and distinguishes that country from all other land. It tingles in the spine of all who hear wolves by night, or who scan their tracks by day. Even without sight or sound of wolf, it is implicit in a hundred small events: the midnight whinny of a pack horse, the rattle of rolling rocks, the bound of a fleeing deer, the way shadows lie under the spruces. Only the ineducable tyro can fail to sense the presence or absence of wolves, or the fact that mountains have a secret opinion about them.

4   My own conviction on this score dates from the day I saw a wolf die. We were eating lunch on a high rimrock, at the foot of which a turbulent river elbowed its way. We saw what we thought was a doe fording the torrent, her breast awash in white water. When she climbed the bank toward us and shook out her tail, we realized our error: it was a

wolf. A half-dozen others, evidently grown pups, sprang from the willows and all joined in a welcoming mêlée of wagging tails and playful maulings. What was literally a pile of wolves writhed and tumbled in the center of an open flat at the foot of our rimrock.

In those days we had never heard of passing up a chance to kill a wolf. In a second we were pumping lead into the pack, but with more excitement than accuracy: how to aim a steep downhill shot is always confusing. When our rifles were empty, the old wolf was down, and a pup was dragging a leg into impassable slide-rocks.

We reached the old wolf in time to watch a fierce green fire dying in her eyes. I realized then, and have known ever since, that there was something new to me in those eyes—something known only to her and to the mountain. I was young then, and full of trigger-itch; I thought that because fewer wolves meant more deer, that no wolves would mean hunters' paradise. But after seeing the green fire die, I sensed that neither the wolf nor the mountain agreed with such a view.

Since then I have lived to see state after state extirpate its wolves. I have watched the face of many a newly wolfless mountain, and seen the south-facing slopes wrinkle with a maze of new deer trails. I have seen every edible bush and seedling browsed, first to anaemic desuetude, and then to death, I have seen every edible tree defoliated to the height of a saddlehorn. Such a mountain looks as if someone had given God a new pruning shears, and forbidden Him all other exercise. In the end the starved bones of the hoped-for deer herd, dead of its own too-much, bleach with the bones of the dead sage, or molder under the high-lined junipers.

I now suspect that just as a deer herd lives in mortal fear of its wolves, so does a mountain live in mortal fear of its deer. And perhaps with better cause, for while a buck pulled down by wolves can be replaced in two or three years, a range pulled down by too many deer may fail of replacement in as many decades.

So also with cows. The cowman who cleans his range of wolves does not realize that he is taking over the wolf's job of trimming the herd to fit the range. He has not learned to think like a mountain. Hence we have dustbowls, and rivers washing the future into the sea.

We all strive for safety, prosperity, comfort, long life, and dullness. The deer strives with his supple legs, the cowman with trap and poison, the statesman with pen, the most of us with machines, votes, and dollars, but it all comes to the same thing: peace in our time. A measure of success in this is all well enough, and perhaps is a requisite to objective thinking, but too much safety seems to yield only danger in the long run. Perhaps this is behind Thoreau's dictum: In wildness is the salvation of the world. Perhaps this is the hidden meaning in the howl of the wolf, long known among mountains, but seldom perceived among men.

✦ Questions for Discussion and Writing

1. How does the mountain's perspective differ from the human one?

2. In what way does the experience of shooting a wolf change Leopold's attitude?

3. What consequences will follow the extermination of wolves, according to Leopold?

4. Is there a condition in the natural environment near you which would take on a different meaning if one thought like a mountain? Describe the circumstances from this objective vantage point. Has the current situation been produced by the attitude Leopold describes as wanting "too much safety"?

5. The presence of the wolves and the mountain impose themselves on Leopold's consciousness; although he does not create a formal dialogue between himself and the wolves or mountain, it would be interesting to know what this dialogue might sound like. Using your journal/diary, create a dialogue between you and an animal or a feature of the environment whose presence is important to you.

William Zinsser

Niagara Falls

◆

William Zinsser, born in 1922, graduated from Princeton University in 1944 and joined the staff of The New York Herald Tribune *in 1946. He worked there until 1959, first as a features editor and then as a drama editor and film critic. In 1959, he became a freelance writer and taught at Yale University between 1971 and 1979. Zinsser is the author of numerous books, including* Pop Goes America *(1966),* On Writing Well *(1976), and* American Places *(1992), in which "Niagara Falls" first appeared.*

Walden Pond and the Concord writers got me thinking about 1
America's great natural places, and I decided to visit Niagara Falls and
Yellowstone Park next. I had been reminded that one of the most radical ideas that Emerson and Thoreau and the other Transcendentalists
lobbed into the 19th-century American air was that nature was not an
enemy to be feared and repelled, but a spiritual force that the people of
a young nation should embrace and take nourishment from. The goal,
as Thoreau put it in his essay "Walking," was to become "an inhabitant,
or a part and parcel of Nature, rather than a member of society," and it
occurred to me that the long and powerful hold of Niagara and Yellowstone on the American imagination had its roots in the gratifying news
from Concord that nature was a prime source of uplift, improvement
and the "higher" feelings.

Niagara Falls existed only in the attic of my mind where collective 2
memory is stored: scraps of songs about honeymooning couples, vistas
by painters who tried to get the plummeting waters to hold still, film
clips of Marilyn Monroe running for her life in *Niagara,* odds and ends
of lore about stuntmen who died going over the falls, and always,
somewhere among the scraps, a boat called *Maid of the Mist,* which took
tourists . . . where? Behind the falls? *Under* the falls? Death hovered at
the edge of the images in my attic, or at least danger. But I had never
thought of going to see the place itself. That was for other people. Now
I wanted to be one of those other people.

One misconception I brought to Niagara Falls was that it consisted 3
of two sets of falls, which had to be viewed separately. I would have to
see the American falls first and then go over to the Canadian side to see
their falls, which, everyone said, were better. But nature hadn't done

anything so officious, as I found when the shuttle bus from the Buffalo airport stopped and I got out and walked, half running, down a path marked FALLS. The sign was hardly necessary; I could hear that I was going in the right direction.

4   Suddenly all the images of a lifetime snapped into place—all the paintings and watercolors and engravings and postcards and calendar lithographs. The river does indeed split into two cataracts, divided by a narrow island called Goat Island, but it was man who put a boundary between them. The eye can easily see them as one spectacle: first the straight line of the American falls, then the island, then the much larger, horseshoe-shaped curve of the Canadian falls. The American falls, 1,060 feet across, are majestic but relatively easy to process—water cascading over a ledge. The Canadian falls, 2,200 feet across, are elusive. Water hurtles over them in such volume that the spray ascends from their circular base as high as the falls themselves, 185 feet, hiding them at the heart of the horseshoe. If the Canadian falls are "better," it's not only because they are twice as big but because they have more mystery, curled in on themselves. Whatever is behind all that spray will remain their secret.

5   My vantage point for this first glimpse was a promenade that overlooks the falls on the American side—a pleasantly landscaped area that has the feeling of a national park, there was none of the souvenir-stand clutter I expected. My strongest emotion as I stood and tried to absorb the view was that I was very glad to be there. So *that's* what they look like! I stayed at the railing for a long time, enjoying the play of light on the tumbling waters; the colors, though the day was gray, were subtle and satisfying. My thoughts, such as they were, were banal—vaguely pantheistic, poor man's Wordsworth. My fellow sightseers were equally at ease, savoring nature with 19th-century scenery, taking pictures of each other against the cataracts. (More Kodak film is sold here than at any place except the Taj Mahal.) Quite a few of the tourists appeared to be honeymooners; many were parents with children; some were elementary schoolteachers with their classes. I heard some foreign accents, but on the whole it was—as it always has been—America-on-the-road. The old icon was still worth taking the kids to see. Today more people visit Niagara Falls than ever before: 10 million a year.

6   Far below, in the gorge where the river reassembles after its double descent, I saw a small boat bobbing in the turbulent water, its passengers bunched at the railing in blue slickers. Nobody had to tell me it was the *Maid of the Mist*—I heard it calling. I took the elevator down to the edge of the river. Even there, waiting at the dock, I could hardly believe that such a freakish trip was possible—or even prudent. What if the boat capsized? What if its engine stopped? What if...? But when the *Maid of the Mist* arrived, there was no question of not getting on it. I was just one more statistic proving the falls' legendary pull—the force

that has beckoned so many daredevils to their death and that compels so many suicides every year to jump.

On the boat, we all got blue raincoats and put them on with due se- 7 riousness. The *Maid of the Mist* headed out into the gorge and immediately sailed past the American falls. Because these falls have famously fallen apart over the years and dumped large chunks of rock at their base, the water glances off the rubble and doesn't churn up as much spray as a straight drop would generate. That gave us a good view of the falls from a fairly close range and got us only moderately wet.

Next we sailed past Goat Island. There I saw a scene so reminiscent 8 of a Japanese movie in its gauzy colors and stylized composition that I could hardly believe it wasn't a Japanese movie. Filtered through the mist, a straggling line of tourists in yellow raincoats was threading its way down a series of wooden stairways and catwalks to reach the rocks in front of the American falls. They were on a tour called "Cave of the Winds," so named because in the 19th century it was possible to go behind the falls into various hollowed-out spaces that have since eroded. Even today nobody gets closer to the falls, or gets wetter, than these stair people. I watched them as I might watch a colony of ants: small yellow figures doggedly following a zigzag trail down a steep embankment to some ordained goal. The sight took me by surprise and was surprisingly beautiful.

Leaving the ants, we proceeded to the Canadian falls. Until then 9 the *Maid of the Mist* had struck me as a normal excursion boat, the kind that might take sightseers around Manhattan. Suddenly it seemed very small. By now we had come within the outer circle of the horseshoe. On both sides of our boat, inconceivable amounts of water were rushing over the edge from the height of a 15-story building. I thought of the word I had seen in so many articles about Niagara's stuntmen: they were going to "conquer" the falls. Conquer! No such emanations were felt in our crowd. Spray was pelting our raincoats, and we peered out at each other from inside our hoods—eternal tourists bonded together by some outlandish event voluntarily entered into. (Am I really riding down the Grand Canyon on a burro? Am I really about to be charged by an African rhino?) The *Maid of the Mist* showed no sign of being afraid of the Canadian falls; it headed straight into the cloud of spray at the heart of the horseshoe. How much farther were we going to go? The boat began to rock in the eddying water. I felt a twinge of fear.

In the 19th-century literature of Niagara Falls, one adjective carries 10 much of the baggage: "sublime." Today it's seldom heard, except in bad Protestant hymns. But for a young nation eager to feel emotions worthy of God's mightiest wonders, the word had a precise meaning— "a mixture of attraction and terror," as the historian Elizabeth McKinsey puts it. Tracing the theory of sublimity to mid-18th-century aestheticians such as Edmund Burke—in particular, to Burke's *Philosophical*

Enquiry into the Origin of Our Ideas of the Sublime and Beautiful—Professor McKinsey says that the experience of early visitors to Niagara Falls called for a word that would go beyond mere awe and fear. "Sublime" was the perfect answer. It denoted "a new capacity to appreciate the beauty and grandeur of potentially terrifying natural objects." Anybody could use it, and everybody did.

11   Whether I was having sublime feelings as I looked up at the falls I will leave to some other aesthetician. By any name, however, I was thinking: This is an amazing place to be. I wasn't having a 19th-century rapture, but I also wasn't connected in any way to 20th-century thought. I was somewhere in a late-Victorian funk, the kind of romanticism that induced Hudson River School artists to paint a rainbow over Niagara Falls more often than they saw one there. Fortunately, in any group of Americans there will always be one pragmatist to bring us back to earth. Just as I was becoming edgy at the thought of being sucked into the vortex, the man next to me said that he had been measuring our progress by the sides of the gorge and we weren't making any progress at all. Even with its engines at full strength, the *Maid of the Mist* was barely holding its own. That was a sufficiently terrifying piece of news, and when the boat finally made a U-turn I didn't protest. A little sublime goes a long way.

12   The first *Maid of the Mist* took tourists to the base of the horseshoe falls in 1846. Now, as the mist enveloped our *Maid*, I liked the idea that I was in the same spot and was having what I assume were the same feelings that those travelers had almost 150 years ago. I liked the idea of a tourist attraction so pure that it doesn't have to be tricked out with improvements. The falls don't tug on our sense of history or on our national psyche. They don't have any intellectual content or take their meaning from what was achieved there. They just do what they do.

13   "When people sit in the front of that boat at the foot of the falls they get a little philosophical," said Christopher M. Glynn, marketing director of the Maid of the Mist Corporation. "They think: There's something bigger than I am that put *this* together. A lot of them have heard about the Seven Wonders of the World, and they ask, 'Is this one of them?'" Glynn's father, James V. Glynn, owner and president of the company, which has been owned by only two families since 1889, often has his lunch on the boat and talks with grandfathers and grandmothers who first visited Niagara on their honeymoon. "Usually," he told me, "they only saw the falls from above. Down here it's a totally different perspective, and they find the power of the water almost unbelievable. You're seeing one of God's great works when you're in that horseshoe."

14   Most Americans come to the falls as a family, said Ray H. Wigle of the Niagara Falls Visitors and Convention Bureau. "They wait until the kids are out of school to visit places like this and the Grand Canyon

and Yellowstone. They say, 'This is part of your education—to see these stupendous works of nature.' On one level today's tourists are conscious of 'the environment,' and they're appreciative of the magnificence of the planet and the fact that something like this has a right to exist by itself—unlike early tourists, who felt that nature was savage and had to be tamed and utilized. But deep down there's still a primal response to uncivilized nature that doesn't change from one century to another. 'I never realized it was like this!' I hear tourists say all the time, and when they turn away from their first look at the falls—when they first connect again with another person—there's always a delighted smile on their face that's universal and childish."

I spent two days at Niagara, looking at the falls at different times of   15
day and night, especially from the Canadian side, where the view of both cataracts across the gorge is the most stunning and—as so many artists have notified us—most pictorial. Even when I wasn't looking at them, even when I was back in my hotel room, I was aware of them, a low rumble in the brain. They are always *there*. Some part of us, as Americans, has known that for a long time.

Sightseers begin coming to Niagara in sizable numbers when the   16
railroads made it easy for them to get there, starting in 1836 with the opening of the Lockport & Niagara Falls line, which brought families traveling on the Erie Canal. Later, workers came over from Rochester on Sunday afternoon after church, and passengers taking Lake Erie steamers came over for a few hours from Buffalo. To stroll in the park beside the falls was an acceptable Victorian thing to do. No other sublime experience of such magnitude was available. People might have heard of the Grand Canyon or the Rockies, but they couldn't get there; vacations were too short and transportation was too slow.

So uplifting were the falls deemed to be that they became a rallying   17
point after the Civil War for religious leaders, educators, artists and scientists eager to preserve them as a sacred grove for the public. This meant wresting them back from the private owners who had bought the adjacent land from New York State, putting up mills, factories and tawdry souvenir shops, and charging admission for a view of God's handiwork through holes in the fence. That the state had sold off its land earlier was not all that surprising; before the Concord poets and philosophers suggested otherwise, the notion that nature should be left intact and simply appreciated was alien to the settler mentality. Land was meant to be cleared, civilized and put to productive use.

Two men in particular inspired the "Free Niagara!" movement: the   18
painter Frederic Edwin Church and the landscape architect Frederick Law Olmsted, designer of New York's great Central Park. Church's seven-foot-long *Niagara*, which has been called the greatest American

painting, drew such worshipful throngs when it was first exhibited in a Broadway showroom in 1857—thousands came every day—that it was sent on a tour of England, where it was unanimously praised by critics, including the sainted John Ruskin. If America could produce such a work, there was hope for the colonies after all. Back home, the painting made a triumphal tour of the South in 1858–59 and was reproduced and widely sold as a chromolithograph. More than any other image, it fixed the falls in the popular imagination as having powers both divine and patriotic: "an earthly manifestation of God's attributes" and a prophecy of "the nation's collective aspirations." Iconhood had arrived; Niagara Falls began to appear in posters and advertisements as the symbol of America. Only the Statue of Liberty would dislodge it.

19   Olmsted, the other man who shaped Niagara's aesthetic, proposed the heretical idea of a public park next to the falls and on the neighboring islands, in which nature would be left alone. This was counter to the prevailing European concept of a park as a formal arrangement of paths and plantings. In the 1870s Olmsted and a coalition of zealous Eastern intellectuals launched a campaign of public meetings, pamphlets, articles and petitions urging state officials to buy back the land and raze everything that man had put on it. Massive political opposition greeted their effort. Not only were the owners of the land rich and influential; many citizens felt that the government in a free society had no right to say, "In the public interest we're taking this land back." The fight lasted 15 years and was narrowly won in 1885 with the creation of the Niagara Reservation, America's first state park. (One hundred thousand people came on opening day.) Olmsted's hands-off landscaping, which preserved the natural character of the area and kept essential roads and buildings unobtrusive, became a model for parks in many other parts of the country.

20   Gradually, however, the adjacent hotels and commercial enterprises began to go to seed, as aging resorts will, and in the early 1960s Mayor E. Dent Lackey of Niagara Falls, New York, decided that only a sharp upgrading of the American side would enable his city to attract enough tourists to keep it healthy. Sublimity was no longer the only option for honeymooners; they could fly to Bermuda as easily as they could fly to Buffalo. Mayor Lackey, riding the 1960s' almost religious belief in urban renewal, tore down much of the "falls area." Like so much '60s renewal, the tearing down far outraced the building back up, but today the new pieces are finally in place: a geological museum, an aquarium, a Native American arts and crafts center, a glass-enclosed botanical garden with 7,000 tropical specimens, an "Artpark," a shopping mall and other such placid amenities. Even the new Burger King is tasteful. The emphasis is on history, culture, education and scenery.

21   By contrast, over on the Canadian side, a dense thoroughfare called Clifton Hill offers a Circus World, a Ripley's Believe It or Not Museum,

a House of Frankenstein, a Guinness Book of Records Museum, several wax museums, a Ferris wheel, a miniature golf course and other such amusements. The result of Mayor Lackey's faith that Americans still want to feel the higher feelings is that tourism has increased steadily ever since he got the call.

> Niag'ra Falls, I'm falling for you,   22
> Niag'ra Falls, with your rainbow hue,
> Oh, the Maid of the Mist
> Has never been kissed,
> Niag'ra, I'm falling for you.

This terrible song is typical of the objects I found in the local his-   23
tory section of the Niagara Falls Public Library, along with 20,000 picture postcards, 15,000 stereopticon slides, books by writers as diverse as Jules Verne and William Dean Howells, and thousands of newspaper and magazine articles. Together, for two centuries, they have sent America the message WISH YOU WERE HERE!, sparing no superlative. Howells, in his novel *Their Wedding Journey*, in 1882, wrote: "As the train stopped, Isabel's heart beat with a child-like exultation, as I believe everyone's heart must who is worthy to arrive at Niagara." Describing the place where Isabel and Basil got off the train as a "sublime destination," Howells says: "Niagara deserves almost to rank with Rome, the metropolis of history and religion; with Venice, the chief city of sentiment and fantasy. In either you are at once made at home by a perception of its greatness . . . and you gratefully accept its sublimity as a fact in no way contrasting with your own insignificance."

What the library gets asked about most often, however, is the   24
"stunts and stunters," according to Donald E. Loker, its local-history specialist. "Just yesterday," he told me, "I got a call from an advertising agency that wanted to use Annie Taylor in an ad campaign." Mrs. Taylor was a schoolteacher who went over the falls in a barrel on October 4, 1901, and survived the plunge, unlike her cat, which she had previously sent over in her barrel for a trial run. Thereby she became the first person to conquer the falls—and also one of the last. Most of the other conquerors tried their luck once too often. Today there is a ban on stunts, but not on ghosts. "Didn't somebody tightrope over this?" is one question that tour guides always get. "People want to see the scene," one of the guides told me. "They want to know: 'How did he do it?'"

Of all those glory-seekers, the most glorious was Jean François   25
Gravelet, known as the great Blondin. A Frenchman trained in the European circus, he came to America in 1859 under the promotional arm of P. T. Barnum and announced that he would cross the Niagara gorge on a tightrope on June 30, 1859. "Blondin was too good a showman to make the trip appear easy," Philip Mason writes in a booklet called "Niagara and the Daredevils." "His hesitations and swayings began to

build a tension that soon had the huge crowd gripped in suspense." In the middle he stopped, lowered a rope to the *Maid of the Mist,* pulled up a bottle and sat down to have a drink. Continuing toward the Canadian shore, "he paused, steadied the balancing pole and suddenly executed a back somersault. Men screamed, women fainted. Those near the rope wept and begged him to come in.... For the rest of the fabulous summer of 1859 he continued to provide thrills for the huge crowds that flocked to Niagara to see him. Never content to merely to repeat his last performance, Blondin crossed his rope on a bicycle, walked it blindfolded, pushed a wheelbarrow, cooked an omelet in the center, and made the trip with his hands and feet manacled."

26   I left the library and went back to the falls for a final look. Far below and far away I saw a tiny boat with a cluster of blue raincoats on its upper deck, vanishing into a tall cloud of mist at the center of the horseshoe falls. Then I didn't see it any more. Would it ever come back out? Historical records going back to 1846 said that it would.

✦ Questions for Discussion and Writing

1. How has the view of nature as a spiritual force shaped Americans' responses to wonders of the natural environment?

2. What role have writers, philosophers, and painters played in the emergence of Niagara Falls as a tourist attraction?

3. Evaluate Zinsser's interweaving of historical accounts with his personal experiences. How effective do you find this mixture in allowing the audience to understand how Niagara Falls came to serve as a symbol of America?

4. Describe a natural scenic wonder, other than Niagara Falls, interweaving historical background with the feelings you experienced.

Le Ly Hayslip

Yearning to Breathe Free

◆────────────

Le Ly Hayslip, the youngest of six children in a close-knit Buddhist family, was twelve years old when U.S. helicopters landed in Ky La, in central Vietnam. Before she was sixteen, Le Ly experienced near starvation, imprisonment, torture, rape, and the deaths of family members. After a courageous escape to America, she settled in Los Angeles with her three sons, where she started the East Meets West Foundation, a charitable relief organization. Her eloquent memoir, When Heaven and Earth Changed Places *(with Jay Wurts, 1989) details her return to Vietnam after thirty years. A 1993 movie,* Heaven and Earth *(directed by Oliver Stone) was based on her experiences. The following account, from* Child of War, Women of Peace *(with James Hayslip, 1993) describes the challenge she faced in emigrating to the United States.*

Honolulu's warm breeze caressed me like a mother's hands. A pretty hula girl put a flowered lei—a victor's garland—around my neck. For the first time in my life, I gulped the heady air of a world at peace. 1

May 27, 1970, the day I stepped onto the ramp at Honolulu International Airport after fleeing the war in Vietnam, marked the beginning of my new life as an apprentice American. It may have been my imagination, but the attendants on the big American jetliner from Saigon seemed exceptionally kind to me and my two boys—three-year-old Jimmy (whose father, a wealthy Saigon industrialist, he never knew) and Tommy, the three-month-old son of my new American husband, Ed Munro, whom we were on our way to join. Liberty and goodwill, like corruption and cruelty, seem to hold each other's hand. 2

Still, Hawaii was too much like Vietnam to really count as the United States. For one, it was a tropical island—covered with palms and sand—and Honolulu, despite its modern hotels and shops and restaurants, was too much like Saigon: filled with Asians and GIs, tawdry bars and taxis, and people in transit, *khong hieu qua khu*—without a past or future, like me. The thrill of great America would have to wait for our next landing. 3

As it turned out, San Diego was another Honolulu, if written on a larger page. Our plane arrived after midnight, not a good time for sightseeing, especially by timid immigrants. In Vietnam, the Viet Cong feared the light, so "friendly" areas—cities, towns, air bases, and out- 4 posts—were lit up like American Christmas trees. Perhaps to show it was safe for GIs coming back from the war, San Diego, too, left its lights burning all night.

5   Ed met us at the arrival gate, just as he'd promised. He had been staying with his mother, Erma, in the suburb of El Cajon. Although he looked tanned and healthy and was a welcome familiar face after thousands of miles of strangers, my heart sagged when I saw him. Born in 1915 (seven years after my mother's birth) in Mount Vernon, Washington, he was old enough to be my father—no twenty-year-old's dream husband. Yet, with two brothers and three sisters, he was no stranger to small towns and big families—one reason, in addition to his own maturity, that he understood me so well. His mother had been a waitress at something called a "drive-in" and his father, like mine, had died. Both had been honest, family-loving men who tackled life barehanded. My father had been a farmer who seldom went farther than a day's walk from our home village of Ky La. Ed's dad had been a carpenter and hunter who ventured to Alaska: a wondrous place where, Ed said, ice fell stinging from the sky. In all, Ed's relatives were solid working-class people. Like my peasant family, they loved one another, loved their country, and lived their values every day.

6   Ed had been married twice before. He knew, as I did, how it felt to lose the game of love. His first wife gave him two sons, Ron and Ed Jr. (navy boys whom we visited in Vietnam), then divorced him and moved to Nevada. His second wife was unfaithful and when Ed found out about it, he did not beat her as a Vietnamese husband would, but sent her a dozen roses and wished her good luck with her new man. In a way, that was what Ed was all about. He put the wishes of those he loved above his own right to be happy. This constant sacrifice, I think, whittled him down and eventually cost him what he treasured most. In this, I would discover, he was not alone among Americans.

7   The long drive from San Diego's Lindbergh Field to El Cajon was not much different from a drive to Saigon's suburbs, except for more cars and fewer motorbikes on the highway's six broad lanes. Off the freeway, we drove through blocks of tidy homes, all dark except for streetlamps standing like GI basketball hoops in the gloom. We parked in the driveway of a pale yellow house—"ranch style," Ed said, although I couldn't smell any animals—and we went up the narrow walk to a front door bright with light. Before Ed could reach the bell, a shadow hobbled up behind the curtain. The door opened onto a large American woman in curlers, backlit in a nightgown as big as a sheet.

8   Startled, I bowed low—to be polite and to put the big creature out of sight while I collected my sleep-starved wits.

9   "Ohhh!" Erma, Ed's sister, screamed, slapping her cheeks, and pulling me to her with beefy arms. "She's so cute—like a little china doll! I want to hug her to pieces!"

She very nearly did—a big, sloppy American bearhug, a show of   10
emotion no proper Vietnamese would dare display on first meeting. It
amazed me how quick Americans were to show affection to strangers,
even those their menfolk had gone so far from home to destroy.

"And the children—?" Erma peeked around my helmet of ratted   11
hair. Ed had shown her pictures of my two sons.

"In the car!" He poked a dad's boastful thumb over his shoulder.   12

"Ooo—I can't wait to see them!" Erma scuttled down the walk.   13
"I'll just eat them up!"

Eat them up—my god! Of course, it was just another American fig-   14
ure of speech. I was beginning to discover that English was as full of
booby traps as the jungle outside Ky La.

Anyway, Ed's new family impressed her, for better *and* for worse.   15
Jimmy was cranky from crossing time zones, and since he spoke mostly
Vietnamese, he cried when this giant brown-haired bear-lady tried to
crush him with her paws. Tommy, however, who had slept fourteen
hours on the plane and was ready for fun, screeched with delight. Erma
knew right away which boy had the bright, upstanding, red-white-
and-blue American father and which child was the pitiful third-world
refugee. First impressions are lasting. I think that midnight meeting
forever biased her in Tommy's favor, although I never dreamed of saying it.

We unloaded the luggage and put the boys to bed, where I stayed   16
with them until they fell asleep. From the depths of this strange-smell-
ing, thick-walled American house, I listened to Ed and Erma chat in too
fast English over coffee. I still didn't know what to make of my new environment: American kitchens smelled like sickly hospitals, reeking of
disinfectant, not *Ong Tao*, "Mr. Stove's," healthy food. The darkness
outside the house was as terrifying as a midnight cadre meeting. I
wanted to join them and gossip and laugh like real family, but I understood only a fraction of what they said and part of that was whispered,
which to me meant danger, not good manners. Fortunately, the deep,
even breathing of the kids won me over and I fell asleep, reminding
myself to pay special attention to any spirits who might visit me in my
first American dream.

My first full day as an American housewife didn't go so well. I   17
slept poorly in Erma's tight-sealed house and my body still awoke and
made water and got hungry on Saigon time. Nobody explained jet lag
to me and I thought my strange waves of sleepiness in the middle of
the day and spunkiness at four in the morning were just signs of how
out of place Orientals were in round-eyed America. I hoped it would
pass, like the flu, without my having to consult the neighborhood psychic or witch doctor.

18　　　My alarm clock on that first day was a playful slap on the rump.

19　　　"Get up, sleepyhead!" Ed yelled with a grin as wide as the band of sunlight streaming in through the window. He looked so happy to have his wife and family with him again that I thought he was going to burst. Like a slug in my mother's garden, I slithered around the sunburst to the shower where I took another ten minutes to wake up.

20　　　I dressed and made up with great care, partly because of my new surroundings (unlike Vietnamese peasant houses, American homes have their owner's fingerprints all over them: no two housewives ever put wastebaskets and tissues in the same place!) and partly because I could take no chances with my appearance. Daylight and in-laws are terrible critics.

21　　　"Hurry up and dress the kids," Ed commanded. "After breakfast, I want you to meet my mother!"

22　　　In Vietnam, meeting in-laws is always a tricky business. This is true especially when the marriage has not been arranged through matchmakers and the couple are of vastly different ages, let alone races—*quen nha ma, la nha chong*, I am at home in my mother's house, but a stranger to my in-laws! I would sooner have met an American battle tank on Erma's lawn than to walk next door unescorted and introduce myself to Ed's mother—which, for some unknown reason, was my husband's harebrained plan.

23　　　When Jimmy was dressed and fed (Tommy was still asleep and nobody had the courage to wake him) Ed booted us out and pointed to the shingled green house next door.

24　　　"Oh, go on!" he laughed. "You girls get acquainted. Mom won't bite your head off!"

25　　　Well, I certainly hoped not, but Ed hadn't met a real Vietnamese mother-in-law. Back in Danang, my mother had never accepted our marriage, and so never treated Ed like a new family-member-in-training, with all the horror the position inspires. I dragged my son across the sunny lawn like a goat on the way to the slaughterhouse.

26　　　I squeezed Jimmy's spit-slick fingers and knocked on the door. Dogbarks from hell—we jumped back! The shadow of a big, Erma-like figure waddled toward us behind lacy curtains. A grandmother's high-pitched voice scolded the yappy dogs.

27　　　Had this been a Vietnamese house, I would have known instantly what to do. I would have bowed low, recited the ritual greeting of an unworthy daughter-in-law to the witch-queen who would transform me over the next few years into a deserving wife for her son, then gone into the kitchen and made us both some tea, humbly serving it with two hands, the old-fashioned way. Then I would have sat silently and waited to be instructed.

28　　　But this was an American house: a great sand-castle trap for a Vietnamese fish out of water. In Vietnam, a matchmaker would have prepared the way—sold my mother-in-law on my maidenly virtues, few as those might be. Now I would have to do my own selling, encumbered with my fatherless child, remembering how I had lost my virginity not once, but *three* times: bodily to the Viet Cong who raped me after my kangaroo court-martial; spiritually to Anh, Jimmy's father, with whom I fell into girlish love; and morally to the sad little GI in Danang who kept my family off the street by paying me four hundred U.S. dollars *green money* for a last happy memory of my country. By any measure, I was unworthy to stand on this fine woman's stoop, let alone pretend to the honors and duties of a daughter-in-law. It was only because of my continuing bad karma that the earth did not swallow me up.

Despite my fears, the door opened onto the most angelic old face I had ever seen.   29

Leatha (whom I would always call "Mom Munro" and *never* impolitely by her first name) was seventy-five and had silver-blond hair that circled her cherub face the way white smoke twists around a storybook cottage. In Vietnam, such women aged like plucked berries: from the blush of virgin freshness to old age it was quick and downhill. Although a woman's post-birth *buon de* ritual, like our daily regimen of outdoor labor, kept our bodies lean and hard, we had no time or money for beauty treatments. Indeed, in a culture where reaching old age was a real accomplishment, we revered our elderly for being one step closer to the ancestors we worshiped. Old women and old men were sometimes mistaken for one another, and that was no cause for shame. In a way, this blending of sexes with its release from the trials of youth—concern for appearance and catching a mate—was one of aging's big rewards.   30

But not for Leatha.   31

Although Ed and Erma later assured me that she was "just an average grandma," I thought her angelic hair, well-fed happy face, plump saggy arms, solid girth, and movie star makeup made her even more spectacular than the painted Buddhas in the shrine beneath Marble Mountain near my village. Her appearance was even more astonishing, since in Vietnam I had seen no American women over fifty. (Most outsiders were men—soldiers or civilian contractors like Ed—or young female nurses.) Although her big hug made me feel better, I continued to stare at her. I tried to imagine my mother's face beneath the silver wreath and felt strangely envious and sad. Until I later found out how most Americans treat their elderly parents, the thought of growing old, fat, and pretty in America seemed to be another dividend of peace.   32

Of course, Leatha knew who I was at once and invited us inside. We talked only a minute before our polite smiles hurt and our rootless conversation slowed to head nods and empty laughter. I volunteered to make tea but she insisted that was the hostess's duty. Unfortunately,   33 such was my mood that even this unexpected kindness seemed like a slap in the face—a reminder of my foreignness and incapacity. How bad must a daughter-in-law be, I thought, not even to merit a stern lecture on family rules?

34   Eventually, Ed and Erma came over with Tommy and I felt more at ease. To be strictly proper, I should have sung the "new bride" song in the presence of both my husband and his mother—a kind of ceremonial acceptance of the collar of obedience:

35   A risen moon is supposed to shine
        Except through clouds, when it is dim and weak,
        I come young and innocent to be your wife
        Please speak of me kindly in your mother's ear.
        People plant trees to grow big and strong,
        People have children to prosper and protect them.
        I cross my arms and bow my head
        To please my husband and his mother.
        If I do something wrong, please teach me right.
        Don't beat me or scold me in public
        For some will laugh and others will say
        The fist is my husband,
        The tongue is she from whence he came.

36   Instead, Ed put his arm around his mother and told her all about Vietnam, leaving out everything of importance in my black and bloody past—most of which he didn't know himself. Instead, he bragged about his mother's blue-ribbon pies at the Skagit Valley Fair, and I nodded enthusiastically even though I hadn't the slightest idea what pies, blue ribbons, or county fairs really were. After Ed's father died, I learned, Leatha had moved south to California where she took up residence next door to Erma, who shared a house with her husband, Larry, and adult son, Larry Jr., who was seldom around.

37   I saw much more of her pixie-faced daughter, Kathy, a young woman about my age, who lived with her husband in the neighboring town of Santee. Why Leatha didn't move in with her daughter, who had more than enough room and could share housekeeping and cooking chores Vietnamese style, was beyond my understanding. I guessed that Americans loved their possessions so much that even a lonely old woman valued her own TV set, kitchen, bathroom, spare bedrooms, and garage for a car she couldn't drive more than living with a daughter in her sunset years.

38   Anyway, the longing in Leatha's eyes told me that she probably would have traded all her possessions for a little room among her family. Her "children" these days were six little dogs that jumped around like kids and yapped at the TV and pestered you for snacks and atten-

tion whenever you sat down. She even bought canned food for them at the store, which I thought was the height of decadence.

In Vietnam, a dog was a guardian first, then a pet, and sometimes 39 dinner. It fed itself by foraging, not at the family's expense. I chalked up Leatha's behavior to American ignorance, and it helped me feel less like a bumpkin in their magnificent homes. After all, if they knew that the soul of the dog was really a transient spirit (usually a greedy person who had to earn a new human body by suffering a dog's life—most of it spent guarding someone else's wealth), they wouldn't be so quick to put them up on pedestals and deny them penance. I shuddered to think how Leatha's six "children" must have laughed among themselves in dogbark about their naive American mistress.

Ed and Leatha gossiped away the morning until Erma's son, Larry, 40 joined us. I soon felt like a decorative china doll Erma had dubbed me when I arrived—just unwrapped and put on a shelf, worthy of an occasional glance but no conversation. Jet lag (as Ed now explained it) soon caught up with me again and, depressed and exhausted, I bowed and apologized in Vietnamese, which I knew would sound more sincere, and went for a nap, leaving Ed to contend with the kids. I fell asleep wondering how quickly Ed's womenfolk would begin to complain about the "lazy new wife" he had brought to California.

When I awoke, most of our things had been moved from Erma's 41 house to Leatha's. Ed preferred the company of his aged mom to imposing on his sister, and I agreed enthusiastically. Whereas Leatha seemed to look down on me as one of her puppies, Erma just seemed to look down. I was not prepared for this reversal of roles, for the sister-in-law was supposed to be the young bride's ally—someone who would comfort her when the rigors of wife-training got too bad. In America, it seems, who you are is more important than the role society gives you. Even as Ed's wife, though, I did not seem to be worth too much.

That evening, Erma and Larry came over and I tried to help the 42 women fix dinner. Unfortunately, between my ignorance of American kitchens and a strong desire to avoid looking dumber than I had already, I didn't contribute much.

The first thing that astounded me was the refrigerator—a two-door 43 monster that dwarfed our knee-high Vietnamese models—every nook and cranny of which was packed with food! It occurred to me that this was why Americans got so big: the bigger the refrigerators, the bigger the people. I thanked fate or luck or god that Jimmy would now grow up to be twice the size of Anh, his wealthy Vietnamese father. For a second I held a fantasy reunion: me, more rich and beautiful than Lien (Anh's wife who had thrown me out of their mansion when I got pregnant); my mother—plump and queenly as Leatha; and Jimmy—called Phung Quoc Hung in Vietnamese—tall and powerful as an American Green Beret, stooping to shake his father's little hand. It was a scene that could never come true, although, as everybody said, all things are possible in America.

44   Erma took out a frosty box with the picture of a glowering green giant (no doubt a character from American fables who devoured children who didn't eat their vegetables), then a slab of meat, frozen solid in a little Styrofoam boat covered with plastic.

45   "How we eat this?" I asked as the clumpy peas, hard as marbles, rattled into a pan. I was not ready to live in a country where vegetables and meat were sucked like ice cubes.

46   "Oh, the peas will cook in no time," Erma said, adding water and flipping on her stove's magic, matchless flame. "The round steak we'll have tomorrow. I'll just defrost it in the fridge."

47   Why not just go to the market and get what you want before you eat it? Maybe that was why Americans had to invent frozen food, so they would have something to put in their expensive freezers. Little by little, I was beginning to understand capitalism.

48   We sat down for my first American dinner and I shyly waited to see what everyone else did first. I knew some Americans said prayers for their food, perhaps to honor the dead animal they were about to eat, but this seemed like a silly custom. There was a time for praying and a time for eating. Did those same people say prayers when they did other ordinary things—when they made love or went shopping or relieved themselves? I just didn't understand their reasoning, particularly since Americans didn't seem like a particularly spiritual people. Their houses lacked shrines for their ancestors where prayers were said. Anyway, I was happy to see the Munros reach for the food all at once—"digging in," as Leatha called it—like an Oriental family, as soon as we sat down.

49   My next hurdle was faking the use of their cumbersome eating utensils. In Vietnam, all food was taken with chopsticks or slurped from a bowl. Here, Americans employed as many utensils as the cook had used to prepare the meal. I was sure I'd never master them all, particularly the fork, which everyone held like a pencil, then juggled like acrobats between hands to cut their meat. Why didn't the cook just slice the food into bite-sized strips the way we did in the Orient? I went along with the game as far as I could, grasping my fork like a club and politely smacking my lips very loudly so that Erma and Leatha would know I enjoyed the meal—despite the rich sauces that filled me up after two bites. Fortunately, after a few seconds of this, nobody looked at me anymore and Jimmy and I finished our meal winking and poking each other at the kids' end of the table.

50   After dinner, I wanted to show my new mother-in-law that I could be a good housewife, so I volunteered to do dishes. At first, I was

shocked by all the uneaten food. In Vietnam, we believed that the more food you waste in this life, the hungrier you'll be in the next. Then I remembered the full refrigerator and guessed that if people rationed their food as we did in Vietnam, all the freezers and freezer makers would be out of business and go hungry; so, in America, waste was really thrift. I began scraping the plates into the garbage can and, predictably, Ed came up behind me and laughed his amused-daddy laugh,

"No, no," he said. "Dump the garbage into the sink." 51

"What?" I knew he must be kidding. "You want to clog drain?" I 52
might be new to America, but I wasn't born yesterday.

"It won't get stopped up. Go ahead. Just dump it down the drain. 53
I'll show you some magic."

I peevishly did as he instructed. *Okay, Mister Smart Man, if you want* 54
to play plumber after your supper, that's okay with me!

When a heap of leavings blocked the drain, I turned on the tap and 55
stood back. Sure enough, the water started to rise. Without blinking an eye, Ed threw a switch over the stove and the pile of sludge became a shaking, squirting volcano, and miraculously, the pile collapsed and disappeared. The grinding earthquake became a hum and Ed turned off the switch. Tap water ran merrily down the drain.

Pale and humiliated—again—I could only look at the floor. Tears 56
came to my eyes.

"Here now," Ed put his arm around me. "I didn't mean to scare 57
you. That's just a garbage disposal. A motor under the sink grinds everything up."

I took the wrapper the peas came in and started to shove it down 58
the monster's rubbery throat.

"No, no," Ed corrected me again. 59

I stopped and blew a wisp of hair from my face. 60

"No paper," Ed warned, "or bones or plastic or anything like that." 61

"But you say put trash in sink!" This American miracle now 62
seemed a little fickle to be real magic.

"No trash. Just soft food." 63

Again, I did as I was told, feeling Erma's critical eyes on my back. 64
With the sink now empty, I could at last get on with washing the dishes—something even an ignorant Vietnamese farm girl knew quite well how to do.

"No, no," Ed said when he saw me stacking the dishes in the sink. 65
"Just load them in the dishwasher." He had the same irritating little smile and I had absolutely no idea if he was making fun of me or trying to be helpful.

"What you talk about?" I slammed the silverware into the sink. I was 66
getting tired again and my tone was not properly humble and subservient. I looked over my shoulder into the dining room. Erma and Leatha politely pretended to be absorbed in their coffee and conversation.

67   "Here—" Ed flipped down the big metal door beside the sink. Inside was a queer wire basket. "Just put the dishes here." He demonstrated with a plate.

68   "Okay, but how we wash them when they inside?" It seemed a logical question, but it only made Ed laugh. Under his close supervision, I loaded all the dishes in the stupid machine, wondering how even these mechanically inclined Americans got greasy plates and the tines of their silly, useless forks clean without rags and fingers. When I was finished, he poured some powder into a little box on the door and shut it tight. He punched a few buttons and turned a big dial and the growling noise began again. I thought for a minute that the dishes would be ground up, but the whirring was friendlier this time and I could hear the water splashing.

69   "See?" Ed smiled proudly. "Nothing to it!"

70   "Okay," I replied, "so how long we wait to dry them?" I fished for a dishtowel.

71   Ed laughed again. "You don't have to wait. You wipe the counter and go watch TV!"

72   *Okay—I can do that!* My first long day in America was coming to an end and I was ready to accept anything he said at face value. I decided I wouldn't even ask about the machine that put the dishes away.

✦ *Questions for Discussion and Writing*

1. How would you characterize Hayslip's first meeting with her new mother-in-law? How did it differ from what would have taken place in Vietnam?

2. What difference in cultural perspectives is revealed in Hayslip's reaction to the material goods, such as dishwasher, garbage disposal, etc., in her new home?

3. How do Hayslip's reactions provide insight into the way in which aging is viewed in Vietnamese and in American cultures?

4. If you have dated someone from a different background, culture, or religion, describe your experiences, feelings, and impressions upon meeting your boyfriend or girlfriend's family for the first time. How did you react to each other?

5. Have you ever been invited by someone from another cultural background to witness or participate in a ceremony or ritual that was important to him or her? Describe your experiences.

Connections

1. What connections can you discover in the accounts of Meriwether Lewis and William Clark, William Zinsser, and Aldo Leopold that provide insight into how the idea of wilderness assumed symbolic importance in American culture?

2. What unfamiliar customs and rituals perplex Meriwether Lewis and William Clark and Le Ly Hayslip?

3. What problem solving abilities do Meriwether Lewis and William Clark and Sir Leonard Woolley display in coping with the challenges that confront them during their respective explorations?

4. Contrast the circumstances, hopes, and dreams of those living in Tijuana who want to come to America (Luis Alberto Urrea, "My Story," Chapter 2) with the circumstances and reactions of Le Ly Hayslip as she tries to adapt to life in southern California.

5. We usually think of the term *culture shock* as meaning the reaction of explorers, like Douchan Gersi ("Initiated into an Iban Tribe of Headhunters," Chapter 5), to unexpected conditions. In what way is it also true that culture shock is experienced by Vietnamese immigrants to the United States, as portrayed by Le Ly Hayslip?

6. What common assumptions about the value of wilderness emerge from the narratives by William Zinsser, Aldo Leopold, Peter Matthiessen ("Snow Leopard," Chapter 11) and Howard Hall ("Playing Tag with Wild Dolphins," Chapter 4)?

10

Politics and Power

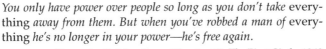

You only have power over people so long as you don't take every-thing away from them. But when you've robbed a man of every-thing he's no longer in your power—he's free again.
—Alexander Solzhenitsyn, Chapter 17, *The First Circle*, 1968

A particularly powerful kind of autobiographical writing that crosses the usual boundaries between literary texts and eyewitness reports is sometimes called the literature of the witness. These works document important moments in history as well as confrontations between the individual and the state. The writers often bear witness to suspension of constitutional rights, arrest, secret detention, and torture. These accounts of human rights abuses transform private horrors into a public record that provides a voice for those who otherwise would not be remembered. For this reason, autobiographies can be political acts with potentially dangerous consequences.

In theory, the legal processes of a society exist to enforce that society's concept of justice and its accompanying norms, laws, and customs. In practice, however, imprisonment and even death are meted out in many societies in far more arbitrary ways. In the former Yugoslavia, for example, the phrase "ethnic cleansing" concealed a genocidal policy in which state power was employed to destroy groups of people because of their nationality and religion. A politicized environment within a state also has an intensely corrosive effect on personal relationships when individual loyalties conflict with officially decreed allegiances.

At no time are conflicts among different points of view greater than they are between citizens and governments when individuals relinquish a degree of freedom in order to gain presumed benefits from collective political and social institutions. Yet, the allegiance that individuals owe their governments and the protection of individual rights that citizens expect in return is often a source of conflict.

"We Have Our State" is Golda Meir's eyewitness account of a moment of great historical importance—the founding of the state of Israel. Tim O'Brien offers a conflicting view of allegiance to the state in "If I Die in a Combat Zone," a description of the inner conflict he experienced while deciding whether to serve in Vietnam. The terrible consequences of political violence in Guatemala form the basis of Rigoberta Menchú's "Things Have Happened to Me as in a Movie." "What Is Poverty?" is Jo Goodwin Parker's heartrending account of the desperate circumstances she and her children endured at the hands of an indifferent federal bureaucracy. The realization of what the war involving Serbia, Croatia, and Bosnia actually means becomes painfully apparent to Slavenka Drakulić in "The Balkan Express."

Golda Meir

We Have Our State

◆

Golda Meir (1898–1978) was born in Russia, and after a teaching career in the United States, she settled in Palestine in 1921. She later served as Israel's minister of labor and foreign affairs before becoming prime minister in 1969. Meir sought peace between Israel and the Arab nations through diplomacy. She was forced to resign in 1974 as a consequence of an unexpected Arab onslaught on Israel a year before. "We Have Our State" is drawn from her autobiography My Life *(1975) and recounts the circumstances surrounding the period just before and at the moment when Israel became a state on May 14, 1948.*

1   On the morning of May 14, I participated in a meeting of the People's Council at which we were to decide on the name of the state and on the final formulation of the declaration. The name was less of a problem than the declaration because there was a last-minute argument about the inclusion of a reference to God. Actually the issue had been brought up the day before. The very last sentence, as finally submitted to the small subcommittee charged with producing the final version of the proclamation, began with the words "With trust in the Rock of Israel, we set our hands in witness to this Proclamation...." Ben-Gurion had hoped that the phrase "Rock of Israel" was sufficiently ambiguous to satisfy those Jews for whom it was inconceivable that the document which established the Jewish state should not contain any reference to God, as well as those who were certain to object strenuously to even the least hint of clericalism in the proclamation.

2   But the compromise was not so easily accepted. The spokesman of the religious parties, Rabbi Fishman-Maimon, demanded that the reference to God be unequivocal and said that he would approve of the "Rock of Israel" only if the words "and its Redeemer" were added, while Aaron Zisling of the left wing of the Labor Party was just as determined in the opposite direction. "I cannot sign a document referring in any way to a God in whom I do not believe," he said. It took Ben-Gurion most of the morning to persuade Maimon and Zisling that the meaning of the "Rock of Israel" was actually twofold: While it signified "God" for a great many Jews, perhaps for most, it could also be considered a symbolic and secular reference to the "strength of the Jewish people." In the end Maimon agreed that the word "Redeemer" should be left out of the text, though, funnily enough, the first English-language

330

translation of the proclamation, released for publication abroad that day, contained no reference at all to the "Rock of Israel" since the military censor had struck out the entire last paragraph as a security precaution because it mentioned the time and place of the ceremony.

The argument itself, however, although it was perhaps not exactly   3
what one would have expected a prime minister-designate to be spending his time on only a few hours before proclaiming the independence of a new state—particularly one threatened by immediate invasion—was far from being just an argument about terminology. We were all deeply aware of the fact that the proclamation not only spelled the formal end to 2,000 years of Jewish homelessness, but also gave expression to the most fundamental principles of the State of Israel. For this reason, each and every word mattered greatly. Incidentally, my good friend Zeev Sharef, the first secretary of the government-to-be (who laid the foundations for the machinery of government), even found time to see to it that the scroll we were about to sign that afternoon should be rushed to the vaults of the Anglo-Palestine Bank after the ceremony, so that it could at least be preserved for posterity—even if the state and we ourselves did not survive for very long.

At about 2 P.M. I went back to my hotel on the seashore, washed my   4
hair and changed into my best black dress. Then I sat down for a few minutes, partly to catch my breath, partly to think—for the first time in the past two or three days—about the children. Menachem was in the United States then—a student at the Manhattan School of Music. I knew that he would come back now that war was inevitable, and I wondered when and how we would meet again. Sarah was in Revivim, and although not so very far away, as the crow flies, we were quite cut off from each other. Months ago, gangs of Palestinian Arabs and armed infiltrators from Egypt had blocked the road that connected the Negev to the rest of the country and were still systematically blowing up or cutting most of the pipelines that brought water to the twenty-seven Jewish settlements that then dotted the Negev. The Haganah had done its best to break the siege. It had opened a dirt track, parallel to the main road, on which convoys managed, now and then, to bring food and water to the 1,000-odd settlers in the south. But who knew what would happen to Revivim or any other of the small, ill-armed ill-equipped Negev settlements when the full-scale Egyptian invasion of Israel began, as it almost certainly would, within only a few hours? Both Sarah and her Zechariah were wireless operators in Revivim, and I had been able to keep in touch with them up till then. But I hadn't heard about or from either of them for several days, and I was extremely worried. It was on youngsters like them, their spirit and their courage, that the future of the Negev and, therefore, of Israel depended, and I shuddered at the thought of their having to face the invading troops of the Egyptian army.

5   I was so lost in my thoughts about the children that I can remember being momentarily surprised when the phone rang in my room and I was told that a car was waiting to take me to the museum. It had been decided to hold the ceremony at the Tel Aviv museum on Rothschild Boulevard, not because it was such an imposing building (which it wasn't), but because it was small enough to be easily guarded. One of the oldest buildings in Tel Aviv, it had originally belonged to the city's first mayor, who had willed it to the citizens of Tel Aviv for use as an art museum. The grand total of about $200 had been allocated for decorating it suitably for the ceremony; the floors had been scrubbed, the nude paintings on the walls modestly draped, the windows blacked out in case of an air raid and a large picture of Theodor Herzl hung behind the table at which the thirteen members of the provisional government were to sit. Although supposedly only the 200-odd people who had been invited to participate knew the details, a large crowd was already waiting outside the museum by the time I arrived there.

6   A few minutes later, at exactly 4 P.M., the ceremony began. Ben-Gurion, wearing a dark suit and tie, stood up and rapped a gavel. According to the plan, this was to be the signal for the orchestra, tucked away in a second floor gallery, to play "Hatikvah." But something went wrong, and there was no music. Spontaneously, we rose to our feet and sang our national anthem. Then Ben-Gurion cleared his throat and said quietly, "I shall now read the Scroll of Independence." It took him only a quarter of an hour to read the entire proclamation. He read it slowly and very clearly, and I remember his voice changing and rising a little as he came to the eleventh paragraph:

7   Accordingly we, the members of the National Council, representing the Jewish people in the Land of Israel and the Zionist movement, have assembled on the day of the termination of the British mandate for Palestine, and, by virtue of our natural and historic right and of the resolution of the General Assembly of the United Nations, do hereby proclaim the establishment of a Jewish state in the Land of Israel—the State of Israel.

8   The State of Israel! My eyes filled with tears, and my hands shook. We had done it. We had brought the Jewish state into existence—and I, Golda Mabovitch Meyerson, had lived to see the day. Whatever happened now, whatever price any of us would have to pay for it, we had recreated the Jewish national home. The long exile was over. From this day on we would no longer live on sufferance in the land of our forefathers. Now we were a nation like other nations, master—for the first time in twenty centuries—of our own destiny. The dream had come true—too late to save those who had perished in the Holocaust, but not too late for the generations to come. Almost exactly fifty years ago, at the close of the First Zionist Congress in Basel, Theodor Herzl had writ-

ten in his diary: "At Basel, I founded the Jewish state. If I were to say this today, I would be greeted with laughter. In five years perhaps, and certainly in fifty, everyone will see it." And so it had come to pass.

As Ben-Gurion read, I thought again about my children and the children that they would have, how different their lives would be from mine and how different my own life would be from what it had been in the past, and I thought about my colleagues in besieged Jerusalem, gathered in the offices of the Jewish Agency, listening to the ceremony through static on the radio, while I, by sheer accident, was in the museum itself. It seemed to me that no Jew on earth had ever been more privileged than I was that Friday afternoon.

Then, as though a signal had been given, we rose to our feet, crying and clapping, while Ben-Gurion, his voice breaking for the only time, read: "The State of Israel will be open to Jewish immigration and the ingathering of exiles." This was the very heart of the proclamation, the reason for the state and the point of it all. I remember sobbing out loud when I heard those words spoken in that hot, packed little hall. But Ben-Gurion just rapped his gavel again for order and went on reading:

"Even amidst the violent attacks launched against us for months past, we call upon the sons of the Arab people dwelling in Israel to keep the peace and to play their part in building the state on the basis of full and equal citizenship and due representation in all its institutions, provisional and permanent."

And: "We extend the hand of peace and good neighborliness to all the states around us and to their peoples, and we call upon them to cooperate in mutual helpfulness with the independent Jewish nation in its land. The State of Israel is prepared to make its contribution in a concerted effort for the advancement of the entire Middle East."

When he finished reading the 979 Hebrew words of the proclamation, he asked us to stand and "adopt the scroll establishing the Jewish state," so once again we rose to our feet. Then, something quite unscheduled and very moving happened. All of a sudden Rabbi Fishman-Maimon stood up, and, in a trembling voice, pronounced the traditional Hebrew prayer of thanksgiving. "Blessed be Thou, O Lord our God, King of the Universe, who has kept us alive and made us endure and brought us to this day. Amen." It was a prayer that I had heard often, but it had never held such meaning for me as it did that day.

Before we came up, each in turn, in alphabetical order, to sign the proclamation, there was one other point of "business" that required our attention. Ben-Gurion read the first decrees of the new state. The White Paper was declared null and void, while, to avoid a legal vacuum, all the other mandatory rules and regulations were declared valid and in temporary effect. Then the signing began. As I got up from my seat to sign my name to the scroll, I caught sight of Ada Golomb, standing not far away. I wanted to go over to her, take her in my arms and tell her that I knew that Eliahu and Dov should have been there in my place, but I couldn't hold up the line of the signatories, so I walked straight to the middle of the table, where Ben-Gurion and Sharett sat with the scroll between them. All I recall about my actual signing of the proclamation is that I was crying openly, not able even to wipe the tears from my face, and I remember that as Sharett held the scroll in place for me, a man called David Zvi Pincus, who belonged to the religious Mizrachi Party, came over to try and calm me. "Why do you weep so much, Golda?" he asked me.

15   "Because it breaks my heart to think of all those who should have been here today and are not," I replied, but I still couldn't stop crying.

16   Only twenty-five members of the People's Council signed the proclamation on May 14. Eleven others were in Jerusalem, and one was in the States. The last to sign was Moshe Sharett. He looked very controlled and calm compared to me—as though he were merely performing a standard duty. Later, when once we talked about that day, he told me that when he wrote his name on the scroll, he felt as though he were standing on a cliff with a gale blowing up all around him and nothing to hold on to except his determination not to be blown over into the raging sea below—but none of this showed at the time.

17   After the Palestine Philharmonic Orchestra played "Hatikvah," Ben-Gurion rapped his gavel for the third time. "The State of Israel is established. This meeting is ended." We all shook hands and embraced each other. The ceremony was over. Israel was a reality.

✦ Questions for Discussion and Writing

1. What details in Meir's account communicate the conflict and compromise that would allow Israel to exist as both a religious and secular state? What role did terminology play in the resolution of this problem?

2. What historical events in the immediate and distant past gave this moment its particular significance?

3. What considerations were uppermost in Meir's mind during this crucial time?

4. What details are effective in communicating the precariousness of the fledgling state?

5. Describe where you were as well as what you thought and felt at the moment an important political event took place in the nation, town, region, or on your campus.

Tim O'Brien

If I Die in a Combat Zone

◆

Tim O'Brien was born in 1946 in Austin, Minnesota, and was educated at Macalester College and Harvard University. Drafted into the army during the Vietnam War, he attained the rank of sergeant and received the Purple Heart. His first published work, If I Die in a Combat Zone, Box Me Up and Ship Me Home *(1973), relates his experiences in Vietnam. This book is an innovative mixture of alternating chapters of fiction and autobiography in which the following nonfiction account first appeared.*

O'Brien's novel Northern Lights *(1974) was followed by the acclaimed work* Going After Cacciato *(1978), which won the National Book Award. His recent works include* The Nuclear Age *(1985) and a collection of stories entitled* The Things They Carried *(1990).*

The summer of 1968, the summer I turned into a soldier, was a good time for talking about war and peace. Eugene McCarthy was bringing quiet thought to the subject. He was winning votes in the primaries. College students were listening to him, and some of us tried to help out. Lyndon Johnson was almost forgotten, no longer forbidding or feared; Robert Kennedy was dead but not quite forgotten; Richard Nixon looked like a loser. With all the tragedy and change that summer, it was fine weather for discussion. 1

And, with all of this, there was an induction notice tucked into a corner of my billfold. 2

So with friends and acquaintances and townspeople, I spent the summer in Fred's antiseptic cafe, drinking coffee and mapping out arguments on Fred's napkins. Or I sat in Chic's tavern, drinking beer with kids from the farms. I played some golf and tore up the pool table down at the bowling alley, keeping an eye open for likely-looking high school girls. 3

Late at night, the town deserted, two or three of us would drive a car around and around the town's lake, talking about the war, very seriously, moving with care from one argument to the next, trying to make it a dialogue and not a debate. We covered all the big questions: justice, tyranny, self-determination, conscience and the state, God and war and love. 4

College friends came to visit: "Too bad, I hear you're drafted. What will you do?" 5

6   I said I didn't know, that I'd let time decide. Maybe something would change, maybe the war would end. Then we'd turn to discuss the matter, talking long, trying out the questions, sleeping late in the mornings.

7   The summer conversations, spiked with plenty of references to the philosophers and academicians of war, were thoughtful and long and complex and careful. But, in the end, careful and precise argumentation hurt me. It was painful to tread deliberately over all the axioms and as-sumptions and corollaries when the people on the town's draft board were calling me to duty, smiling so nicely.

8   "It won't be bad at all," they said. "Stop in and see us when it's over."

9   So to bring the conversations to a focus and also to try out in real words my secret fears, I argued for running away.

10   I was persuaded then, and I remain persuaded now, that the war was wrong. And since it was wrong and since people were dying as a result of it, it was evil. Doubts, of course, hedged all this: I had neither the expertise nor the wisdom to synthesize answers; most of the facts were clouded, and there was no certainty as to the kind of government that would follow a North Vietnamese victory or, for that matter, an American victory, and the specifics of the conflict were hidden away— partly in men's minds, partly in the archives of government, and partly in buried, irretrievable history. The war, I thought, was wrongly con-ceived and poorly justified. But perhaps I was mistaken, and who re-ally knew, anyway?

11   Piled on top of this was the town, my family, my teachers, a whole history of the prairie. Like magnets, these things pulled in one direction or the other, almost physical forces weighting the problem, so that, in the end, it was less reason and more gravity that was the final influ-ence.

12   My family was careful that summer. The decision was mine and it was not talked about. The town lay there, spread out in the corn and watching me, the mouths of old women and Country Club men poised in a kind of eternal readiness to find fault. It was not a town, not a Min-neapolis or New York, where the son of a father can sometimes escape scrutiny. More, I owed the prairie something. For twenty-one years I'd lived under its laws, accepted its education, eaten its food, wasted and guzzled its water, slept well at night, driven across its highways, dirtied and breathed its air, wallowed in its luxuries. I'd played on its Little League teams. I remembered Plato's *Crito*, when Socrates, facing certain death—execution, not war—had the chance to escape. But he reminded himself that he had seventy years in which he could have left the coun-try, if he were not satisfied or felt the agreements he'd made with it were unfair. He had not chosen Sparta or Crete. And, I reminded myself, I hadn't thought much about Canada until that summer.

The summer passed this way. Gold afternoons on the golf course, a   13
comforting feeling that the matter of war would never touch me, nights
in the pool hall or drug store, talking with towns-folk, turning the
questions over and over, being a philosopher.

Near the end of that summer the time came to go to the war. The   14
family indulged in a cautious sort of Last Supper together, and afterward my father, who is brave, said it was time to report at the bus depot. I moped down to my bedroom and looked the place over, feeling
quite stupid, thinking that my mother would come in there in a day or
two and probably cry a little. I trudged back up to the kitchen and put
my satchel down. Everyone gathered around, saying so long and good
health and write and let us know if you want anything. My father took
up the induction papers, checking on times and dates and all the last-
minute things, and when I pecked my mother's face and grabbed the
satchel for comfort, he told me to put it down, that I wasn't supposed
to report until tomorrow.

After laughing about the mistake, after a flush of red color and a   15
flood of ribbing and a wave of relief had come and gone, I took a long
drive around the lake, looking again at the place. Sunset Park, with its
picnic table and little beach and a brown wood shelter and some families swimming. The Crippled Children's School. Slater Park, more kids.
A long string of split level houses, painted every color.

The war and my person seemed like twins as I went around the   16
town's lake. Twins grafted together and forever together, as if a separation would kill them both.

The thought made me angry.   17

In the basement of my house I found some scraps of cardboard and   18
paper. With devilish flair, I printed obscene words on them, declaring
my intention to have no part of Vietnam. With delightful viciousness, a
secret will, I declared the war evil, the draft board evil, the town evil in
its lethargic acceptance of it all. For many minutes, making up the
signs, making up my mind, I was outside the town. I was outside the
law, all my old ties to my loves and family broken by the old crayon in
my hand. I imagined strutting up and down the sidewalks outside the
depot, the bus waiting and the driver blaring his horn, the *Daily Globe*
photographer trying to push me into line with the other draftees, the
frantic telephone calls, my head buzzing at the deed.

On the cardboard, my strokes of bright red were big and ferocious   19
looking. The language was clear and certain and burned with a hard,
defiant, criminal, blasphemous sound. I tried reading it aloud.

Later in the evening I tore the signs into pieces and put the shreds   20
in the garbage can outside, clanging the gray cover down and trapping
the messages inside. I went back into the basement. I slipped the crayons into their box, the same stubs of color I'd used a long time before to
chalk in reds and greens on Roy Rogers' cowboy boots.

21   I'd never been a demonstrator, except in the loose sense. True, I'd taken a stand in the school newspaper on the war, trying to show why it seemed wrong. But, mostly, I'd just listened.

22   "No war is worth losing your life for," a college acquaintance used to argue. "The issue isn't a moral one. It's a matter of efficiency: what's the most efficient way to stay alive when your nation is at war? That's the issue."

23   But others argued that no war is worth losing your country for, and when asked about the case when a country fights a wrong war, those people just shrugged.

24   Most of my college friends found easy paths away from the problem, all to their credit. Deferments for this and that. Letters from doctors or chaplains. It was hard to find people who had to think much about the problem. Counsel came from two main quarters, pacifists and veterans of foreign wars.

25   But neither camp had much to offer. It wasn't a matter of peace, as the pacifists argued, but rather a matter of when and when not to join others in making war. And it wasn't a matter of listening to an ex-lieutenant colonel talk about serving in a right war, when the question was whether to serve in what seemed a wrong one.

26   On August 13, I went to the bus depot. A Worthington *Daily Globe* photographer took my picture standing by a rail fence with four other draftees.

27   Then the bus took us through corn fields, to little towns along the way—Lismore and Rushmore and Adrian—where other recruits came aboard. With some of the tough guys drinking beer and howling in the back seats, brandishing their empty cans and calling one another "scum" and "trainee" and "GI Joe," with all this noise and hearty farewelling, we went to Sioux Falls. We spent the night in a YMCA. I went out alone for a beer, drank it in a corner booth, then I bought a book and read it in my room.

28   By noon the next day our hands were in the air, even the tough guys. We recited the proper words, some of us loudly and daringly and others in bewilderment. It was a brightly lighted room, wood paneled. A flag gave the place the right colors, there was some smoke in the air. We said the words, and we were soldiers.

29   I'd never been much of a fighter. I was afraid of bullies. Their ripe muscles made me angry: a frustrated anger. Still, I deferred to no one. Positively lorded myself over inferiors. And on top of that was the matter of conscience and conviction, uncertain and surface-deep but pure nonetheless: I was a confirmed liberal, not a pacifist; but I would have cast my ballot to end the Vietnam war immediately, I would have voted

for Eugene McCarthy, hoping he would make peace. I was not soldier material, that was certain.

But I submitted. All the personal history, all the midnight conversations and books and beliefs and learning, were crumpled by abstention, extinguished by forfeiture, for lack of oxygen, by a sort of sleepwalking default. It was no decision, no chain of ideas or reasons, that steered me into the war.

It was an intellectual and physical stand-off, and I did not have the energy to see it to an end. I did not want to be a soldier, not even an observer to war. But neither did I want to upset a peculiar balance between the order I knew, the people I knew, and my own private world. It was not that I valued that order. But I feared its opposite, inevitable chaos, censure, embarrassment, the end of everything that had happened in my life, the end of it all.

And the stand-off is still there. I would wish this book could take the form of a plea for everlasting peace, a plea from one who knows, from one who's been there and come back, an old soldier looking back at a dying war.

That would be good. It would be fine to integrate it all to persuade my younger brother and perhaps some others to say no to wars and other battles.

Or it would be fine to confirm the odd beliefs about war: it's horrible, but it's a crucible of men and events and, in the end, it makes more of a man out of you.

But, still, none of these notions seems right. Men are killed, dead human beings are heavy and awkward to carry, things smell different in Vietnam, soldiers are afraid and often brave, drill sergeants are boors, some men think the war is proper and just and others don't and most don't care. Is that the stuff for a morality lesson, even for a theme?

Do dreams offer lessons? Do nightmares have themes, do we awaken and analyze them and live our lives and advise others as a result? Can the foot soldier teach anything important about war, merely for having been there? I think not. He can tell war stories.

✦ Questions for Discussion and Writing

1. What competing pressures caused O'Brien to experience such intense inner conflict when he was drafted?

2. Of all the factors weighing upon O'Brien, which in your view has the most significant influence on his decision whether or not to go to Vietnam?

3. What do you think you would have done if you were in O'Brien's shoes? What would you do now if another war like Vietnam were underway, the draft was reinstated, and both men and women were expected to serve?

4. The Tim O'Brien we get to know from reading this account probably appeared very different to the townspeople. Describe a person you know who seems to be one way publicly but may be completely different in private. Your character sketch of this person should support your impressions with particular incidents or a single dramatic event.

5. O'Brien describes being at a crossroads in his life. If you keep a journal, look back over a path you did not take, and imagine what your life would be like today if you had taken it .

Rigoberta Menchú

Things Have Happened to Me as in a Movie

◆————————————◆

Rigoberta Menchú, a Quiché Indian, was born in the hamlet of Chimel in northwestern Guatemala in 1959. Her life reflects experiences common to ethnic Indians in communities throughout Central America. When she was eight years old, she started picking coffee and cotton for pennies a pound. She later left the Guatemalan highlands, home of her native Quiché people, for Guatemala City to work as a maid for a family that expected her to submit to having sex with their sons. She survived a genocide that destroyed her family and community: her brother, father, and mother were killed in acts of savagery following the Garcia Lucas regime's rise to power in 1978. Menchú fled to Mexico in 1981 after receiving death threats for her human rights work. There she met the anthropologist Elisabeth Burgos-Debray, herself from Latin America, who undertook an ambitious program of interviews with Menchú. The result is a book unique in contemporary literature, I, Rigoberta Menchú: An Indian Woman in Guatemala *(1983), translated by Ann Wright—a powerful work that speaks of the struggle to maintain Indian culture and tradition. In recognition of her work as an international activist for the rights of Guatemalan Indians, Menchú was awarded the Nobel Peace Prize in 1992. The Guatemalan government denounced the award. The following essay, from an interview with César Chelala and translated by Regina M. Kreger, graphically describes the horrifying incidents of savagery that destroyed Menchú's family and drove her into exile.*

I am Rigoberta Menchú; I am a native of the Quiché people of Gua-   1
temala. My life has been a long one. Things have happened to me as in a movie. My parents were killed in the repression. I have hardly any relatives living, or if I have, I don't know about them. It has been my lot to live what has been the lot of many, many Guatemalans.

We were a very poor family. All their lives my parents worked cut-   2
ting cotton, cutting coffee. We lived about four months of the year on the high plain of Guatemala, where my father had a small piece of land; but that only supported us a short time, and then we had to go down to the plantations to get food.

During the whole time my mother was pregnant with me, she was   3
on the plantation cutting coffee and cotton. I was paid twenty cents,

341

many years ago, when I started to work in my town in Guatemala. There, the poor, the children, didn't have the opportunity for school; we did not have the opportunity to achieve any other life but working for food and to help our parents buy medicine for our little brothers and sisters. Two of my brothers died on the plantation cutting coffee. One of them got sick, couldn't be cured, and died. The other died when the landowner ordered the cotton sprayed while we were in the field. My brother was poisoned, there was no way to cure him and he died on the plantation, where we buried him.

4   We didn't know why those things happened. It's a miracle we were saved several times. When we got sick our mother looked for plants to cure us. The natives in Guatemala depended very much on nature. My mother cured us many times with the leaves of plants, with roots. That is how we managed to grow up. At ten years old, I started to work more in collaboration with my community, where my father, a local, native Mayan leader, was known by all the Indians of the region.

5   Little by little, my father got us involved in the concerns of the community. And so we grew up with that consciousness. My father was a catechist, and in Guatemala, a catechist is a leader of the community, and what he does especially is preach the Gospel. We, his children, began to evolve in the Catholic religion, and became catechists.

6   Little by little, we grew up—and really you can't say we started fighting only a short time ago, because it has been twenty-two years since my father fought over the land. The landowners wanted to take away our land, our little bit of land, and so my father fought for it. So he went to speak with the mayors, and with the judges in various parts of Guatemala. Afterwards, my father joined INTA, the land reform institution in Guatemala. For many years, my father was tricked because he did not speak Spanish. None of us spoke Spanish. So they made my father travel all over Guatemala to sign papers, letters, telegrams, which meant that not only he, but the whole community, had to sacrifice to pay the travel expenses. All this created an awareness in us from a very young age.

7   In the last years, my father was imprisoned many times, the first of those in 1954. My father landed in jail when he was accused of causing unrest among the population. When our father was in jail, the army kicked us out of our houses. They burned our clay pots. In our community we don't use iron or steel; we use clay pots, which we make ourselves with earth. But the army broke everything, and it was really hard for us to understand this situation.

8   Then my father was sentenced to eighteen years in prison, but he didn't serve them because we were able to work with lawyers to get him released. After a year and two months, my father got out of prison and returned home with more courage to go on fighting and much angrier because of what had happened. When that was over my mother

had to go right to work as a maid in the city of Santa Cruz del Quiché, and all of us children had to go down to work on the plantations.

A short time later, my father was tortured by the landowners' bodyguards. Some armed men came to my house and took my father away. We got the community together and found my father lying in the road, far away, about two kilometers from home. My father was badly beaten and barely alive. The priests of the region had to come out to take my father to the hospital. He had been in the hospital for six months when we heard he was going to be taken out and killed. The landowners had been discussing it loudly, and the information came to us by way of their servants, who are also natives, and with whom we were very close. And so we had to find another place for my father, a private clinic the priests found for him so he would heal. But my father could no longer do hard work like he did before. A little later my father dedicated himself exclusively to working for the community, traveling, living off the land.

Several years passed, and again, in the year 1977, my father was sentenced to death. He landed in jail again. When we went to see him in the Pantán jail, the military told us they didn't want us to see my father, because he had committed many crimes. My mother went to Santa Cruz to find lawyers, and from them we learned that my father was going to be executed. When the time of the execution came, many union workers, students, peasants and some priests demonstrated for my father's freedom. My father was freed, but before he left he was threatened; he was told that he was going to be killed anyway for being a communist. From that moment on, my father had to carry out his activities in secret. He had to change the rhythm of his life. He lived hidden in several houses in Quiché, and then he went to the capital city. And so he became a leader of struggle for the peasants. It was then that my father said, "We must fight as Christians," and from there came the idea, along with other catechists, of forming Christian organizations which would participate in the process.

For us it was always a mystery how my father could carry out all those activities, which were very important, despite being illiterate. He never learned to read or write in his life. All his children were persecuted because of his activities, and our poverty really didn't help us defend ourselves, because we were in very sad circumstances.

All my father's activities had created a resentment in us because we couldn't have our parents' affection, because there were a lot of us children and a bigger worry was how to survive. On top of all this were the problems of the land, which upset my father very much. Many years before, rocks had fallen from the mountain and we had to go down from where we lived. When we went down and cultivated new land, the landowners appeared with documents and they told us the land was theirs before we came. But we knew very well the land had no owner before we got there.

13   They couldn't catch my father, but in the year 1979, they kidnapped one of my little brothers. He was sixteen. We didn't know who did it. We only knew that they were five armed men, with their faces covered. Since my father couldn't go out, we went with my mother and members of the community to make a complaint to the army, but they said they didn't know anything about what had happened to my brother. We went to City Hall, we went to all the jails in Guatemala, but we didn't find him. After many trips all over my mother was very upset. It had taken a lot for my brother to survive, and so for my mother it was very hard to accept his disappearance.

14   At that time the army published a bulletin saying there was going to be a guerrilla council. They said they had some guerrillas in their custody and that they were going to punish them in public. My mother said, "I hope to God my son shows up. I hope to God my son is there. I want to know what has happened to him." So we went to see what was happening. We walked for one day and almost the whole night to get to the other town. There were hundreds of soldiers who had almost the whole town surrounded, and who had gathered the people together to witness what they were going to do. There were natives of other areas as well as natives of that town. After a while an army truck arrived with twenty people who had been tortured in different ways. Among them we recognized my brother, who, along with the other prisoners, had been tortured for fifteen days. When my mother saw my little brother she almost gave herself away, but we had to calm her down, telling her that if she give herself away she was going to die right there for being family of a guerrilla. We were crying, but almost all the rest of the people were crying also at the sight of the tortured people. They had pulled out my little brother's fingernails, they had cut off parts of his ears and other parts of his body, his lips, and he was covered with scars and swollen all over. Among the prisoners was a woman and they had cut off parts of her breasts and other parts of her body.

15   An army captain gave us a very long speech, almost three hours, in which he constantly threatened the people, saying that if we got involved with communism the same things were going to happen to us. Then he explained to us one by one the various types of torture they had applied to the prisoners. After three hours, the officer ordered the troops to strip the prisoners, and said: "Part of the punishment is still to come." He ordered the prisoners tied to some posts. The people didn't know what to do and my mother was overcome with despair in those few moments. And none of us knew how we could bear the situation. The officer ordered the prisoners covered with gasoline and they set fire to them, one by one.

+ *Questions for Discussion and Writing*

1. What impression do you get of Menchú's father? What effect do his life and activities have on Menchú herself?

2. What features of Menchú's account suggest that her family's circumstances were not atypical?

3. How does the torture and execution of Menchú's little brother illustrate the predicament of the Quiché Indians in Guatemala?

4. Do you think the title of this account is a good one? If so, why; and if not, why not? What would you have used as a title?

5. Is there any idea or belief so important to you that you would be prepared to undergo imprisonment and/or torture to defend it? Discuss why this idea or belief means so much to you.

Jo Goodwin Parker

What Is Poverty?

◆————◆

Jo Goodwin Parker's poignant and realistic account of the shame, humili-
ation, and outrage of being poor was first given as a speech in Deland,
Florida, on December 27, 1965, and was published in America's Other
Children: Public Schools Outside Suburbia, *edited by George Hender-*
son (1971). Parker reveals in graphic detail the hard choices she was
forced to make in an ever-losing battle to preserve the health of her three
children.

1   You ask me what is poverty? Listen to me. Here I am, dirty, smelly,
and with no "proper" underwear on and with the stench of my rotting
teeth near you. I will tell you. Listen to me. Listen without pity. I cannot
use your pity. Listen with understanding. Put yourself in my dirty,
worn out, ill-fitting shoes, and hear me.

2   Poverty is getting up every morning from a dirt- and illness-
stained mattress. The sheets have long since been used for diapers.
Poverty is living in a smell that never leaves. This is a smell of urine,
sour milk, and spoiling food sometimes joined with the strong smell of
long-cooked onions. Onions are cheap. If you have smelled this smell,
you did not know how it came. It is the smell of the outdoor privy. It is
the smell of young children who cannot walk the long dark way in the
night. It is the smell of the mattresses where years of "accidents" have
happened. It is the smell of the milk which has gone sour because the
refrigerator long has not worked, and it costs money to get it fixed. It is
the smell of rotting garbage. I could bury it, but where is the shovel?
Shovels cost money.

3   Poverty is being tired. I have always been tired. They told me at the
hospital when the last baby came that I had chronic anemia caused
from poor diet, a bad case of worms, and that I needed a corrective operation. I listened politely—the poor are always polite. The poor always listen. They don't say that there is no money for iron pills, or
better food, or worm medicine. The idea of an operation is frightening
and costs so much that, if I had dared, I would have laughed. Who
takes care of my children? Recovery from an operation takes a long
time. I have three children. When I left them with "Granny" the last
time I had a job, I came home to find the baby covered with fly specks,
and a diaper that had not been changed since I left. When the dried diaper came off, bits of my baby's flesh came with it. My other child was

playing with a sharp bit of broken glass, and my oldest was playing alone at the edge of a lake. I made twenty-two dollars a week, and a good nursery school costs twenty dollars a week for three children. I quit my job.

Poverty is dirt. You say in your clean clothes coming from your clean house, "Anybody can be clean." Let me explain about housekeeping with no money. For breakfast I give my children grits with no oleo or cornbread without eggs and oleo. This does not use up many dishes. What dishes there are, I wash in cold water and with no soap. Even the cheapest soap has to be saved for the baby's diapers. Look at my hands, so cracked and red. Once I saved for two months to buy a jar of Vaseline for my hands and the baby's diaper rash. When I had saved enough, I went to buy it and the price had gone up two cents. The baby and I suffered on. I have to decide every day if I can bear to put my cracked, sore hands into the cold water and strong soap. But you ask, why not hot water? Fuel costs money. If you have a wood fire it costs money. If you burn electricity, it costs money. Hot water is a luxury. I do not have luxuries. I know you will be surprised when I tell you how young I am. I look so much older. My back has been bent over the wash tubs every day for so long, I cannot remember when I ever did anything else. Every night I wash every stitch my school age child has on and just hope her clothes will be dry by morning.

Poverty is staying up all night on cold nights to watch the fire, knowing one spark on the newspaper covering the walls means your sleeping children die in flames. In summer poverty is watching gnats and flies devour your baby's tears when he cries. The screens are torn and you pay so little rent you know they will never be fixed. Poverty means insects in your food, in your nose, in your eyes, and crawling over you when you sleep. Poverty is hoping it never rains because diapers won't dry when it rains and soon you are using newspapers. Poverty is seeing your children forever with runny noses. Paper handkerchiefs cost money and all your rags you need for other things. Even more costly are antihistamines. Poverty is cooking without food and cleaning without soap.

Poverty is asking for help. Have you ever had to ask for help, knowing your children will suffer unless you get it? Think about asking for a loan from a relative, if this is the only way you can imagine asking for help. I will tell you how it feels. You find out where the office is that you are supposed to visit. You circle that block four or five times. Thinking of your children, you go in. Everyone is very busy. Finally, someone comes out and you tell her that you need help. That never is the person you need to see. You go see another person, and after spilling the whole shame of your poverty all over the desk between you, you find that this isn't the right office after all—you must repeat the whole process, and it never is any easier at the next place.

7   You have asked for help, and after all it has a cost. You are again told to wait. You are told why, but you don't really hear because of the red cloud of shame and the rising black cloud of despair.

8   Poverty is remembering. It is remembering quitting school in junior high because "nice" children had been so cruel about my clothes and my smell. The attendance officer came. My mother told him I was pregnant. I wasn't, but she thought that I could get a job and help out. I had jobs off and on, but never long enough to learn anything. Mostly I remember being married. I was so young then. I am still young. For a time, we had all the things you have. There was a little house in another town, with hot water and everything. Then my husband lost his job. There was unemployment insurance for a while and what few jobs I could get. Soon, all our nice things were repossessed and we moved back here. I was pregnant then. This house didn't look so bad when we first moved in. Every week it gets worse. Nothing is ever fixed. We now had no money. There were a few odd jobs for my husband, but everything went for food then, as it does now. I don't know how we lived through three years and three babies, but we did. I'll tell you something, after the last baby I destroyed my marriage. It had been a good one, but could you keep on bringing children in this dirt? Did you ever think how much it costs for any kind of birth control? I knew my husband was leaving the day he left, but there were no good-bys between us. I hope he has been able to climb out of this mess somewhere. He never could hope with us to drag him down.

9   That's when I asked for help. When I got it, you know how much it was? It was, and is, seventy-eight dollars a month for the four of us; that is all I ever can get. Now you know why there is no soap, no needles and thread, no hot water, no aspirin, no worm medicine, no hand cream, no shampoo. None of these things forever and ever and ever. So that you can see clearly, I pay twenty dollars a month rent, and most of the rest goes for food. For grits and cornmeal, and rice and milk and beans. I try my best to use only the minimum electricity. If I use more, there is that much less for food.

10   Poverty is looking into a black future. Your children won't play with my boys. They will turn to other boys who steal to get what they want. I can already see them behind the bars of their prison instead of behind the bars of my poverty. Or they will turn to the freedom of alcohol or drugs, and find themselves enslaved. And my daughter? At best, there is for her a life like mine.

11   But you say to me, there are schools. Yes, there are schools. My children have no extra books, no magazines, no extra pencils, or crayons, or paper and the most important of all, they do not have health. They have worms, they have infections, they have pink-eye all summer. They do not sleep well on the floor, or with me in my one bed. They do not suffer from hunger, my seventy-eight dollars keeps us alive, but

they do suffer from malnutrition. Oh yes, I do remember what I was taught about health in school. It doesn't do much good. In some places there is a surplus commodities program. Not here. The county said it cost too much. There is a school lunch program. But I have two children who will already be damaged by the time they get to school.

But, you say to me, there are health clinics. Yes, there are health clinics and they are in the towns. I live out here eight miles from town. I can walk that far (even if it is sixteen miles both ways), but can my little children? My neighbor will take me when he goes; but he expects to get paid, *one way or another*. I bet you know my neighbor. He is that large man who spends his time at the gas station, the barbershop, and the corner store complaining about the government spending money on the immoral mothers of illegitimate children.   12

Poverty is an acid that drips on pride until all pride is worn away. Poverty is a chisel that chips on honor until honor is worn away. Some of you say that you would do *something* in my situation, and maybe you would, for the first week or the first month, but for year after year after year?   13

Even the poor can dream. A dream of a time when there is money. Money for the right kinds of food, for worm medicine, for iron pills, for toothbrushes, for hand cream, for a hammer and nails and a bit of screening, for a shovel, for a bit of paint, for some sheeting, for needles and thread. Money to pay *in money* for a trip to town. And, oh, money for hot water and money for soap. A dream of when asking for help does not eat away the last bit of pride. When the office you visit is as nice as the offices of other governmental agencies, when there are enough workers to help you quickly, when workers do not quit in defeat and despair. When you have to tell your story to only one person, and that person can send you for other help and you don't have to prove your poverty over and over and over again.   14

I have come out of my despair to tell you this. Remember I did not come from another place or another time. Others like me are all around you. Look at us with an angry heart, anger that will help you help me. Anger that will let you tell of me. The poor are always silent. Can you be silent too?   15

+ *Questions for Discussion and Writing*

1. Of the many details mentioned by Parker, which made the greatest impression on you about what being poor actually means on a daily basis?

2. What are the obstacles Parker faces in simply trying to keep her three children clean and fed? What are the trade-offs she is constantly forced to consider because she does not have enough money?

3. What sequence of events led to Parker's present situation?

4. How does Parker answer critics who suggest ways she might improve her situation? For example, what does she reveal about the amount of money she receives from public relief, what it will buy, the opportunities offered by public schools, food giveaway programs, school lunch programs, and health clinics? How, in each case, does she answer the objections that well-meaning people might raise?

5. What damaging consequences for her children does Parker foresee because of her inability to help them in the present?

6. What evidence does Parker offer to illustrate that being poor and a woman means that she is in constant danger of being exploited by men?

7. How did reading this article change preconceptions you may have had about the poor?

8. If you or anyone you know has ever had to rely on public assistance, such as welfare, unemployment compensation, or disability compensation, were the experiences similar to or different from those described by Parker? Are there any details that Parker does not mention that you might add?

9. Did you ever have to get by on very little money? What trade-offs did you make, as Parker did, when she had to choose between buying food or soap? How did you make one thing serve several purposes, such as using one kind of soap for dishes, baths, and as shampoo?

Slavenka Drakulić

The Balkan Express

—————————◆—————————

Slavenka Drakulić is a leading Croatian journalist and novelist. Her insightful commentary on East European affairs first appeared in her columns in the magazine Danas, *published in Zagreb. She is a regular contributor to* The Nation, The New Republic, *and* The New York Times Magazine. *Drakulić is the author of a novel,* Holograms of Fear *(1992), and several works of nonfiction, including* How We Survived Communism and Even Laughed *(1991). This chapter, from her book of essays,* The Balkan Express *(1993), presents a heartfelt account of the war involving Serbia, Croatia, and Bosnia-Herzegovina, from which she escaped to live in New York.*

Early Sunday morning a mist hovered over the Vienna streets like whipped cream, but the sunshine piercing the lead-grey clouds promised a beautiful autumn day, a day for leafing through magazines at the Museum Kaffe, for taking a leisurely walk along the Prater park and enjoying an easy family lunch. Then perhaps a movie or the theatre—several films were premiering.

But when I entered the Südbanhof, the South Station, the milky Viennese world redolent with café au lait, fresh rolls and butter or apple strudel and the neat life of the ordinary Viennese citizens was far behind me. As soon as I stepped into the building I found myself in another world; a group of men cursed someone's mother in Serbian, their greasy, sodden words tumbling to the floor by their feet, and a familiar slightly sour odour, a mixture of urine, beer and plastic-covered seats in second-class rail compartments, wafted through the stale air of the station. Here in the heart of Vienna I felt as if I were already on territory occupied by another sort of people, a people now second-class. Not only because they had come from a poor socialist country, at least not any more. Now they were second-class because they had come from a country collapsing under the ravages of war. War is what made them distinct from the sleepy Viennese, war was turning these people into ghosts of the past—ghosts whom the Viennese are trying hard to ignore. They'd rather forget the past, they cannot believe that history is repeating itself, that such a thing is possible: bloodshed in the Balkans, TV images of burning buildings and beheaded corpses, a stench of fear spreading from the south and east through the streets, a stench brought here by refugees. War is like a brand on the brows of Serbs who curse

Croat mothers, but it is also a brand on the faces of Croats leaving a country where all they had is gone. The first are branded by hatred, the second by the horror that here in Vienna no one really understands them. Every day more and more refugees arrive from Croatia. Vienna is beginning to feel the pressure from the Südbanhof and is getting worried. Tormented by days spent in bomb shelters, by their arduous journey and the destruction they have left behind, the exiles are disembarking—those who have the courage and the money to come so far—stepping first into the vast hall of the warehouse-like station. From there they continue out into the street, but once in the street they stop and stare at the fortress-like buildings, at the bolted doors and the doormen. They stand there staring at this metropolis, this outpost of Western Europe, helplessly looking on as Europe turns its back on them indifferently behind the safety of closed doors. The exiles feel a new fear now: Europe is the enemy, the cold, rational, polite and fortified enemy who still believes that the war in Croatia is far away, that it can be banished from sight, that the madness and death will stop across the border.

3   But it's too late. The madness will find its way, and with it, death. Standing on the platform of the Karlsplatz subway, I could hardly believe I was still in the same city: here at the very nerve centre of the city, in the trams, shops, at 'Kneipe,' German was seldom heard. Instead everyone seems to speak Croatian or Serbian (in the meantime, the language has changed its name too), the languages of people at war. One hundred thousand Yugoslavs are now living in Vienna, or so I've heard. And seventy thousand of them are Serbs. In a small park near Margaretenstrasse I came across a carving on a wooden table that read 'This is Serbia.' Further along, on a main street, I saw the graffiti 'Red Chetniks,' but also 'Fuck the Red Chetniks' scrawled over it. War creeps out of the cheap apartments near the Gurtel and claims its victims.

4   I am one of a very few passengers, maybe twenty, heading southeast on a train to Zagreb. I've just visited my daughter who, after staying some time in Canada with her father, has come to live in Vienna. There are three of us in the compartment. The train is already well on its way, but we have not yet spoken to one another. The only sound is the rattling of the steel wheels, the rhythmic pulse of a long journey. We are wrapped in a strange, tense silence. All three of us are from the same collapsing country (betrayed by the tell-tale, 'Excuse me, is this seat taken?' 'No, it's free'), but we feel none of the usual camaraderie of travel when passengers talk or share snacks and newspapers to pass the time. Indeed, it seems as if we are afraid to exchange words which might trap us in that small compartment where our knees are so close they almost rub. If we speak up, our languages will disclose who is a Croat and who a Serb, which of us is the enemy. And even if we are all

Croats (or Serbs) we might disagree on the war and yet there is no other topic we could talk about. Not even the landscape because even the landscape is not innocent any more. Slovenia has put real border posts along the border with Croatia and has a different currency. This lends another tint to the Slovenian hills, the colour of sadness. Or bitterness. Or anger. If we three strike up a conversation about the green woods passing us by, someone might sigh and say, 'Only yesterday this was my country too.' Perhaps then the other two would start in about independence and how the Slovenes were clever while the Croats were not, while the Serbs, those bastards . . .

The war would be there, in our words, in meaningful glances, and in the faces reflecting our anxiety and nausea. In that moment the madness we are travelling towards might become so alive among us that we wouldn't be able perhaps to hold it back. What if one of us is a Serb? What if he says a couple of ordinary, innocent words? Would we pretend to be civilized or would we start to attack him? What if the hypothetical Serb among us keeps silent because he is not really to blame? Are there people in this war, members of the aggressor nation, who are not to blame? Or maybe he doesn't want to hurt our feelings, thinking that we might have family or friends in Vukovar, Osijek, Šibenik, Dubrovnik, those cities under the heaviest fire? Judging from our silence, growing more and more impenetrable as we approach the Croatian border, I know that we are more than mere strangers—surly, unfamiliar, fellow passengers—just as one cannot be a mere bank clerk. In war one loses all possibility of choice. But for all that, I think the unbearable silence between us that verges on a scream is a good sign, a sign of our unwillingness to accept the war, our desire to distance ourselves and spare each other, if possible.

So we do not talk to each other. The man on my left stares out of the window, the woman opposite sleeps with her mouth half open. From time to time she wakes up and looks around, confused; then she closes her eyes again, thinking that this is the best she can do, close her eyes and pretend the world doesn't exist. I pick up a newspaper, risking recognition—one betrays oneself by the newspapers one reads—but my fellow travellers choose not to see it. At the Südbanhof newspaper stand there were no papers from Croatia, only *Borba*, one of the daily papers published in Serbia. As I leaf through the pages I come across a description of an atrocity of war, supposedly committed by the Ustashe—the Croatian Army—which freezes the blood in my veins. When you are forced to accept war as a fact, death becomes something you have to reckon with, a harsh reality that mangles your life even if it leaves you physically unharmed. But the kind of death I met with on the second page of the *Borba* paper was by no means common and therefore acceptable in its inevitability: . . . *and we looked down the well in the back yard. We pulled up the bucket—it was full of testicles, about 300 in all*. An image as if fabricated to manufacture horror. A long line of men, hundreds of them, someone's hands, a lightning swift jab of a knife, then blood, a jet of thick dark blood cooling on someone's hands, on clothing, on the ground. Were the men alive when it happened, I wondered, never questioning whether the report was true. The question of truth, or any other question for that matter, pales next to the swirling pictures, the whirlpool of pictures that sucks me in, choking me. At that moment, whatever the truth, I can imagine nothing but the bucket full of testicles, slit throats, bodies with gory holes where hearts had been, gouged eyes—death as sheer madness. As I rest my forehead on the cold windowpane I notice that there is still a little light outside, and other scenes are flitting by, scenes of peaceful tranquillity. I don't believe in tranquillity any more. It is just a thin crust of ice over a deadly treacherous river. I know I am travelling towards a darkness that has the power, in a single sentence in a newspaper, to shatter in me the capacity to distinguish real from unreal, possible from impossible. Hardly anything seems strange or dreadful now—not dismembered bodies, not autopsy reports from Croatian doctors, claiming that the victims were forced by Serbians to eat their own eyes before they were killed.

7   Only on the train heading southeast, on that sad 'Balkan Express' did I understand what it means to report bestialities as the most ordinary facts. The gruesome pictures are giving birth to a gruesome reality; a man who, as he reads a newspaper, forms in his mind a picture of the testicles being drawn up from the well will be prepared to do the same tomorrow, closing the circle of death.

8   I fold the paper. I don't need it for any further 'information.' Now I'm ready for what awaits me upon my return. I have crossed the internal border of the warring country long before I've crossed the border outside, and my journey with the two other silent passengers, the newspaper and the seed of madness growing in each of us is close to its end. Late that night at home in Zagreb I watch the news on television. The anchor man announces that seven people have been slaughtered in a Slavonian village. I watch him as he utters the word 'slaughtered' as if it were the most commonplace word in the world. He doesn't flinch, he doesn't stop, the word slips easily from his lips. The chill that emanates from the words feels cold on my throat, like the blade of a knife. Only then do I know that I've come home, that my journey has ended here in front of the TV screen, plunged in a thick, clotted darkness, a darkness that reminds me of blood.

✦ *Questions for Discussion and Writing*

1. In what ways, overt and subtle, has the war affected the relationships of the passengers traveling on the train to Zagreb?

2. In what ways is Drakulić a different person at the end of the journey from the person she was at the beginning?

3. How has reading about the atrocities changed her?

4. Have you ever had the experience of witnessing firsthand how a highly politicized environment affects human relationships? Describe what you saw and felt.

Connections

1. Compare the levels of commitment between Israeli citizens in Meir's account and Tim O'Brien's, as he faced the prospect of fighting in Vietnam.

2. Compare Tim O'Brien's position and Jo Goodwin Parker's with respect to governmental agencies: what do citizens owe the government and what does the government owe its citizens?

3. How do the accounts of Slavenka Drakulić and Rigoberta Menchú illustrate the devastating effects on people's lives of governmental repression and civil disorder?

4. Compare Menchú's picture of life as a Quiché Indian with accounts by Mary Crow Dog ("Civilize Them with a Stick," Chapter 6) and Tadeusz Borowski ("This Way for the Gas, Ladies and Gentlemen," Chapter 12) in terms of the dehumanizing effect of the misuse of governmental power.

5. What do the accounts by Jo Goodwin Parker and Luis Alberto Urrea ("My Story," Chapter 2) reveal about the psychological effects of poverty?

6. What similarities can you discover between the methods used to condition slaves, as described by Frederick Douglass, ("Learning to Read and Write," Chapter 6) and the training of new army recruits, as described by Tim O'Brien?

7. How do the accounts by Slavenka Drakulić and Tadeusz Borowski ("This Way for the Gas, Ladies and Gentlemen," Chapter 12) reveal the social and psychological effects on citizens when governments play one group off against another?

11

Facing the Unknown

◆

Is there any thing beyond?—who *knows?*
— Lord Byron, *Byron's Letters and Journals,*
Vol. 3, February 18, 1814

The prospect of imminent death, whether on the battlefield, from disease, or from a hazardous environment, and the possibility of an existence after death are the driving forces behind the diaries, letters, journals, and autobiographical essays in this chapter. The writers of these works ask themselves profound questions about the meaning and limitations of human existence. The need to clarify and interpret one's past at moments when there may not be a future produces accounts that aim at understanding what was said, acted, or lived during an entire life. Many of these documents are quite literally the last opportunity the authors have to communicate with those who will never see them again. When writers confront the final limits of life, spiritual concerns become uppermost.

At one time or another in their lives most people reflect on their relationship to a higher order of existence, whether it is perceived as an eternal force or as a defined spiritual entity that answers to the basic human need for a sense of order behind the turbulent appearance of everyday life. Some people are content to continue within the religious traditions in which they were raised, while others are drawn towards systems of belief that match their needs and perceptions of the spiritual dimension.

Sullivan Ballou, a Civil War soldier writing to his wife on the eve of battle, eloquently expresses his feelings in "Letter." The last diary entries recorded by Robert Falcon Scott on the disastrous expedition to the South Pole, in "Scott's Last March," offer an unflinching appraisal of what went wrong. In "The Snow Leopard" Peter Matthiessen draws

357

on the wisdom of Buddhist spiritual masters to sustain him on a precarious journey across the Himalayas. "The Cancer Journals" of Audre Lorde offer a courageous account of a poet facing a terminal disease. The psychiatrist Brian L. Weiss, M.D., in "Many Lives, Many Masters," recounts experiences that make him question the finality of death.

Sullivan Ballou

Letter

◆

Sullivan Ballou served as a major in the Union army during the Civil War. He was assigned to the Second Rhode Island Volunteers. Ballou wrote this moving letter to his wife, Sarah, a week before the first battle of Bull Run on July 21, 1861. Ballou's premonition of his fate was indeed fulfilled, because he was killed in that battle.

July 14, 1861
Camp Clark, Washington

My very dear Sarah:

1   The indications are very strong that we shall move in a few days—perhaps tomorrow. Lest I should not be able to write again, I feel impelled to write a few lines that may fall under your eye when I shall be no more....

2   I have no misgivings about, or lack of confidence in the cause in which I am engaged, and my courage does not halt or falter. I know how strongly American Civilization now leans on the triumph of the Government, and how great a debt we owe to those who went before us through the blood and sufferings of the Revolution. And I am willing—perfectly willing—to lay down all my joys in this life, to help maintain this Government, and to pay that debt....

3   Sarah my love for you is deathless, it seems to bind me with mighty cables that nothing but Omnipotence could break; and yet my love of Country comes over me like a strong wind and bears me unresistibly on with all these chains to the battle field.

4   The memories of the blissful moments I have spent with you come creeping over me, and I feel most gratified to God and to you that I have enjoyed them so long. And hard it is for me to give them up and burn to ashes the hopes of future years, when, God willing, we might still have lived and loved together, and seen our sons grown up to honorable manhood, around us. I have, I know, but few and small claims upon Divine Providence, but something whispers to me—perhaps it is the wafted prayer of my little Edgar, that I shall return to my loved ones unharmed. If I do not my dear Sarah, never forget how much I love you, and when my last breath escapes me on the battle field, it will whisper your name. Forgive my many faults, and the many pains I have caused you. How thoughtless and foolish I have often times been!

How gladly would I wash out with my tears every little spot upon
your happiness....

5   But, O Sarah! if the dead can come back to this earth and flit unseen
around those they loved, I shall always be near you; in the gladdest
days and in the darkest nights...*always, always,* and if there be a soft
breeze upon your cheek, it shall be my breath, as the cool air fans your
throbbing temple, it shall be my spirit passing by. Sarah do not mourn
me dead; think I am gone and wait for thee, for we shall meet again....

✦ Questions for Discussion and Writing

1. What imminent event is behind Ballou's decision to write this letter to
   his wife, Sarah?

2. How would you characterize the tone of this letter? What words or
   phrases are especially effective in communicating the writer's feelings?

3. Write a short letter to someone who is very important to you as though
   you will never communicate with that person again.

Robert Falcon Scott

Scott's Last March

◆

Robert Falcon Scott (1869–1912), British explorer and naval officer, led two expeditions into Antarctica. The first expedition (1901–1904) opened up previously unexplored southern latitudes. The second, begun in June 1910, with the objective of reaching the as-yet unattained South Pole, ended disastrously when, after travelling 1,842 miles by pony, sledge, and foot, Scott and his men discovered that they had been beaten to the Pole by the Norwegian, Roald Amundsen, and his party. Eight hundred miles into the return trip, Scott and his men died from the effects of exhaustion, frostbite, and the lack of food. At the time, they were only eleven miles from food and shelter. The final stages of the eight hundred mile sledge-haul back to the Base Camp are recorded here from Scott's diary, found when the frozen bodies of Scott and two of his men (Wilson and Bowers) were discovered by a relief party eight months later. The original diaries, now in the British Museum, are among the most moving documents in the English language.

Monday, February 19—R. 33. Temp. –17°. We have struggled out 4.6   1
miles in a short day over a really terrible surface—it has been like pulling over desert sand, without the least glide in the world. If this goes
on we shall have a bad time, but I sincerely trust it is only the result of
the windless area close to the coast and that, as we are making steadily
outwards, we shall shortly escape it. It is perhaps premature to be anxious about covering distance. In all other respects things are improving.
We have our sleeping-bags spread on the sledge and they are drying,
but, above all, we have our full measure of food again. To-night we had
a sort of stew fry of pemmican and horseflesh, and voted it the best
hoosh we had ever had on a sledge journey. The absence of poor Evans
is a help to the commissariat, but if he had been here in a fit state we
might have got along faster. I wonder what is in store for us, with some
little alarm at the lateness of the season.

Friday, March 2.—Lunch. Misfortunes rarely come singly. We   2
marched to the [Middle Barrier] depôt fairly easily yesterday afternoon, and since that have suffered three distinct blows which have
placed us in a bad position. First we found a shortage of oil; with most
rigid economy it can scarce carry us to the next depôt on this surface

---

*At Shambles Camp on February 18 they had picked up a supply of horsemeat.

[71 miles away]. Second, Titus Oates disclosed his feet, the toes showing very bad indeed, evidently bitten by the late temperatures. The third blow came in the night, when the wind, which we had hailed with some joy, brought dark overcast weather. It fell below –40° in the night, and this morning it took 1½ hours to get our foot-gear on, but we got away before eight. We lost cairn and tracks together and made as steady as we could N. by W., but have seen nothing. Worse was to come—the surface is simply awful. In spite of strong wind and full sail we have only done 5½ miles. We are in a *very* queer street, since there is no doubt we cannot do the extra marches and feel the cold horribly.

3   *Sunday, March 4.*—Lunch. Things looking *very* black indeed. As usual we forgot our trouble last night, got into our bags, slept splendidly on good hoosh, woke and had another, and started marching. Sun shining brightly, tracks clear, but surface covered with sandy frostrime. All the morning we had to pull with all our strength, and in 4½ hours we covered 3½ miles. Last night it was overcast and thick, surface bad; this morning sun shining and surface as bad as ever. Under the immediate surface crystals is a hard sastrugi surface, which must have been excellent for pulling a week or two ago. We are about 42 miles from the next depôt and have a week's food, but only about 3 to 4 days' fuel—we are as economical of the latter as one can possibly be, and we cannot afford to save food and pull as we are pulling. We are in a very tight place indeed, but none of us despondent *yet*, or at least we preserve every semblance of good cheer, but one's heart sinks as the sledge stops dead at some sastrugi behind which the surface sand lies thickly heaped. For the moment the temperature is in the –20°—an improvement which makes us much more comfortable, but a colder snap is bound to come again soon. I fear that Oates at least will weather such an event very poorly. Providence to our aid! We can expect little from man now except the possibility of extra food at the next depôt. It will be real bad if we get there and find the same shortage of oil. Shall we get there? Such a short distance it would have appeared to us on the summit! I don't know what I should do if Wilson and Bowers weren't so determinedly cheerful over things.

4   *Monday, March 5.*—Lunch. Regret to say going from bad to worse. We got a slant of wind yesterday afternoon, and going on 5 hours we converted our wretched morning run of 3½ miles into something over 9. We went to bed on a cup of cocoa and pemmican solid with the chill off. (R. 47.) The result is telling on all, but mainly on Oates, whose feet are in a wretched condition. One swelled up tremendously last night and he is very lame this morning. We started march on tea and pemmican as last night—we pretend to prefer the pemmican this way. Marched for 5 hours this morning over a slightly better surface covered

with high moundy sastrugi. Sledge capsized twice; we pulled on foot, covering about 5½ miles. We are two pony marches and 4 miles about from our depôt. Our fuel dreadfully low and the poor Soldier nearly done. It is pathetic enough because we can do nothing for him; more hot food might do a little, but only little, I fear. We none of us expected these terribly low temperatures, and of the rest of us Wilson is feeling them most; mainly, I fear, from his self-sacrificing devotion in doctoring Oates' feet. We cannot help each other, each has enough to do to take care of himself. We get cold on the march when the trudging is heavy, and the wind pierces our worn garments. The others, all of them, are unendingly cheerful when in the tent. We mean to see the game through with a proper spirit, but it's tough work to be pulling harder than we ever pulled in our lives for long hours, and to feel that the progress is so slow. One can only say "God help us!" and plod on our weary way, cold and very miserable, though outwardly cheerful. We talk of all sorts of subjects in the tent, not much of food now, since we decided to take the risk of running a full ration. We simply couldn't go hungry at this time.

Wednesday, March 7.—A little worse, I fear. One of Oates' feet *very* bad this morning; he is wonderfully brave. We still talk of what we will do together at home.   5

We only made 6½ miles yesterday. This morning in 4½ hours we did just over 4 miles. We are 16 from our depôt. If we only find the correct proportion of food there and this surface continues, we may get to the next depôt [Mt. Hooper, 72 miles farther] but not to One Ton Camp. We hope against hope that the dogs have been to Mt. Hooper; then we might pull through. If there is a shortage of oil again we can have little hope. One feels that for poor Oates the crisis is near, but none of us are improving, though we are wonderfully fit considering the really excessive work we are doing. We are only kept by good food. No wind this morning till a chill northerly air came ahead. Sun bright and cairns showing up well. I should like to keep the track to the end.   6

Thursday, March 8.—Lunch. Worse and worse in morning; poor Oates' left foot can never last out, and time over foot-gear something awful. Have to wait in night foot-gear for nearly an hour before I start changing, and then am generally first to be ready. Wilson's feet giving trouble now. We did 4½ miles this morning and are now 8½ miles from the depôt—a ridiculously small distance to feel in difficulties, yet on this surface we know we cannot equal half our old marches, and that for that effort we expend nearly double the energy. The great question is, What shall we find at the depôt? If the dogs have visited it we may get along a good distance, but if there is another short allowance of fuel, God help us indeed. We are in a very bad way, I fear, in any case.   7

8   *Saturday, March 10.*—Things steadily downhill. Oates' foot worse. He has rare pluck and must know that he can never get through. He asked Wilson if he had a chance this morning, and of course Bill had to say he didn't know. In point of fact he has none. Apart from him, if he went under now, I doubt whether we could get through. With great care we might have a dog's chance, but no more. The weather conditions are awful, and our gear gets steadily more icy and difficult to manage. At the same time, of course, poor Titus is the greatest handicap. He keeps us waiting in the morning until we have partly lost the warming effect of our good breakfast, when the only wise policy is to be up and away at once; again at lunch. Poor chap! it is too pathetic to watch him; one cannot but try to cheer him up.

9   Yesterday we marched up the depôt, Mt. Hooper. Cold comfort. Shortage on our allowance all round.

10   This morning it was calm when we breakfasted, but the wind came from the W.N.W. as we broke camp. It rapidly grew in strength. After travelling for a half an hour I saw that none of us could go on facing such conditions. We were forced to camp and are spending the rest of the day in a comfortless blizzard camp, wind quite foul. [R. 52.]

11   *Sunday, March 11.*—Titus Oates near the end, one feels. What we or he will do, God only knows. We discussed the matter after breakfast; he is a brave fine fellow and understands the situation, but he practically asked for advice. Nothing could be said but to urge him to march as long as he could. One satisfactory result to the discussion; I practically ordered Wilson to hand over the means of ending our troubles to us, so that any one of us may know how to do so. Wilson had no choice between doing so and our ransacking the medicine case. We have 30 opium tabloids apiece and he is left with a tube of morphine. So far the tragical side of our story.

12   The sky was completely overcast when we started this morning. We could see nothing, lost the tracks, and doubtless have been swaying a good deal since—3.1 miles for the forenoon—terribly heavy dragging—expected it. Know that 6 miles is about the limit of our endurance now, if we get no help from wind or surfaces. We have 7 days' food and should be about 55 miles from One Ton Camp to-night, 6 × 7 = 42, leaving us 13 miles short of our distance, even if things get no worse. Meanwhile the season rapidly advances.

13   *Monday, March 12.*—We did 6.9 miles yesterday, under our necessary average. Things are left much the same, Oates not pulling much, and now with hands as well as feet pretty well useless. We did 4 miles this morning in 4 hours 20 min.—we may hope for 3 this afternoon, 7 × 6 = 42. We shalt be 47 miles from the depôt. I doubt if we can possibly do it. The surface remains awful, the cold intense, and our physical

condition running down. God help us! Not a breath of favourable wind for more than a week, and apparently [we are] liable to head winds at any moment.

Wednesday, March 14.—No doubt about the going downhill, but everything going wrong for us. Yesterday we woke to a strong northerly wind with temp. –37°. Couldn't face it, so remained in camp till 2, then did 5¼ miles. Wanted to march later, but party feeling the cold badly as the breeze (N.) never took off entirely, and as the sun sank the temp. fell. Long time getting supper in dark.

This morning started with southerly breeze, set sail and passed another cairn at good speed; half-way, however, the wind shifted to W. by S. or W.S.W., blew through our wind clothes and into our mits. Poor Wilson horribly cold, could [not] get off ski for some time. Bowers and I practically made camp, and when we got into the tent at last we were all deadly cold. Then temp. now midday down –43° and the wind strong. We *must* go on, but now the making of every camp must be more difficult and dangerous. It must be near the end, but a pretty merciful end. Poor Oates got it again in the foot. I shudder to think what it will be like to-morrow. It is only with greatest pains rest of us keep off frostbites. No idea there could be temperatures like this at this time of year with such winds. Truly awful outside the tent. Must fight it out to the last biscuit, but can't reduce rations.

Friday, March 16, or Saturday 17.—Lost track of dates, but think the last correct. Tragedy all along the line. At lunch, the day before yesterday, poor Titus Oates said he couldn't go on; he proposed we should leave him in his sleeping-bag. That we could not do, and we induced him to come on, on the afternoon march. In spite of its awful nature for him he struggled on and we made a few miles. At night he was worse and we knew the end had come.

Should this be found I want these facts recorded. Oates' last thoughts were of his Mother, but immediately before he took pride in thinking that his regiment would be pleased with the bold way in which he met his death. We can testify to his bravery. He has borne intense suffering for weeks without complaint, and to the very last was able and willing to discuss outside subjects. He did not—would not—give up hope till the very end. He was a brave soul. This was the end. He slept through the night before last, hoping not to wake; but he woke in the morning—yesterday. It was blowing a blizzard. He said, "I am just going outside and may be some time." He went out into the blizzard and we have not seen him since.

I take this opportunity of saying that we have stuck to our sick companions to the last. In case of Edgar Evans, when absolutely out of food and he lay insensible, the safety of the remainder seemed to demand his abandonment, but Providence mercifully removed him at this critical moment. He died a natural death, and we did not leave him till two hours after his death. We knew that poor Oates was walking to his death, but though we tried to dissuade him, we knew it was the act of a brave man and an English gentleman. We all hope to meet the end with a similar spirit, and assuredly the end is not far.

19   I can only write at lunch and then only occasionally. The cold is intense, –40° at midday. My companions are unendingly cheerful, but we are all on the verge of serious frostbites, and though we constantly talk of fetching through, I don't think any one of us believes it in his heart.

20   We are cold on the march now, and at all times except meals. Yesterday we had to lie up for a blizzard and to-day we move dreadfully slowly. We are at No. 14 pony camp, only two pony marches from One Ton Depôt. We leave here our theodolite, a camera, and Oates' sleeping-bags. Diaries, etc., and geological specimens carried at Wilson's special request, will be found with us or on our sledge.

21   *Sunday, March 18.*—To-day, lunch, we are 21 miles from the depôt. Ill fortune presses, but better may come. We have had more wind and drift from ahead yesterday; had to stop marching; wind N.W., force 4, temp. –35°. No human being could face it, and we are worn out *nearly.*

22   My right foot has gone, nearly all the toes—two days ago I was proud possessor of best feet. These are the steps of my downfall. Like an ass I mixed a small spoonful of curry powder with my melted pemmican—it gave me violent indigestion. I lay awake and in pain all night; woke and felt done on the march; foot went and I didn't know it. A very small measure of neglect and I have a foot which is not pleasant to contemplate. Bowers takes first place in condition, but there is not much to choose after all. The others are still confident of getting through—or pretend to be—I don't know! We have the last *half* fill of oil in our primus and a very small quantity of spirit—this alone between us and thirst. The wind is fair for the moment, and that is perhaps a fact to help. The mileage would have seemed ridiculously small on our outward journey.

23   *Monday, March 19.*—Lunch. We camped with difficulty last night and were dreadfully cold till after our supper of cold pemmican and biscuit and a half a pannikin of cocoa cooked over the spirit. Then, contrary to expectation, we got warm and all slept well. To-day we started in the usual dragging manner. Sledge dreadfully heavy. We are 15½ miles from the depôt and ought to get there in three days. What progress! We have two days' food, but barely a day's fuel. All our feet are getting bad—Wilson's best, my right foot worse, left all right. There is no chance to nurse one's feet till we can get hot food into us. Ampu-

tation is the least I can hope for now, but will the trouble spread? This is the serious question. The weather doesn't give us a chance—the wind from N. to N.W. and –40° temp. to-day.

Wednesday, March 21.—Got within 11 miles of depôt Monday night;* had to lie up all yesterday in severe blizzard. To-day forlorn hope, Wilson and Bowers going to depôt for fuel. 24

22 and 23.—Blizzard bad as ever—Wilson and Bowers unable to start—to-morrow last chance—no fuel and only one or two† of food left—must be near the end. Have decided it shall be natural—we shall march for the depôt with or without our effects and die in our tracks. 25

[*Thursday*] *March 29.*—Since the 21st we have had a continuous gale from W.S.W. and S.W. We had fuel to make two cups of tea apiece and bare food for two days on the 20th. Every day we have been ready to start for our depôt 11 *miles* away, but outside the door of the tent it remains a scene of whirling drift. I do not think we can hope for any better things now. We shall stick it out to the end, but we are getting weaker, of course, and the end cannot be far. 26

It seems a pity, but I do not think I can write more. 27

R. SCOTT.

Last entry. For God's sake look after our people. 28

[*During the Antarctic summer, eight months later, a relief party discovered the frozen bodies of Scott and two of his men, Wilson and Bowers. Wilson and Bowers were in their sleeping bags, while Scott had thrown back the flaps of his sleeping bag and opened his coat. Three notebooks were found. With the diaries in the tent were found the following letters:*] 29

To Mrs. E. A. Wilson

My Dear Mrs. Wilson, 30

If this letter reaches you, Bill [Dr. Wilson] and I will have gone out together. We are very near it now and I should like you to know how splendid he was at the end—everlastingly cheerful and ready to sacrifice himself for others, never a word of blame to me for leading him into this mess. He is not suffering, luckily, at least only minor discomforts.

His eyes have a comfortable blue look of hope and his mind is peaceful with the satisfaction of his faith in regarding himself as part of the great scheme of the Almighty. I can do no more to comfort you 31

---

*The sixtieth camp from the Pole.
†Word missing: evidently "rations."

than to tell you that he died as he lived, a brave, true man—the best of comrades and staunchest of friends.

32   My whole heart goes out to you in pity....

Yours,
R. Scott

To Mrs. Bowers

33   *My Dear Mrs. Bowers,*

34   I am afraid this will reach you after one of the heaviest blows of your life.

35   I write when we are very near the end of our journey, and I am finishing it in company with two gallant, noble gentlemen. One of these is your son [Lt. Bowers]. He had come to be one of my closest and soundest friends, and I appreciate his wonderful upright nature, his ability and energy. As the troubles have thickened his dauntless spirit ever shone brighter and he has remained cheerful, hopeful, and indomitable to the end.

36   The ways of Providence are inscrutable, but there must be some reason why such a young, vigorous, and promising life is taken.

37   To the end he has talked of you and his sisters. One sees what a happy home he must have had, and perhaps it is well to look back on nothing but happiness.

38   He remains unselfish, self-reliant and splendidly hopeful to the end, believing in God's mercy to you....

Yours,
R. Scott

To Sir J. M. Barrie

39   *My Dear Barrie,*

We are showing that Englishmen can still die with a bold spirit, fighting it out to the end. It will be known that we have accomplished our object in reaching the Pole, and that we have done everything possible, even to sacrificing ourselves in order to save sick companions. I think this makes an example for Englishmen of the future, and that the country ought to help those who are left behind to mourn us. I leave my poor girl and your godson, Wilson leaves a widow, and Edgar Evans also a widow in humble circumstances. Do what you can to get their claims recognized. Good-bye. I am not at all afraid of the end, but sad to miss many a humble pleasure which I had planned for the future on our long marches. I may not have proved a great explorer, but we have done the greatest march ever made and come very near to great success.... We are in a desperate state, feet frozen, etc. No fuel and a long way from food, but it would do your heart good to be in our tent, to hear our songs and the cheery conversation as to what we will do when we get to Hut Point.

Later.—We are very near the end, but have not and will not lose   40
our good cheer. We have had four days of storm in our tent and no-where's food or fuel. We did intend to finish ourselves when things proved like this, but we have decided to die naturally in the track.

As a dying man, my dear friend, be good to my wife and child.   41
Give the boy a chance in life if the State won't do it. He ought to have good stuff in him.... I never met a man in my life whom I admired and loved more than you [Sir J. M. Barrie], but I could never show you how much your friendship meant to me, for you had much to give and I nothing.

Yours ever,
R. Scott

Message to the Public

The causes of the disaster are not due to faulty organisation, but to   42
misfortune in all risks which had to be undertaken.

1. The loss of pony transport in March 1911 obliged me to start   43
later than I had intended, and obliged the limits of stuff transported to be narrowed.
2. The weather throughout the outward journey, and especially   44
the long gale in 83° S., stopped us.
3. The soft snow in lower reaches of glacier again reduced pace.   45

We fought these untoward events with a will and conquered, but it   46
cut into our provision reserve.

Every detail of our food supplies, clothing and depôts made on the   47
interior icesheet and over that long stretch of 700 miles to the Pole and back, worked out to perfection. The advance party would have returned to the glacier in fine form and with surplus of food, but for the astonishing failure of the man whom we had least expected to fail. Edgar Evans was thought the strongest man of the party.

The Beardmore Glacier is not difficult in fine weather, but on our   48
return we did not get a single completely fine day; this with a sick companion enormously increased our anxieties.

As I have said elsewhere, we got into frightfully rough ice and   49
Edgar Evans received a concussion of the brain—he died a natural death, but left us a shaken party with the season unduly advanced.

But all the facts above enumerated were as nothing to the surprise   50
which awaited us on the Barrier. I maintain that our arrangements for

returning were quite adequate, and that no one in the world would have expected the temperatures and surfaces which we encountered at this time of the year. On the summit in lat 85°, 86° we had −20°, −30°. On the Barrier in lat 82°, 10,000 feet lower, we had −30° in the day, −47° at night pretty regularly, with continuous head wind during our day marches. It is clear that these circumstances came on very suddenly, and our wreck is certainly due to this sudden advent of severe weather, which does not seem to have any satisfactory cause. I do not think human beings ever came through such a month as we have come through, and we should have got through in spite of the weather but for the sickening of a second companion, Captain Oates, and a shortage of fuel in our depôts for which I cannot account,[*] and finally, but for the storm which has fallen on us within 11 miles of the depôt at which we hoped to secure our final supplies. Surely misfortune could scarcely have exceeded this last blow. We arrived within 11 miles of our old One Ton Camp with fuel for one last meal and food for two days. For four[†] days we have been unable to leave the tent—the gale howling about us. We are weak, writing is difficult, but for my own sake I do not regret this journey, which has shown that Englishmen can endure hardships, help one another, and meet death with as great a fortitude as ever in the past. We took risks, we knew we took them; things have come out against us, and therefore we have no cause for complaint, but bow to the will of Providence, determined still to do our best to the last. But if we have been willing to give our lives to this enterprise, which is for the honour of our country, I appeal to our countrymen to see that those who depend on us are properly cared for.

51   Had we lived, I should have had a tale to tell of the hardihood, endurance, and courage of my companions which would have stirred the heart of every Englishman. These rough notes and our dead bodies must tell the tale, but surely, surely, a great rich country like ours will see that those who are dependent on us are properly provided for.

R. Scott

✦ Questions for Discussion and Writing

1. Why was it important for Scott to continue keeping his diary when he knew that he and his men would perish and the diary might never be found?

2. How did Scott wish himself and his men to be remembered by his countrymen in England?

[*]*The fuel had evaporated.*
[†]*They lasted for six more days after this.*

3. What did the episode involving Titus Oates tell about both Oates's heroism and Scott's sense of responsibility toward his men?

4. Summarize the main reasons, according to Scott, why the expedition failed.

5. What specific details convey the fact that the situation Scott and his men were in got progressively worse?

6. What in the narrative reveals why Scott wanted to lead his men on an expedition into the Antarctic?

7. What specific examples from the diary show that Scott wished it to provide an objective account of the expedition?

8. What do the letters that Scott wrote to the families of his men reveal about Scott himself?

9. Have you ever been on a trip that became life endangering? Describe your experiences.

Peter Matthiessen

The Snow Leopard

————————◆————————

*Peter Matthiessen, born in 1927, is a novelist as well as a prolific author
of nonfiction accounts growing out of his extensive travels throughout the
world. As a writer, he is most concerned with alerting the public to cata-
strophic environmental effects on endangered species. His works include*
Wildlife in America *(1959),* The Snow Leopard *(1978), from which
the following autobiographical account is drawn, and* In the Spirit of
Crazy Horse *(1983). Throughout his life Matthiessen has been a student
of Zen Buddhism and embarked on a quest in northwest Nepal on a journey by foot of 250 miles across the Himalayas in the hope of getting a
glimpse of the rarest of the great cats, the snow leopard. But, as we soon
become aware, this was for him an inner journey as well.*

October 14

1   Last night, for the first time in my life, I was conscious of hallucinat-
ing in a dream. I was sitting in the shadows of a hut, outside of which
the figure of a friend was sitting with a dog beside a rock. Then everything became vibrant, luminous, and plastic, as in psychedelic vision,
and the figure outside was seized up by some dreadful force and cast
down, broken and dead. Throughout, it seemed to me that I stood apart,
watching myself dreaming, watching myself stand free of my body: I
could have gone away from it but hesitated, afraid of being unable to return. In this fear, I awoke—or rather, I *decided* to awake, for the waking-
and dream-states seemed no different. Then I slept again, and a yellow-
throated marten—the large Himalayan weasel whose droppings we
have seen along the trail—jumped with cub in mouth into a tree. As it
set the cub down in a crotch of branches, a squirrel leaped from a higher
limb, and the marten intercepted it in midair. For seconds, gazing at me,
the marten remained suspended in the air beside the tree, mouth gro-
tesquely spread by the squirrel's body; then it was on its branch again,
gutting the squirrel, and letting fall the head and skin of it. From the
ground, the squirrel's eyes in its head gazed up at me, alive and bright.
Both dreams seemed more like hallucinations, experienced in the waiting state, and left me with a morbid feeling in the morning.

These dreams do not seem to evaporate—can I be dead? It is as if I had entered what Tibetans call the Bardo—literally, between-two-existences—a dreamlike hallucination that precedes reincarnation, not necessarily in human form; typical of the dream-state visions is the skull cup full of blood, symbolizing the futility of carnal existence, with its endless thirsting, drinking, quenching, and thirsting anew.

In case I should need them, instructions for passage through the Bardo are contained in the Tibetan "Book of the Dead" which I carry with me—a guide for the living, actually, since it teaches that a man's last thoughts will determine the quality of his reincarnation. Therefore, every moment of life is to be lived calmly, mindfully, as if it were the last, to insure that the most is made of the precious human state—the only one in which enlightenment is possible. And only the enlightened can recall their former lives; for the rest of us, the memories of past existences are but glints of light, twinges of longing, passing shadows, disturbingly familiar, that are gone before they can be grasped, like the passage of that silver bird on Dhaulagiri.

Thus one must seek to "regard as one this life, the next life, and the life between, in the Bardo." This was a last message to his disciples of Tibet's great poet-saint the Lama Milarepa,[1] born in the tenth century, in the Male Water-Dragon Year, to a woman known as "the White Garland of the Nyang." Milarepa is called Mila Repa because as a great yogin and master of "mystical heat" he wore only a simple white cloth, or *repa*, even in deepest winter: his "songs" or hortatory verses, as transcribed by his disciples, are still beloved in Tibet. Like Sakyamuni,[2] he is said to have attained nirvana in a single lifetime, and his teaching as he prepared for death might have been uttered by the Buddha:

> All worldly pursuits have but the one unavoidable and inevitable end, which is sorrow: acquisitions end in dispersion; buildings, in destruction; meetings, in separation; births, in death. Knowing this, one should from the very first renounce acquisition and heaping-up, and building and meeting, and ... set about realizing the Truth.... Life is short, and the time of death is uncertain; so apply yourselves to meditation....[3]

Meditation has nothing to do with contemplation of eternal questions, or of one's own folly, or even of one's navel, although a clearer

---

[1]Lama Milarepa—In the Buddhism of Tibet, a monk or priest. The chief of the lamas is the Dalai Lama.

[2]Sakyamuni—one of the names of Buddha.

[3] W. Y. Evans-Wentz, *Tibet's Great Yogi: Milarepa* (New York: Oxford University Press, 1969), p 35.

view on all of these enigmas may result. It has nothing to do with thought of any kind—with anything at all, in fact, but intuiting the true nature of existence, which is why it has appeared, in one form or another, in almost every culture known to man. The entranced Bushman staring into fire, the Eskimo using a sharp rock to draw an ever-deepening circle into the flat surface of a stone achieves the same obliteration of the ego (and the same power) as the dervish or the Pueblo sacred dancer. Among Hindus and Buddhists, realization is attained through inner stillness, usually achieved through the *samadhi* state of sitting yoga.[4] In Tantric practice, the student may displace the ego by filling his whole being with the real or imagined object of his concentration;[5] in Zen, one seeks to empty out the mind, to return it to the clear, pure stillness of a seashell or a flower petal.[6] When body and mind are one, then the whole being, scoured clean of intellect, emotions, and the senses, may be laid open to the *experience* that individual existence, ego, the "reality" of matter and phenomena are no more than fleeting and illusory arrangements of molecules. The weary self of masks and screens, defenses, preconceptions, and opinions that, propped up by ideas and words, imagines itself to be some sort of entity (in a society of like entities) may suddenly fall away, dissolve into formless flux where concepts such as "death" and "life," "time" and "space," "past" and "future" have no meaning. There is only a pearly radiance of Emptiness, the Uncreated, without beginning, therefore without end.[7]

---

[4]In the absence of a meaningful vocabulary, one must fall back on nebulous terms, on grandiose capital letters and on Sanskrit. But Sanskrit terms are differently defined by Hindus and Buddhists, and even within Buddhism, they blur and overlap a little, like snakes swallowing their tails in that ancient symbol of eternity: *samadhi* (one-pointedness, unification) may lead to *sunyata* (transparency, void) which can open out in a sudden *satori* (glimpse) which may evolve into the *prajna* (transcendent wisdom) of *nirvana* (beyond delusion, beyond all nature, life, and death, beyond becoming), which might be seen as eternal *samadhi*. Thus the circle is complete, every state is conditioned by each of the others, and all are inherent in meditation, which is itself a realization of the way.

[5]Tantric—in Hinduism and in Buddhism, the esoteric tradition of ritual and yoga that uses mantras or mystical words, mandalas, sacred diagrams, and other means to achieve a oneness with the universe.

[6]Zen Buddhism—Buddhist sect of Japan and China based on the practice of meditation rather than adherence to a particular scriptural doctrine.

[7]Lawrence Le Shan, in *The Medium, the Mystic, and the Physicist* (New York: Grossman, 1974), has suggested that some such plane or trancelike state in which one becomes a vehicle or "medium," beyond thought or feelings, laid open to the energies and *knowing* that circulate freely through the universe may be the one on which telepathy, precognition, and even psychic healing are transmitted.

Like the round-bottomed Bodhidharma doll,[8] returning to its cen-   7
ter, meditation represents the foundation of the universe to which all
returns, as in the stillness of the dead of night, the stillness between
tides and winds, the stillness of the instant before Creation. In this
"void," this dynamic state of rest, without impediments, lies ultimate
reality, and here one's own true nature is reborn, in a return from what
Buddhists speak of as "great death." This is the Truth of which Milarepa speaks.

At daybreak comes a light patter of rain on the tent canvas, al-   8
though there had been stars all night before, and GS, who is not often
profane, is cursing in his tent. As soon as the rain ceases, we break
camp. Setting out ahead, I meet almost immediately with a hoopoe,
oddly tame. Such tameness must be a good omen, of which we are in
need, for the hoopoe walks around before my feet on the wet grass under the oaks as if waiting to conduct us farther.

The path enters a narrowing ravine that climbs to a high cleft be-   9
tween boulders, and the cleft is reached at the strike of the rising sun,
which fills this portal with a blinding light. I emerge in a new world
and stare about me. A labyrinth of valleys mounts toward the snows,
for the Himalaya is as convoluted as a brain. Churen Himal looms in
high mist, then vanishes. A pheasant hen and then three more sail
down off a lichened rock face with sweet chortlings; the crimson cock
stays hidden. Far below, over dark gorges where no sun has reached, a
griffon circles in the silence. The forest on this ridge is oak and maple,
and a mist of yellow leaves softens the ravine sides all around: on a
golden wind comes a rich humus smell of autumn.

Now GS comes, and we climb quickly to 12,000 feet. The paths   10
around these mountainsides are narrow, there is no room for a misstep,
and at this altitude, one is quickly out of breath. Gradually I have
learned to walk more lightly, legs loose, almost gliding, and this helps a
lot in times of vertigo. Some of the cliffside trail is less than two feet
wide—I measure it—and skirts sheer precipice; nor is the rest very
much better, for these mountainsides of shining grass are so precipi-
tous, so devoid of trees or even shrubs, that a stumbler might tumble
and roll thousands of feet, then drop into the dark where the sun ends,
for want of anything to catch hold of.

My sense of dread is worsened by last night's lingering dreams.   11
"The dream . . . wherein phenomena and mind were seen as one was a
teacher: did you not so understand it?" I have not quite apprehended
this idea—that man's world, man's dreams are both dream-states—but
Milarepa has been of help in other ways. Returning to his village after
many years (he was born about fifty miles north of Kathmandu, on the

[8]Bodhidharma—reference to the legendary fifth century founder of Zen Buddhism in
China.

Tibetan side of the present-day frontier), Mila discovers the decayed corpse of his mother, no more than a mound of dirt and rags in her fallen hut; shaken by grief and horror, he remembers the instruction of his guru, the Lama Marpa, to embrace all that he most fears or finds repugnant, the better to realize that everything in the Universe, being inseparably related, is therefore holy. And so he makes a headrest of the sad remains of the erstwhile White Garland of the Nyang and lies upon them for seven days, in a deep, clear state of *samadhi*. This Tantric discipline to overcome ideas of "horror," often performed while sitting on a corpse or in the graveyard in the dark of night, is known as *chöd*. Since trusting to life must finally mean making peace with death, I perform some mild *chöd* of my own, forcing myself to look over the precipice whenever I can manage it. The going in the weeks ahead is bound to worsen, and hardening myself might make less scary some evil stretch of ledge in the higher mountains. It helps to pay minute attention to details—a shard of rose quartz, a cinnamon fern with spores, a companionable mound of pony dung. When one pays attention to the present, there is great pleasure in awareness of small things; I think of the comfort I took yesterday in the thin bouillon and stale biscuits that shy Dawa brought to my leaking tent.

12   The trees die out in a rock garden of dwarf rhododendron, birch, and fire-colored ash, set about with strap fern, edelweiss, and unknown alpine florets, fresh mineral blue. Then a woodpecker of vivid green appears, and though I *know* that I am awake, that I actually see such a bird, the blue flowers and green woodpecker have no more reality, or less, than the yellow-throated marten of my dream.

13   Sun comes and goes. The monsoon is not done with us, there is wind and weather in the east, but to the south, the sky of India is clear. GS says, "Do you realize we haven't heard even a distant motor since September?" And this is true. No airplane crosses such old mountains. We have strayed into another century.

14   This wayfaring in shifting sun, in snow and cloud worlds, so close to the weather, makes me happy; the morbid feeling of this dawn has passed away. I would like to reach the Crystal Monastery, I would like to see a snow leopard, but if I do not, that is all right, too. In this moment, there are birds—red-billed choughs, those queer small crows of the high places, and a small buteo, black against the heavens, and southbound finches bounding down the wind, in their wake a sprinkling of song. A lark, a swift, a lammergeier, and more griffons: the vultures pass at eye level, on creaking wings.

15   At a low pass stands a small cairn topped with sticks and rags, and an opening on the eastern side for offerings: the rag strips or wind prayers bring good luck to travelers who are crossing a pass for the first time. Perhaps because we ignore the cairn, the mountain gods greet us with a burst of hail, then sun, then both together. A patter of ice dies

away as the clouds turn. We wait. Tukten, an hour behind us, is a good half hour ahead of all the rest and, for his pains, is chastised by GS as representative of the lead-footed porter breed. Slowly, he puts down the load that he has humped two thousand feet uphill, observing GS in the equable way in which he observes everything: giving thanks for his arrival at the pass, he places a small stone upon the cairn.

The Tamangs come, then the Tarakots, and we descend steeply to a brushy gulley, where the porters throw their baskets down and start a fire, in preparation for the first of their two meals. After their hard climb, this is understandable, but after our wait of an hour and a half, it is damned frustrating; in the long delay, we assumed they must have eaten. We curse them as we have each day for not taking this main meal before starting out, when fires are already built, and water boiling; this two-hour stop, more days than not, has meant wasting warm sunny hours on the trail and setting up camp in rain, cold, and near-darkness.

The new delay makes GS desperate: we are sure to miss the blue-sheep rut if we don't move faster. But the porters can see the snow that fills the north end of this canyon; chivvy them as we may, they will go no farther than that snow this afternoon.

Ranging back and forth, GS nags Phu-Tsering about wasting sugar and cooking precious rice instead of using the potatoes, which are heavy and still locally available. The cook's happy-go-lucky ways can be exasperating, although GS learned in eastern Nepal that his merry smile more than compensates for any failings. And the sherpas accept his reprimands in good spirit, since GS is faithfully considerate of their feelings and concerned about their welfare, and rarely permits their childlike natures to provoke him.

Since no brush occurs between this point and the far side of Jang La, we scavenge shrubby birch and rhododendron and gather old sods of bamboo, which flowers every twelve or thirteen years, then dies over vast areas. In a semicave I find some faggots left half-burnt by other travelers, and bind them across my rucksack with the rest.

The trail ascends the torrent called Seng Khola, under looming cliffs, and in this gloom, in the roar of the gray water, I half expect the visage of a mountain god to peer over the knife edge of the rim. Clouds creep after us, up the canyon, and for once skies look more promising ahead: a shaft of sun that lights the snow at the head of the Seng Khola is a beacon. Then come the first gray drops of rain, the cold rain with a cold wind behind it that overtakes us every afternoon. The river is som-ber, with broken waterfalls and foaming rock, in a wasteland of sere stubble and spent stone, and I wonder why, in this oppressive place, I feel so full of well-being, striding on through the rain, and grateful in some unnameable way—to what? On the path, the shadow of my close-cropped head is monkish, and the thump of my stave resounds in the still mountains: I feel inspired by Milarepa as described by one of his disciples, walking "free as an unbridled lion in the snowy ranges."

21   At a canyon bend stands the headman of Tarakot, who wears Hindu puttees and carries no pack of any kind. He is pointing at the bouldered slopes across the stream. *"Na!"* he cries. *"Na!"* Then he goes on. A pale form jumps across a gully, followed quickly by six more; the animals move up a steep slope to a haze of green between the rocks and snow. I watch them climb until, at snow line, they are swept up and consumed by clouds that have rushed up the valley from the south: this wonderful silver-blue-gray creature is the bharal, the blue sheep of the Himalaya—in Tibetan, *na*—that we have come so far to see.

22   We camp on a flat ledge by the river, just beneath the snows. A dipper plunges into the cold torrent, and a pair of redstarts pursue some tardy insect over the black boulders. The altitude is nearly 13,000 feet, says GS as he comes up: it is dark and cold. GS, too, has seen blue sheep, and later, after tents are pitched, he goes out and finds more. He returns at dusk, delighted—"The first data in a month and a half!" he cries. And I tell him of a small find of my own. Back down the trail there was a solitary print, as if a dog had crossed the path and gone its way, leaving no trace on the stony ground to either side. There were no signs of human travelers on the wet earth, and the print was fresh. Therefore a dog seemed most unlikely, and having assumed it was a wolf, which still occurs in the wilder regions of Tibet, I had not checked for foretoes on the print. "This is perfect country for the snow leopard," says GS. The headman of Tarakot declares that snow leopards occur here in the Jang region, but the all-knowing Tukten shakes his head. "Only on Dolpo side," says Tukten, "not in Nepal." Dolpo lies on the Tibetan Plateau, and it interests me that he regards it as a foreign land.

23   In his abrupt way, more in exuberance than rudeness, my friend hurls goggles through my tent flap, to protect my eyes from tomorrow's sun and snow. Excited, I lie awake much of the night, my head out of the tent. The night is clear, clear, clear and very cold. Before dawn, black turns black-blue over the mountains, and there is fireglow high in the heavens.

◆ *Questions for Discussion and Writing*

1. What significance does the Tibetan "Book of the Dead" have for Matthiessen? What connections does he draw between Tibetan philosophy and the dreams he had the previous night?

2. Of what significance is the concept of meditation, its purposes, and its objectives for Matthiessen?

3. Where do Matthiessen's accounts of forests, wildlife, mountains, and weather suggest he is seeing the environment from a spiritual perspective?

4. Why, for Matthiessen, is the quest to see the snow leopard less important than the transformation he experiences in overcoming physical and psychological obstacles on his hazardous journey?

5. Have you ever tried meditating? Describe your experience. Was it beneficial to you? Why or why not?

6. Matthiessen drew on the sensory details, characters, symbols, images, impressions, observations, and colors in his dream as he experienced its message in everyday life. If you keep a journal, you might set down a few of your recurring and/or powerful dreams, using the following technique:

   1. Write a narrative of the dream, identifying yourself with an important character or symbol.
   2. Express your experiences in the first person.
   3. Try to speculate on the message of the dream and what you have learned from it. If you have a recurring dream, you might wish to give it a title that identifies a significant feeling, symbol, or character, for example, "An Endless Highway," "An All-You-Can-Eat Buffet," "Nude in Public."

Audre Lorde

The Cancer Journals

◆

Audre Lorde (1934–1992) was born and educated in New York City. She received a B.A. from Hunter College, an M.L.S. from Columbia University, and worked as a librarian for the City University of New York. Lorde taught creative writing at John Jay College in New York and was a professor of English at Hunter College.

A prolific writer, Lorde was the author of six collections of verse and a fictionalized memoir, Zami: A New Spelling of My Name *(1982). This account of her struggle with breast cancer is drawn from* The Cancer Journals *(1980), from which the following excerpt is reprinted. The selection gives us insight into the way Lorde's personal writings have served as a source of inspiration.*

1   *There is a commonality of isolation and painful reassessment which is shared by all women with breast cancer, whether this commonality is recognized or not. It is not my intention to judge the woman who has chosen the path of prosthesis, of silence and invisibility, the woman who wishes to be "the same as before." She has survived on another kind of courage, and she is not alone. Each of us struggles daily with the pressures of conformity and the loneliness of difference from which those choices seem to offer escape. I only know that those choices do not work for me, nor for other women who, not without fear, have survived cancer by scrutinizing its meaning within our lives, and by attempting to integrate this crisis into useful strengths for change.*

2   THESE SELECTED JOURNAL ENTRIES, *which begin six months after my modified radical mastectomy for breast cancer, exemplify the process of integrating this crisis into my life.*

1/26/79

3   I'm not feeling very hopeful these days, about selfhood or anything else. I handle the outward motions of each day while pain fills me like a puspocket and every touch threatens to breech the taut membrane that keeps it from flowing through and poisoning my whole existence. Sometimes despair sweeps across my consciousness like lunar winds across a barren moonscape. Ironshod horses rage back and forth over

every nerve. Oh Seboulisa ma, help me remember what I have paid so much to learn. I could die of difference, or live—myriad selves.

2/5/79

The terrible thing is that nothing goes past me these days, nothing. Each horror remains like a steel vise in my flesh, another magnet to the flame. Buster has joined the roll call of useless wasteful deaths of young Black people; in the gallery today everywhere ugly images of women offering up distorted bodies for whatever fantasy passes in the name of male art. Gargoyles of pleasure. Beautiful laughing Buster, shot down in a hallway for ninety cents. Shall I unlearn that tongue in which my curse is written? 4

3/1/79

It is such an effort to find decent food in this place, not to just give up and eat the old poison. But I must tend my body with at least as much care as I tend the compost, particularly now when it seems so beside the point. Is this pain and despair that surround me a result of cancer, or has it just been released by cancer? I feel so unequal to what I always handled before, the abominations outside that echo the pain within. And yes I am completely self-referenced right now because it is the only translation I can trust, and I do believe not until every woman traces her weave back strand by bloody self-referenced strand, will we begin to alter the whole pattern. 5

4/16/79

The enormity of our task, to turn the world around. It feels like turning my life around, inside out. If I can look directly at my life and my death without flinching I know there is nothing they can ever do to me again. I must be content to see how really little I can do and still do it with an open heart. I can never accept this, like I can't accept that turning my life around is so hard, eating differently, sleeping differently, moving differently, being differently. Like Martha said, I want the old me, bad as before. 6

4/22/79

I must let this pain flow through me and pass on. If I resist or try to stop it, it will detonate inside me, shatter me, splatter my pieces against every wall and person that I touch. 7

5/1/79

Spring comes, and still I feel despair like a pale cloud waiting to consume me, engulf me like another cancer, swallow me into immobil- 8 ity, metabolize me into cells of itself; my body, a barometer. I need to remind myself of the joy, the lightness, the laughter so vital to my living and my health. Otherwise, the other will always be waiting to eat me up into despair again. And that means destruction. I don't know how, but it does.

9 There is no room around me in which to be still, to examine and explore what pain is mine alone—no device to separate my struggle within from my fury at the outside world's viciousness, the stupid brutal lack of consciousness or concern that passes for the way things are. The arrogant blindness of comfortable white women. What is this work all for? What does it matter whether I ever speak again or not? I try. The blood of black women sloshes from coast to coast and Daly says race is of no concern to women. So that means we are either immortal or born to die and no note taken, un-women.

10/3/79

10 I don't feel like being strong, but do I have a choice? It hurts when even my sisters look at me in the street with cold and silent eyes. I am defined as other in every group I'm a part of. The outsider, both strength and weakness. Yet without community there is certainly no liberation, no future, only the most vulnerable and temporary armistice between me and my oppression.

11/19/79

11 I want to write rage but all that comes is sadness. We have been sad long enough to make this earth either weep or grow fertile. I am an anachronism, a sport, like the bee that was never meant to fly. Science said so. I am not supposed to exist. I carry death around in my body like a condemnation. But I do live. The bee flies. There must be some way to integrate death into living, neither ignoring it nor giving in to it.

1/1/80

12 Faith is the last day of Kwanza, and the name of the war against despair, the battle I fight daily. I become better at it. I want to write about that battle, the skirmishes, the losses, the small yet so important victories that make the sweetness of my life.

1/20/80

13 The novel is finished at last. It has been a lifeline. I do not have to win in order to know my dreams are valid, I only have to believe in a process of which I am a part. My work kept me alive this past year, my work and the love of women. They are inseparable from each other. In the recognition of the existence of love lies the answer to despair. Work is that recognition given voice and name.

2/18/80

I am forty-six years living today and very pleased to be alive, very [14] glad and very happy. Fear and pain and despair do not disappear. They only become slowly less and less important. Although sometimes I still long for a simple orderly life with a hunger sharp as that sudden vegetarian hunger for meat.

4/6/80

Somedays, if bitterness were a whetstone, I could be sharp as grief. [15]

5/30/80

Last spring was another piece of the fall and winter before, a pro- [16] gression from all the pain and sadness of that time, ruminated over. But somehow this summer which is almost upon me feels like a part of my future. Like a brand-new time, and I'm pleased to know it, wherever it leads. I feel like another woman, de-chrysalised and become a broader, stretched-out me, strong and excited, a muscle flexed and honed for action.

6/20/80

I do not forget cancer for very long, ever. That keeps me armed and [17] on my toes, but also with a slight background noise of fear. Carl Simonton's book, *Getting Well Again,* has been really helpful to me, even though his smugness infuriates me sometimes. The visualizations and deep relaxing techniques that I learned from it help make me a less anxious person, which seems strange, because in other ways, I live with the constant fear of recurrence of another cancer. But fear and anxiety are not the same at all. One is an appropriate response to a real situation which I can accept and learn to work through just as I work through semi-blindness. But the other, anxiety, is an immobilizing yield to things that go bump in the night, a surrender to namelessness, formlessness, voicelessness, and silence.

But on the day before my mastectomy I wrote in my journal: [18]

September 21, 1978

The anger that I felt for my right breast last year has faded, and I'm [19] glad because I have had this extra year. My breasts have always been so very precious to me since I accepted having them it would have been a shame not to have enjoyed the last year of one of them. And I am prepared to lose it now in a way I was not quite ready to last November, because now I really see it as a choice between my breast and my life, and in that view there cannot be any question.

Somehow I always knew this would be the final outcome, for it [20] never did seem like a finished business for me. This year between was like a hiatus, an interregnum in a battle within which I could so easily be a casualty, since I certainly was a warrior. And in that brief time the sun shone and the birds sang and I wrote important words and have loved richly and been loved in return. And if a lifetime of furies is the cause of this death in my right breast, there is still nothing I've never been able to accept before that I would accept now in order to keep my breast. It was a twelve-month reprieve in which I could come to accept the emotional fact/truths I came to see first in those horrendous weeks last year before the biopsy. If I do what I need to do because I want to do it, it will matter less when death comes, because it will have been an ally that spurred me on.

21   I was relieved when the first tumor was benign, but I said to Frances at the time that the true horror would be if they said it was benign and it wasn't. I think my body knew there was a malignancy there somewhere, and that it would have to be dealt with eventually. Well, I'm dealing with it as best I can. I wish I didn't have to, and I don't even know if I'm doing it right, but I sure am glad that I had this extra year to learn to love me in a different way.

22   I'm going to have the mastectomy, knowing there are alternatives, some of which sound very possible in the sense of right thinking, but none of which satisfy me enough.... Since it is my life that I am gambling with, and my life is worth even more than the sensual delights of my breast, I certainly can't take that chance.

23   *7.30 P.M.* And yet if I cried for a hundred years I couldn't possibly express the sorrow I feel right now, the sadness and the loss. How did the Amazons of Dahomey feel? They were only little girls. But they did this willingly, for something they believed in. I suppose I am too but I can't feel that now.

✦ *Questions for Discussion and Writing*

1. As clearly as you can, try to identify the stages by which Lorde comes to terms with cancer.

2. To what extent does Lorde appear to go through the process of denial, anger, bargaining, depression, and acceptance that Elisabeth Kubler-Ross discovered in her clinical work with terminally ill patients (reported in *Stages of Dying* [1972])?

3. What details make you aware that being an African American feminist poet and writer was of crucial importance to Lorde in sustaining her during this difficult time?

4. Lorde's journal reveals a complicated bargaining process with her fate that required her to come to terms with her sorrow. If you keep a journal, try to compose a short list of three to eight events or people for

whom you have not adequately grieved, and acknowledge the emotions that you did not express at the time.

5. Keep a diary for a few weeks in which you record your changing reactions to a pressing personal issue; try to gain insight into the problem by looking at it in its societal and philosophical dimensions as well. One practical technique you might try is to create a journal dialogue between yourself and any strong emotion personified as a character you experienced during this time (for example, jealousy, fear, hate, joy, anger, elation,... etc.).

Brian L. Weiss

Many Lives, Many Masters

——————◆——————

Brian L. Weiss graduated magna cum laude from Columbia University in 1966, received his medical degree from Yale Medical School in 1970, and, after his internship at New York University Medical Center, became the chief resident in the Department of Psychiatry at Yale University School of Medicine. Dr. Weiss is currently chairman of the Department of Psychiatry at Mt. Sinai Medical Center, Miami Beach, Florida, and clinical associate professor, Department of Psychiatry at the University of Miami. He is the author of 37 scientific papers and chapters in the field of biological psychiatry. Many Lives, Many Masters *(1988) records the interaction between Weiss and his patient, who under hypnosis became a channel for information that raises profound questions about conventional views of life and death.*

1   "I see a square white house with a sandy road in front. People on horses are going back and forth." Catherine was speaking in her usual dreamy whisper. "There are trees... a plantation, a big house with a bunch of smaller houses, like slave houses. It's very hot. It's in the South... Virginia?" She thought the date was 1873. She was a child.

2   "There are horses and lots of crops... corn, tobacco." She and the other servants ate in a kitchen of the big house. She was black, and her name was Abby. She felt a foreboding, and her body tensed. The main house was on fire, and she watched it burn down. I progressed her fifteen years in time to 1888.

3   "I'm wearing an old dress, cleaning a mirror on the second floor of a house, a brick house with windows... with lots of of panes. The mirror is wavy, not straight, and it has knobs on the end. The man who owns the house is named James Manson. He has a funny coat with three buttons and a big black collar. He has a beard.... I don't recognize him [as someone in Catherine's present lifetime]. He treats me well. I live in a house on the property. I clean the rooms. There is a schoolhouse on the property, but I'm not allowed in the school. I make butter, too!"

4   Catherine was whispering slowly, using very simple terms and paying great attention to detail. Over the next five minutes, I learned how to make butter. Abby's knowledge of churning butter was new to Catherine, too. I moved her ahead in time.

5   "I am with somebody, but I don't think we are married. We sleep together... but we don't always live together. I feel okay about him,

386

but nothing special. I don't see any children. There are apple trees and
ducks. Other people are in the distance. I'm picking apples. Something
is making my eyes itch." Catherine was grimacing with her eyes
closed. "It's the smoke. The wind is blowing it this way... the smoke
from burning wood. They're burning up wooden barrels." She was
coughing now. "It happens a lot. They're making the inside of the barrels black... tar... to waterproof."

After the excitement of last week's session, I was eager to reach the
in-between state again. We had already spent ninety minutes exploring
her lifetime as a servant. I had learned about bedspreads, butter, and
barrels; I was hungry for a more spiritual lesson. Forsaking my patience, I advanced her to her death.

"It's hard to breathe. My chest hurts so much." Catherine was
gasping, in obvious pain. "My heart hurts; it's beating fast. I'm so
cold... my body's shaking." Catherine began to shiver. "People are in
the room giving me leaves to drink [a tea]. It smells funny. They're rubbing a liniment on my chest. Fever... but I feel very cold." She quietly
died. Floating up to the ceiling, she could see her body in the bed, a
small, shriveled woman in her sixties. She was just floating, waiting for
someone to come and help her. She became aware of a light, feeling
herself drawn toward it. The light was becoming brighter, and more luminous. We waited in silence as minutes slowly passed. Suddenly she
was in another lifetime, thousands of years before Abby.

Catherine was softly whispering, "I see lots of garlic, hanging in an
open room. I can *smell* it. It is believed to kill many evils in the blood
and to cleanse the body, but you must take it every day. The garlic is
outside too, on top of a garden. Other herbs are there... figs, dates, and
other herbs. These plants help you. My mother is buying garlic and the
other herbs. Somebody in the house is sick. These are strange roots.
Sometimes you just keep them in your mouth, or ears, or other openings. You just keep them in.

"I see an old man with a beard. He's one of the healers in the village.
He tells you what to do. There is some type of... plague... killing the
people. They're not embalming because they're afraid of the disease.
People are just buried. The people are unhappy about this. They feel the
soul cannot pass on this way [contrary to Catherine's after-death re-
ports]. But so many have died. The cattle are dying, too. Water...
floods... people are sick because of the floods. [She apparently just realized this bit of epidemiology.] I also have some disease from the water. It
makes your stomach hurt. The disease is of the bowel and stomach. You
lose so much water from the body. I'm by the water to bring more back,
but that's what is killing us. I bring the water back. I see my mother and
brothers. My father has already died. My brothers are very sick."

I paused before progressing her in time. I was fascinated by the
way her conceptions of death and the afterlife changed so much from

lifetime to lifetime. And yet her *experience* of death itself was so uniform, so similar, every time. A conscious part of her would leave the body around the moment of death, floating above and then being drawn to a wonderful, energizing light. She would then wait for someone to come and help her. The soul automatically passed on. Embalming, burial rituals, or any other procedure after death had nothing to do with it. It was automatic, no preparation necessary, like walking through a just-opened door.

11   "The land is barren and dry.... I see no mountains around here, just land, very flat and dry. One of my brothers has died. I'm feeling better, but the pain is still there." However, she did not live much longer. "I'm lying on a pallet with some type of covering." She was very ill, and no amount of garlic or other herbs could prevent her death. Soon she was floating above her body, drawn to the familiar light. She waited patiently for someone to come to her.

12   Her head began to roll slowly from side to side, as if she were scanning some scene. Her voice was again husky and loud.

13   "They tell me there are many gods, for God is in each of us."

14   I recognized the voice from the in-between–lives state by its huskiness as well as by the decidedly spiritual tone of the message. What she said next left me breathless, pulling the air from my lungs.

15   "Your father is here, and your son, who is a small child. Your father says you will know him because his name is Avrom, and your daughter is named after him. Also, his death was due to his heart. Your son's heart was also important, for it was backward, like a chicken's. He made a great sacrifice for you out of his love. His soul is very advanced.... His death satisfied his parents' debts. Also he wanted to show you that medicine could only go so far, that its scope is very limited."

16   Catherine stopped speaking, and I sat in an awed silence as my numbed mind tried to sort things out. The room felt icy cold.

17   Catherine knew very little about my personal life. On my desk I had a baby picture of my daughter, grinning happily with her two bottom baby teeth in an otherwise empty mouth. My son's picture was next to it. Otherwise Catherine knew virtually nothing about my family or my personal history. I had been well schooled in traditional psychotherapeutic techniques. The therapist was supposed to be a tabula rasa, a blank tablet upon which the patient could project her own feelings, thoughts, and attitudes. These then could be analyzed by the therapist, enlarging the arena of the patient's mind. I had kept this therapeutic distance with Catherine. She really knew me only as a psychiatrist, nothing of my past or of my private life. I had never even displayed my diplomas in the office.

18   The greatest tragedy in my life had been the unexpected death of our firstborn son, Adam, who was only twenty-three days old when he

died, early in 1971. About ten days after we had brought him home from the hospital, he had developed respiratory problems and projectile vomiting. The diagnosis was extremely difficult to make. "Total anomalous pulmonary venous drainage with an atrial septal defect," we were told. "It occurs once in approximately every ten million births." The pulmonary veins, which were supposed to bring oxygenated blood back to the heart, were incorrectly routed, entering the heart on the wrong side. It was as if his heart were turned around, *backward.* Extremely, extremely rare.

Heroic open-heart surgery could not save Adam, who died several days later. We mourned for months, our hopes and dreams dashed. Our son, Jordan, was born a year later, a grateful balm for our wounds.

At the time of Adam's death, I had been wavering about my earlier choice of psychiatry as a career. I was enjoying my internship in internal medicine, and I had been offered a residency position in medicine. After Adam's death, I firmly decided that I would make psychiatry my profession. I was angry that modern medicine, with all of its advanced skills and technology, could not save my son, this simple, tiny baby.

My father had been in excellent health until he experienced a massive heart attack early in 1979, at the age of sixty-one. He survived the initial attack, but his heart wall had been irretrievably damaged, and he died three days later. This was about nine months before Catherine's first appointment.

My father had been a religious man, more ritualistic than spiritual. His Hebrew name, Avrom, suited him better than the English, Alvin. Four months after his death, our daughter, Amy, was born, and she was named after him.

Here, in 1982, in my quiet, darkened office, a deafening cascade of hidden, secret truths was pouring upon me. I was swimming in a spiritual sea, and I loved the water. My arms were gooseflesh. Catherine could not possibly know this information. There was no place even to look it up. My father's *Hebrew* name, that I had a son who died in infancy from a one-in-ten-million heart defect, my brooding about medicine, my father's death, and my daughter's naming—it was too much, too specific, too true. This unsophisticated laboratory technician was a conduit for transcendental knowledge. And if she could reveal these truths, what else was there? I needed to know more.

"Who," I sputtered, "who is there? Who tells you these things?"

"The Masters," she whispered, "the Master Spirits tell me. They tell me I have lived eighty-six times in physical state."

Catherine's breathing slowed, and her head stopped rolling from side to side. She was resting. I wanted to go on, but the implications of what she had said were distracting me. Did she really have eighty-six previous lifetimes? And what about "the Masters"? Could it be? Could our lives be guided by spirits who have no physical bodies but who seem to possess great knowledge. Are there steps on the way to God? Was this real? I found it difficult to doubt, in view of what she had just revealed, yet I still struggled to believe. I was overcoming years of alternative programming. But in my head and my heart and my gut, I knew she was right. She was revealing truths.

27   And what about my father and my son? In a sense, they were still alive; they had never really died. They were talking to me, years after their burials, and proving it by providing specific, very secret information. And since all that was true, was my son as advanced spiritually as Catherine had said? Did he indeed agree to be born to us and then die twenty-three days later in order to help us with our karmic debts and, in addition, to teach me about medicine and humankind, to nudge me back to psychiatry? I was very heartened by these thoughts. Beneath my chill, I felt a great love stirring, a strong feeling of oneness and connection with the heavens and the earth. I had missed my father and my son. It was good to hear from them again.

28   My life would never be the same again. A hand had reached down and irreversibly altered the course of my life. All of my reading, which had been done with careful scrutiny and skeptical detachment, fell into place. Catherine's memories and messages were true. My intuitions about the accuracy of her experiences had been correct. I had the facts. I had the proof.

29   Yet, even in that very instant of joy and understanding, even in that moment of the mystical experience, the old and familiar logical and doubting part of my mind lodged in objection. Perhaps it's just ESP or some psychic skill. Granted, it's quite a skill, but it doesn't prove reincarnation or Master Spirits. Yet this time I knew better. The thousands of cases recorded in the scientific literature, especially those of children speaking foreign languages to which they had never been exposed, of having birthmarks at the site of previous mortal wounds, of these same children knowing where treasured objects were hidden or buried thousands of miles away and decades or centuries earlier, all echoed Catherine's message. I knew Catherine's character and her mind. I knew what she was and what she wasn't. No, my mind could not fool me this time. The proof was too strong and too overwhelming. This was real. She would verify more and more as our sessions progressed.

30   At times over the succeeding weeks I would forget the power and immediacy of this session. At times I would fall back into the rut of everyday life, worrying about the usual things. Doubts would surface. It was as if my mind, when not focused, tended to drift back into the old patterns, beliefs, and skepticism. But then I would remind myself—this actually happened! I appreciated how difficult it is to believe these con-

cepts without having personal experience. The experience is necessary to add emotional belief to intellectual understanding. But the impact of experience always fades to some degree.

At first, I was not aware of why I was changing so much. I knew I was more calm and patient, and others were telling me how peaceful I looked, how I seemed more rested and happier. I felt more hope, more joy, more purpose, and more satisfaction in my life. It dawned on me that I was losing the fear of death. I wasn't afraid of my own death or of nonexistence. I was less afraid of losing others, even though I would certainly miss them. How powerful the fear of death is. People go to such great lengths to avoid the fear: mid-life crises, affairs with younger people, cosmetic surgeries, exercise obsessions, accumulating material possessions, procreating to carry on a name, striving to be more and more youthful, and so on. We are frightfully concerned with our own deaths, sometimes so much so that we forget the real purpose of our lives. 31

I was also becoming less obsessive. I didn't need to be in control all the time. Although I was trying to become less serious, this transformation was difficult for me. I still had much to learn. 32

My mind was indeed now open to the possibility, even the probability, that Catherine's utterances were real. The incredible facts about my father and my son could not be obtained through the usual senses. Her knowledge and abilities certainly proved an outstanding psychic ability. It made sense to believe her, but I remained wary and skeptical about what I read in the popular literature. Who are these people reporting psychic phenomena, life after death, and other amazing paranormal events? Are they trained in the scientific method of observation and validation? Despite my overwhelming and wonderful experience with Catherine, I knew my naturally critical mind would continue to scrutinize every new fact, every piece of information. I would check to see if it fit into the framework being built with every session. I would examine it from every angle, with a scientist's microscope. And yet I could no longer deny that the framework was already there. 33

✦ Questions for Discussion and Writing

1. How does Weiss's training and background make him more skeptical in critically evaluating the phenomena of past life regression?

2. What logical possibilities, explanations, and alternatives does Weiss consider and then reject?

3. Why were Catherine's revelations under hypnosis about Weiss's family so unsettling? How did this experience alter Weiss's preconceptions?

4. Can you think of any other explanation for the phenomena Weiss describes? Have you or anyone you know had an experience that suggested the existence of reincarnation? In a short essay, discuss your views on this subject.

5. Weiss's experiences led him to believe that people may have lived before and may live again without being aware that this is the case. Write a letter to your future self, sharing important details about your life that you would want remembered from one life to another.

Connections

1. Compare Sullivan Ballou's letter with Robert Falcon Scott's journal entries to discover similarities about (a) the conditions under which each account was written, and (b) the way each writer wished to be remembered.

2. How do Peter Matthiessen and Brian L. Weiss, each coming from a very different perspective, approach the possibility of life beyond death?

3. What do the journal entries of Audre Lorde and Robert Falcon Scott reveal about each writer's values in the face of almost certain death?

4. Compare the motivations and objectives of Robert Falcon Scott to those of Meriwether Lewis and William Clark ("The Journals of Lewis and Clark," Chapter 9) in writing such detailed journals.

5. How did the traditional training Brian L. Weiss and Jean Henri Fabre ("The Praying Mantis," Chapter 4) received in their respective disciplines of psychiatry and entomology enable each one to objectively react to unfamiliar phenomena?

12

Autobiographical Fiction: A Boundary Genre

---◆---

I write fiction and I'm told it's autobiography, I write autobiography and I'm told it's fiction, so since I'm so dim and they're so smart, let them decide what it is or it isn't.

—Philip Roth, *Deception*, 1990

There is no longer any such thing as fiction or non-fiction; there is only narrative.

—E. L. Doctorow, *New York Times Book Review*,
January 27, 1988

The boundary between autobiographical narratives and works of fiction is not as distinct as one might imagine. Both kinds of writing can communicate intense, complex, deeply felt responses to human experiences. Like fiction writers, autobiographers reinvent what has already occurred by reconstructing the meaning and significance of past events. The autobiographies we have read in previous chapters offer insight into the process by which one's own past, and indeed one's self, is constructed or discovered anew. In this sense, autobiography does not simply retell the past, but it confers meanings on experiences that these events did not possess at the time they occurred.

In both fiction and nonfiction, the interpretive act of remembering creates new relationships between the past and the present, so that perceiving a life narrative often becomes indistinguishable from inventing one. The motives for writing autobiography and fiction stem from a desire to understand one's own experience by conferring form and order on events and relationships that otherwise would remain ill-defined.

Moreover, the act of writing always entails selective recollections that fuse aspects of identity that have previously gone unarticulated.

Yet there are important differences between fiction and autobiography. Fiction writers have greater flexibility in restructuring their narratives in ways that create suspense and conflict. They can add to or take away from the known facts, expand or compress time, add imaginative details, or even invent new characters or a narrator through whose eyes the story is told. Thus, fiction acts to transform what is real into what can be imagined. By contrast, autobiographical works move in the opposite direction. The writer's wish to repossess a lost or dispersed self entails a search for a more authentic prefictional self conceived without falsification or dramatization.

In each of the following works, we can observe the writers using the freedom offered by fiction to question and enlarge the meaning of experiences that these events did not have when they occurred. In each case, the goal is to create an imagined self whose story makes sense of the past.

Natsume Soseki uses the fictional vantage point provided by a household pet, in "I Am a Cat," to make telling observations about a Japanese professor and his family. Based on Tadeusz Borowski's harrowing experiences in the Auschwitz concentration camp, "This Way for the Gas, Ladies and Gentlemen" offers an uncompromising picture of the extremes to which prisoners will go in order to survive. In "Black Hair," Gary Soto dramatizes his plight as a Mexican American working at a low-paying job in a tire factory. In "Two Kinds," Amy Tan ruefully reminisces about trying to meet her mother's expectation that her daughter would become a doctor by profession and an accomplished pianist for recreation.

Natsume Soseki

I Am a Cat

◆

Natsume Soseki (1867–1916) was one of Japan's most distinguished writers. He taught English at Tokyo University and was literary editor of the Asahi Newspaper. *Considered to be a milestone in Japanese literature, I Am a Cat (1905) brought Soseki instant recognition as an incisive observer of Japanese bourgeois life. This work was translated into English by Katsue Shibata and Motomari Kai in 1961. Soseki's work, like that of other twentieth-century Japanese writers, reveals the influence of the West on Japanese life and culture. The first chapter from* I Am a Cat *introduces a professor of English and his family as they appear through the eyes of a cat who has taken up residence in their home.*

1   I am a cat but as yet I have no name.

2   I haven't the faintest idea of where I was born. The first thing I do remember is that I was crying "meow, meow," somewhere in a gloomy damp place. It was there that I met a human being for the first time in my life. Though I found this all out at a later date, I learned that this human being was called a Student, one of the most ferocious of the human race. I also understand that these Students sometimes catch us, cook us and then take to eating us. But at that time, I did not have the slightest idea of all this so I wasn't frightened a bit. When this Student placed me on the palm of his hand and lifted me up lightly, I only had the feeling of floating around. After a while, I got used to this position and looked around. This was probably the first time I had a good look at a so-called "human being." What impressed me as being most strange still remains deeply imbedded in my mind: the face which should have been covered with hair was a slippery thing similar to what I now know to be a teakettle. I have since come across many other cats but none of them are such freaks. Moreover, the center of the Student's face protruded to a great extent, and from the two holes located there, he would often emit smoke. I was extremely annoyed by being choked by this. That this was what they term as tobacco, I came to know only recently.

3   I was snuggled up comfortably in the palm of this Student's hand when, after a while, I started to travel around at a terrific speed. I was unable to find out if the Student was moving or if it was just myself that was in motion, but in any case I became terribly dizzy and a little

sick. Just as I was thinking that I couldn't last much longer at this rate, I heard a thud and saw sparks. I remember everything up till that moment but think as hard as I can, I can't recall what took place immediately after this.

When I came to, I could not find the Student anywhere. Nor could I find the many cats that had been with me either. Moreover, my dear mother had also disappeared. And the extraordinary thing was that this place, when compared to where I had been before, was extremely bright—ever so bright. I could hardly keep my eyes open. This was because I had been removed from my straw bed and thrown into a bamboo bush.

Finally, mustering up my strength, I crawled out from his bamboo grove and found myself before a large pond. I sat on my haunches and tried to take in the situation. I didn't know what to do but suddenly I had an idea. If I could attract some attention by meowing, the Student might come back to me. I commenced but this was to no avail; nobody came.

By this time, the wind had picked up and came blowing across the pond. Night was falling. I sensed terrible pangs of hunger. Try as I would, my voice failed me and I felt as if all hope were lost. In any case, I resolved to get myself to a place where there was food and so, with this decision in mind, I commenced to circle the water by going around to the left.

This was very difficult but at any rate, I forced myself along and eventually came to a locality where I sensed Man. Finding a hole in a broken bamboo fence, I crawled through, having confidence that it was worth the try, and lo! I found myself within somebody's estate. Fate is strange; if that hole had not been there, I might have starved to death by the roadside. It is well said that every tree may offer shelter. For a long time afterwards, I often used this hole for my trips to call on Mike, the tomcat living next door.

Having sneaked into the estate, I was at a loss as to what the next step should be. Darkness had come and my belly cried for food. The cold was bitter and it started to rain. I had no time to fool around any longer so I went in to a room that looked bright and cozy. Coming to think of it now, I had entered somebody's home for the first time. It was there that I was to confront other humans.

The first person I met was the maid Osan. This was a human much worse than the Student. As soon as she saw me, she grabbed me by the neck and threw me outdoors. I sensed I had no chance against her sudden action so I shut my eyes and let things take their course. But I couldn't endure the hunger and the cold any longer. I don't know how many times I was thrown out but because of this, I came to dislike Osan all through. That's one reason why I stole the fish the other day and why I felt so proud of myself.

10   When the maid was about to throw me out for the last time, the master of the house made his appearance and asked what all the row was about. The maid turned to him with me hanging limp from her hand, and told him that she had repeatedly tried throwing this stray cat out but that it always kept sneaking into the kitchen again—and that she didn't like it at all. The master, twisting his moustache, looked at me for a while and then told the maid to let me in. He then left the room. I took it that the master was a man of few words. The maid, still mad at me, threw me down on the kitchen floor. In such a way, I was able to establish this place as my home.

11   At first it was very seldom that I got to see my master. He seemed to be a schoolteacher. Coming home from school he'd shut himself up in his study and would hardly come out for the rest of the day. His family thought him to be very studious and my master also made out as if he were. But actually, he wasn't as hard working as they all believed him to be. I'd often sneak up and look into his study only to find him taking a nap. Sometimes I would find him drivelling on the book he had been reading before dozing off.

12   He was a man with a weak stomach so his skin was somewhat yellowish. He looked parched and inactive, yet he was a great consumer of food. After eating as much as he possibly could, he'd take a dose of Taka-diastase and then open a book. After reading a couple of pages, however, he'd become drowsy and again commence drooling. This was his daily routine. Though I am a cat myself, at times I think that schoolteachers are very fortunate. If I were to be reborn a man, I would, without doubt, become a teacher. If you can keep a job and still sleep as much as my master did, even cats could manage such a profession. But according to my master—and he makes it plain—there's nothing so hard as teaching. Especially when his friends come to visit him, he does a lot of complaining.

13   When I first came to this home, nobody but the master was nice to me. Wherever I went, they would kick me around and I was given no other consideration. The fact that they haven't given me a name even as of today goes to show how much they care for me. That's why I try to stay close to my master.

14   In the morning, when my master reads the papers, I always sit on his lap; and when he takes his nap, I perch on his back. This doesn't mean that he likes it, but then, on the other hand, it doesn't mean that he dislikes it—it has simply become a custom.

15   Experience taught me that it is best for me to sleep on the container for boiled rice in the mornings as it is warm, and on a charcoal-burning foot warmer in the evenings. I generally sleep on the veranda on fine days. But most of all, I like to crawl into the same bed with the children

of the house at night. By children, I mean the girls who are five and three years old respectively. They sleep together in the same bed in their own room. In some way or other, I try to slip into their bed and crawl in between them. But if one of them wakes up, then it is terrible. The girls—especially the smaller one—raise an awful cry in the middle of the night and holler, "There's that cat in here again!" At this, my weak-stomached master wakes up and comes in to help them. It was only the other day that he gave me a terrible whipping with a ruler for indulging in this otherwise pleasant custom.

In coming to live with human beings, I have had the chance to ob- 16
serve them and the more I do the more I come to the conclusion that they are terribly spoiled, especially the children. When they feel like it, they hold you upside down or cover your head with a bag; and at times, they throw you around or try squeezing you into the cooking range. And on top of that, should you so much as bare a claw to try to stop them, the whole family is after you. The other day, for instance, I tried sharpening my claws just for a second on the straw mat of the living room when the Mrs. noticed me. She got furious and from then on, she won't let me in the sitting room. I can be cold and shivering in the kitchen but they never take the trouble to bother about me. When I met Shiro across the street whom I respected, she kept telling me there was nothing as inconsiderate as humans.

Only the other day, four cute little kittens were born to Shiro. But 17
the Student who lives with the family threw all four of them into a pond behind the house on the third day. Shiro told me all this in tears and said that in order for us cats to fulfill parental affection and to have a happy life, we will have to overthrow the human race. Yes, what she said was all very logical. Mi-ke, next door, was extremely furious when I told him about Shiro. He said that humans did not understand the right of possession of others. With us cats, however, the first one that finds the head of a dried sardine or the navel of a gray mullet gets the right to eat it. Should anyone try to violate this rule, we are allowed to use force in order to keep our find. But humans depend on their great strength to take what is legally ours away from us and think it right.

Shiro lives in the home of a soldier and Mi-ke in the home of a law- 18
yer. I live in the home of a schoolteacher and, in comparison, I am far more optimistic about such affairs than either of them. I am satisfied only in trying to live peacefully day after day. I don't believe that the human race will prosper forever so all I have to do is to relax and wait for the time when cats will reign.

Coming to think of the way they act according to their whims—an- 19
other word for selfishness—I'm going to tell you more about my master. To tell the truth, my master can't do anything well but he likes to stick his nose into everything. Going in for composing *haiku*, he contributes his poems to the *Hototogisu* magazine, or writes some modern

poetry for the *Myojo* magazine; or at times, he composes a piece in English, but all grammatically wrong. Then again, he finds himself engrossed in archery or tries singing lyrical plays; or maybe he tries a hand at playing discordant tunes on the violin. What is most disheartening is the fact that he cannot manage any of them well. Though he has a weak stomach, he does his best.

20   When he enters the toilet, he commences chanting so he is nicknamed "Mr. Mensroom" by his neighbors. Yet, he doesn't mind such things and continues his chanting: "This is Taira-no-Munemori...." Everybody says, "There goes Munemori again," and then bursts out laughing. I don't know exactly what had come over him about a month after I first established myself at his place, but one pay day he came home all excited carrying with him a great big bundle. I couldn't help feeling curious about the contents.

21   The package happened to contain a set of water colors, brushes and drawing paper. It seems that he had given up lyrical plays and writing verses and was going in for painting. The following day, he shut himself up in his study and without even taking his daily nap, he drew pictures. This continued day after day. But what he drew remained a mystery because others could not even guess what they were. My master finally came to the conclusion that he wasn't as good a painter as he had thought himself to be. One day he came home with a man who considers himself an aesthetic and I heard them talking to each other.

22   "It's funny but it's difficult to draw as well as you want. When a painting is done by others, it looks so simple. But when you do a work with a brush yourself, it's quite a different thing," said my master. Coming to think of it, he did have plenty of proof to back up his statement.

23   His friend, looking over his gold-rimmed glasses, said, "You can't expect to draw well right from the beginning. In the first place, you can't expect to draw anything just from imagination, and by shutting yourself up in a room at that. Once the famous Italian painter Andrea del Sarto said that to draw, you have to interpret nature in its original form. The stars in the sky, the earth with flowers shining with dew, the flight of birds and the running animals, the ponds with their goldfish, and the black crow in a withered tree—nature is the one great panorama of the living world. How about it? If you want to draw something recognizable, why not do some sketching?"

24   "Did del Sarto really say all those things? I didn't know that. All right, just as you say," said my master with admiration. The eyes behind the gold-rimmed glasses shone, but with scorn.

25   The following day, as I was peacefully enjoying my daily nap on the veranda, my master came out from his study, something quite out of the ordinary, and sat down beside me. Wondering what he was up to, I slit my eyes open just a wee bit and took a look. I found him trying out Andrea del Sarto's theory on me. I could not suppress a smile. Hav-

ing been encouraged by his friend, my master was using me as a model.

I tried to be patient and pretended to continue my nap. I wanted to yawn like anything but when I thought of my master trying his best to sketch me, I felt sorry for him, and so I killed it. He first drew my face in outline and then began to add colors. I'd like to make a confession here: as far as cats are concerned, I have to admit that I'm not one of those you'd call perfect or beautiful; my back, my fur or even my face cannot be considered superior in any way to those of other cats. Yet, even though I may be uncomely, I am hardly as ugly as what my master was painting. In the first place, he shaded my color all wrong. I am really somewhat like a Persian cat, a light gray with a shade of yellow with lacquer-like spots—as can be vouched by anyone. But according to my master's painting, my color was not yellow nor was it black. It wasn't gray or brown. It wasn't even a combination of these colors but something more like a smearing together of many tones. What was most strange about the drawing was that I had no eyes. Of course, I was being sketched while taking a nap so I won't complain too much, but you couldn't even find the location of where they should have been. You couldn't tell if I was a sleeping cat or a blind cat. I thought, way down inside me, that if this is what they called the Andrea del Sarto way of drawing pictures, it wasn't worth a sen.

But as to the enthusiasm of my master, I had to bow my head humbly. I couldn't disappoint him by moving but, if you'll excuse my saying so, I had wanted to go outside to relieve myself from a long while back. The muscles of my body commenced fidgeting and I felt that I couldn't hold out much longer. So, trying to excuse myself, I stretched out my forelegs, gave my neck a little twist and indulged in a long slow yawn. Going this far, there was no need for me to stay still any longer because I had changed my pose. I then stepped outside to accomplish my object.

But my master, in disappointment and rage, shouted from within the room, "You fool!" My master, in abusing others, has the habit of using this expression. "You fool!" This is the best he can manage as he doesn't know any other way to swear. Even though he had not known how long I had endured the urgent call of nature, I still consider him uncivilized for this. If he had ever given me a smile or some other encouragement when I climbed onto his back, I could have forgiven him this time, but the fact is that he never considers my convenience. That he should holler, "You fool!" only because I was about to go and relieve myself was more than I could stand. In the first place, humans take too much for granted. If some power doesn't appear to control them better, there's no telling how far they will go in their excesses.

I could endure their being so self-willed but I've heard many other complaints regarding mankind's lack of virtue, and they are much worse.

30   Right in back of the house, there is a patch of tea plants. It isn't large but it is nice and sunny. When the children of the house are so noisy that I can't enjoy my naps peacefully or when, because of idleness, my digestion is bad, I usually go out to the tea patch to enjoy the magnanimous surroundings. One lovely autumn day about two o'clock in the afternoon, after taking my after-lunch nap, I took a stroll through this patch. I walked along, smelling each tea plant as I went, until I reached a cryptomeria hedge at the west end.

31   There I found a large cat sleeping soundly, using a withered chrysanthemum in lieu of a mat. It seemed as if he didn't notice me coming, for he kept snoring loudly. I was overwhelmed at his boldness;—after sneaking into somebody else's yard. He was a big black cat.

32   The sun, now past midday, cast its brilliant rays upon his body and reflected themselves to give the impression of flames bursting from his soft fur. He had such a big frame that he seemed fit to be called a king of the feline family. He was more than twice my size. Admiration and a feeling of curiosity made me forget the past and the future, and I could only stare at him.

33   The soft autumn breeze made the branches of the paulawnia above quiver lightly and a couple of leaves came fluttering down upon the thicket of dead chrysanthemums. Then the great "king" opened his eyes. I can still feel the thrill of that moment. The amber light in his eyes shone much brighter than the jewels man holds as precious. He did not move at all. The glance he shot at me concentrated on my small forehead, and he abruptly asked me who I was. The great king's directness betrayed his rudeness. Yet, there was a power in his voice that would have terrified dogs, and I found myself shaking with fear. But thinking it inadvisable not to pay my respects, I said, "I am a cat though, as yet, I don't have any name." I said this while pretending to be at ease but actually my heart was beating away at a terrific speed. Despite my courteous reply, he said, "A cat? You don't say so! Where do you live?" He was extremely audacious.

34   "I live here in the schoolteacher's house."

35   "I thought so. You sure are skinny." Gathering from his rudeness I couldn't imagine him coming from a very good family. But, judging from his plump body, he seemed to be well fed and able to enjoy an easy life. As for myself, I couldn't refrain from asking, "And you are you?"

36   "Me? Huh—I'm Kuro, living at the rickshawman's place."

37   So this was the cat living at the rickshawman's house! He was known in the vicinity as being awfully unruly. Actually he was admired within the home of the rickshawman but, having no education, nobody else befriended him. He was a hoodlum from whom others shied. When I heard him tell me who he was, I felt somewhat uneasy

and, at the same time, I felt slightly superior. With the intention of finding out how much learning he had, I asked him some more questions.

"I was just wondering which of the two is the greater—the rickshawman or the schoolteacher." 38

"What a question! The rickshawman, naturally. Just take a look at your teacher—he's all skin and bones," he snorted. 39

"You look extremely strong. Most probably, living at the rickshawman's house, you get plenty to eat." 40

"What? I don't go unfed anywhere! Stick with me for a while instead of going around in circles in the tea patch and you'll look better yourself in less than a month." 41

"Sure, some day, maybe. But to me, it seems as though the schoolteacher lives in a bigger house than the rickshawman," I purred. 42

"Huh! What if the house is big? That doesn't mean you get your belly full there, does it?" 43

He seemed extremely irritated and, twitching his pointed ears, he walked away without saying another word. This was my first encounter with Kuro of the house of the rickshawman, but not the last. 44

Since then, we've often talked together. Whenever we do, Kuro always commences bragging, as one living with a rickshawman would. 45

One day, we were lying in the tea patch and indulging in some small talk. As usual, he kept bragging about the adventures he had had, and then he got around to asking me, "By the way, how many rats have you killed?" 46

Intellectually I am much more developed than Kuro but when it comes to using strength and showing bravado, there is no comparison. I was prepared for something like this but when he actually asked me the question, I felt extremely embarrassed. But facts are facts; I could not lie to him: "To tell the truth, I have been wanting to catch one for a long time but the opportunity has never come." 47

Kuro twitched the whiskers which stood out straight from his muzzle and laughed hard. Kuro is conceited, as those who brag usually are, so when I find him being sarcastic I try to say something to appease him. In this way, I am able to manage him pretty well. Having learned this during our first meeting, I stayed calm when he laughed. I realized that it would be foolish to commit myself now by giving unasked-for reasons. I figured it best, at this stage, to let him brag about his own adventures and so I purred quietly, "Being as old as you are, you've probably caught a lot of rats yourself." I was trying to get him to talk about himself. And, as I had expected, he took the bait. 48

"Well, can't say a lot—maybe about thirty or forty." He was very proud of this and continued, "I could handle one or two hundred rats alone but when it comes to weasels, they're not to my liking. A weasel once gave me a terrible time." 49

50   "So? And what happened?" I chimed in. Kuro blinked several times before he continued. "It was at the time of our annual house-cleaning last summer. The master crawled under the veranda to put away a sack of lime, and—what do you think? He surprised a big weasel which came bouncing out."

51   "Oh?" I pretended to admire him.

52   "As you know, a weasel is only a little bigger than a rat. Thinking him to be just another big mouse, I cornered him in a ditch."

53   "You did?"

54   "Yeah. Just as I was going in for the *coup-de-grace*—can you imagine what he did? Well, it raised its tail and—ooph! You ought to have taken a whiff. Even now when I see a weasel I get giddy." So saying, he rubbed his nose with one of his paws as if he were still trying to stop the smell. I felt somewhat sorry for him so, with the thought of trying to liven him up a little, I said, "But when it comes to rats, I hardly believe they would have a chance against you. Being such a famous rat catcher, you probably eat nothing else and that's why you're so plump and glossy, I'm sure."

55   I had said this to get him into a better mood but actually it had the contrary effect. He let a big sigh escape and replied, "When you come to think of it, it's not all fun. Rats are interesting but, you know, there's nobody as crafty as humans in this world. They take all the rats I catch over to the police box. The policeman there doesn't know who actually catches them so he hands my master five sen per head. Because of me, my master has made a neat profit of one yen and fifty sen, but yet he doesn't give me any decent food. Do you know what humans are? Well, I'll tell you. They're men, yes, but thieves at heart."

56   Even Kuro, who was not any too bright, understood such logic and he bristled his back in anger. I felt somewhat uneasy so I murmured some excuse and went home. It was because of this conversation that I made up my mind never to catch rats. But, on the other hand, neither do I go around hunting for other food. Instead of eating an extravagant dinner, I simply go to sleep. A cat living with a schoolteacher gets to become, in nature, just like a teacher himself. If I'm not careful I might still become just as weak in the stomach as my master.

57   Speaking of my master the schoolteacher, it finally dawned upon him that he could not ever hope to get anywhere with water-color painting. He wrote the following entry in his diary, dated December 1:

58   Met a man today at a party. It's said that he's a debauchee and he looked like one. Such individuals are liked by women, so it may be quite proper to say that such people cannot help becoming dissipated. His wife was formerly a geisha girl and I envy him. Most of the people who criticize debauchees generally have no chance to become one themselves. Still, others who claim to be debauchees have no qualifications to become so worldly. They simply force themselves into that position. Just

as in the case of my water-color painting, there was absolutely no fear of my making good. But indifferent to others, I might think that I was good at it. If some men are considered worldly only because they drink *sake* at restaurants, frequent geisha houses and stop over for the night, and go through all the necessary motions, then it stands to reason that I should be able to call myself a remarkable painter. But my water-color paintings will never be a success.

In regard to this theory, I cannot agree. That a schoolteacher should   59
envy a man who has a wife who was once a geisha shows how foolish and inferior my master is. But his criticism of himself as a water-color painter is unquestionably true. Though my master understands many of his own shortcomings, he cannot get over being terribly conceited. On December 4, he wrote:

> Last night, I attempted another painting but I have finally come to un-   60
> derstand that I have no talent. I dreamed that somebody had framed the pictures I have laying around, and had hung them on the wall. Upon seeing them framed, I suddenly thought that I was an excellent painter. I felt happy and kept looking but, when the day dawned, I awoke and again clearly realized that I am still a painter of no talent.

Even in his dreams, my master seemed to regret his having given   61
up painting. This is characteristic of a learned man, a frustrated water-color painter and one who can never become a man of the world.

The day after my master had had his dream, his friend, the man of   62
arts, came to see him again. The first question he asked my master was "How are the pictures getting along?"

My master calmly answered, "According to your advice I'm work-   63
ing hard at sketching. Just as you said, I am finding interesting shapes and detailed changes of colors which I had never noticed before. Due to the fact that artists in Western countries have persisted in sketching, they have reached the development we see today. Yes, all this must be due to Andrea del Sarto." He did not mention what he had written in his diary, but only continued to show his admiration for del Sarto.

The artist scratched his head and commenced to laugh, "That was   64
all a joke, my friend."

"What's that?" My master didn't seem to understand.   65

"Andrea del Sarto is only a person of my own highly imaginative   66
creation. I didn't think you'd take it so seriously. Ha, ha, ha." The artist was greatly enjoying himself.

Listening to all this from the veranda, I couldn't help wondering   67
what my master would write in his diary about that conversation. This artist was a person who took great pleasure in fooling others. As if he did not realize how his joke about Andrea del Sarto hurt my master, he boasted more: "When playing jokes, some people take them so seriously that they reveal great comic beauty, and it's a lot of fun. The other

day I told a student that Nicholas Nickleby had advised Gibbon to translate his great story of the French Revolution from a French text-book and to have it published under his own name. This student has an extremely good memory and made a speech at the Japanese Literature Circle quoting everything I had told him. There were about a hundred people in the audience and they all listened very attentively. Then there's another time. One evening, at a gathering of writers, the conversation turned to Harrison's historical novel *Theophano*. I said that it was one of the best historical novels ever written, especially the part where the heroine dies. 'That really gives you the creeps'—that's what I said. An author who was sitting opposite me was one of those types who cannot and will not say no to anything. He immediately voiced the opinion that that was a most famous passage. I knew right away that he had never read any more of the story than I had."

68   With wide eyes, my nervous and weak-stomached master asked, "What would you have done if the other man had really read the story?"

69   The artist did not show any excitement. He thought nothing of fooling other people. The only thing that counted was not to be caught in the act.

70   "All I would have had to do is to say that I had made a mistake in the title or something to that effect." He kept on laughing. Though this artist wore a pair of gold-rimmed glasses, he looked somewhat like Kuro of the rickshawman's.

71   My master blew a few smoke rings but he had an expression on his face that showed he wouldn't have the nerve to do such a thing. The artist, with a look in his eyes as if saying, "That's why you can't paint pictures," only continued. "Jokes are jokes but, getting down to facts, it's not easy to draw. They say that Leonardo da Vinci once told his pupils to copy a smear on a wall. That's good advice. Sometimes when you're gazing at water leaking along the wall in a privy, you see some good patterns. Copy them carefully and you're bound to get some good designs."

72   "You're only trying to fool me again."

73   "No, not this time. Don't you think it's a wonderful idea? Just what da Vinci himself would have suggested."

74   "Just as you say," replied my master, half surrendering. But he still hasn't made any sketches in the privy—at least not yet.

75   Kuro of the rickshawman's wasn't looking well. His glossy fur began to fade and fall out. His eyes, which I formerly compared to amber, began to collect mucus. What was especially noticeable was his lack of energy. When I met him in the tea patch, I asked him how he felt.

"I'm still disgusted with the weasel's stink and with the fisherman. 76
The fish seller hit me with a pole again the other day."

The red leaves of the maple tree were beginning to show contrast to 77
the green of the pines here and there. The maples shed their foliage like
dreams of the past. The fluttering petals of red and white fell from the
tea plants one after another until there were none remaining. The sun
slanted its rays deeper and deeper into the southern veranda and seldom did a day pass that the late autumn wind didn't blow. I felt as
though my napping hours were being shortened.

My master still went to school every day and, coming home, he'd 78
still bottle himself up in his study. When he had visitors he'd continue
to complain about his job. He hardly ever touched his water colors
again. He had discontinued taking Taka-diastase for his indigestion,
saying that it didn't do him any good. It was wonderful now that the
little girls were attending kindergarten every day but returning home,
they'd sing loudly and bounce balls and, at times, they'd still pick me
up by the tail.

I still had nothing much to eat so I did not become very fat but I 79
was healthy enough. I didn't become sick like Kuro and, as always, I
took things as they came. I still didn't try to catch rats, and I still hated
Osan, the maid. I still didn't have a name but you can't always have
what you want. I resigned myself to continue living here at the home of
this schoolteacher as a cat without a name.

✦ Questions for Discussion and Writing

1. Why would a cat, from its own perspective, assume faces should be
   covered with hair? Why would it perceive the center of the student's
   face to be protruding to a great extent?

2. How is the cat's process of justifying the act of stealing the fish quite
   similar to the human characteristic of rationalizing? How do both
   practices involve attributing reasons after the fact to justify an action
   one performed?

3. What standards of behavior can you infer that the cat applies to the behavior of humans in general and to its master in particular? Why is it
   ironic for a cat to call a human "uncivilized"?

4. What additional insights about the master does the cat provide, which
   the schoolteacher has concealed from his family? How does the cat's
   viewpoint complete the picture of the master, showing him as he really
   is compared to the way he would like to be seen?

5. Discuss the subtle or overt similarities between each cat and the characteristics of its owner. For example, how is the unnamed cat like the schoolteacher, Mi-ke like the lawyer, and Kuro like the rickshawman?

6. How does the December 1 entry from the diary show that the schoolteacher deceives himself about the quality of his artistic endeavors?

7. What actions did a pet of yours once take that demonstrated evidence of self-awareness, intelligence, and true emotions? Describe this action or event, and reply to someone who believed that you wanted to interpret it in this way.

8. What could your pet say about you that no one else knows?

9. What choices did you consider in deciding on your pet's name? What important character traits does this name reveal about both you and your pet? What name would you give the cat in Soseki's story, and why?

10. Have you ever observed people address one another indirectly through a pet? To what extent do pets function, in your opinion, as a buffer or foil, that allows people to express real feelings—negative and positive—that they could not express to each other directly?

Tadeusz Borowski

This Way for the Gas, Ladies and Gentlemen

◆

Tadeusz Borowski (1922–1951) was born in the Soviet Ukraine of Polish parents and was educated by attending secret lectures at Warsaw University during the Nazi occupation of Poland. He published his first volume of verse, Whenever the Earth, *in 1942. The following year he was arrested by the Gestapo and ultimately sent to Auschwitz, where he survived by working as a hospital orderly. After the war, Borowski returned to Warsaw, where he lectured at the University. In 1946, the first of three collections based on his concentration camp experiences was published in Munich.* Farewell to Maria *and* A World of Stone *were published in Poland in 1948. The experience of his own dehumanization in the brutalizing conditions of Auschwitz formed the basis for his most significant work on the Holocaust, ironically titled, "This Way for the Gas, Ladies and Gentlemen" (1967). Borowski's searing, unsentimental portrayal of life in the concentration camps is told from the viewpoint of Vorabeiter ("foreman") Tadeusz, a narrator with whom Borowski himself is identified. Tragically, Borowski, who had survived the gas chambers and was seen as the bright hope of Polish literature, took his own life in July of 1951 at the age of 29 by turning on the gas.*

All of us walk around naked. The delousing is finally over, and our striped suits are back from the tanks of Cyclone B solution, an efficient killer of lice in clothing and of men in gas chambers. Only the inmates in the blocks cut off from ours by the "Spanish goats"[1] still have nothing to wear. But all the same, all of us walk around naked: the heat is unbearable. The camp has been sealed off tight. Not a single prisoner, not one solitary louse, can sneak through the gate. The labour Kommandos have stopped working. All day, thousands of naked men shuffle up and down the roads, cluster around the squares, or lie against the walls and on top of the roofs. We have been sleeping on plain boards, since our mattresses and blankets are still being disinfected. From the rear blockhouses we have a view of the F.K.L.—*Frauen Konzentration Lager;* there too the delousing is in full swing. Twenty-eight thousand

---

[1]Crossed wooden beams wrapped in barbed wire.

women have been stripped naked and driven out of the barracks. Now they swarm around the large yard between the blockhouses.

2   The heat rises, the hours are endless. We are without even our usual diversion: the wide roads leading to the crematoria are empty. For several days now, no new transports have come in. Part of "Canada"[2] has been liquidated and detailed to a labour Kommando—one of the very toughest—at Harmenz. For there exists in the camp a special brand of justice based on envy: when the rich and mighty fall, their friends see to it that they fall to the very bottom. And Canada, our Canada, which smells not of maple forests but of French perfume, has amassed great fortunes in diamonds and currency from all over Europe.

3   Several of us sit on the top bunk, our legs dangling over the edge. We slice the neat loaves of crisp, crunchy bread. It is a bit coarse to the taste, the kind that stays fresh for days. Sent all the way from Warsaw— only a week ago my mother held this white loaf in her hands ... dear Lord, dear Lord ...

4   We unwrap the bacon, the onion, we open a can of evaporated milk. Henri, the fat Frenchman dreams aloud of the French wine brought by the transports from Strasbourg, Paris, Marseille ... Sweat streams down his body.

5   "Listen, *mon ami,* next time we go up on the loading ramp, I'll bring you real champagne. You haven't tried it before, eh?"

6   "No. But you'll never be able to smuggle it through the gate, so stop teasing. Why not try and 'organize' some shoes for me instead— you know, the perforated kind, with a double sole, and what about that shirt you promised me long ago?"

7   "*Patience, patience.* When the new transports come, I'll bring all you want. We'll be going on the ramp again!"

8   "And what if there aren't any more 'cremo' transports?" I say spitefully. "Can't you see how much easier life is becoming around here: no limit on packages, no more beatings? You even write letters home ... One hears all kind of talk, and, dammit, they'll run out of people!"

9   "Stop talking nonsense." Henri's serious fat face moves rhythmically, his mouth full of sardines. We have been friends for a long time, but I do not even know his last name. "Stop talking nonsense," he repeats, swallowing with effort. "They can't run out of people, or we'll starve to death in this blasted camp. All of us live on what they bring."

10   "All? We have our packages ..."

11   "Sure, you and your friend, and ten other friends of yours. Some of you Poles get packages. But what about us, and the Jews, and the

---

[2]"Canada" designated wealth and well-being in the camp. More specifically, it referred to the members of the labour gang, or Kommando, who helped to unload the incoming transports of people destined for the gas chambers.

Russkis? And what if we had no food, no 'organization' from the transports, do you think you'd be eating those packages of yours in peace? We wouldn't let you!"

"You would, you'd starve to death like the Greeks. Around here, 12 whoever has grub, has power."

"Anyway, you have enough, we have enough, so why argue?" 13

Right, why argue? They have enough. I have enough, we eat to- 14 gether and we sleep on the same bunks. Henri slices the bread, he makes a tomato salad. It tastes good with the commissary mustard.

Below us, naked, sweat-drenched men crowd the narrow barracks 15 aisles or lie packed in eights and tens in the lower bunks. Their nude, withered bodies stink of sweat and excrement; their cheeks are hollow. Directly beneath me, in the bottom bunk, lies a rabbi. He has covered his head with a piece of rag torn off a blanket and reads from a Hebrew prayer book (there is no shortage of this type of literature at the camp), wailing loudly, monotonously.

"Can't somebody shut him up? He's been raving as if he'd caught 16 God himself by the feet."

"I don't feel like moving. Let him rave. They'll take him to the oven 17 that much sooner."

"Religion is the opium of the people," Henri, who is a Communist 18 and a *rentier*, says sententiously. "If they didn't believe in God and eternal life, they'd have smashed the crematoria long ago."

"Why haven't you done it then?" 19

The question is rhetorical: the Frenchman ignores it. 20

"Idiot," he says simply, and stuffs a tomato in his mouth. 21

Just as we finish our snack, there is a sudden commotion at the 22 door. The Muslims[3] scurry in fright to the safety of their bunks, a messenger runs into the Block Elder's shack. The Elder, his face solemn, steps out at once.

"Canada! *Antreten!* But fast! There's a transport coming!" 23

"Great God!" yells Henri, jumping off the bunk. He swallows the 24 rest of his tomato, snatches his coat, screams *"Raus"* at the men below, and in a flash is at the door. We can hear a scramble in the other bunks. Canada is leaving for the ramp.

"Henri, the shoes!" I call after him. 25

"Keine Angst!" he shouts back already outside. 26

I proceeded to put away the food. I tie a piece of rope around the 27 suitcase where the onions and the tomatoes from my father's garden in Warsaw mingle with Portuguese sardines, bacon from Lublin (that's from my brother), and authentic sweetmeats from Salonica. I tie it all up, pull on my trousers, and slide off the bunk.

---

[3]"Muslim" was the camp name for a prisoner who had been destroyed physically and spiritually, and who had neither the strength nor the will to go on living—a man ripe for the gas chamber.

28   *"Platz!"* I yell, pushing my way through the Greeks. They step aside. At the door I bump into Henri.

29   *"Was ist los?"*

30   "Want to come with us on the ramp?"

31   "Sure, why not?"

32   "Come along then, grab your coat! We're short of a few men. I've already told the Kapo," and he shoves me out of the barracks door.

33   We line up. Someone has marked down our numbers, someone up ahead yells, "March, march," and now we are running towards the gate, accompanied by the shouts of a multilingual throng that is already being pushed back to the barracks. Not everybody is lucky enough to be going on the ramp... We have almost reached the gate. *Links, zwei, drei, viter! Mutzen ab!* Erect, arms stretched stiffly along our hips, we march past the gate briskly, smartly, almost gracefully. A sleepy S.S. man with a large pad in his hand checks us off, waving us ahead in groups of five.

34   *"Hundert!"* he calls after we have all passed.

35   *"Stimmt!"* comes a hoarse answer from out front.

36   We march fast, almost as a run. There are guards all around, young men with automatics. We pass camp 11 B, then some deserted barracks and a clump of unfamiliar green—apple and pear trees. We cross the circle of watchtowers and, running, burst on to the highway. We have arrived. Just a few more yards. There, surrounded by trees, is the ramp.

37   A cheerful little station, very much like any other provincial railway stop: a small square framed by tall chestnuts and paved with yellow gravel. Not far off, beside the road, squats a tiny wooden shed, uglier and more flimsy than the ugliest and flimsiest railway shack; farther along lie stacks of old rails, heaps of wooden beams, barracks parts, bricks, paving stones. This is where they load freight for Birkenau: supplies for the construction of the camp, and people for the gas chambers. Trucks drive around, load up lumber, cement, people—a regular daily routine.

38   And now the guards are being posted along the rails, across the beams, in the green shade of the Silesian chestnuts, to form a tight circle around the ramp. They wipe the sweat from their faces and sip out of their canteens. It is unbearably hot; the sun stands motionless at its zenith.

39   "Fall out!"

40   We sit down in the narrow streaks of shade along the stacked rails. The hungry Greeks (several of them managed to come along. God only knows how) rummage underneath the rails. One of them finds some pieces of mildewed bread, another a few half-rotten sardines. They eat.

41   *"Schweinedreck,"* spits a young, tall guard with corn-coloured hair and dreamy blue eyes. "For God's sake, any minute you'll have so much food to stuff down your guts, you'll bust!" He adjusts his gun, wipes his face with a handkerchief.

"Hey you, fatso!" His boot lightly touches Henri's shoulder. *"Pass* 42
mal auf, want a drink?"

"Sure, but I haven't got any marks," replies the Frenchman with a 43
professional air.

"*Schade,* too bad." 44

"Come, come, Herr Posten, isn't my word good enough any more? 45
Haven't we done business before? How much?"

"One hundred. *Gemacht?*" 46

"*Gemacht.*" 47

We drink the water, lukewarm and tasteless. It will be paid for by 48
the people who have not yet arrived.

"Now you be careful." says Henri, turning to me. He tosses away the 49
empty bottle. It strikes the rails and bursts into tiny fragments. "Don't
take any money, they might be checking. Anyway, who the hell needs
money? You've got enough to eat. Don't take suits either, or they'll think
you're planning to escape. Just get a shirt, silk only, with a collar. And a
vest. And if you find something to drink, don't bother calling me. I know
how to shift for myself, but you watch your step or they'll let you have it."

"Do they beat you up here?" 50

"Naturally. You've got to have eyes in your ass. *Arschaugen.*" 51

Around us sit the Greeks, their jaws working greedily, like huge 52
human insects. They munch on stale lumps of bread. They are restless,
wondering what will happen next. The sight of the large beams and the
stacks of rails has them worried. They dislike carrying heavy loads.

"*Was wir arbeiten?*" they ask. 53

"*Niks. Transport kommen, alles Krematorium. compris?*" 54

"*Alles verstehen,*" they answer in crematorium Esperanto. All is 55
well—they will not have to move the heavy rails or carry the beams.

In the meantime, the ramp has become increasingly alive with ac- 56
tivity, increasingly noisy. The crews are being divided into those who
will open and unload the arriving cattle cars and those who will be
posted by the wooden steps. They receive instructions on how to proceed most efficiently. Motor cycles drive up, delivering S.S. officers, be-
medalled, glittering with brass, beefy men with highly polished boots
and shiny, brutal faces. Some have brought their briefcases, others hold
thin, flexible whips. This gives them an air of military readiness and
agility. They walk in and out of the commissary—for the miserable little shack by the road serves as their commissary, where in the summer-
time the drink mineral water, *Studentenquelle,* and where in winter they
can warm up with a glass of hot wine. They greet each other in the
state-approved way, raising an arm Roman fashion, then shake hands
cordially, exchanging warm smiles, discuss mail from home, their children, their families. Some stroll majestically on the ramp. The silver
squares on their collars glitter, the gravel crunches under their boots,
their bamboo whips snap impatiently.

57   We lie against the rails in the narrow streaks of shade, breathe unevenly, occasionally exchange a few words in our various tongues, and gaze listlessly at the majestic men in green uniforms, at the green trees, and at the church steeple of a distant village.

58   "The transport is coming," somebody says. We spring to our feet, all eyes turn in one direction. Around the bend, one after another, the cattle cars begin rolling in. The train backs into the station, a conductor leans out, waves his hand, blows a whistle. The locomotive whistles back with a shrieking noise, puffs, the train rolls slowly alongside the ramp. In the tiny barred windows appear pale, wilted, exhausted human faces, terror-stricken women with tangled hair, unshaven men. They gaze at the station in silence. And then, suddenly, there is a stir inside the cars and a pounding against the wooden boards.

59   "Water! Air!"—weary, desperate cries.

60   Heads push through the windows, mouths gasp frantically for air. They draw a few breaths, then disappear; others come in their place, then also disappear. The cries and moans grow louder.

61   A man in a green uniform covered with more glitter than any of the others jerks his head impatiently, his lips twist in annoyance. He inhales deeply, then with a rapid gesture throws his cigarette away and signals to the guard. The guard removes the automatic from his shoulder, aims, sends a series of shots along the train. All is quiet now. Meanwhile, the trucks have arrived, steps are being drawn up, and the Canada men stand ready at their posts by the train doors. The S.S. officer with the briefcase raises his hand.

62   "Whoever takes gold, or anything at all besides food, will be shot for stealing Reich property. Understand? *Verstanden?*"

63   "*Jawohl!*" we answer eagerly.

64   "*Also los!* Begin!"

65   The bolts crack, the doors fall open. A wave of fresh air rushes inside the train. People . . . inhumanly crammed, buried under incredible heaps of luggage, suitcases, trunks, packages, crates, bundles of every description (everything that had been their past and was to start their future). Monstrously squeezed together, they have fainted from heat, suffocated, crushed one another. Now they push towards the opened doors, breathing like fish cast out on the sand.

66   "Attention! Out, and take your luggage with you! Take out everything. Pile all your stuff near the exits. Yes, your coats too. It is summer. March to the left. Understand?"

67   "Sir, what's going to happen to us?" They jump from the train on to the gravel, anxious, worn-out.

68   "Where are you people from?"

69   "Sosnowiec-Bedzin. Sir, what's going to happen to us?" They repeat the question stubbornly, gazing into our tired eyes.

70   "I don't know, I don't understand Polish."

It is the camp law: people going to their death must be deceived to   71
the very end. This is the only permissible form of charity. The heat is
tremendous. The sun hangs directly over our heads, the white, hot sky
quivers, the air vibrates, an occasional breeze feels like a sizzling blast
from a furnace. Our lips are parched, the mouth fills with the salty taste
of blood, the body is weak and heavy from lying in the sun. Water!

A huge, multicoloured wave of people loaded down with luggage   72
pours from the train like a blind, mad river trying to find a new bed.
But before they have a chance to recover, before they can draw a breath
of fresh air and look at the sky, bundles are snatched from their hands,
coats ripped off their backs, their purses and umbrellas taken away.

"But please sir, it's for the sun. I cannot..."   73

"*Verboten!*" one of us barks through clenched teeth. There is an S.S.   74
man standing behind your back, calm, efficient, watchful.

"*Meine herrschaften,* this way, ladies and gentlemen, try not to   75
throw your things around, please. Show some goodwill," he says cour-
teously, his restless hands playing with the slender whip.

"Of course, of course," they answer as they pass, and now they   76
walk alongside the train somewhat more cheerfully. A woman reaches
down quickly to pick up her handbag. The whip flies, the woman
screams, stumbles, and falls under the feet of the surging crowd. Behind her, a child cries in a thin little voice "Mamele!"—a very small girl
with tangled black curls.

The heaps grow. Suitcases, bundles, blankets, coats, handbags that   77
open as they fall, spilling coins, gold, watches; mountains of bread
pile up at the exits, heaps of marmalade, jams, masses of meat, sausages; sugar spills on the gravel. Trucks, loaded with people, start up
with a deafening roar and drive off amidst the wailing and screaming
of the women separated from their children, and the stupefied silence
of the men left behind. They are the ones who had been ordered to
step to the right—the healthy and the young who will go to the camp.
In the end, they too will not escape death, but first they must work.

Trucks leave and return, without interruption, as on a monstrous   78
conveyor belt. A Red Cross van drives back and forth, back and forth,
incessantly: it transports the gas that will kill these people. The enormous cross on the hood, red as blood, seems to dissolve in the sun.

The Canada men at the trucks cannot stop for a single moment,   79
even to catch their breath. They shove the people up the steps, pack
them in tightly, sixty per truck, more or less. Near by stands a young,
clean-shaven "gentleman," an S.S. officer with a notebook in his hand.
For each departing truck he enters a mark; sixteen gone means one
thousand people, more or less. The gentleman is calm, precise. No
truck can leave without a signal from him, or a mark in his notebook:
Ordnung muss sein. The marks swell into thousands, the thousands into
whole transports, which afterwards we shall simply call "from Salon-

ica," "from Strasbourg." "from Rotterdam." This one will be called "Sosnowiec-Bedzin." The new prisoners from Sosnowiec-Bedzin will receive serial numbers 131–2—thousand, of course, though afterwards we shall simply say 131–2, for short.

80   The transports swell into weeks, months, years. When the war is over, they will count up marks in their notebooks—all four and a half million of them. The bloodiest battle of the war, the greatest victory of the strong, united Germany. *Ein Reich, ein Volk, ein Führer*—and four crematoria.

81   The train has been emptied. A thin, pock-marked S.S. man peers inside, shakes his head in disgust and motions to our group, pointing his finger at the door.

82   *"Rein.* Clean it up!"

83   We climb inside. In the corners amid human excrement and abandoned wristwatches lie squashed, trampled infants, naked little monsters with enormous heads and bloated bellies. We carry them out like chickens, holding several in each hand.

84   "Don't take them to the trucks, pass them on to the women," says the S.S. man, lighting a cigarette. His cigarette lighter is not working properly; he examines it carefully.

85   "Take them, for God's sake!" I explode as the women run from me in horror, covering their eyes.

86   The name of God sound strangely pointless, since the women and the infants will go on the trucks, every one of them, without exception. We all know what this means, and we look at each other with hate and horror.

87   "What, you don't want to take them?" asks the pock-marked S.S. man with a note of surprise and reproach in his voice, and reaches for his revolver.

88   "You mustn't shoot, I'll carry them." A tall grey-haired woman takes the little corpses out of my hands and for an instant gazes straight into my eyes.

89   "My poor boy," she whispers and smiles at me. Then she walks away, staggering along the path. I lean against the side of the train. I am terribly tired. Someone pulls at my sleeve.

90   *"En avant,* to the rails, come on!"

91   I look up, but the face swims before my eyes, dissolves, huge and transparent, melts into the motionless trees and the sea of people...I blink rapidly: Henri.

92   "Listen, Henri, are we good people?"

93   "That's stupid. Why do you ask?"

94   "You see, my friend, you see, I don't know why, but I am furious, simply furious with these people—furious because I must be here because of them. I feel no pity. I am not sorry they're going to the gas

chamber. Damn them all! I could throw myself at them, beat them with my fists. It must be pathological, I just can't understand..."

"Ah, on the contrary, it is natural, predictable, calculated. The ramp exhausts you, you rebel—and the easiest way to relieve your hate is to turn against someone weaker. Why, I'd even call it healthy. It's simple logic, *compris?*" He props himself up comfortably against the heap of rails. "Look at the Greeks, they know how to make the best of it! They stuff their bellies with anything they find. One of them has just devoured a full jar of marmalade." 95

"Pigs! Tomorrow half of them will die of the shits." 96

"Pigs! You've been hungry." 97

"Pigs!" I repeat furiously. I close my eyes. The air is filled with ghastly cries, the earth trembles beneath me, I can feel sticky moisture on my eyelids. My throat is completely dry. 98

The morbid procession streams on and on—trucks growl like mad dogs. I shut my eyes tight, but I can still see corpses dragged from the train, trampled infants, cripples piled on top of the dead, wave after wave... freight cars roll in, the heaps of clothing, suitcases and bundles grow, people climb out, look at the sun, take a few breaths, beg for water, get into the trucks, drive away. And again freight cars roll in, again people... The scenes become confused in my mind—I am not sure if all of this is actually happening, or if I am dreaming. There is a humming inside my head. I feel that I must vomit. 99

Henri tugs at my arm. 100

"Don't sleep, we're off to load up the loot." 101

All the people are gone. In the distance, the last few trucks roll along the road in clouds of dust, the train has left, several S.S. officers promenade up and down the ramp. The silver glitters on their collars. Their boots shine, their red, beefy faces shine. Among them there is a woman—only now I realize she has been here all along—withered, flat-chested, bony, her thin, colourless hair pulled back and tied in a "Nordic" knot; her hands are in the pockets of her wide skirt. With a rat-like resolute smile glued on her thin lips she sniffs around the corners of the ramp. She detests feminine beauty with the hatred of a woman who is herself repulsive, and knows it. Yes, I have seen her many times before and I know her well: she is the commandant of the F.K.L. She has come to look over the new crop of women, for some of them, instead of going on the trucks, will go on foot—to the concentration camp. There our boys, the barbers from Zauna, will shave their heads and will have a good laugh at their "outside world" modesty. 102

We proceed to load the loot. We lift huge trunks, heave them on to the trucks. There they are arranged in stacks, packed tightly. Occasionally somebody slashes one open with a knife, for pleasure or in search of vodka and perfume. One of the crates falls open; suits, shirts, books 103 drop out on the ground... I pick up a small, heavy package. I unwrap it—gold, about two handfuls, bracelets, rings, brooches, diamonds...

104   "*Gib hier*," an S.S. man says calmly, holding up his briefcases already full of gold and colourful foreign currency. He locks the case, hands it to an officer, takes another, an empty one, and stands by the next truck, waiting. The gold will go to the Reich.

105   It is hot, terribly hot. Our throats are dry, each word hurts. Anything for a sip of water! Faster, faster, so that it is over, so that we may rest. At last we are done, all the trucks have gone. Now we swiftly clean up the remaining dirt: there must be "no trace left of the *Schweinerei*." But just as the last truck disappears behind the trees and we walk, finally, to rest in the shade, a shrill whistle sounds around the bend. Slowly, terribly slowly, a train rolls in, the engine whistles back with a deafening shriek. Again weary, pale faces at the windows, flat as though cut out of paper, with huge, feverishly burning eyes. Already trucks are pulling up, already the composed gentleman with the notebook is at his post, and the S.S. men emerge from the commissary carrying briefcases for the gold and money. We unseal the train doors.

106   It is impossible to control oneself any longer. Brutally we tear suitcases from their hands, impatiently pull off their coats. Go on, go on, vanish! They go, they vanish. Men, women, children. Some of them know.

107   Here is a woman—she walks quickly, but tries to appear calm. A small child with a pink cherub's face runs after her and, unable to keep up, stretched out his little arms and cries: "Mama! Mama!"

108   "Pick up your child, woman!"

109   "It's not mine, sir, not mine!" she shouts hysterically and runs on, covering her face with her hands. She wants to hide, she wants to reach those who will not ride the trucks, those who will go on foot, those who will stay alive. She is young, healthy, good-looking, she wants to live.

110   But the child runs after her, wailing loudly: "Mama, mama, don't leave me."

111   "It's not mine, not mine, no!"

112   Andrei, a sailor from Sevastopol, grabs hold of her. His eyes are glassy from vodka and the heat. With one powerful blow he knocks her off her feet, then, as she falls, takes her by the hair and pulls her up again. His face twitches with rage.

113   "Ah, you bloody Jewess! So you're running from your own child! I'll show you, you whore." His huge hand chokes her, he lifts her in the air and heaves her on to the truck like a heavy sack of grain.

114   "Here! And take this with you, bitch!" and he throws the child at her feet.

115   "*Gut gemacht*, good work. That's the way to deal with degenerate mothers," says the S.S. man standing at the foot of the truck "*Gut, gut, Russki.*"

"Shut your mouth," growls Andrei through clenched teeth, and 116
walks away. From under a pile of rags he pulls out a canteen, unscrews
the cork, takes a few deep swallows, passes it to me. The strong vodka
burns the throat. My head swims, my legs are shaky, again I feel like
throwing up.

And suddenly, above the teeming crowd pushing forward like a 117
river driven by an unseen power, a girl appears. She descends lightly
from the train, hops on to the gravel, looks around inquiringly, as if
somewhere surprised. Her soft, blonde hair has fallen on her shoulders
in a torrent, she throws it back impatiently. With a natural gesture she
runs her hands down her blouse, casually straightens her skirt. She
stands like this for an instant, gazing at the crowd, then turns and with
a gliding look examines our faces, as though searching for someone.
Unknowingly, I continue to stare at her, until our eyes meet.

"Listen, tell me, where are they taking us?" 118

I look at her without saying a word. Here, standing before me, is a 119
girl, a girl with enchanting blonde hair, with beautiful breasts, wearing
a little cotton blouse, a girl with a wise, mature look in her eyes. Here
she stands, gazing straight into my face, waiting. And over there is the
gas chamber; communal death, disgusting and ugly. And over in the
other direction is the concentration camp, the shaved head, the heavy
Soviet trousers in sweltering heat, the sickening, stale odour of dirty,
damp female bodies, the animal hunger, the inhuman labour, and later
the same gas chamber, only an even more hideous, more terrible
death...

Why did she bring it? I think to myself, noticing a lovely gold 120
watch on her delicate wrist. They'll take it away from her anyway.

"Listen, tell me," she repeats. 121

I remain silent. Her lips tighten. 122

"I know," she says with a shade of proud contempt in her voice, 123
tossing her head. She walks off resolutely in the direction of the trucks.
Someone tries to stop her; she boldly pushes him aside and runs up the
steps. In the distance I can only catch a glimpse of her blonde hair flying in the breeze.

I go back inside the train; I carry out dead infants; I unload lug- 124
gage. I touch corpses, but I cannot overcome the mounting, uncontrol-
lable terror. I try to escape from the corpses, but they are everywhere:
lined up on the gravel on the cement edge of the ramp, inside the cattle
cars. Babies, hideous naked women, men twisted by convulsions. I run
off as far as I can but immediately a whip slashes across my back. Out
of the corner of my eye I see an S.S. man, swearing profusely. I stagger
forward and run, lose myself in the Canada group. Now, at last, I can
once more rest against the stack of rails. The sun has leaned low over
the horizon and illuminates the ramp with a reddish glow; the shadows of the trees have become elongated, ghostlike. In silence that set-

tles over nature at this time of day, the human cries seem to rise all the way to the sky.

125   Only from this distance does one have a full view of the inferno on the teeming ramp. I see a pair of human beings who have fallen to the ground locked in a last desperate embrace. The man has dug his fingers into the woman's flesh and has caught her clothing with his teeth. She screams hysterically, swears, cries, until at last a large boot comes down over her throat and she is silent. They are pulled apart and dragged like cattle to the truck. I see four Canada men lugging a corpse: a huge, swollen female corpse. Cursing, dripping wet from the strain, they kick out of their way some stray children who have been running all over the ramp, howling like dogs. The men pick them up by the collars, heads, arms, and toss them inside the trucks, on top of the heaps. The four men have trouble lifting the fat corpse on to the car, they call others for help, and all together they hoist up the mound of meat. Big, swollen, puffed-up corpses are being collected from all over the ramp: on top of them are piled the invalids, the smothered, the sick, the unconscious. The heap seethes, howls, groans. The driver starts the motor, the truck begins rolling.

126   "Halt! Halt!" an S.S. man yells after them. "Stop, damn you!"

127   They are dragging to the truck an old man wearing tails and a band around his arm. His head knocks against the gravel and pavement; he moans and wails in an uninterrupted monotone: *"ich will mit dem Herrn Kommandanten sprechen—I wish to speak with the commandant..."* With senile stubbornness he keeps repeating these words all the way. Thrown on the truck, trampled by others, choked, he still wails: *"Ich will mit dem..."*

128   "Look here, old man!" a young S S. man calls, laughing jovially. "In half an hour you'll be talking to the top commandant! Only don't forget to greet him with a *Heil Hitler!"*

129   Several other men are carrying a small girl with only one leg. They hold her by the arms and the one leg. Tears are running down her face and she whispers faintly: "Sir, it hurts, it hurts..." They throw her on the truck on top of the corpses. She will burn alive along with them.

130   The evening has come, cool and clear. The stars are out. We lie against the rails. It is incredibly quiet. Anaemic bulbs hang from the top of the high lamp-posts; beyond the circle of light stretches an impenetrable darkness. Just one step, and a man could vanish for ever. But the guards are watching, their automatics ready.

131   "Did you get the shoes?" asks Henri.

132   "No."

133   "Why?"

134   "My God, man, I am finished, absolutely finished!"

135   "So soon? After only two transports? Just look at me, I...since Christmas, at least a million people have passed through my hands.

The worst of all are the transports from around Paris—one is always bumping into friends."

"And what do you say to them?"   136

"That first they will have a bath, and later we'll meet at the camp.   137
What would you say?"

I do not answer. We drink coffee with vodka; somebody opens a tin   138
of cocoa and mixes it with sugar. We scoop it up by the handful, the cocoa sticks to the lips. Again coffee, again vodka.

"Henri, what are we waiting for?"   139

"There'll be another transport."   140

"I'm not going to unload it! I can't take any more."   141

"So, it's got you down? Canada is nice, eh?" Henri grins indul-   142
gently and disappears into the darkness. In a moment he is back again.

"All right. Just sit quietly and don't let an S.S. man see you. I'll try   143
to find you your shoes."

"Just leave me alone. Never mind the shoes." I want to sleep. It is   144
very late.

Another whistle, another transport. Freight cars emerge out of the   145
darkness, pass under the lamp-posts, and again vanish in the night.
The ramp is small, but the circle of lights is smaller. The unloading will
have to be done gradually. Somewhere the trucks are growling. They
back up against the steps, black, ghostlike, their searchlights flash
across the trees. *Wasser! Luft!* The same all over again, like a late showing or the same film: a volley of shots, the train falls silent. Only this
time a little girl pushes herself halfway through the small windows and
losing her balance, falls out on to the gravel. Stunned, she lies still for a
moment, then stands up and begins walking around in a circle, faster
and faster, waving her rigid arms in the air, breathing loudly and spas-
modically, whining in a faint voice. Her mind has given way in the inferno inside the train. The whining is hard on the nerves: an S.S. man
approaches calmly, his heavy book strikes between her shoulders. She
falls. Holding her down with his foot, he draws his revolver, fires once,
then again. She remains face down, kicking the gravel with her feet,
until she stiffens. They proceed to unseal the train.

I am back on the ramp, standing by the doors. A warm, sickening   146
smell gushes from inside. The mountain of people filling the car almost
halfway up to the ceiling is motionless, horribly tangled, but still
steaming.

"*Ausladen*" comes the command. An S.S. man steps out from the   147
darkness. Across his chest hangs a portable searchlight. He throws a
stream of light inside.

"Why are you standing about like sheep? Start unloading!" His   148
whip flies and falls across our backs. I seize a corpse by the hand; the
fingers close tightly around mine. I pull back with a shriek and stagger
away. My heart pounds, jumps up to my throat. I can no longer control

the nausea. Hunched under the train I begin to vomit. Then, like a drunk, I weave over to the stack of rails.

149   I lie against the cool, kind metal and dream about returning to the camp, about my bunk, on which there is no mattress, about sleep among comrades who are not going to the gas tonight. Suddenly I see the camp as a haven of peace. It is true, others may be dying, but one is somehow still alive, one has enough food, enough strength to work . . .

150   The lights on the ramp flicker with a spectral glow, the wave of people—feverish, agitated, stupefied people—flows on and on, endlessly. They think that now they will have to face a new life in the camp, and they prepare themselves emotionally for the hard struggle ahead. They do not know that in just a few moments they will die, that the gold, money, and diamonds which they have so prudently hidden in their clothing and on their bodies are now useless to them. Experienced professionals will probe into every recess of their flesh, will pull the gold from under the tongue and the diamonds from the uterus and the colon. They will rip out gold teeth. In lightly sealed crates they will ship them to Berlin.

151   The S.S. men's black figures move about, dignified, businesslike. The gentleman with the notebook puts down his final marks, rounds out the figures: fifteen thousand.

152   Many, very many, trucks have been driven to the crematoria today.

153   It is almost over. The dead are being cleared off the ramp and piled into the last truck. The Canada men weighed down under a load of bread, marmalade and sugar, and smelling of perfume and fresh linen, line up to go. For several days the entire camp will live off this transport. For several days the entire camp will talk about "Sosnowiec-Bedzin." "Sosnowiec-Bedzin" was a good, rich transport.

154   The stars are already beginning to pale as we walk back to the camp. The sky grows translucent and opens high above our heads—it is getting light.

155   Great columns of smoke rise from the crematoria and merge up above into a huge black river which very slowly floats across the sky over Birkenau and disappears beyond the forests in the direction of Trzebinia. The "Sosnowiec-Bedzin" transport is already burning.

156   We pass a heavily armed S.S. detachment on its way to change guard. The men march briskly, in step, shoulder to shoulder, one mass, one will. *"Und morgen die ganze Welt . . ."* they sing at the top of their lungs. *"Rechts ran!* To the right march!" snaps a command from up front. We move out of their way.

✦ *Questions for Discussion and Writing*

   1. What task is performed by Tadeusz's labor battalion within the camp? For their work, what rewards and privileges does Tadeusz's group receive?

2. Explain how the lack of concern regarding fellow prisoners was a way of shielding oneself from a terrible reality. For example, why was there so much joking in a situation where it would seem humor could not exist?

3. What does Tadeusz reveal about his inner torment regarding the kind of person he has become in order to survive?

4. What is the effect of Borowski maintaining a first-person point of view throughout his narrative?

5. How does Borowski use irony in his account of the SS officers conversing while prisoners are being unloaded from the trains?

6. How does the equation of humans and insects symbolize the reduced value of human beings in the camp?

7. How does the episode centering on the young girl with one leg dramatize the indifference of the labor battalion toward the masses of people who have been and will be killed?

8. How does Borowski, through his account of the arrival and unloading of prisoners, control the pacing of his narrative?

9. Discuss what you learned about the phenomena of dehumanization from Borowski's narrative.

10. Describe other environments that degrade people psychologically and/or physically and produce an attitude of "every man for himself."

11. In light of this account, what might explain why Borowski, many years after he was released from the camp and on the verge of becoming Poland's greatest writer, committed suicide?

Gary Soto

Black Hair

◆

Gary Soto was born in 1952 in Fresno, California, where he grew up. He received a B.A. from California State University at Fresno and an M.F.A., in 1976, from the University of California at Irvine. He is currently teaching in the English Department at the University of California at Berkeley. A prolific writer of both poetry and prose, Soto has written several books, including an autobiography, Living Up the Street *(1985), from which "Black Hair" is taken,* Baseball in April *(1990) and* Pieces of the Heart: New Chicano Fiction *(1993). In the following piece we see the author as a young Mexican boy confronting the harsh realities of work experiences.*

1   There are two kinds of work: One uses the mind and the other uses muscle. As a kid I found out about the latter. I'm thinking of the summer of 1969 when I was a seventeen-year-old runaway who ended up in Glendale, California, to work for Valley Tire Factory. To answer an ad in the newspaper I walked miles in the afternoon sun, my stomach slowly knotting on a doughnut that was breakfast, my teeth like bright candles gone yellow.

2   I walked in the door sweating and feeling ugly because my hair was still stiff from a swim at the Santa Monica beach the day before. Jules, the accountant and part owner, looked droopily through his bifocals at my application and then at me. He tipped his cigar in the ashtray, asked my age as if he didn't believe I was seventeen, but finally after a moment of silence, said, "Come back tomorrow. Eight-thirty."

3   I thanked him, left the office, and went around to the chain link fence to watch the workers heave tires into a bin; others carted uneven stacks of tires on hand trucks. Their faces were black from tire dust and when they talked—or cussed—their mouths showed a bright pink.

4   From there I walked up a commercial street, past a cleaners, a motorcycle shop, and a gas station where I washed my face and hands; before leaving I took a bottle that hung on the side of the Coke machine, filled it with water, and stopped it with a scrap of paper and a rubber band.

5   The next morning I arrived early at work. The assistant foreman, a potbellied Hungarian, showed me a timecard and how to punch in. He showed me the Coke machine, the locker room with its slimy shower, and also pointed out the places where I shouldn't go: The ovens where

the tires were recapped and the customer service area, which had a slashed couch, a coffee table with greasy magazines, and an ashtray. He introduced me to Tully, a fat man with one ear, who worked the buffers that resurfaced the white walls. I was handed an apron and a face mask and shown how to use the buffer: Lift the tire and center, inflate it with a footpedal, press the buffer against the white band until cleaned, and then deflate and blow off the tire with an air hose.

With a paint brush he stirred a can of industrial preserver. "Then 6 slap this blue stuff on." While he was talking a co-worker came up quietly from behind him and goosed him with the air hose. Tully jumped as if he had been struck by a bullet and then turned around cussing and cupping his genitals in his hands as the other worker walked away calling out foul names. When Tully turned to me smiling his gray teeth, I lifted my mouth into a smile because I wanted to get along. He has to be on my side, I thought. He's the one who'll tell the foreman how I'm doing.

I worked carefully that day, setting the tires on the machine as if 7 they were babies, since it was easy to catch a finger in the rim that expanded to inflate the tire. At the day's end we swept up the tire dust and emptied the trash into bins.

At five the workers scattered for their cars and motorcycles while I 8 crossed the street to wash at a burger stand. My hair was stiff with dust and my mouth showed pink against the backdrop of my dirty face. I then ordered a hotdog and walked slowly in the direction of the abandoned house where I had stayed the night before. I lay under the trees and within minutes was asleep. When I woke my shoulders were sore and my eyes burned when I squeezed the lids together.

From the backyard I walked dully through a residential street, and 9 as evening came on, the TV glare in the living rooms and the headlights of passing cars showed against the blue drift of dusk. I saw two children coming up the street with snow cones, their tongues darting at the packed ice. I saw a boy with a peach and wanted to stop him, but felt embarrassed by my hunger. I walked for an hour only to return and discover the house lit brightly. Behind the fence I heard voices and saw a flashlight poking at the garage door. A man on the back steps mumbled something about the refrigerator to the one with the flashlight.

I waited for them to leave, but had the feeling they wouldn't be- 10 cause there was the commotion of furniture being moved. Tired, even more desperate, I started walking again with a great urge to kick things and tear the day from my life. I felt weak and my mind kept drifting because of hunger. I crossed the street to a gas station where I sipped at the water fountain and searched the Coke machine for change. I started walking again, first up a commercial street, then into a residential area where I lay down on someone's lawn and replayed a scene at home— my Mother crying at the kitchen table, my stepfather yelling with food in his mouth. They're cruel, I thought, and warned myself that I should never forgive them. How could they do this to me.

11   When I got up from the lawn it was late. I searched out a place to sleep and found an unlocked car that seemed safe. In the back seat, with my shoes off, I fell asleep but woke up startled about four in the morning when the owner, a nurse on her way to work, opened the door. She got in and was about to start the engine when I raised my head up from the backseat to explain my presence. She screamed so loudly when I said "I'm sorry" that I sprinted from the car with my shoes in hand. Her screams faded, then stopped altogether, as I ran down the block where I hid behind a trash bin and waited for a police siren to sound. Nothing. I crossed the street to a church where I slept stiffly on cardboard in the balcony.

12   I woke up feeling tired and greasy. It was early and a few street lights were still lit, the east growing pink with dawn. I washed myself from a garden hose and returned to the church to break into what looked like a kitchen. Paper cups, plastic spoons, a coffee pot littered on a table. I found a box of Nabisco crackers which I ate until I was full.

13   At work I spent the morning at the buffer, but was then told to help Iggy, an old Mexican, who was responsible for choosing tires that could be recapped without the risk of exploding at high speeds. Every morning a truck would deliver used tires, and after I unloaded them Iggy would step among the tires to inspect them for punctures and rips on the side walls.

14   With a yellow chalk he marked circles and Xs to indicate damage and called out "junk." For those tires that could be recapped, he said "goody" and I placed them on my hand truck. When I had a stack of eight I kicked the truck at an angle and balanced them to another work area where Iggy again inspected the tires, scratching Xs and calling out "junk."

15   Iggy worked only until three in the afternoon, at which time he went to the locker room to wash and shave and to dress in a two-piece suit. When he came out he glowed with a bracelet, watch, rings, and a shiny fountain pen in his breast pocket. His shoes sounded against the asphalt. He was the image of a banker stepping into sunlight with millions on his mind. He said a few low words to workers with whom he was friendly and none to people like me.

16   I was seventeen, stupid because I couldn't figure out the difference between an F 78 14 and 750 14 at sight. Iggy shook his head when I brought him the wrong tires, especially since I had expressed interest in being his understudy. "Mexican, how can you be so stupid?" he would yell at me, slapping a tire from my hands. But within weeks I learned a lot about tires, from sizes and makes to how they are molded in iron forms to how Valley stole from other companies. Now and then we received a truckload of tires, most of them new or nearly new, and they

were taken to our warehouse in the back where the serial numbers were ground off with a sander. On those days the foreman handed out Cokes and joked with us as we worked to get the numbers off.

Most of the workers were Mexican or black, though a few redneck whites worked there. The base pay was a dollar sixty-five, but the average was three dollars. Of the black workers, I knew Sugar Daddy the best. His body carried two hundred and fifty pounds, armfuls of scars, and a long knife that made me jump when he brought it out from his boot without warning. At one time he had been a singer, and had cut a record in 1967 called *Love's Chance*, which broke into the R and B charts. But nothing came of it. No big contract, no club dates, no tours. He made very little from the sales, only enough for an operation to pull a steering wheel from his gut when, drunk and mad at a lady friend, he slammed his Mustang into a row of parked cars.

"Touch it," he smiled at me one afternoon as he raised his shirt, his black belly kinked with hair. Scared, I traced the scar that ran from his chest to the left of his belly button, and I was repelled but hid my disgust.

Among the Mexicans I had few friends because I was different, a *pocho* who spoke bad Spanish. At lunch they sat in tires and laughed over burritos, looking up at me to laugh even harder. I also sat in tires while nursing a Coke and felt dirty and sticky because I was still living on the street and had not had a real bath in over a week. Nevertheless, when the border patrol came to round up the nationals, I ran with them as they scrambled for the fence or hid among the tires behind the warehouse. The foreman, who thought I was an undocumented worker, yelled at me to run, to get away. I did just that. At the time it seemed fun because there was no risk, only a goodhearted feeling of hide-and-seek, and besides it meant an hour away from work on company time. When the police left we came back and some of the nationals made up stories of how they were almost caught—how they out-raced the police. Some of the stories were so convoluted and unconvincing that everyone laughed *mentiras,* especially when one described how he overpowered a policeman, took his gun away, and sold the patrol car. We laughed and he laughed, happy to be there to make up a story.

If work was difficult, so were the nights. I still had not gathered enough money to rent a room, so I spent the nights sleeping in parked cars or in the balcony of a church. After a week I found a newspaper ad for room for rent, phoned, and was given directions. Finished with work, I walked the five miles down Mission Road looking back into the traffic with my thumb out. No rides. After eight hours of handling tires I was frightening, I suppose, to drivers since they seldom looked at me; if they did, it was a quick glance. For the next six weeks I would try to hitchhike, but the only person to stop was a Mexican woman who gave me two dollars to take the bus. I told her it was too much and that no bus ran from Mission Road to where I lived, but she insisted that I keep the money and trotted back to her idling car. It must have hurt her to see me day after day walking in the heat and looking very much the dirty Mexican to the many minds that didn't know what it meant to work at hard labor. That woman knew. Her eyes met mine as she opened the car door, and there was a tenderness that was surprisingly true—one for which you wait for years but when it comes it doesn't help. Nothing changes. You continue on in rags, with the sun still above you.

21   I rented a room from a middle-aged couple whose lives were a mess. She was a school teacher and he was a fireman. A perfect set up, I thought. But during my stay there they would argue with one another for hours in their bedroom.

22   When I rang at the front door both Mr. and Mrs. Van Deusen answered and didn't bother to disguise their shock at how awful I looked. But they let me in all the same. Mrs. Van Deusen showed me around the house, from the kitchen and bathroom to the living room with its grand piano. On her fingers she counted out the house rules as she walked me to my room. It was a girl's room with lace curtains, scenic wallpaper of a Victorian couple enjoying a stroll, canopied bed, and stuffed animals in a corner. Leaving, she turned and asked if she could do laundry for me and, feeling shy and hurt, I told her no; perhaps the next day. She left and I undressed to take a bath, exhausted as I sat on the edge of the bed probing my aches and my bruised places. With a towel around my waist I hurried down the hallway to the bathroom where Mrs. Van Deusen had set out an additional towel with a tube of shampoo. I ran the water in the tub and sat on the toilet, lid down, watching the steam curl toward the ceiling. When I lowered myself into the tub I felt my body sting. I soaped a wash cloth and scrubbed my arms until they lightened, even glowed pink, but still I looked unwashed around my neck and face no matter how hard I rubbed. Back in the room I sat in bed reading a magazine, happy and thinking of no better luxury than a girl's sheets, especially after nearly two weeks of sleeping on cardboard at the church.

23   I was too tired to sleep, so I sat at the window watching the neighbors move about in pajamas, and, curious about the room, looked through the bureau drawers to search out personal things—snapshots, a messy diary, and a high school yearbook. I looked up the Van Deusen's daughter, Barbara, and studied her face as if I recognized her from my own school—a face that said "promise," "college," "nice clothes in the closet." She was a skater and a member of the German Club; her greatest ambition was to sing at the Hollywood Bowl.

24   After awhile I got into bed and as I drifted toward sleep I thought about her. In my mind I played a love scene again and again and altered it slightly each time. She comes home from college and at first is

indifferent to my presence in her home, but finally I overwhelm her with deep pity when I come home hurt from work, with blood on my shirt. Then there was another version: Home from college she is immediately taken with me, in spite of my work-darkened face, and invites me into the family car for a milkshake across town. Later, back at the house, we sit in the living room talking about school until we're so close I'm holding her hand. The truth of the matter was that Barbara did come home for a week, but was bitter toward her parents for taking in boarders (two others besides me). During that time she spoke to me only twice: Once, while searching the refrigerator, she asked if we had any mustard; the other time she asked if I had seen her car keys.

But it was a place to stay. Work had become more and more diffi- 25 cult. I not only worked with Iggy, but also with the assistant foreman who was in charge of unloading trucks. After they backed in I hopped on top to pass the tires down by bouncing them on the tailgate to give them an extra spring so they would be less difficult to handle on the other end. Each truck was weighed down with more than two hundred tires, each averaging twenty pounds, so that by the time the truck was emptied and swept clean I glistened with sweat and my T-shirt stuck to my body. I blew snot threaded with tire dust onto the asphalt, indifferent to the customers who watched from the waiting room.

The days were dull. I did what there was to do from morning until 26 the bell sounded at five; I tugged, pulled, and cussed at tires until I was listless and my mind drifted and caught on small things, from cold sodas to shoes to stupid talk about what we would do with a million dollars. I remember unloading a truck with Hamp, a black man.

"What's better than a sharp lady?" he asked me as I stood sweaty 27 on a pile of junked tires. "Water. With ice," I said.

He laughed with his mouth open wide. With his fingers he pinched 28 the sweat from his chin and flicked at me. "You be too young, boy. A woman can make you a god."

As a kid I had chopped cotton and picked grapes, so I knew work. 29 I knew the fatigue and the boredom and the feeling that there was a good possibility you might have to do such work for years, if not for a lifetime. In fact, as a kid I imagined a dark fate: To marry Mexican poor, work Mexican hours, and in the end die a Mexican death, broke and in despair.

But this job at Valley Tire Company confirmed that there was some- 30 thing worse than field work, and I was doing it. We were all doing it, from foreman to the newcomers like me, and what I felt heaving tires for eight hours a day was felt by everyone—black, Mexican, redneck. We all despised those hours but didn't know what else to do. The workers were unskilled, some undocumented and fearful of deportation, and all struck with an uncertainty at what to do with their lives. Although everyone bitched about work, no one left. Some had worked there for as long as twelve years; some had sons working there. Few quit; no one was ever fired. It amazed me that no one gave up when the border patrol jumped from their vans, baton in hand, because I couldn't imagine any work that could be worse—or any life. What was out there, in the world, that made men run for the fence in fear?

31   Iggy was the only worker who seemed sure of himself. After five hours of "junking," he brushed himself off, cleaned up in the washroom, and came out gleaming with an elegance that humbled the rest of us. Few would look him straight in the eye or talk to him in our usual stupid way because he was so much better. He carried himself as a man should—with that old world "dignity"—while the rest of us muffed our jobs and talked dully about dull things as we worked. From where he worked in his open shed he would now and then watch us with his hands on his hips. He would shake his head and click his tongue in disgust.

32   The rest of us lived dismally. I often wondered what the others' homes were like; I couldn't imagine that they were much better than our work place. No one indicated that his outside life was interesting or intriguing. We all looked defeated and contemptible in our filth at the day's end. I imagined the average welcome at home: Rafael, a Mexican national who had worked at Valley for five years, returned to a beaten house of kids who were dressed in mismatched clothes and playing kick-the-can. As for Sugar Daddy, he returned home to a stuffy room where he would read and reread old magazines. He ate potato chips, drank beer, and watched TV. There was no grace in dipping socks into a wash basin where later he would wash his cup and plate.

33   There was no grace at work. It was all ridicule. The assistant foreman drank Cokes in front of the newcomers as they laced tires in the afternoon sun. Knowing that I had a long walk home, Rudy, the college student, passed me waving and yelling "Hello," as I started down Mission Road on the way home to eat out of cans. Even our plump secretary got into the act by wearing short skirts and flaunting her milky legs. If there was love, it was ugly. I'm thinking of Tully and an older man whose name I can no longer recall fondling one another in the washroom. I had come in cradling a smashed finger to find them pressed together in the shower, their pants undone and partly pulled down. When they saw me they smiled their pink mouths but didn't bother to push away.

34   How we arrived at such a place is a mystery to me. Why anyone would stay for years is even a deeper concern. You showed up, but from where? What broken life? What ugly past? The foreman showed you the

Coke machine, the washroom, and the yard where you'd work. When you picked up a tire, you were amazed at the black it could give off.

◆ *Questions for Discussion and Writing*

1. What circumstances led Soto to become homeless?

2. How does the idea of black hair enter into Soto's account?

3. What is the effect of Soto's comparison of the Van Deusens' lifestyle and emotional life with his own condition?

4. What is significant about the qualities Soto admires in his co-worker Iggy?

5. Why did Soto's co-workers not leave the tire factory to get other jobs?

Amy Tan

Two Kinds

◆

Amy Tan was born in Oakland, California, in 1952, two and a half years after her parents immigrated to the United States in 1949, just before the Communist Revolution. She has worked as a consultant to programs for disabled children and as a freelance writer. Of her first visit to China in 1987 she says, "As soon as my feet touched China, I became Chinese."

"Two Kinds" is from Tan's first book, The Joy Luck Club *(1989), a work that explores conflicts between different cultures, and generations, of Chinese mothers and daughters in America.*

1   My mother believed you could be anything you wanted to be in America. You could open a restaurant. You could work for the government and get good retirement. You could buy a house with almost no money down. You could become rich. You could become instantly famous.

2   "Of course you can be prodigy, too," my mother told me when I was nine. "You can be best anything. What does Auntie Lindo know? Her daughter, she is only best tricky."

3   America was where all my mother's hopes lay. She had come here in 1949 after losing everything in China: her mother and father, her family home, her first husband, and two daughters, twin baby girls. But she never looked back with regret. There were so many ways for things to get better.

We didn't immediately pick the right kind of prodigy. At first my mother thought I could be a Chinese Shirley Temple. We'd watch Shirley's old movies on TV as though they were training films. My mother would poke my arm and say, *"Ni kan"*—You watch. And I would see Shirley tapping her feet, or singing a sailor song, or pursing her lips into a very round O while saying, "Oh my goodness."

4   *"Ni kan,"* said my mother as Shirley's eyes flooded with tears. "You already know how. Don't need talent for crying!"

5   Soon after my mother got this idea about Shirley Temple, she took me to a beauty training school in the Mission district and put me in the

hands of a student who could barely hold the scissors without shaking. Instead of getting big fat curls, I emerged with an uneven mass of crinkly black fuzz. My mother dragged me off to the bathroom and tried to wet down my hair.

"You look like Negro Chinese," she lamented, as if I had done this   6
on purpose.

The instructor of the beauty training school had to lop off these   7
soggy clumps to make my hair even again. "Peter Pan is very popular these days," the instructor assured my mother. I now had hair the length of a boy's, with straight-across bangs that hung at a slant two inches above my eyebrows. I liked the haircut and it made me actually look forward to my future fame.

In fact, in the beginning, I was just as excited as my mother, maybe   8
even more so. I pictured this prodigy part of me as many different images, trying each one on for size. I was a dainty ballerina girl standing by the curtains, waiting to hear the right music that would send me floating on my tiptoes. I was like the Christ child lifted out of the straw manger, crying with holy indignity. I was Cinderella stepping from her pumpkin carriage with sparkly cartoon music filling the air.

In all of my imaginings, I was filled with a sense that I would soon   9
become *perfect*. My mother and father would adore me. I would be beyond reproach. I would never feel the need to sulk for anything.

But sometimes the prodigy in me became impatient. "If you don't   10
hurry up and get me out of here, I'm disappearing for good," it warned. "And then you'll always be nothing."

Every night after dinner, my mother and I would sit at the Formica   11
kitchen table. She would present new tests, taking her examples from stories of amazing children she had read in *Ripley's Believe It or Not,* or *Good Housekeeping, Reader's Digest,* and a dozen other magazines she kept in a pile in our bathroom. My mother got these magazines from people whose houses she cleaned. And since she cleaned many houses each week, we had a great assortment. She would look through them all, searching for stories about remarkable children.

The first night she brought out a story about a three-year-old boy   12
who knew the capitals of all the states and even most of the European countries. A teacher was quoted as saying the little boy could also pronounce the names of the foreign cities correctly.

"What's the capital of Finland?" my mother asked me, looking at   13
the magazine story.

All I knew was the capital of California, because Sacramento was   14
the name of the street we lived on in Chinatown. "Nairobi!" I guessed,

saying the most foreign word I could think of. She checked to see if that was possibly one way to pronounce "Helsinki" before showing me the answer.

15   The tests got harder—multiplying numbers in my head, finding the queen of hearts in a deck of cards, trying to stand on my head without using my hands, predicting the daily temperatures in Los Angeles, New York, and London.

16   One night I had to look at a page from the Bible for three minutes and then report everything I could remember. "Now Jehoshaphat had riches and honor in abundance and . . . that's all I remember, Ma," I said.

17   And after seeing my mother's disappointed face once again, something inside of me began to die. I hated the tests, the raised hopes and failed expectations. Before going to bed that night, I looked in the mirror above the bathroom sink and when I saw only my face staring back—and that it would always be this ordinary face—I began to cry. Such a sad, ugly girl! I made high-pitched noises like a crazed animal, trying to scratch out the face in the mirror.

18   And then I saw what seemed to be the prodigy side of me—because I had never seen that face before. I looked at my reflection, blinking so I could see more clearly. The girl staring back at me was angry, powerful. This girl and I were the same. I had new thoughts, willful thoughts, or rather thoughts filled with lots of won'ts. I won't let her change me, I promised myself. I won't be what I'm not.

19   So now on nights when my mother presented her tests, I performed listlessly, my head propped on one arm, I pretended to be bored. And I was. I got so bored I started counting the bellows of the foghorns out on the bay while my mother drilled me in other areas. The sound was comforting and reminded me of the cow jumping over the moon. And the next day, I played a game with myself, seeing if my mother would give up on me before eight bellows. After a while I usually counted only one, maybe two bellows at most. At last she was beginning to give up hope.

20   Two or three months had gone by without any mention of my being a prodigy again. And then one day my mother was watching *The Ed Sullivan Show* on TV. The TV was old and the sound kept shorting out. Every time my mother got halfway up from the sofa to adjust the set, the sound would go back on and Ed would be talking. As soon as she sat down, Ed would go silent again. She got up, the TV broke into loud piano music. She sat down. Silence. Up and down, back and forth, quiet and loud. It was like a stiff embraceless dance between her and the TV set. Finally she stood by the set with her hand on the sound dial.

She seemed entranced by the music, a little frenzied piano piece   21
with this mesmerizing quality, sort of quick passages and then teasing
lilting ones before it returned to the quick playful parts.

"*Ni kan*," my mother said, calling me over with hurried hand ges-   22
tures, "Look here."

I could see why my mother was fascinated by the music. It was be-   23
ing pounded out by a little Chinese girl, about nine years old, with a
Peter Pan haircut. The girl had the sauciness of a Shirley Temple. She
was proudly modest like a proper Chinese child. And she also did this
fancy sweep of a curtsy, so that the fluffy skirt of her white dress cas-
caded slowly to the floor like the petals of a large carnation.

In spite of these warning signs, I wasn't worried. Our family had   24
no piano and we couldn't afford to buy one, let alone reams of sheet
music and piano lessons. So I could be generous in my comments when
my mother bad-mouthed the little girl on TV.

"Play note right, but doesn't sound good! No singing sound," com-   25
plained my mother.

"What are you picking on her for?" I said carelessly. "She's pretty   26
good. Maybe she's not the best, but she's trying hard." I knew almost
immediately I would be sorry I said that.

"Just like you," she said. "Not the best. Because you not trying." She   27
gave a little huff as she let go of the sound dial and sat down on the sofa.

The little Chinese girl sat down also to play an encore of "Anitra's   28
Dance" by Grieg. I remember the song, because later on I had to learn
how to play it.

Three days after watching *The Ed Sullivan Show,* my mother told me   29
what my schedule would be for piano lessons and piano practice. She
had talked to Mr. Chong, who lived on the first floor of our apartment
building. Mr. Chong was a retired piano teacher and my mother had
traded housecleaning services for weekly lessons and a piano for me to
practice on every day, two hours a day, from four until six.

When my mother told me this, I felt as though I had been sent to   30
hell. I whined and then kicked my foot a little when I couldn't stand it
anymore.

"Why don't you like me the way I am? I'm *not* a genius! I can't play   31
the piano. And even if I could, I wouldn't go on TV if you paid me a
million dollars!" I cried.

My mother slapped me. "Who ask you be genius?" she shouted.   32
"Only ask you be your best. For you sake. You think I want you be genius? Hnnh! What for! Who ask you!"

"So ungrateful," I heard her mutter in Chinese. "If she had as much   33
talent as she has temper, she would be famous now."

34   Mr. Chong, whom I secretly nicknamed Old Chong, was very strange, always tapping his fingers to the silent music of an invisible orchestra. He looked ancient in my eyes. He had lost most of the hair on top of his head and he wore thick glasses and had eyes that always looked tired and sleepy. But he must have been younger than I thought, since he lived with his mother and was not yet married.

35   I met Old Lady Chong once and that was enough. She had this peculiar smell like a baby that had done something in its pants. And her fingers felt like a dead person's, like an old peach I once found in the back of the refrigerator; the skin just slid off the meat when I picked it up.

36   I soon found out why Old Chong had retired from teaching piano. He was deaf. "Like Beethoven!" he shouted to me. "We're both listening only in our head!" And he would start to conduct his frantic silent sonatas.

37   Our lessons went like this. He would open the book and point to different things, explaining their purpose: "Key! Treble! Bass! No sharps or flats! So this is C major! Listen now and play after me!"

38   And then he would play the C scale a few times, a simple chord, and then, as if inspired by an old, unreachable itch, he gradually added more notes and running trills and a pounding bass until the music was really something quite grand.

39   I would play after him, the simple scale, the simple chord, and then I just played some nonsense that sounded like a cat running up and down on top of garbage cans. Old Chong smiled and applauded and then said, "Very good! But now you must learn to keep time!"

40   So that's how I discovered that Old Chong's eyes were too slow to keep up with the wrong notes I was playing. He went through the motions in half-time. To help me keep rhythm, he stood behind me, pushing down on my right shoulder for every beat. He balanced pennies on top of my wrists so I would keep them still as I slowly played scales and arpeggios. He had me curve my hand around an apple and keep that shape when playing chords. He marched stiffly to show me how to make each finger dance up and down, staccato like an obedient little soldier.

41   He taught me all these things, and that was how I also learned I could be lazy and get away with mistakes, lots of mistakes. If I hit the wrong notes because I hadn't practiced enough, I never corrected myself. I just kept playing in rhythm. And Old Chong kept conducting his own private reverie.

42   So maybe I never really gave myself a fair chance. I did pick up the basics pretty quickly, and I might have become a good pianist at that young age. But I was so determined not to try, not to be anybody different that I learned to play only the most ear-splitting preludes, the most discordant hymns.

43   Over the next year, I practiced like this, dutifully in my own way. And then one day I heard my mother and her friend Lindo Jong both

talking in a loud bragging tone of voice so others could hear. It was after church, and I was leaning against the brick wall wearing a dress with stiff white petticoats. Auntie Lindo's daughter, Waverly, who was about my age, was standing farther down the wall about five feet away, We had grown up together and shared all the closeness of two sisters squabbling over crayons and dolls. In other words, for the most part, we hated each other. I thought she was snotty. Waverly Jong had gained a certain amount of fame as "Chinatown's Littlest Chinese Chess Champion."

"She bring home too many trophy," lamented Auntie Lindo that 44 Sunday. "All day she play chess. All day I have no time do nothing but dust off her winnings." She threw a scolding look at Waverly, who pretended not to see her.

"You lucky you don't have this problem," said Auntie Lindo with a 45 sigh to my mother.

And my mother squared her shoulders and bragged: "Our prob- 46 lem worser than yours. If we ask Jing-Mei wash dish, she hear nothing but music. It's like you can't stop this natural talent."

And right then, I was determined to put a stop to her foolish pride. 47

A few weeks later, Old Chong and my mother conspired to have 48 me play in a talent show which would be held in the church hall. By then, my parents had saved up enough to buy me a secondhand piano, a black Wurlitzer spinet with a scarred bench. It was the showpiece of our living room.

For the talent show, I was to play a piece called "Pleading Child" 49 from Schumann's *Scenes from Childhood*. It was a simple, moody piece that sounded more difficult than it was. I was supposed to memorize the whole thing, playing the repeat parts twice to make the piece sound longer. But I dawdled over it, playing a few bars and then cheating, looking up to see what notes followed. I never really listened to what I was playing. I daydreamed about being somewhere else, about being someone else.

The part I liked to practice best was the fancy curtsy: right foot out, 50 touch the rose on the carpet with a pointed foot, sweep to the side, left leg bends, look up and smile.

My parents invited all the couples from the Joy Luck Club to wit- 51 ness my debut. Auntie Lindo and Uncle Tin were there. Waverly and her two older brothers had also come. The first two rows were filled with children both younger and older than I was. The littlest ones got to go first. They recited simple nursery rhymes, squawked out tunes on miniature violins, twirled Hula Hoops, pranced in pink ballet tutus, and when they bowed or curtsied, the audience would sigh in unison, "Awww," and then clap enthusiastically.

52   When my turn came, I was very confident. I remember my childish excitement. It was as if I knew, without a doubt, that the prodigy side of me really did exist. I had no fear whatsoever, no nervousness. I remember thinking to myself, This is it! This is it! I looked out over the audience, at my mother's blank face, my father's yawn, Auntie Lindo's stiff-lipped smile, Waverly's sulky expression. I had on a white dress layered with sheets of lace, and a pink bow in my Peter Pan haircut. As I sat down I envisioned people jumping to their feet and Ed Sullivan rushing up to introduce me to everyone on TV.

53   And I started to play. It was so beautiful. I was so caught up in how lovely I looked that at first I didn't worry how I would sound. So it was a surprise to me when I hit the first wrong note and I realized something didn't sound quite right. And then I hit another and another followed that. A chill started at the top of my head and began to trickle down. Yet I couldn't stop playing, as though my hands were bewitched. I kept thinking my fingers would adjust themselves back, like a train switching to the right track. I played this strange jumble through two repeats, the sour notes staying with me all the way to the end.

54   When I stood up, I discovered my legs were shaking. Maybe I had just been nervous and the audience, like Old Chong, had seen me go through the right motions and had not heard anything wrong at all. I swept my right foot out, went down on my knee, looked up and smiled. The room was quiet, except for Old Chong, who was beaming and shouting, "Bravo! Bravo! Well done!" But then I saw my mother's face, her stricken face. The audience clapped weakly, and as I walked back to my chair, with my whole face quivering as I tried not to cry, I heard a little boy whisper loudly to his mother, "That was awful," and the mother whispered back, "Well, she certainly tried."

55   And now I realized how many people were in the audience, the whole world it seemed. I was aware of eyes burning into my back. I felt the shame of my mother and father as they sat stiffly throughout the rest of the show.

56   We could have escaped during intermission. Pride and some strange sense of honor must have anchored my parents to their chairs. And so we watched it all: the eighteen-year-old boy with a fake mustache who did a magic show and juggled flaming hoops while riding a unicycle. The breasted girl with white makeup who sang from *Madama Butterfly* and got honorable mention. And the eleven-year-old boy who won first prize playing a tricky violin song that sounded like a busy bee.

57   After the show, the Hsus, the Jongs, and the St. Clairs from the Joy Luck Club came up to my mother and father.

58   "Lots of talented kids," Auntie Lindo said vaguely, smiling broadly.

"That was somethin' else," said my father, and I wondered if he   59
was referring to me in a humorous way, or whether he even remembered what I had done.

Waverly looked at me and shrugged her shoulders. "You aren't a   60
genius like me," she said matter-of-factly. And if I hadn't felt so bad, I
would have pulled her braids and punched her stomach.

But my mother's expression was what devastated me: a quiet,   61
blank look that said she had lost everything. I felt the same way, and it
seemed as if everybody were now coming up, like gawkers at the scene
of an accident, to see what parts were actually missing. When we got
on the bus to go home, my father was humming the busy-bee tune and
my mother was silent. I kept thinking she wanted to wait until we got
home before shouting at me. But when my father unlocked the door to
our apartment, my mother walked in and then went to the back, into
the bedroom. No accusations. No blame. And in a way, I felt disappointed. I had been waiting for her to start shouting, so I could shout
back and cry and blame her for all my misery.

I assumed my talent-show fiasco meant I never had to play the pi-   62
ano again. But two days later, after school, my mother came out of the
kitchen and saw me watching TV.

"Four clock," she reminded me as if it were any other day. I was   63
stunned, as though she were asking me to go through the talent-show
torture again. I wedged myself more tightly in front of the TV.

"Turn off TV," she called from the kitchen five minutes later.   64

I didn't budge. And then I decided. I didn't have to do what my   65
mother said anymore. I wasn't her slave. This wasn't China. I had listened to her before and look what happened. She was the stupid one.

She came out from the kitchen and stood in the arched entryway of   66
the living room. "Four clock," she said once again, louder.

"I'm not going to play anymore," I said nonchalantly. "Why should   67
I? I'm not a genius."

She walked over and stood in front of the TV. I saw her chest was   68
heaving up and down in an angry way.

"No!" I said, and I now felt stronger, as if my true self had finally   69
emerged. So this was what had been inside me all along.

"No! I won't!" I screamed.   70

She yanked me by the arm, pulled me off the floor, snapped off the   71
TV. She was frighteningly strong, half pulling, half carrying me toward
the piano as I kicked the throw rugs under my feet. She lifted me up
and onto the hard bench. I was sobbing by now, looking at her bitterly.
Her chest was heaving even more and her mouth was open, smiling
crazily as if she were pleased I was crying.

72   "You want me to be someone that I'm not!" I sobbed. "I'll never be the kind of daughter you want me to be!"

73   "Only two kinds of daughters," she shouted in Chinese. "Those who are obedient and those who follow their own mind! Only one kind of daughter can live in this house. Obedient daughter!"

74   "Then I wish I wasn't your daughter. I wish you weren't my mother," I shouted. As I said these things I got scared. It felt like worms and toads and slimy things crawling out of my chest, but it also felt good, as if this awful side of me had surfaced, at last.

75   "Too late change this," said my mother shrilly.

76   And I could sense her anger rising to its breaking point. I wanted to see it spill over. And that's when I remembered the babies she had lost in China, the ones we never talked about. "Then I wish I'd never been born!" I shouted. "I wish I were dead! Like them."

77   It was as if I had said the magic words. Alakazam!—and her face went blank, her mouth closed, her arms went slack, and she backed out of the room, stunned, as if she were blowing away like a small brown leaf, thin, brittle, lifeless.

It was not the only disappointment my mother felt in me. In the years that followed, I failed her so many times, each time asserting my own will, my right to fall short of expectations. I didn't get straight As. I didn't become class president. I didn't get into Stanford. I dropped out of college.

78   For unlike my mother, I did not believe I could be anything I wanted to be. I could only be me.

79   And for all those years, we never talked about the disaster at the recital or my terrible accusations afterward at the piano bench. All that remained unchecked, like a betrayal that was now unspeakable. So I never found a way to ask her why she had hoped for something so large that failure was inevitable.

80   And even worse, I never asked her what frightened me the most: Why had she given up hope?

81   For after our struggle at the piano, she never mentioned my playing again. The lessons stopped. The lid to the piano was closed, shutting out the dust, my misery, and her dreams.

82   So she surprised me. A few years ago, she offered to give me the piano, for my thirtieth birthday. I had not played in all those years. I saw the offer as a sign of forgiveness, a tremendous burden removed.

83   "Are you sure?" I asked shyly. "I mean, won't you and Dad miss it?"

84   "No, this your piano," she said firmly. "Always your piano. You only one can play."

85   "Well, I probably can't play anymore," I said. "It's been years."

86   "You pick up fast," said my mother, as if she knew this was certain. "You have natural talent. You could been genius if you want to."

"No I couldn't." 87

"You just not trying," said my mother. And she was neither angry 88
nor sad. She said it as if to announce a fact that could never be dis-
proved. "Take it," she said.

But I didn't at first. It was enough that she had offered it to me. 89
And after that, every time I saw it in my parents' living room, standing
in front of the bay windows, it made me feel proud, as if it were a shiny
trophy I had won back.

Last week I sent a tuner over to my parents' apartment and had the 90
piano reconditioned, for purely sentimental reasons. My mother had
died a few months before and I had been getting things in order for my
father, a little bit at a time. I put the jewelry in special silk pouches. The
sweaters she had knitted in yellow, pink, bright orange—all the colors I
hated—I put those in moth-proof boxes. I found some old Chinese silk
dresses, the kind with little slits up the sides. I rubbed the old silk
against my skin, then wrapped them in tissue and decided to take them
home with me.

After I had the piano tuned, I opened the lid and touched the keys. 91
It sounded even richer than I remembered. Really, it was a very good
piano. Inside the bench were the same exercise notes with handwritten
scales, the same secondhand music books with their covers held together with yellow tape.

I opened up the Schumann book to the dark little piece I had 92
played at the recital. It was on the left-hand side of the page, "Pleading
Child." It looked more difficult than I remembered. I played a few bars,
surprised at how easily the notes came back to me.

And for the first time, or so it seemed, I noticed the piece on the 93
righthand side. It was called "Perfectly Contented." I tried to play this
one as well. It had a lighter melody but the same flowing rhythm and
turned out to be quite easy. "Pleading Child" was shorter but slower;
"Perfectly Contented" was longer, but faster. And after I played them
both a few times, I realized they were two halves of the same song.

✦ Questions for Discussion and Writing

1. Why is it so important to Jing-Mei's mother to have her daughter become a prodigy of some kind? How does this expectation shape Jing-
   Mei's early childhood? How does Jing-Mei react to the pressure of living up to her mother's expectations? Left to her own devices, do you
   feel she would have preferred to be just an ordinary child and not
   stand out from the crowd?

2. How was it that Jing-Mei did not know that she had little talent for the
   piano? Why weren't her teacher, her mother, or Jing-Mei herself able to

determine this? Why did it have to get to the point where she gave a horrible recital for everyone to realize she couldn't play the piano?

3. Describe the conflict Jing-Mei feels in trying to search for her own identity, while at the same time trying to make her mother happy by becoming a child prodigy. Do you think Jing-Mei misunderstood her mother and transformed her mother's desire for her to "be her best" into the expectation that she would become a prodigy?

4. What evidence is there within the story that this account was written many years after the events described took place? How do we know that at a later point Jing-Mei saw her mother was only trying to do what was best for her? What evidence is there that the narrator is much older, has greater understanding of what her mother was trying to do, and has more compassion toward her mother? How does the different perspective from which she remembers the situation enable her to grasp it in a way she could not as a child?

5. How does Jing-Mei's treatment of the old piano, which she "reconditioned, for purely sentimental reasons," symbolize her attitude toward her childhood?

6. How do the two pieces of music mentioned in the story ("Pleading Child" and "Perfectly Contented") refer to her role as daughter and to the outcome of attempting to fulfill her mother's expectations? In what way do these two pieces of music represent different sides of her personality?

7. Children of immigrants feel pressured to take advantage of opportunities offered by American society as a way of repaying sacrifices made by their parents. What kinds of pressures did Tan's account reveal?

8. You need not be the child of a first-generation immigrant to experience the kinds of pressures Tan describes. For example, did your parents try to live vicariously through your achievements in Little League or other sports? What experiences have you had that gave you insight into Jing-Mei Woo's dilemma?

9. Were you encouraged to or forced to take lessons on the piano or on another musical instrument when you were a child? Were your experiences similar to or different from those of Jing-Mei Woo?

10. Interview an older member of your family who immigrated to the United States. What obstacles did he or she have to overcome? In an essay, discuss how his or her experiences have influenced your entire family's attitude towards America, as well as shaped their ambitions, expectations, hopes and dreams.

Connections

1. What signals do Natsume Soseki and Amy Tan use to make the reader aware that each narrator's view of the world should be taken ironically?

2. Tadeusz Borowski's dramatization of his experiences in Auschwitz and Gary Soto's fictionalized account of working in a tire factory reveal that people can react differently to harsh and degrading environments. In your view, why do some people retain their humanity while others become dehumanized?

3. Compare Natsume Soseki's portrait of the Japanese schoolteacher with Mark Salzman's portrayal of his teacher, Pan ("Lessons," Chapter 6). What differences can you observe in teaching methods, in attitudes towards the subjects taught, and in the personalities of the two teachers?

4. How are Jing-Mei Woo and Christy Brown ("The Letter 'A'," Chapter 8) each influenced by his or her mother's aspirations and expectations?

5. How do Christy Brown's narrative ("The Letter 'A'," Chapter 8) and Natsume Soseki's fictionalized account rely on narrators who perceive and understand but cannot communicate with others?

6. Contrast Tadeusz Borowski's account with Robert Falcon Scott's ("Scott's Last March," Chapter 11) to discover why men facing imminent death will, in some cases, be concerned with the welfare of others and, in other instances, think only of themselves.

7. To more fully appreciate Natsume Soseki's ingenuity, try rewriting the accounts by Howard Hall ("Playing Tag with Wild Dolphins," Chapter 4) and E. B. White ("Death of a Pig," Chapter 4) from the perspective of the dolphins and the pig, respectively.

Rhetorical Index

MEMOIRS

NEWSPAPER COLUMNS

REPORTAGE

SPEECHES

Index of Authors and Titles

◆

Acknowledgments

———————◆———————

Annie Dillard, "So This Was Adolescence" from *An American Childhood*. Copyright © 1987 by Annie Dillard. Reprinted by permission of HarperCollins Publishers, Inc.

Slavenka Drakulić, "The Balkan Express" from *The Balkan Express: Fragments from the Other Side of War*, translated by Maja Soljan. Copyright © 1993 by Slavenka Drakulić. English translation copyright © 1993 by Maja Soljan. Reprinted by permission of W. W. Norton & Company, Inc.

Nawal el-Saadawi, "Circumcision of Girls" from *The Hidden Face of Eve: Women in the Arab World*, translated and edited by Sherif Hetata (London: Zed Books, 1980).

Nora Ephron, "A Few Words About Breasts" from *Crazy Salad*. Copyright © 1975 by Nora Ephron. Reprinted by permission of International Creative Management, Inc.

Douchan Gersi, "Initiated in an Iban Tribe of Headhunters" from *Explorer* (New York: Jeremy P. Tarcher, 1987). Copyright © 1987 by Douchan Gersi. Reprinted with the permission of The Putnam Publishing Group, Inc.

Mikal Gilmore, "My Brother, Gary Gilmore" from "Family Album," *GRANTA* 37 (Fall 1991). Copyright © 1991 by Mikal Gilmore. Reprinted with the permission of the author c/o Arthur Pine Associates.

Nancy Bazelon Goldstone, "A Trader in London," *New York Times Magazine* (January 29, 1987), "Hers" column. Copyright © 1987 by The New York Times Company. Reprinted by permission.

Howard Hall, "Playing Tag with Wild Dolphins" from *The Fireside Diver*, edited by Bonnie Cardone (Birmingham: Menasha Ridge Press, 1992). Copyright © 1992 by Howard Hall. Reprinted with the permission of the author.

Patricia Hampl, "Grandmother's Sunday Dinner" from *A Romantic Education*. Copyright © 1981 by Patricia Hampl from the book *A Romantic Education* published by Houghton Mifflin. Reprinted by permission granted by The Rhoda Weyr Agency, New York.

Barbara Grizzuti Harrison, "Growing Up Apocalyptic" from *Off Center*. Copyright © 1980 by Barbara Grizzuti Harrison. Reprinted by permission of Georges Borchardt, Inc. for the author. "Growing Up Apocalyptic" first appeared in *Ms.*

Le Ly Hayslip, "Yearning to Breathe Free" from *Child of War, Woman of Peace*. Copyright © 1993 by Le Ly Hayslip and Charles Jay Warts. Used by permission of Doubleday, a division of Bantam Doubleday Dell Publishing Group, Inc.

Lesley Hazleton, "Confessions of a Fast Woman" from *Confessions of a Fast Woman*. Copyright © 1992 by Lesley Hazleton. Reprinted by permission of Addison-Wesley Publishing Company, Inc.

Aldo Leopold, "Thinking Like a Mountain" from *A Sand County Almanac: And Sketches Here and There*. Copyright © 1949, 1977 by Oxford University Press, Inc. Reprinted by permission.

Audre Lorde, "The Cancer Journals (1/26/79–6/20/80)" from *The Cancer Journals* (San Francisco: Aunt Lute Books, 1980). Copyright © 1980 by Audre Lorde. Reprinted by permission of the Charlotte Sheedy Literary Agency, Inc, 41 King Street, New York, NY 10014, (212) 633-2289.

Peter Matthiessen, "The Snow Leopard" from *The Snow Leopard*. Copyright © 1978 by Peter Matthiessen. Used by permission of Viking Penguin, a division of Penguin Books USA Inc.

Melton A. McLaurin, "Bobo" from *Separate Pasts*. Copyright © 1987 by Melton A. McLaurin. Reprinted with the permission of The University of Georgia Press.

Golda Meir, "We Have Our State" from *My Life*. Copyright © 1975 by Golda Meir. Reprinted with the permission of The Putnam Publishing Group, Inc.

Rigoberta Menchú, "Things Have Happened to Me as in a Movie" from *You Can't Drown the Fire: Latin American Women Writing in Exile*, edited by Alicia Partnoy (San Francisco: Cleis Press, 1988). Copyright © 1988 by Alicia Partnoy. Reprinted with the permission of Alicia Partnoy.

Lydia Minatoya, "Transformation" from *Talking to High Monks in the Snow*. Copyright © 1992 by Lydia Minatoya. Reprinted by permission of HarperCollins Publishers, Inc.

Paul Monette, "Becoming a Man" (editors' title) from *Becoming a Man: Half a Life Story*. Copyright © 1992 by Paul Monette. Reprinted with the permission of Harcourt Brace & Company.

Jill Nelson, "Number One!" from *Volunteer Slavery*. Copyright © 1993 by Jill Nelson. *Volunteer Slavery*, Penguin Books, (ISBN 0-14-023716-X), is available in paperback. Reprinted with the permission of Jill Nelson.

Itabari Njeri, "Hair Piece" from *Every Goodbye Ain't Gone*. Copyright © 1982, 1983, 1984, 1986, 1990 by Itabari Njeri. Reprinted by permission of Times Books, a division of Random House, Inc.

Tim O'Brien, "If I Die in a Combat Zone" from *If I Die in a Combat Zone*. Copyright © 1973 by Tim O'Brien. Used by permission of Delacorte Press/Seymour Lawrence, a division of Bantam Doubleday Dell Publishing Group, Inc.

Jo Goodwin Parker, "What Is Poverty?" from *America's Other Children*, edited by George Henderson. Copyright © 1971. Reprinted with the permission of University of Oklahoma Press.

Fritz Peters, "Gurdjieff Remembered" from *Gurdjieff Remembered* (New York: Samuel Weiser, 1971). Copyright © 1965 by Fritz Peters. Reprinted with the permission of Tale Weaver Publishing.

Sylvia Plath, "Letters Home (June 1953)" from *Letters Home By Sylvia Plath: Correspondence 1950–1963*. Copyright © 1975 by Aurelia Schober Plath. Reprinted with the permission of HarperCollins Publishers, Inc.

Richard Rhodes, "A Hole in the World" from *A Hole in the World* (New York: Simon & Schuster, 1990). Copyright © 1990 by Richard Rhodes. Reprinted with the permission of Janklow & Nesbit Associates.

Mike Royko, "Farewell to Fitness," *Chicago Sun Times* (1980). Copyright © 1980. Reprinted with the permission of Tribune Media Services.

Tepilit Ole Saitoti, "The Initiation of a Masai Warrior" from *The Worlds of a Masai Warrior.* Copyright © 1986 by Tepilit Ole Saitoti. Reprinted by permission of Random House, Inc.

Mark Salzman, "Lessons" from *Iron and Silk.* Copyright © 1986 by Mark Salzman. Reprinted by permission of Random House, Inc.

Margaret Sanger, "The Turbid Ebb and Flow of Misery" from *The Autobiography of Margaret Sanger* (New York: W. W. Norton & Company, 1938). Reprinted with the permission of Sanger Resources and Management, Inc.

Natsume Soseki, "I Am a Cat" from *I Am a Cat*, translated by Katsue Shibata and Motonari Kai. English translation copyright © 1961 by Kenkyusha Ltd. Tokyo. Reprinted with the permission of The Putnam Publishing Group, Inc.

Gary Soto, "Black Hair" from *Living Up the Street*, Dell Publishing. Copyright © 1985 by Gary Soto. Used by permission of the author.

Amy Tan, "Jing Mei Woo: Two Kinds" from *The Joy Luck Club.* Copyright © 1989 by Amy Tan. Reprinted with the permission of The Putnam Publishing Group.

Luis Alberto Urrea, "My Story" from *Across the Wire: Life & Hard Times.* Copyright © 1993 by Luis Alberto Urrea. Used by permission of Doubleday, a division of Bantam Doubleday Dell Publishing Group, Inc.

Jane van Lawick-Goodall, "First Observations" from *In the Shadow of Man.* Copyright © 1971 by Hugo and Jane van Lawick-Goodall. Reprinted with the permission of Houghton Mifflin Company and Weidenfeld & Nicolson.

Brian L. Weiss, excerpt from *Many Lives, Many Masters* (New York: Fireside, 1988). Copyright © 1988 by Brian L. Weiss. Reprinted with the permission of International Creative Management.

E. B. White, "Death of a Pig" from *The Second Tree from the Corner.* Copyright 1947 by E. B. White. Copyright renewed. First appeared in *Atlantic Monthly.* Reprinted by permission of HarperCollins Publishers, Inc.

Tennessee Williams, "The Man in the Overstuffed Chair" from *Antaeus*, Spring/Summer 1982, edited by Daniel Halpern. Copyright © 1982 by *Antaeus*, New York, NY. First published by The Ecco Press in 1982. Reprinted by permission.

William Zinsser, "Niagara Falls" from *American Places.* Copyright © 1992 by William K. Zinsser. Reprinted by permission of the author.